Copyright © 2001 A.D.A. EDITA Tokyo Co., Ltd.
3-12-14 Sendagaya, Shibuya-ku, Tokyo 151-0051, Japan
All rights reserved. No part of this publication may be reproduced,
stored in a retrieval system, or transmitted, in any form or by any means,
electronic, mechanical, photocopying, recording, or otherwise,
without permission in writing from the publisher.

Copyright of photographs
© 2001 GA photographers

Logotype design: Gan Hosoya

First published in 2001
Reprinted in 2015

Printed and bound in Japan

ISBN978-4-87140-571-3 C1352

MUSEUM 1

Edited and Photographed by Yukio Futagawa

GA Contemporary Architecture 01 — MUSEUM 1

6	1950-51	**Junzo Sakakura:** Museum of Modern Art, Kamakura, Kanagawa, Japan 坂倉準三：神奈川県立近代美術館
10	1953-58	**Affonso Eduardo Reidy:** Museum of Modern Art, Rio de Janeiro, Brazil アルフォンソ・エドゥアルド・レイディ：リオ・デ・ジャネイロ近代美術館
16	1958-73	**Alvar Aalto:** Museum in Aalborg, Aalborg, Denmark アルヴァ・アアルト：オルボーの美術館
20	1961-68	**Kevin Roche John Dinkeloo:** Oakland Museum, Oakland, California, U.S.A. ケヴィン・ローチ ジョン・ディンケルー：オークランド・ミュージアム
24	1962-68	**Mies van der Rohe:** New National Gallery, Berlin, Germany ミース・ファン・デル・ローエ：ニュー・ナショナル・ギャラリー
30	1966-72	**Louis I. Kahn:** Kimbell Art Museum, Fort Worth, Texas, U.S.A. ルイス・I・カーン：キンベル美術館
36	1969-74	**Louis I. Kahn:** Center for British Art and Studies, Yale University, New Haven, Connecticut, U.S.A. ルイス・I・カーン：イェール大学イギリス美術研究センター
42	1971-74/ 1992-97	**Arata Isozaki:** Gumma Prefectural Museum of Fine Arts, Gumma, Japan 磯崎新：群馬県立近代美術館
50	1971-77	**Piano/Rogers:** Georges Pompidou Cultural Center, Paris, France ピアノ／ロジャース：ジョルジュ・ポンピドゥ文化センター
60	1972-82	**Hans Hollein:** Abteiberg Museum, Mönchengladbach, Germany ハンス・ホライン：アプタイベルク美術館
68	1974-78/ 1988-91	**Norman Foster:** Sainsbury Centre for Visual Arts, Norwich, U.K. ノーマンフォスター：セインズベリー視覚芸術センター
74	1977-84	**James Stirling, Michael Wilford:** Staatsgalerie Extension and New Chamber Theater, Stuttgart, Germany ジェームズ・スターリング，マイケル・ウィルフォード：シュトゥットガルト国立美術館
84	1979-84	**O. M. Ungers:** German Architecture Museum, Frankfurt am Main, Germany O・M・ウンガース：ドイツ建築美術館
88	1979-85	**Richard Meier:** Museum for Decorative Arts, Frankfurt am Main, Germany リチャード・マイヤー：フランクフルト装飾工芸美術館
96	1981-83	**Yoshio Taniguchi:** Ken Domon Museum of Photography, Yamagata, Japan 谷口吉生：土門拳記念館
102	1981-86	**Arata Isozaki:** Museum of Contemporary Art, Los Angeles, California, U.S.A. 磯崎新：ロサンジェルス現代美術館
110	1981-86	**Renzo Piano:** Menil Collection Museum, Houston, Texas, U.S.A. レンゾ・ピアノ：メニル・コレクション美術館
116	1981-87	**Jean Nouvel + Architecture Studio:** Arab World Institute, Paris, France ジャン・ヌヴェル＋アーキテクチュア・スタジオ：アラブ世界研究所
122	1982-84	**Frank O. Gehry:** California Aerospace Museum and Theater, Los Angeles, California, U.S.A. フランク・O・ゲーリー：カリフォルニア航空宇宙博物館
126	1982-90	**Günter Behnisch:** German Postal Museum, Frankfurt am Main, Germany ギュンター・ベーニッシュ：ドイツ郵便・通信博物館
132	1982-91	**Hans Hollein:** Museum for Modern Art, Frankfurt am Main, Germany ハンス・ホライン：フランクフルト現代美術館
140	1983-86	**Fumihiko Maki:** National Museum of Modern Art, Kyoto, Japan 槇文彦：京都国立近代美術館
148	1986-88	**Hiroshi Hara:** Iida City Museum, Nagano, Japan 原広司：飯田市美術博物館
156	1987-92	**Henri Ciriani:** Historical Museum of World War, Péronne, France アンリ・シリアニ：世界大戦記念館
162	1987-95	**Richard Meier:** Museum of Contemporary Art, Barcelona, Spain リチャード・マイヤー：バルセロナ現代美術館
170	1988-91	**Toyo Ito:** Yatsushiro Municipal Museum, Kumamoto, Japan 伊東豊雄：八代市立博物館・未来の森ミュージアム

178	1988-92	**Tadao Ando:** Naoshima Contemporary Art Museum, Kagawa, Japan 安藤忠雄：直島コンテンポラリーアートミュージアム
186	1988-93	**Jo Coenen:** Netherlands Architecture Institute, Rotterdam, The Netherlands ヨー・クーネン：オランダ建築協会
192	1988-93	**Fumihiko Maki:** Center for Arts Yerba Buena Gardens, San Francisco, California, U.S.A. 槇文彦：YBG芸術センター
198	1989-91	**Sverre Fehn:** Glacier Museum, Fjaerland, Balestrand, Norway スヴェーレ・フェーン：氷河博物館
202	1989-91	**Ricardo Legorreta:** MARCO Museum of Contemporary Art, Monterrey, Mexico リカルド・レゴレッタ：モンテレー現代美術館
208	1989-97	**Peter Zumthor:** Art Museum, Bregenz, Austria ピーター・ズントー：ブレゲンツ美術館
212	1989-98	**Daniel Libeskind:** Berlin Museum with Jewish Museum, Berlin, Germany ダニエル・リベスキンド：ユダヤ美術館
218	1990-96	**Tod Williams Billie Tsien:** Phoenix Art Museum, Phoenix, Arizona, U.S.A. トッド・ウィリアムズ ビリー・ツィン：フェニックス美術館
226	1991-94	**Tadao Ando:** Suntory Museum+Plaza, Osaka, Japan 安藤忠雄：サントリーミュージアム＋マーメイド広場
232	1991-94	**Balkrishna V. Doshi:** Hussain-Doshi Gufa Museum, Ahmedabad, India バルクリシュナ・V・ドーシ：フセイン／ドーシ美術館
236	1991-94	**Arata Isozaki:** Nagi Museum of Contemporary Art/Nagi Town Library, Okayama, Japan 磯崎新：奈義町現代美術館・奈義町立図書館
242	1991-94	**Jean Nouvel:** Cartier Foundation, Paris, France ジャン・ヌヴェル：カルティエ財団
246	1991-95	**Yoshio Taniguchi:** Toyota Municipal Museum of Art, Aichi, Japan 谷口吉生：豊田市美術館
256	1991-96	**Oscar Niemeyer:** Museum of Contemporary Art, Rio de Janeiro, Brazil オスカー・ニーマイヤー：リオ・デ・ジャネイロ現代美術館
260	1991-97	**Frank O. Gehry:** Guggenheim Bilbao Museum, Bilbao, Spain フランク・O・ゲーリー：グッゲンハイム・ビルバオ・ミュージアム
272	1991-99	**Álvaro Siza:** Contemporary Art Museum of Oporto, Oporto, Portugal アルヴァロ・シザ：ポルト現代美術館
280	1992-94	**Tadao Ando:** Nariwa Museum, Okayama, Japan 安藤忠雄：成羽町美術館
286	1992-96	**I. M. Pei:** Miho Museum, Shiga, Japan I・M・ペイ：ミホ・ミュージアム
294	1992-97	**Steven Holl:** KIASMA Museum of Contemporary Art, Helsinki, Finland スティーヴン・ホール：ヘルシンキ現代美術館
302	1993-94	**Coop Himmelblau:** Groninger Museum East Pavilion, Groningen, The Netherlands コープ・ヒンメルブラウ：フローニンヘン美術館東館
310	1995-99	**Kazuyo Sejima + Ryue Nishizawa:** O-Museum, Nagano, Japan 妹島和世＋西沢立衛：飯田市小笠原資料館
316	1994-2000	**Herzog & De Meuron:** Tate Modern, London, U.K. ヘルツォーク＆ド・ムーロン：テート・モダン
324	1998-2000	**Kengo Kuma:** Bato Machi Hiroshige Museum, Tochigi, Japan 隈研吾：馬頭町広重美術館
330	1994-2000	**Norman Foster:** Queen Elizabeth II Great Court, British Museum, London, U.K. ノーマン・フォスター：大英博物館クイーン・エリザベスII世グレート・コート

* 〈Museum〉 is published in two volumes.　　「ミュージアム」は二巻に分けて紹介いたします。

1950–51
JUNZO SAKAKURA

MUSEUM OF MODERN ART, KAMAKURA
Kanagawa, Japan

View toward main entrance メイン・エントランスを見る

Terrace on south 南側テラス

In 1939, Junzo Sakakura has regained his homeground from his practice abroad under Le Corbusier. This museum of contemporary art marks the beginning of his professional activities in post-war Japan.

The site is placed in the woods, facing a pond within the precincts of Tsurugaoka Hachimangu Shrine in the center of Kamakura City. The two-storied, steel-framed museum with a total floor space of 1,575 square meters was finished in a short period of time, approximately one year from the design competition. Its square plan is composed of a central patio surrounded by exhibition rooms and other facilities. The main spaces including the exhibition rooms are raised to the second floor on top of the pilotis.

Indoor exhibitions are illuminated by external light from the light-diffusing louvers on the ceiling. Sequences of exhibition space can be reorganized with mobile partitions, and spaces are given between each exhibition room for visitors to perceive the surrounding nature.

In this museum, harmony among the building and its natural environment follows the close relationship between buildings and gardens typical of Japanese traditional architecture. The patio is no exception, as it is open in order to connect with the exterior. The choices seen in the material—natural and gentle, such as Oya stone used in the first-floor exterior, or the finishing—simple and plain, such as asbestos boards and aluminium joints used in the second-floor external walls, are characteristic of Japanese architectural tradition. Here, elements of modernism that Le Corbusier has proposed through his house building during the 1920s reach a common ground with traditional spaces of Japanese architecture, and a cohabitation is realized. Sakakura has developed his design for Japan Pavilion of 1937 International Exhibition in Paris into this museum, but further in line with the Japanese context. An apex of modernism in Japanese architecture of the time.

Extension and renovation works have been executed in 1966 by Sakakura himself.

1939年、ル・コルビュジエのもとから帰国した坂倉準三は、第二次大戦後、日本国内における本格的な活動をこの近代美術館から開始することになった。

鎌倉市の中心に位置する鶴岡八幡宮の境内の、森に囲まれ池に面した敷地に、鉄骨造2階建て、延床面積1,575平方メートルの美術館は、コンペから一年余という短期間で完成させられた。方形のプランで、中庭を中心とし、その周囲を展示室や他の機能が取り囲む構成となっている。展示室などの主要空間はピロティによって2階に持ち上げられている。

室内の展示室は、天井に設けられた散光ルーバーからの外光により照らされた。展示空間のシークエンスは可動パーティションにより自由に作られ、各展示室の間には外部の自然を認知させる空間が与えられている。

この美術館では、建物を囲む自然環境との調和が、日本の伝統建築における建物と庭園との密接な関係に則っている。中庭においても、閉ざすことなく外部と繋がりを持たせている。1階の外装

Aerial view 航空写真

材に用いられる大谷石に代表される自然の優しい素材や、2階外壁のアスベスト・ボードにアルミ・ジョイント留めなどの質素な仕上げの選択は日本に固有の建築伝統に通じるものであり、ル・コルビュジエが1920年代の住宅建築において提唱したモダニズムの要素と日本の伝統空間との接点、共存を実現している。この美術館は、坂倉自身による'37年のパリ万博での日本館のデザインをより日本のコンテクストに沿った形で発展させた、当時の日本におけるモダニズム建築の頂点に到達する建築であった。

66年、坂倉自身による増改築が行われた。

Terrace of southeast corner テラス南東隅部

South view: main building (left) and annex (right) 南より見る：本館（左）と新館（右）

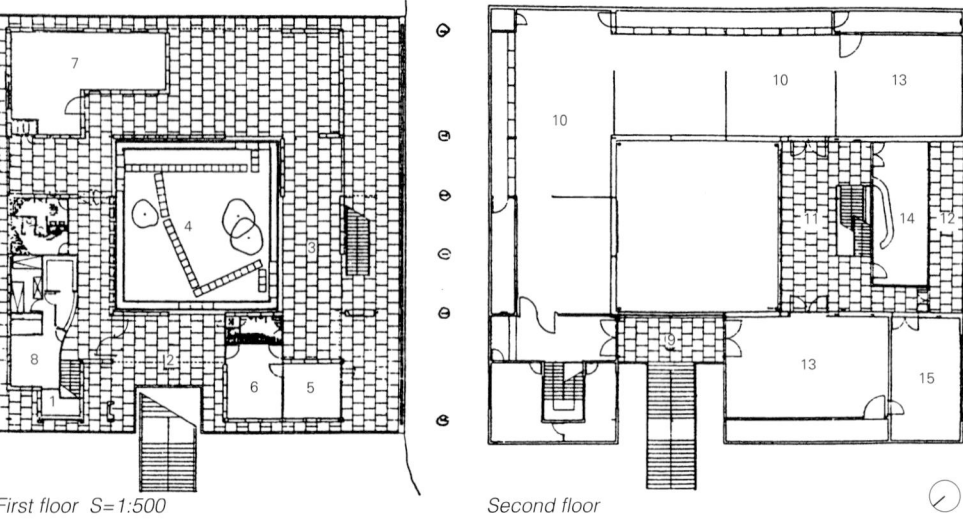

First floor S=1:500

Second floor

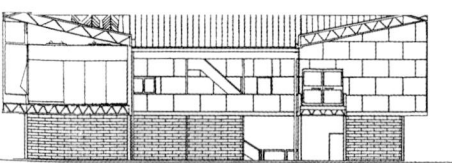

Section

1 TICKETS
2 ENTRANCE HALL
3 SCULPTURE ROOM
4 COURTYARD
5 DIRECTOR'S ROOM
6 ARCHIVE
7 MECHANICAL
8 OFFICE
9 MAIN ENTRANCE
10 EXHIBITION ROOM
11 SCULPTURE ROOM
12 TERRACE
13 EXTRA EXHIBITION ROOM
14 CAFE
15 GUEST ROOM

Annex　新館　△▽

1953–58
AFFONSO EDUARDO REIDY

MUSEUM OF MODERN ART, RIO DE JANEIRO
Rio de Janeiro, Brazil

Section

Aerial view 航空写真

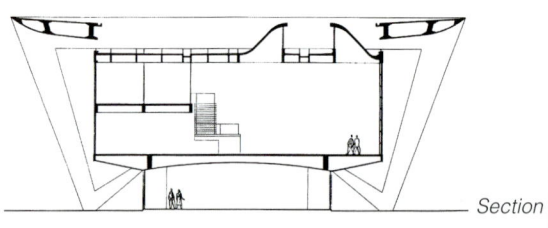

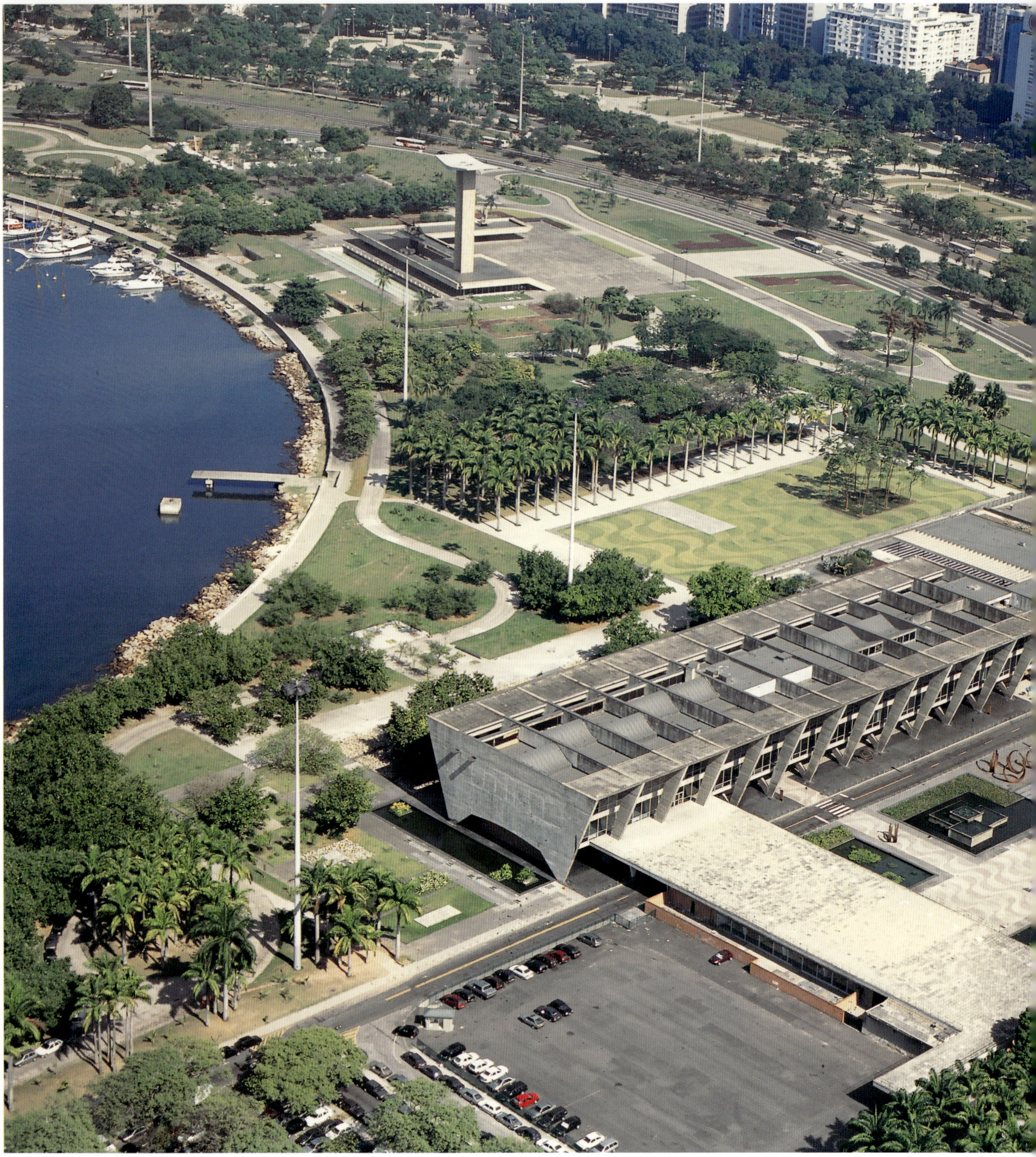

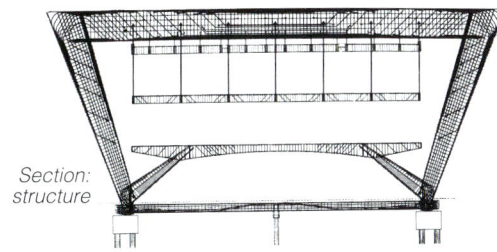

Section: structure

South elevation　南面

Terrace of east wing　東棟のテラス

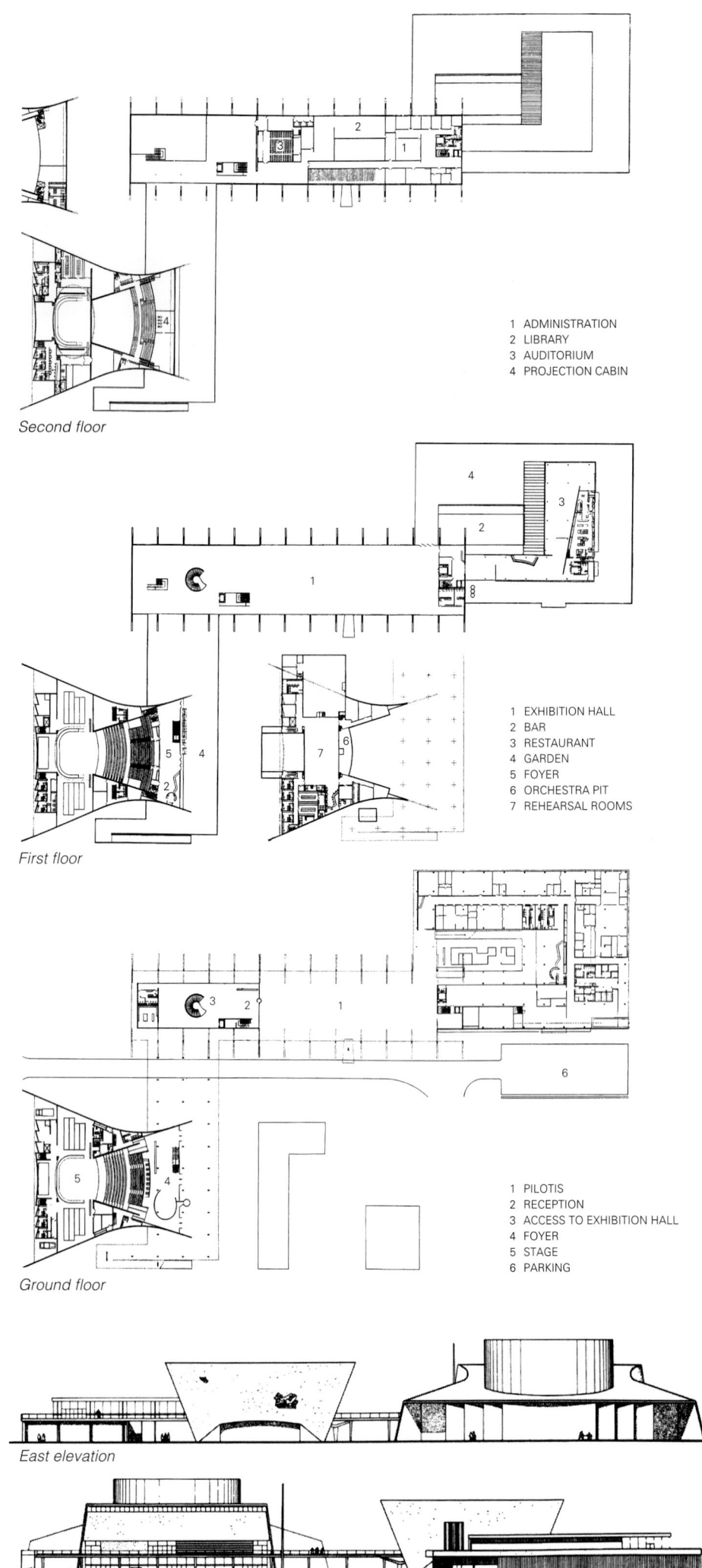

This museum of modern art has been planned and constructed as a cultural core of Rio de Janeiro's newly developed waterfront, the reclaimed land of Flamengo, that the architect himself has taken charge of the master plan. A theater was originally planned adjacent to the museum, but this one has never been materialized. With its oblong plan set along to the new shoreline, the museum features 14 units of U-shaped, in situ concrete frame arranged at 10-meter intervals to the longitudinal direction, from which floor slabs for the third and fourth levels are suspended. The second-floor slab housing the main space is raised over the pilotis. Such structure enables to realize the main three gallery levels with no pillars, where various forms of exhibition can be accommodated using partitions and installations.

The volume of exposed concrete and dynamic expressions of its texture provide a lucid explanation to this systemized organization. By lifting up the exhibitions spaces onto the pilotis, the museum allows not only the magnificent marine view to be seen at its foot from inside the city, but also to uninterruptedly call in activities from the park sharing the same reclaimed land.

In 1978, a fire broke out and damaged the interior of the building, but its sturdy body frame was left intact, as if proving that this very structure were the museum's identity itself. It is now under reconstruction, with a new enclosure given onto the remaining body.

この近代美術館は、建築家自らがマスタープランを担当したリオ・デ・ジャネイロ市の新しい水際、フラメンゴ埋立地の開発計画における文化的中心として計画、建設された。新しい海岸線に沿って置かれた長方形のプランを持つ美術館は、当初、その横に劇場も計画されていたが、こちらは実現しなかった。美術館は、長手方向に10m間隔で並べられた14枚のコの字型現場打ちコンクリート・フレームと、それらから吊り下げられた3、4階スラブ、ピロティ上に持ち上げられた主要空間である2階スラブからなる構成である。これによって、主要の3層ギャラリーを無柱空間にすることが出来るため、パーティションやインスタレーションによって様々な展示形態に対応することができる。

打放しコンクリートの量感とテクスチャーの力強い表現により、このシステム構成が明解に見て取れる。また、展示空間のボリュームをピロティによって持ち上げることでその足元において、街側からは素晴らしい海側の風景を建物が遮ることはなく、また、埋め立て地に作られた公園からのアクティビティを連続的に美術館に迎え入れることに成功している。

建物は1978年、火災に遭い内部を焼失するが、その強固なコンクリートの躯体は残った。躯体システム自体がこの美術館の主体そのものであったことを証明するかのように、美術館は残された躯体に再びエンクロージャーを与えられて、再建されている。

Pilotis ピロティ

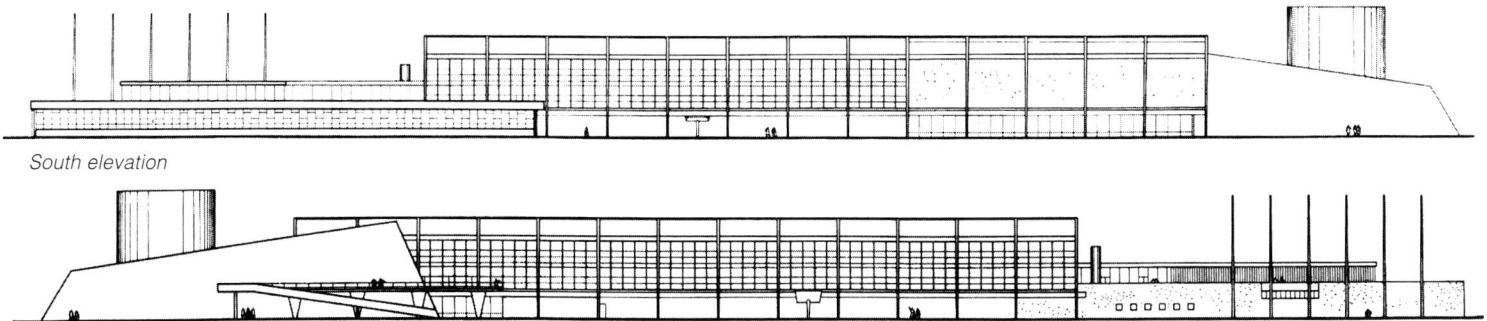

Entrance: spiral staircase エントランス：螺旋階段

South elevation

North elevation

Exhibition hall on first floor　2階展示室

Exhibition hall: west view　展示室：西を見る

Exhibition hall: east view　展示室：東を見る

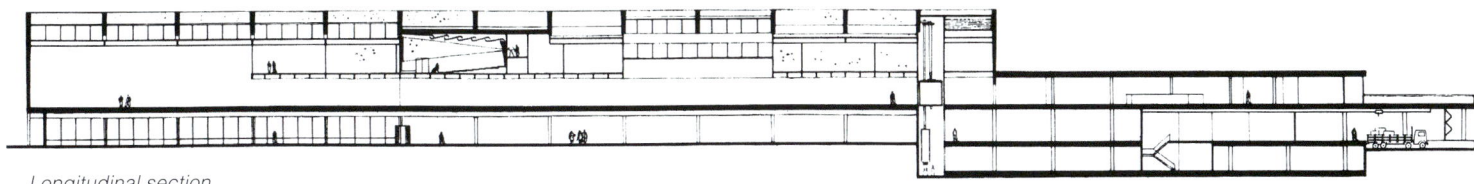

Longitudinal section

Staircase to second floor　3階への階段

1958–73
ALVAR AALTO

MUSEUM IN AALBORG
Aalborg, Denmark

Overall view 全景

Lecture room on left 左は講義室

The site is a land with inclination in the midst of a beech wood. Its difference in levels made it possible of lifting up the piloti and using the lower-level as parking space. The single-floor, main exhibition space lies on the piloti. It is divided into two rooms: one for general use and the other for large-sized exhibitions. The former is a single volume with partition system that allows to reconfigure the room in a variety of space layouts, whereas the latter is a lofty volume with large walls on its four sides and a high ceiling, complying with massive installations nowadays. The open-air amphitheater is a place to enjoy the blessings of the surrounding nature, as well as a home and meeting place of activities happening inside and outside the building.

Aalto was an architect whose approach in designing museums had involved treatment of light in the same manner as dealing with acoustics in concert-hall design. Introduction of light controlled in various aspects has enriched his architectural spaces. There are two main lighting systems adopted to this museum. Lighting inside the general exhibition room in the western part of the building features five slots of skylight equipped with asymmetrical reflection boards, oriented to the east and west to make full use of natural light. Asymmetry of reflecting boards is a result of elaborate study over light's characteristic of transforming its own properties according to the direction of entry. Lighting inside the larger exhibition room on the east features a pyramid-shaped skylight which provides quality lighting from three directions

Section

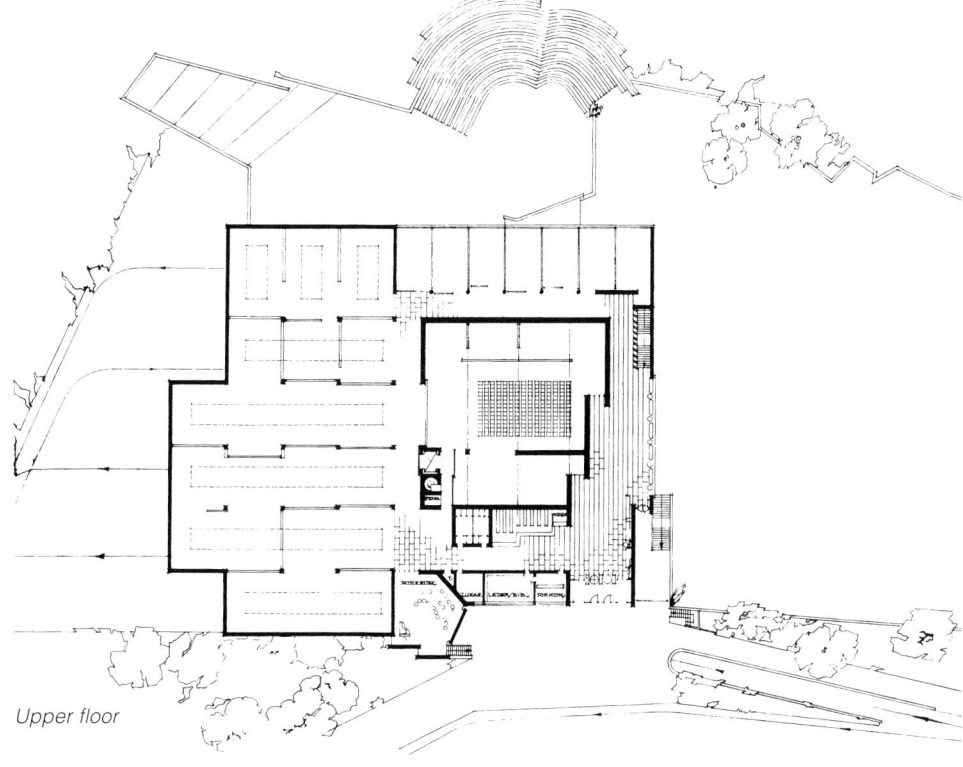
Upper floor

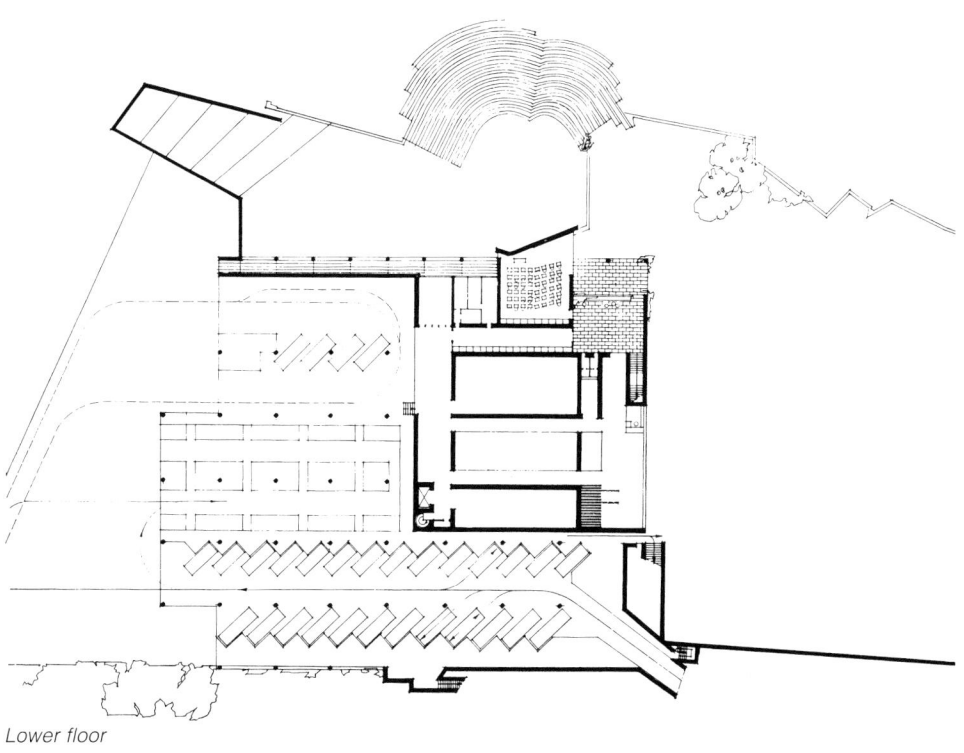
Lower floor

but the south, so that all wall surfaces can be used for exhibition.

　敷地はぶな林に囲まれた傾斜地で、この高低差を利用して、建物はピロティで持ち上げられ、下層階を駐車場に利用している。主要の展示空間はピロティ上の一層分に収められている。展示空間は大きく一般展示室と大型展示室に分けられている。一般展示室は一室空間で、パーティション・システムによって様々なレイアウトが可能になっている。それに対して階高のある大型展示室は四方を大きな壁に囲まれた、昨今の大きなインスタレーションにも対応するヴォリュームの空間である。また、周囲の自然の恵みを享受するように、野外には円形劇場が設けられ、建物内外のアクティビティを生まれさせ、相互に結びつけている。

　アアルトは、美術館を設計する際、コンサートホールの設計における音響設計と同様に光の取り扱い方を考察した建築家であった。様々な光の性格をコントロールして用いることで、建築空間をゆたかに演出した。この美術館では大きく2つの採光システムが導入されている。一つは建物の西側に位置する一般展示空間における採光である。ここでは非対称の反射板を持つスカイライトの帯を東西方向に5本配置することで自然光を積極的に採り入れている。非対称の反射板の形状は、入ってくる方向によって全く異なる光の性質をスタディした結果である。もう一つは、東側の大展示室の採光である。ここではピラミッド型のスカイライトによって、南側を除く三方から良い光が得られるので、すべての壁面が展示に利用される。

△▽ Main exhibition space　一般展示室

Entrance　エントランス

Entrance hall　エントランス・ホール

Large-sized exhibition space　大型展示室

Main exhibition space　一般展示室

1961–68
KEVIN ROCHE JOHN DINKELOO

OAKLAND MUSEUM
Oakland, California, U.S.A.

![Entrance]

Entrance　エントランス

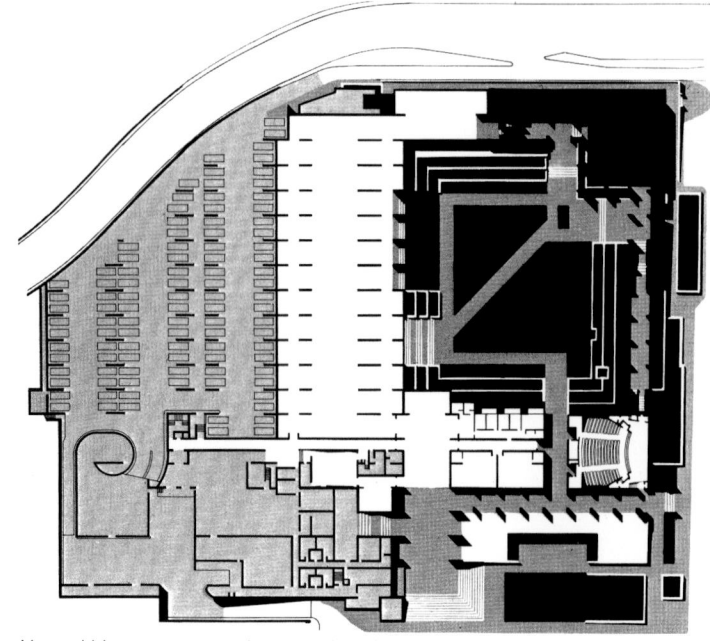

Natural history museum+lower parking level

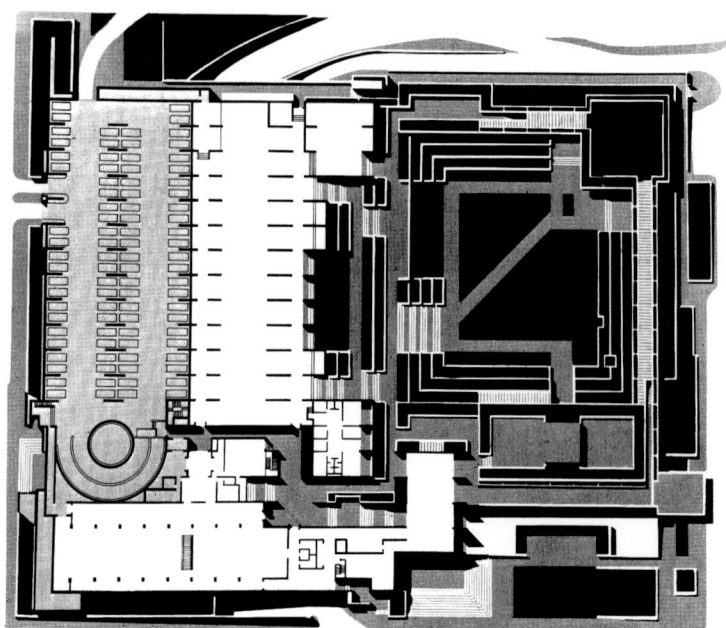

Cultural history museum+upper parking level

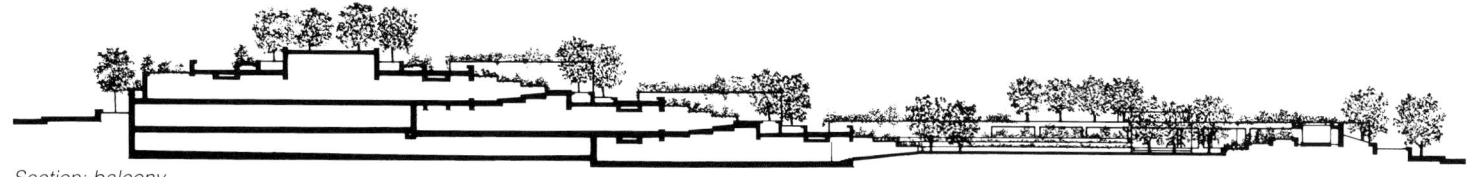
Section: balcony

Staircase from garden　庭園側階段

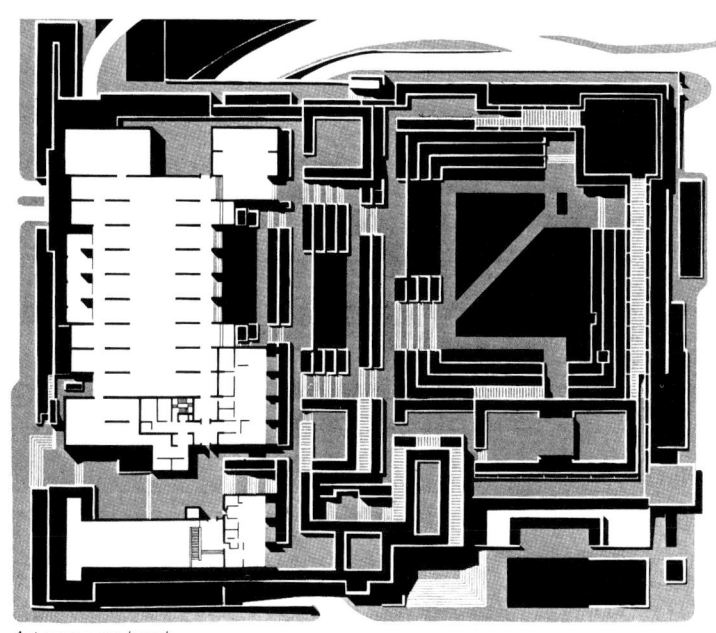
Art museum level

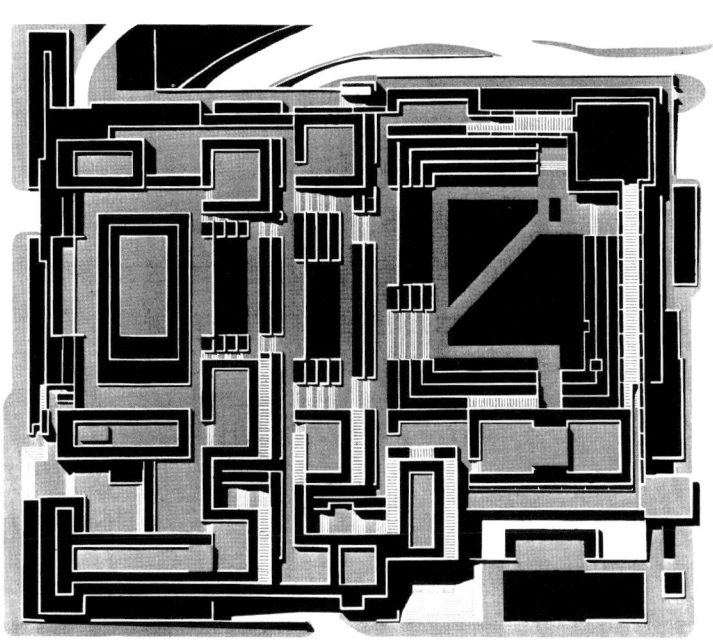
Garden level

Aerial view　航空写真

View from garden　庭園より見る

The City of Oakland's original intention was to construct an art museum, a natural history museum and a cultural history museum. It was agreed that these separate entities could be combined into one complex with a common architecture, and that they could share a common objective — to create a regional museum of California and its environs. The building, which occupies four blocks, is conceived as a walled garden with large welcoming entrances. The galleries are so arranged that the roof of one becomes the terrace of another. A pedestrian street connects the different levels and the other functions. Each area opens directly onto lawns, terraces, trellised passages and broad flights of stairs. The entire museum is built of a light colored concrete with a sandblasted finish. The wide walls which surround the planting are just the right height to sit on. The planting has begun to do what it was hoped it would, to grow over the entire building, gradually submerging its form and creating a lush, colorful garden.

建設プログラムでは、美術館、自然博物館、文化博物館の三つを建設することが要求されていた。その後、関係諸団体との討論のなかで、これらの別々の機能をひとつの建物に統合することが認められた。美術館がカリフォルニアとその周辺地域に対して広域美術館の役割をはたすことも確認された。オークランド市の歴史と将来の可能性を調査した結果、このプロジェクトが下町地区の再生の核になりうることがはっきりしたが、それには、敷地を美術館としてだけでなく公園としても利用すべきだという結論が得られた。建物は四つの街区を占めている。デザインは、壁をめぐらした庭園をイメージしていた。大きな入口が、人々を迎え入れるように開いている。各館のギャラリーの屋上は他の館のギャラリーのテラスになっており、テラスは互いに歩道で結ばれている。講堂、教室、ギャラリー、オフィス、レストランなどの諸施設も、この歩道で連絡されている。各エリアは、芝生、テラス、格子棚に覆われた歩道、広い階段に面している。建物は明るい色彩のコンクリート造で、サンドブラスト仕上げがほどこされている。植栽をとりまく厚い壁は、腰掛けるのにちょうどよい高さにしてある。建物が完成してから開館までの間に植栽は期待通りに成長して建物を覆いはじめている。それは、やがて建物の形態を包み込み、色彩豊かな庭園をつくり出すだろう。

View toward main entrance メイン・エントランス方向を見る

Exhibition room 展示室 △▽

1962–68
MIES VAN DER ROHE

NEW NATIONAL GALLERY
Berlin, Germany

Overall view 全景

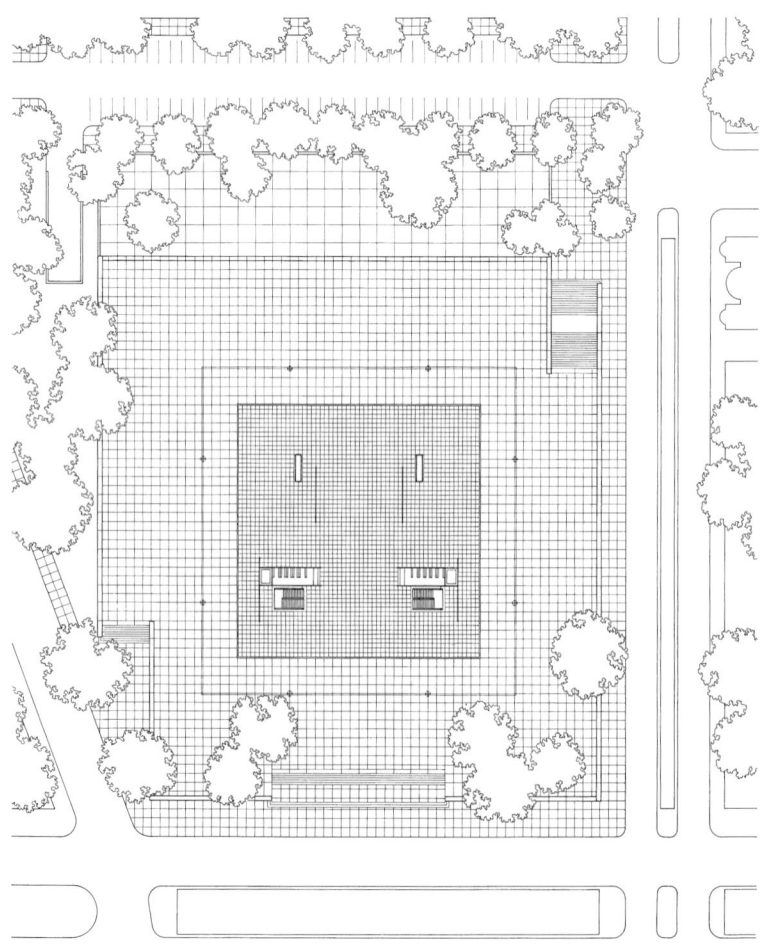

Main floor S=1:1500

Situated in close proximity to the wall which had divided Berlin during the Cold War, this museum was originally planned as part of a cultural complex of the western side, along with Hans Scharoun's concert hall and a library among others. It has a square plan, surrounded by glass walls, and is built onto a vast terrace. The main floor is a glass box, a space for temporary exhibitions. Underneath are housed the exhibition space for 20th-century fine arts—the museum's permanent collection, administrative offices, and storage spaces. The site itself inclines to the west. In fact the terrace, which is given an adequate size, serves as a courtyard to provide lighting for the lower floor. It is a podium accentuating the building's temple-like facet. The iron roof is 64.8 m square and 1.8 m thick. Its orthogonal grid consists of welded web girders. Beams on the perimeter are fixed by ribs. Each side is supported by a pair of cross-shaped, steel frame columns.

The temporary exhibition space is enclosed

Section

Elevation

within glass walls set 7.2 m back from the roof perimeter, leaving room for the arcades outside. The ceiling is 8.4 m high. Both the terrace and the temporary exhibition hall are paved with the same granite tiles measuring 1.2 m square.

The lower-level space for permanent exhibitions is of reinforced concrete. The exhibition room is a white space, in contrast with the transparent space of the upper floor defined by glass walls and fringed by black steel frames. The beauty of such proportion and details indicate the presence of an unshakable truth.

Dynamism of the iron roof emphasizing horizontality; accuracy of the surrounding glass walls; continuity of material generated by granite pavement inside and outside the building; steel-frame structure that never interrupts the lines of vision nor of motion—this space of intense transparency is the acme of 'universal space', a concept that the architect has been pursuing since his Barcelona Pavilion. A fruit of Mies' architectural philosophy, a masterpiece that he has finally come to realize in his home country, among his numerous works in the United States during the postwar period.

冷戦期のベルリンを東西に分断していた壁に程近い地区の、ハンス・シャロウンのコンサート・ホールや図書館等とともに西側の文化施設群の一つとして計画された美術館である。ガラス壁に囲まれた正方形プランの美術館は広いテラスの上に建つ。そのガラスの箱である基準階は特別展示のための空間であり、その階下は常設の20世紀美術コレクションのための展示空間と事務所、倉庫を収める。西に向かって敷地は傾斜し、テラスは階下の採光のためのコートヤードを形成している。十分な広さを持つテラスはこの建物の神殿的な性格を強調する基壇である。鉄製の屋根は64.8m角の正方形で、1.8mの厚さを持ち、溶接によるウェブ・ガーターで正方形の格子を形成している。外周の梁はリブによって固定され、各辺、2本ずつの十字形の鉄骨柱によって支持されている。

特別展示の空間は屋根外周から7.2m内側にセットバックしたガラス壁で囲われ、周囲にアーケードを残している。天井高は8.4m、テラスと特別展示のホールは同じ1.2m角の御影石が敷き詰められている。

下層の常設展示の空間は鉄筋コンクリート造で、展示室は、黒い鉄骨に縁取られガラスに囲まれる上階の透明な空間とは対照的に、白い空間となっている。その美しいプロポーションやディテールには揺るぎのない真実がある。

水平性を強調する力強い鉄の屋根、四方のガラス壁の正確さ、内外に敷き詰められる御影石の連続する質感、視界や動線を遮らない鉄骨の構造――透明性の高い空間はバルセロナ・パヴィリオン以降探求していた「ユニバーサル・スペース」の到達点であり、戦後のアメリカでの仕事とともにミースの建築哲学の結実、戦後の祖国に実現した傑作であった。

Terrace テラス

Steel roof 鉄製の屋根

Detail ディテール

Exhibition space on main floor 主階展示室 △▽▷

1966–72
LOUIS I. KAHN

KIMBELL ART MUSEUM
Fort Worth, Texas, U.S.A.

Because the site is placed inside a vast garden, a building with minimum height was a prerequisite from the very beginning. It is a museum accommodating art pieces from 19th century and antiquity that are rather small in size and scale.

The building is of reinforced concrete with architectural surfaces. Vaults covered with travertine are arranged into three and six rows on the longitudinal and latitudinal sides respectively, on top of the ground-floor volume that may be compared to an architectural terracing. These 30-meter by 6.5-meter units make up the museum's plan. Between the vaulted units are service spaces, 2.5-meter wide with ceilings lower than the vaults and housing various facilities and staircases.

Kahn's belief about this museum was that these works of art ought to be contemplated under natural lighting. Two types of natural light would be captured inside the museum in order to light up the exhibition: one being the 'silver light' from the sky, and the other the 'green light' from the courtyard. 'Silver light' comes through aluminium skylight units in the center of vaults. Since the vaults' shape has been defined by cycloid curves designed to create an even distribution of light, the skylight's silvery light induces such curved silhouettes to emerge, then softly pervades the gallery. 'Green light' comes from three courtyards that are all different in size, scattered among the vaults and planted with greenery. Light passing through them adds an unique accent to exhibition spaces.

With its sequenced cycloid vaults, the museum's profile is of great beauty and gentleness, in harmony with the surrounding nature. Travertine and concrete covering the wall surfaces may be disparate in terms of value, but in fact, both prove to us the fact that they share an intense affinity and close proximity with each other. They have been chosen as ideal materials for this building to exist and be evaluated over the times: travertine as symbol of 'classics' and concrete as a building's 'vital root'. Inside, each spatial unit of vault, complete in itself, is tied up to bring about diverse effects, and create spatial variation.

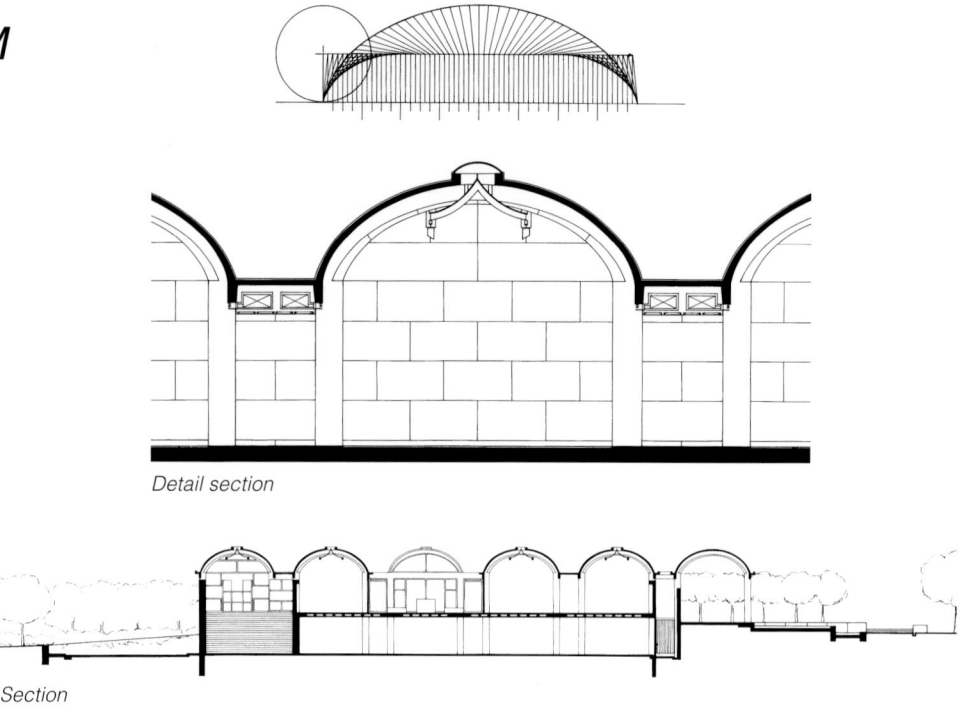
Detail section

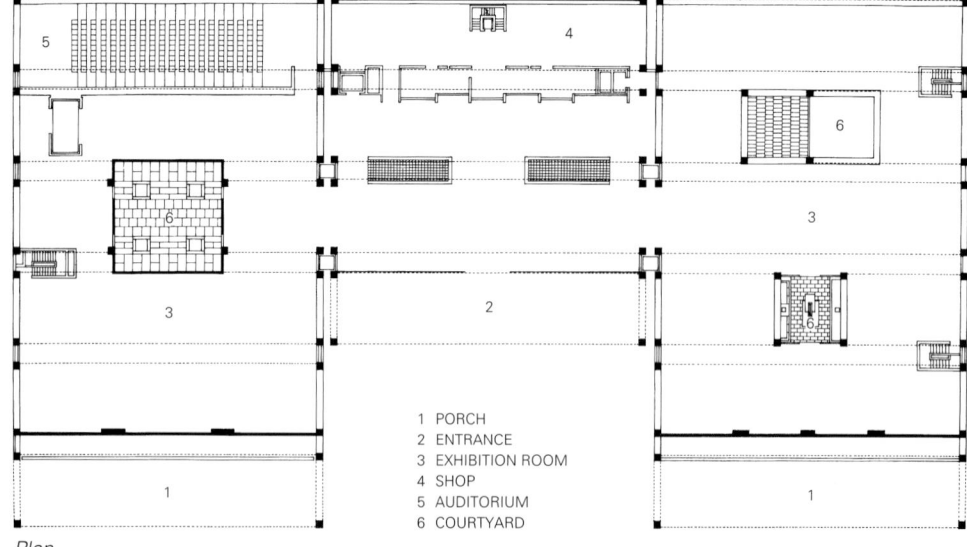
Section

Plan

1 PORCH
2 ENTRANCE
3 EXHIBITION ROOM
4 SHOP
5 AUDITORIUM
6 COURTYARD

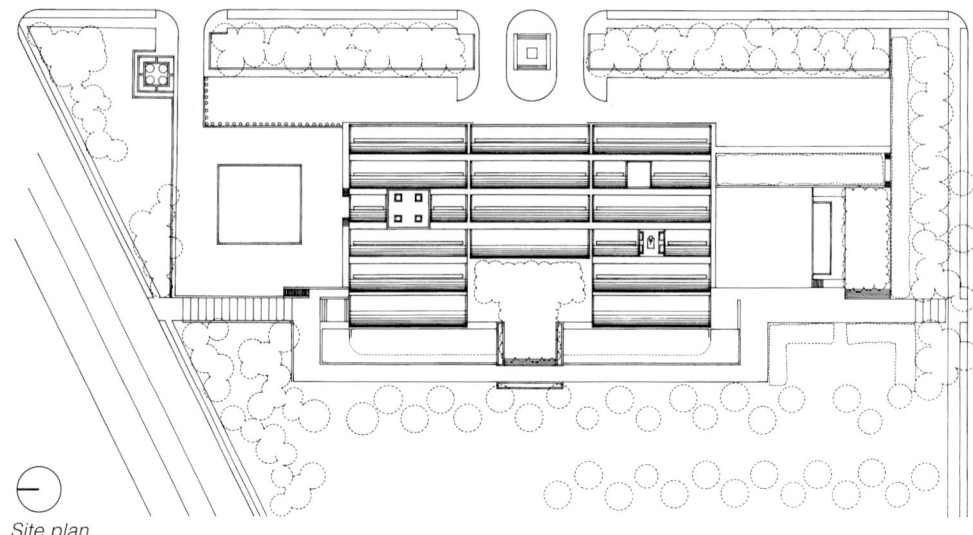
Site plan

敷地は広大な庭園の中であり、建物の高さを抑えることが当初からの条件であった。収められるのは19世紀と古代の美術作品であり、比較的小規模の作品のための美術館である。

建物はコンクリート造でコンクリート部分は打放し仕上げである。基壇に見立てられる1階部分のヴォリューム上に、トラバーチンが張られた30×6.5mのヴォールトを長手方向に3列、短手方向に6列並べている。このヴォールトを単位として美術館の平面は構成されている。ヴォールトのユニット間に取られるサーヴァント・スペースはヴォールトに対して天井高が低く、幅は2.5mで、設備や階段室などにあてられている。

この美術館でカーンは作品を自然光で鑑賞すべきであると考えた。そしてここで二種類の自然光を美術館の中に採り入れて展示照明にした。一つは天空からの「銀色の光」であり、もう一つはコートヤードの「緑色の光」であった。「銀色の光」はヴォールト中央に設けられたアルミニウムのスカイライト・ユニットによる。ヴォールトの形状はサイクロイド曲線によって、一様な光量分布が生まれるように計算されていたため、スカイライトの銀色の光はそのカーブを浮かび上がらせ、ギャラリーに柔らかな光を満たす。「緑色の光」はヴォールト群の中に作られた大小3つのコートヤードからの光による。コートヤードには植栽が与えられ、その緑を通った光は展示空間にアクセントを与えることになる。

サイクロイド・ヴォールトが連続する外観の美しく優しいシルエットは、周囲の緑の中に調和している。その壁面のトラバーチンとコンクリートは一見、価値の全く異なる素材同士であるが、実は高い親和性と近似性があるという事実を証明している。トラバーチンは「古典」、コンクリートは建造物の「根源」を意味するものであるかのように、この建物が時代を超えて、評価され、存在するための素材として選ばれている。内部において、一つの完全なヴォールトの空間ユニットは繋ぎ合わされて、様々な効果をもたらして、空間のバリエーションを造り出している。

Aerial view 航空写真

Overall view 全景

31

South elevation　南面

Porch on west　西側ポーチ

View toward courtyard 中庭を見る

Fountain 泉

Entrance　エントランス

Exhibition room　展示室

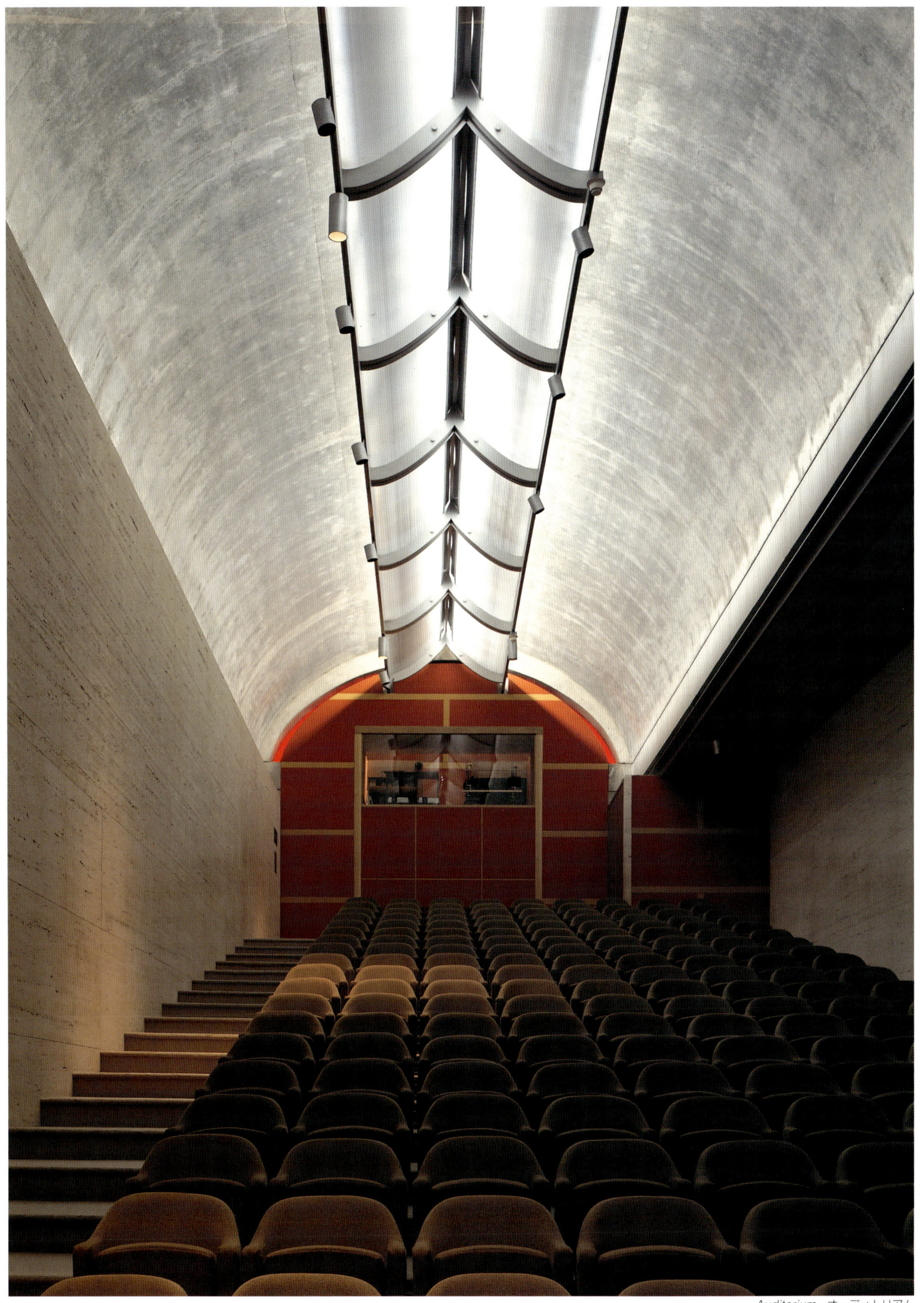

Auditorium　オーディトリアム

1969–74
LOUIS I. KAHN

CENTER FOR BRITISH ART AND STUDIES, YALE UNIVERSITY
New Haven, Connecticut, U.S.A.

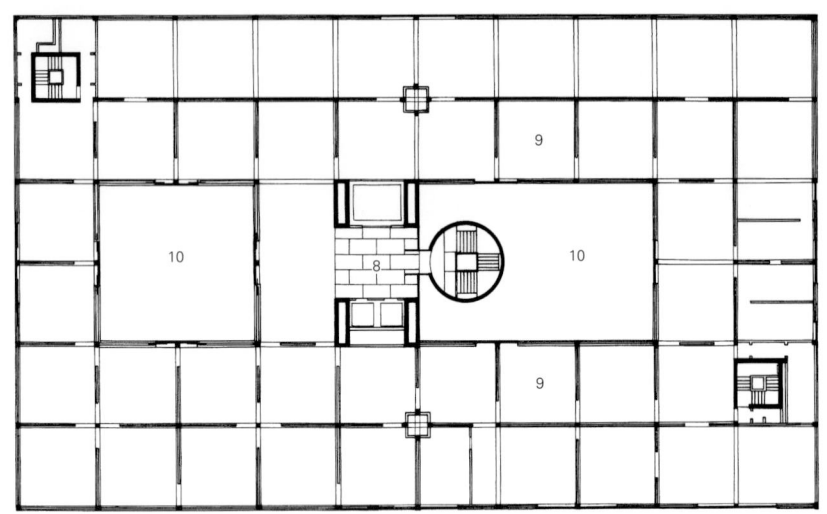

Fourth floor

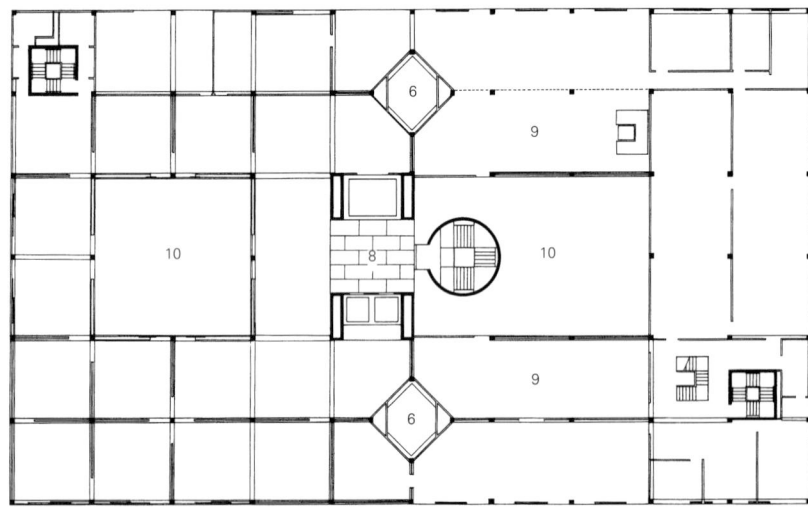

Third floor

First floor

Standing across the street from the Art Gallery—completed in 1953, also designed by Kahn—this building is a research facility for British art comprising an exhibition space. It features a uniform, concrete frame structure. Stainless and white oak panels are set inside these exposed concrete frames for exterior and interior finishings respectively: the combination of two different materials forms a smooth and harmonious surface. The external stainless panels are dotted with glass windows in a random manner as if added posteriorly from necessity, bringing rhythm to the facade's uniformity.

The rectangular plan is precisely divided into 6x10 grids, and the structural body in concrete is built in accordance with these grids. An atrium with a four-level height that constitutes the entrance court, and three levels of spaces with a columned staircase are arranged along the longitudinal axis. Such highly symmetric structure attributes a classical and strict character to the space like a temple. Exhibition spaces are organized around these two major spaces. Skylights are opened throughout the whole roof. They grow out of the coffered ceiling with some taper, and are given solid forms in delicate balance with the size and depth of each opening to let natural light pervade the atrium and exhibition spaces.

Application of precise geometry in the decision of appropriate sizes of the modules, together with the spatial effects produced, seem to have stopped the flow of time in this particular place, with an immutable sense of conclusion. This is an extraordinary example of modernism sublimated into a spatial value equal to the classics, an achievement that Kahn has accomplished through a series of works.

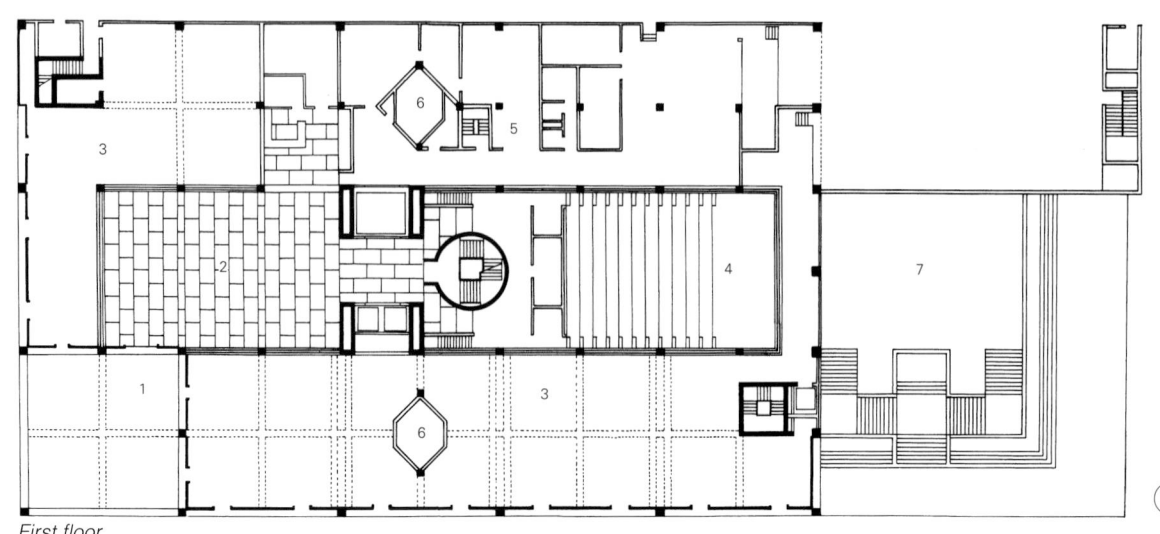

1 PORCH
2 COURTYARD
3 ATELIER
4 AUDITORIUM
5 OFFICE
6 DUCTS SPACE
7 SUNKEN GARDEN
8 LOBBY
9 EXHIBITION ROOM
10 LIGHT COURT

Street view 道路より見る

同じくカーン設計、1953年竣工のアート・ギャラリーと道を挟んで向かいに建つこの建物は、英国美術の研究施設で展示空間を持つ。構造は均質なコンクリート・フレーム架構による。外装材としてステンレス・パネル、内部においてホワイト・オーク材のパネルがその打放しコンクリート・フレームの内側にはめ込まれる。2素材の組み合わせによる調和のとれたスムーズな表面を形成している。外部のステンレス・パネルには必要に応じて空けられたかのようにランダムなガラス窓が均質なファサードにリズムを与えている。

長方形の平面は6×10のグリッドに正確に分割され、コンクリートの構造体はこのグリッドに従って建ち上げられている。エントランス・コートである4層吹抜けのアトリウム空間と円柱の階段室のある3層の空間が長手軸上に並べられ、この強いシンメトリー構成が神殿のような古典的で厳格な性格を空間に与えている。展示空間はこれら二つの大空間の周りに配置される。屋根全体にわたって設置されたスカイライトは、天井面のグリッドからテーパーをかけて建ち上げられ、その開口の大きさと深さの絶妙なバランスを与えられた立体的な形状をもち、これによってもたらされる自然光がアトリウムや展示空間を満たす。

厳格な幾何学形態を用いて、そのモジュールの寸法の適切な決定とそれが造り出す空間効果は、変更しようのない完結性をもってこの場所の時間を止めてしまっているかのようである。一連のカーンの仕事に見られる偉業である、モダニズムの古典レベルの空間価値への昇華は、ここで見事に完成している。

Northwest elevation 北西面

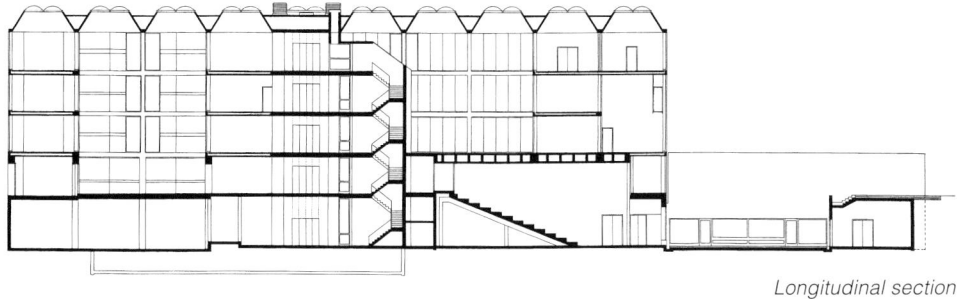

Longitudinal section

Light court on southeast 南東側光庭

Light court on northwest　北西側光庭

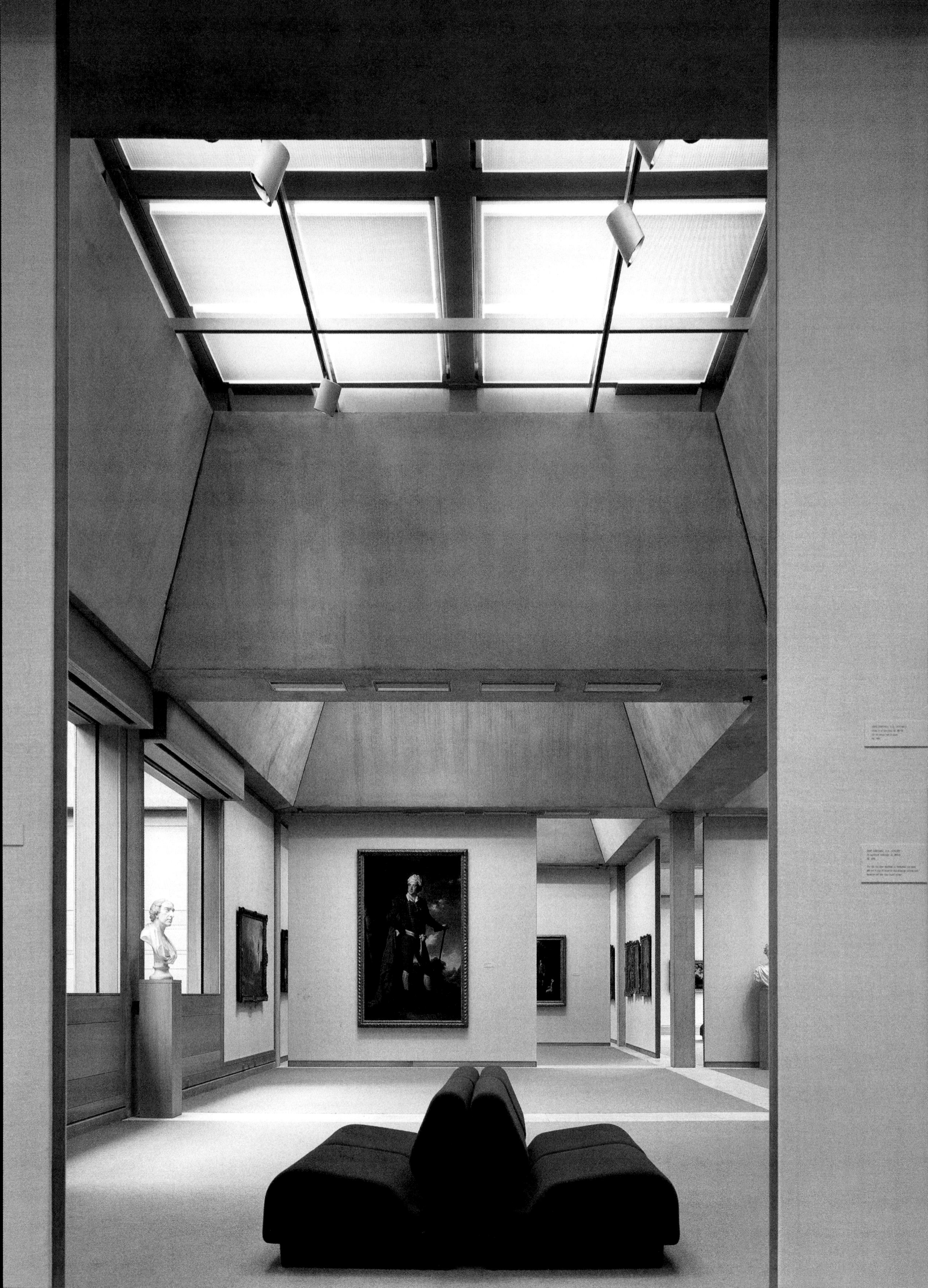

Skylight of staircase　階段室のスカイライト

Fourth floor: detail　4階：ディテール

◁ *Exhibition room on fourth floor*　4階展示室

Staircase　階段室

Skylight　スカイライト

41

1971–74 / 1992–97 (renovation & Contemporary Art Wing)
ARATA ISOZAKI

GUMMA PREFECTURAL MUSEUM OF FINE ARTS
Gumma, Japan

Overall view 全景

View from southwest 南西より見る

Entrance hall　エントランス・ホール △▽

Fusaichiro Inoue of Takasaki, Gumma Prefecture has patronized cultural activities in his city over the course of a lifetime. Before the Second World War, he invited Bruno Taut, who had sought refuge in Japan, and found a home for Taut in a detached house on the grounds of a local monastery. After the war, he commissioned Antonin Raymond to design a concert hall, which permitted an orchestra to establish roots in a provincial city, something that has rarely happened in Japan.

For a long time Inoue had tried to convince the prefecture of the necessity of building an art museum, and when there were problems in appropriating a budget for the project, he went so far as to start a gallery himself in his own office as a preliminary measure. After the idea of constructing a prefectural museum had been accepted, Inoue held discussions with Teiichi Hijikata, the director of the Kanagawa Prefectural Museum of Modern Art designed by Junzo Sakakura, and began the selection of the architect. He interviewed Masato Otaka, Fumihiko Maki, and me, and I was ultimately selected to design the museum. (Otaka has since designed a prefectural museum of natural history on an adjoining site, and Maki is expected to design a museum of modern literature for the same prefecture.)

Getting this public commission at a time when I was recovering from the crisis after Expo'70 was extremely fortunate from the point of view of my career as an architect. I decided to concentrate on developing a new method. I had already begun to experiment in the work in Fukuoka, but I really gained confidence designing this museum.

The approach I used has much in common with mannerism and conceptualism in art. It is practically impossible to reduce architecture, which must accommodate various functions, to a sculptural object. However, the code generating meaning in a material object that has been reduced to abstract signs and the code suggesting conventional architectural meaning can be made to alternately appear and disappear, resulting in a new multilayered code.

The double-layered code appears in my subsequent works. At times the two layers are only slightly distinguishable, and at other times they offer a clear contrast. I began to feel that my design style demanded that I avoid using just one code.

Arata Isozaki

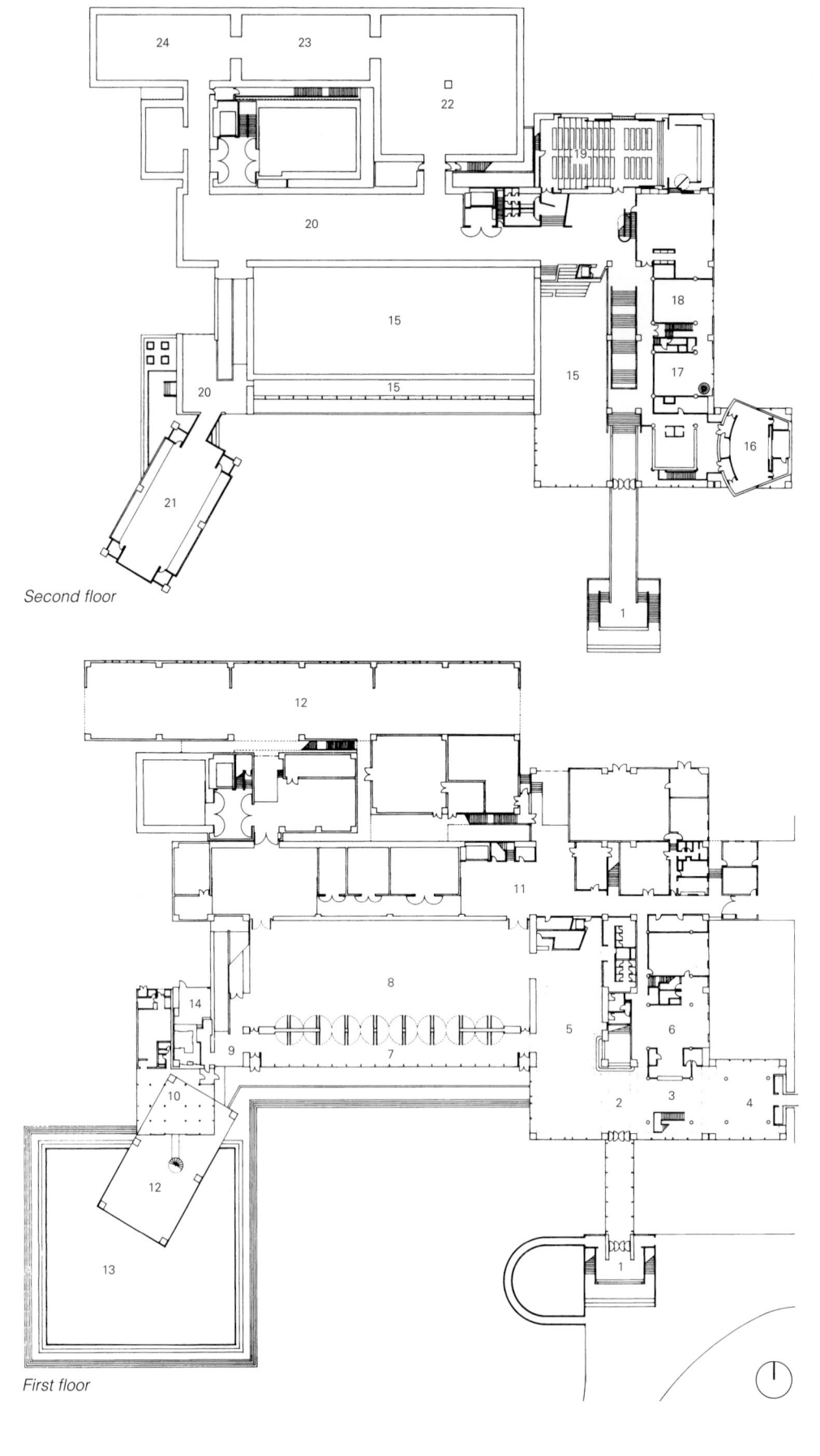

Second floor

First floor

1	ENTRANCE	15	VOID
2	ENTRANCE HALL	16	HDTV THEATER
3	RECEPTION	17	CURATORS' ROOM
4	SHOP	18	LIBRARY
5	HALL	19	LECTURE HALL
6	OFFICE	20	PERMANENT EXHIBITION ROOM
7	GALLERY	21	EXHIBITION ROOM FOR JAPANESE ARTS
8	TEMPORARY EXHIBITION ROOM	22	EXHIBITION ROOM 3 (Contemporary Art Wing)
9	LOUNGE	23	EXHIBITION ROOM 4 (Contemporary Art Wing)
10	RESTAURANT		
11	LOADING		
12	PILOTIS	24	EXHIBITION ROOM 5 (Contemporary Art Wing)
13	POOL		
14	TEA CEREMONY ROOM		

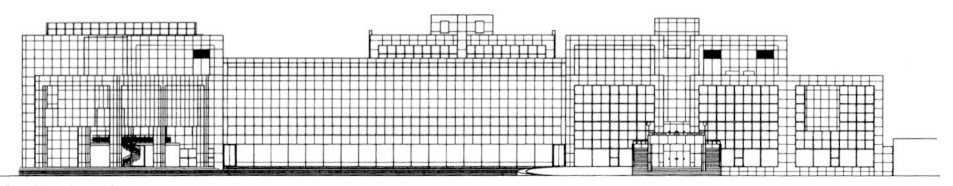

South elevation

Entrance hall: north view エントランス・ホール：北を見る

South elevation: view toward entrance
エントランス方向を見る

　群馬県高崎市在住の井上房一郎氏は、生涯かけて、この都市における文化活動をパトロネージしてきている。戦前には、日本に亡命したブルーノ・タウトをこの地に招聘し、3年間にわたって、ひとつの寺院の離れ家に住むことを補助した。戦後は、アントニン・レーモンドにコンサートホールの設計を依頼した。地方都市にオーケストラを根づかせた、日本では稀な活動であった。

　井上氏は早くから美術館建設の必要を県に説いたが、容易に予算化されなかったので、みずからの事務所を建設の準備のために、ギャラリーとしてその活動をはじめたほどであった。県立の美術館として、建設の構想が立てられてから、井上氏は坂倉準三氏の設計になる神奈川県立近代美術館長の土方定一氏と相談して建築家の選考をはじめ、大高正人、槇文彦、磯崎新の三名をインタビュウして、私が最終的に美術館の設計者にえらばれた。（その後、大高正人氏は隣接地に県立博物館を設計し、槇文彦氏は、同じく県立の近代文学館を設計する予定になっている。）

　EXPO'70の後におとずれたクライシスからの回復時期に、このパブリック・コミッションを得たことは、私の建築家としてのキャリアにとっても僥倖であった。この仕事に、私は新しい方法的投企を集中することにした。その一部分は既に福岡の仕事で実験的にはじめていたのだが、この美術館の設計を通じて、確信をもてるにいたった。

　それは美術におけるミニマリズムあるいはコンセプチュアリズムと通底している。建築であるからには、各種の用途を包含せねばならないので、それ自身を彫刻的物体に還元することはほとんど不可能だろう。だがその抽象的記号に還元された物体の意味が生産されるコードと、具体的な用途をもち、通念としての建築の意味を呈示するコードとの境界が、見えがくれして、あらためて重層したコードの解読へと導くことを可能にした。

　この二重コードは、それ以後の私の仕事にあらためて操作的にあらわれるようになる。みわけがつかない程のかすかな状態から、明瞭な対位法として構成されるまで、様態を変えながら、たえず出現する。そして、敢えて、単一のコードのみに陥るのをさけることが私のデザインのスタイルだと語るようになりはじめる。

（磯崎新）

Entrance hall: north wall　エントランス・ホール：北壁面

Entrance hall: south view　エントランス・ホール：南を見る

Entrance hall: north view　エントランス・ホール：北を見る

Exhibition room on first floor　1階展示室

Exhibition room 3 in contemporary art wing (1997)　現代美術棟（1997）の展示室3

Exhibition room 5 in contemporary art wing 現代美術棟の展示室5

1971–77
PIANO / ROGERS

GEORGES POMPIDOU CULTURAL CENTER
Paris, France

The building is situated in the center of historic Paris within 1.1 kilometers of Notre Dame, the Louvre, and the edge of the densely populated medieval Marais quarter. At the time of the competition there were no sizeable open activity spaces in central Paris.

As a general concept it was decided that it was to be a "live center of information, entertainment and culture". The building was to be both a flexible container and a dynamic machine, highly serviced and made from prefabricated pieces, aimed at attracting as wide a public as possible by cutting across the traditional cultural-institutional limits.

Over half of the square was left as an open "piazza" for a wide variety of public events. The roads were closed over a large area so that shops could spill out over the pedestrian area.

The client specified a number of specialized cultural activities. The aim was to generalize the brief while not forgetting specialist needs; and to create a center for both tourists and people who live in neighborhood, a true dynamic meeting-place where activities overlap in flexible well-serviced space. The view taken was that the greater the public involvement, the greater the success.

建物は、ノートルダム、ルーヴルなどパリの歴史的な中心から1.1キロの範囲内、そして中世の面影を残し人口の集中するマレ地区との境界に位置している。コンペが行われた当時、パリ中心部には一般に開放された広いアクティビティ・スペースは存在しなかった。

全体的なコンセプトは、〈情報、エンタテイメント、文化のライヴ・センター〉とすることである。建物はフレキシブルなコンテナであると同時にダイナミックなマシンであり、高度なサービスを行い、プレファブ部材で構成し、従来の文化施設の限界を切り開いて、出来る限り広範な大衆の関心を惹きつけるものとすることが目的であった。

広場の半分以上が、さまざまな一般のイベントを行える開放的な"ピアッツァ"として残された。この広いエリアの周囲は車両通行止めにされているので、歩行者エリア全体に店を広げることができる。

クライアント側は、相当数の特別な文化活動が行われることを明記していた。専門家の必要とするものに対処する一方で、ツーリストや近隣住民双方のためのセンターとすること。柔軟で、サービスの行き届いたスペースのなかに、さまざまな活動が重層する、真にダイナミックな出会いの場をつくりだすこと。大衆を巻き込むことができればできるほど、建物は成功したものとなる、というのがその意図であった。

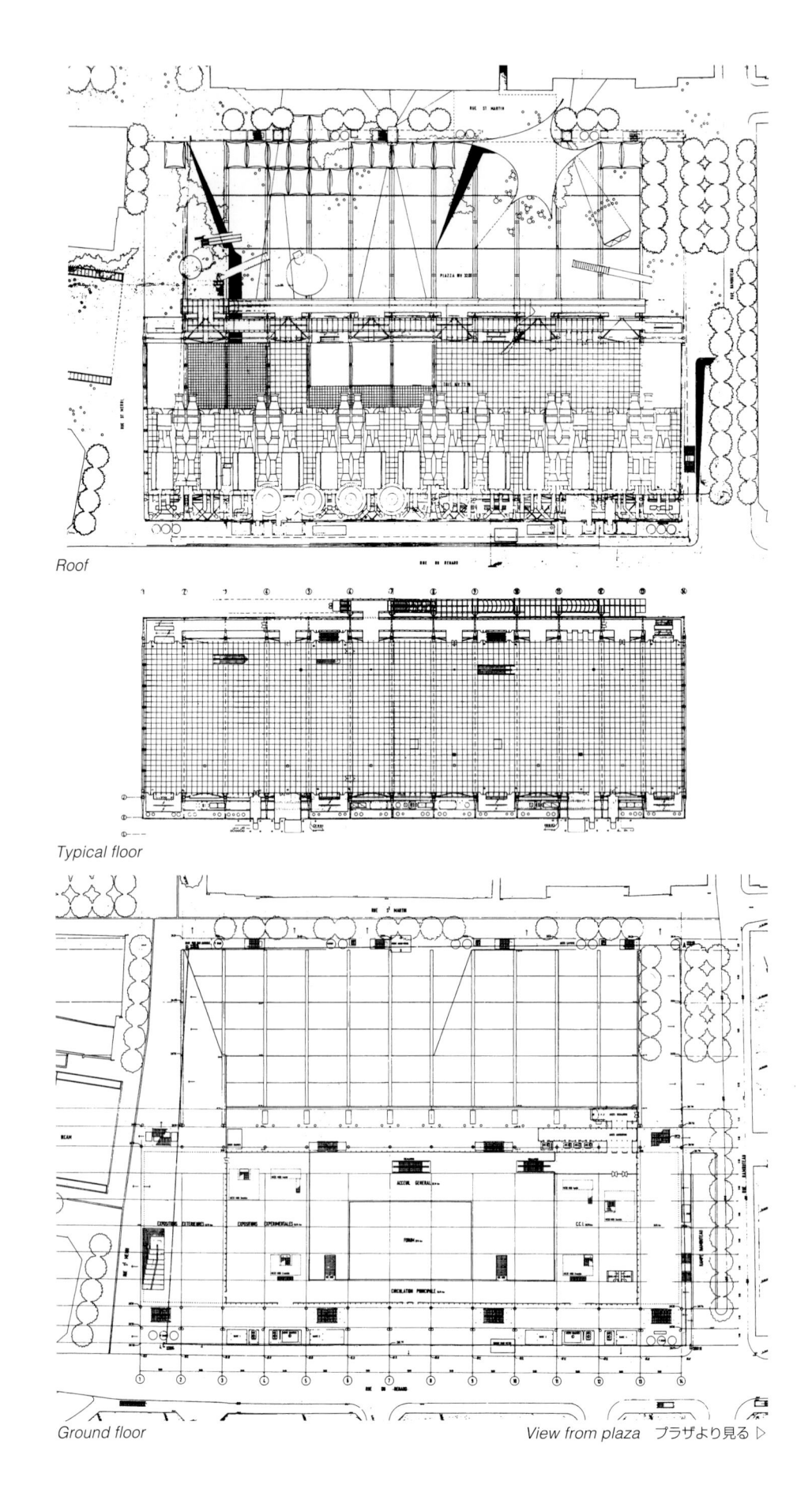

Roof

Typical floor

Ground floor

View from plaza プラザより見る ▷

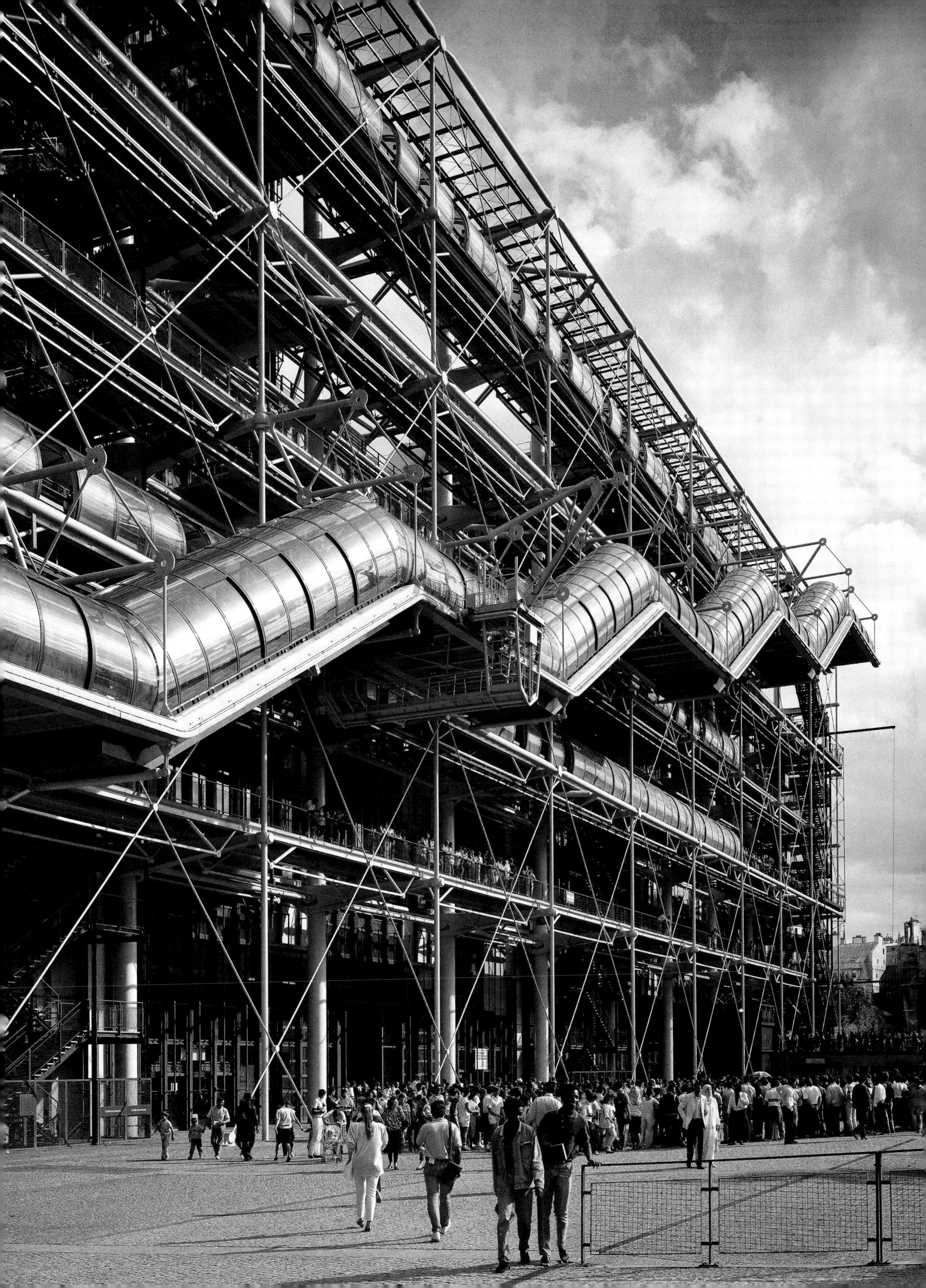

West elevation 西面

South elevation 南面

Plaza プラザ

△▽ *Entrance hall: view toward north*　エントランス・ホール：北を見る

Entrance hall: view toward west　エントランス・ホール：西を見る

Interior of museum　美術館内部

View from northeast　北東より見る

East elevation

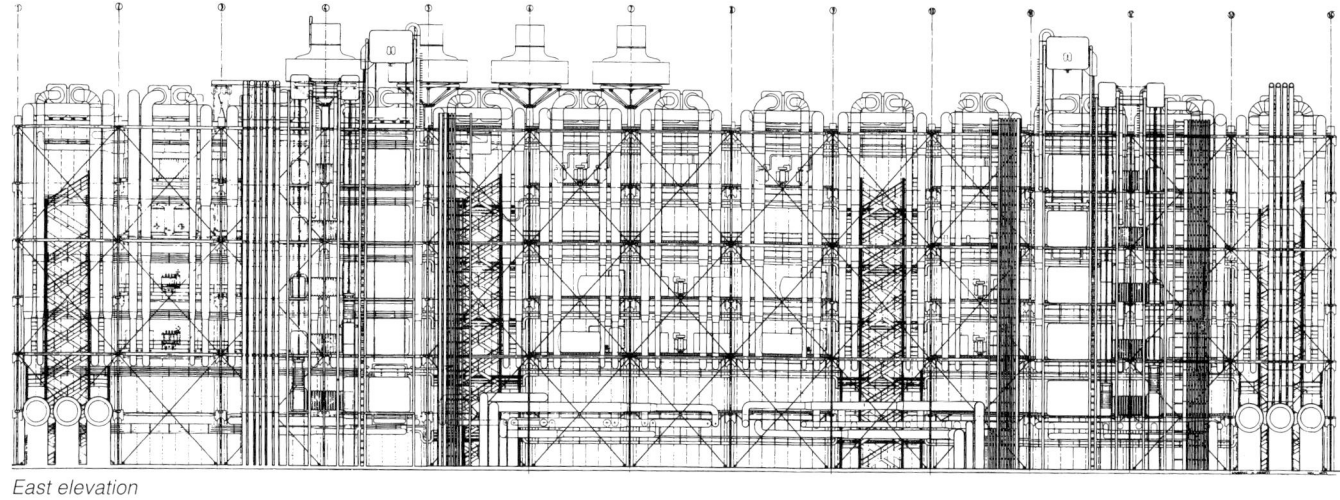

Interior of museum　美術館内部

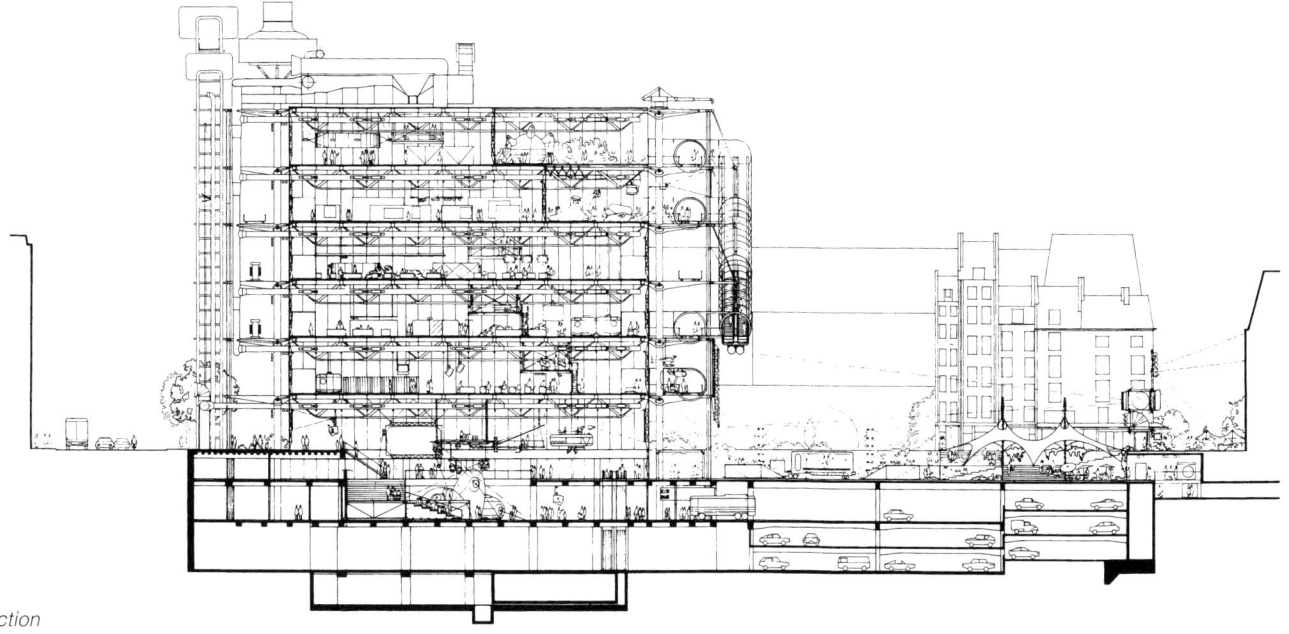

Cross section

Escalator system and support structure　エスカレータ・システムと支持構造

Circulation　通路

View from roof terrace　屋上テラスからの眺め

Structure　構造

1972–82
HANS HOLLEIN

ABTEIBERG MUSEUM
Mönchengladbach, Germany

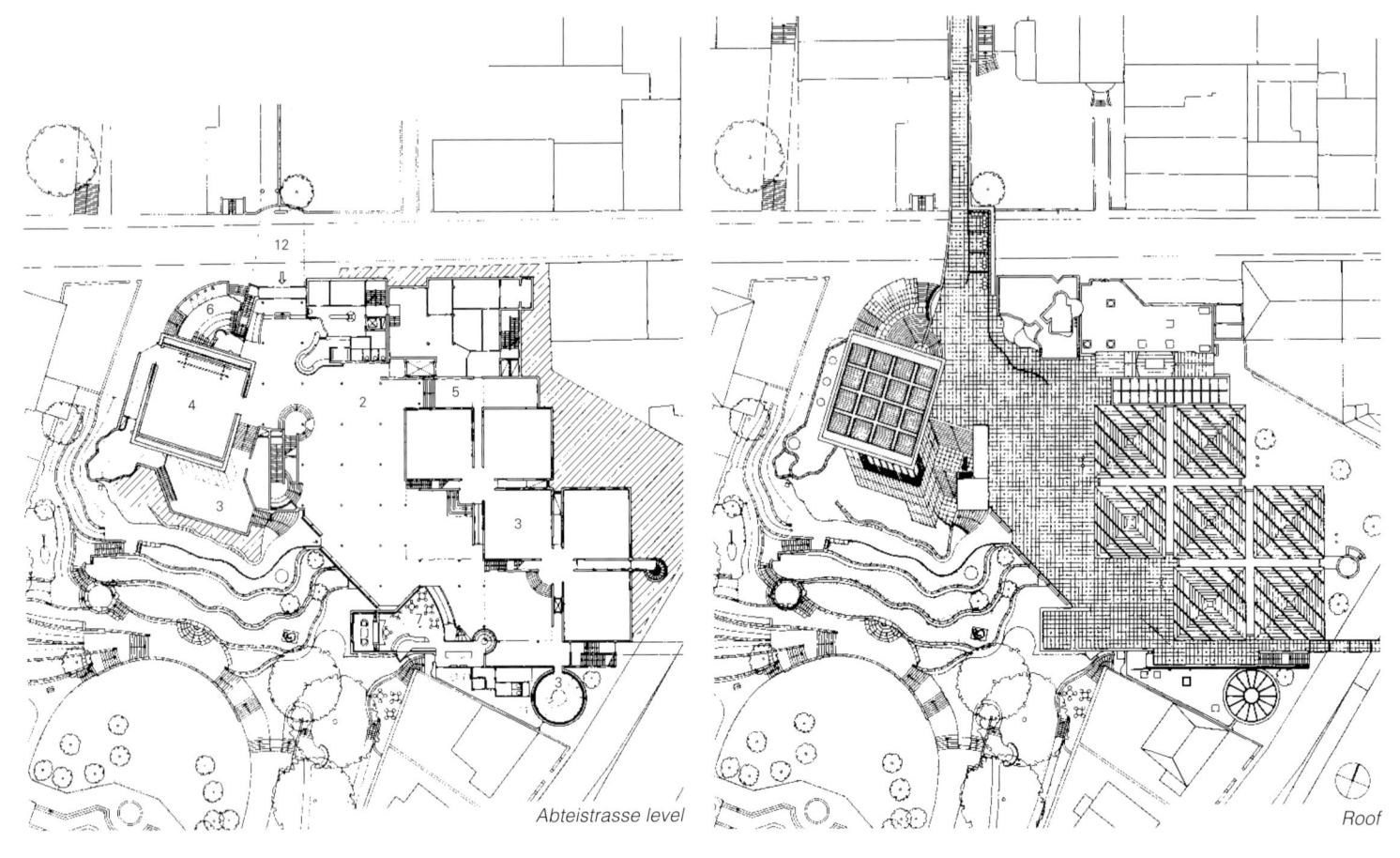

Abteistrasse level

Roof

1. ENTRANCE
2. EXHIBITION HALL
3. EXHIBITION ROOM
4. TEMPORARY EXHIBITION HALL
5. GALLERY
6. AUDIO-VISUAL ROOM
7. CAFETERIA
8. LECTURE HALL
9. LECTURE ROOM
10. CURATORS' ROOM
11. TERRACE
12. SUB-ENTRANCE
13. PEDESTRIAN TERRACE

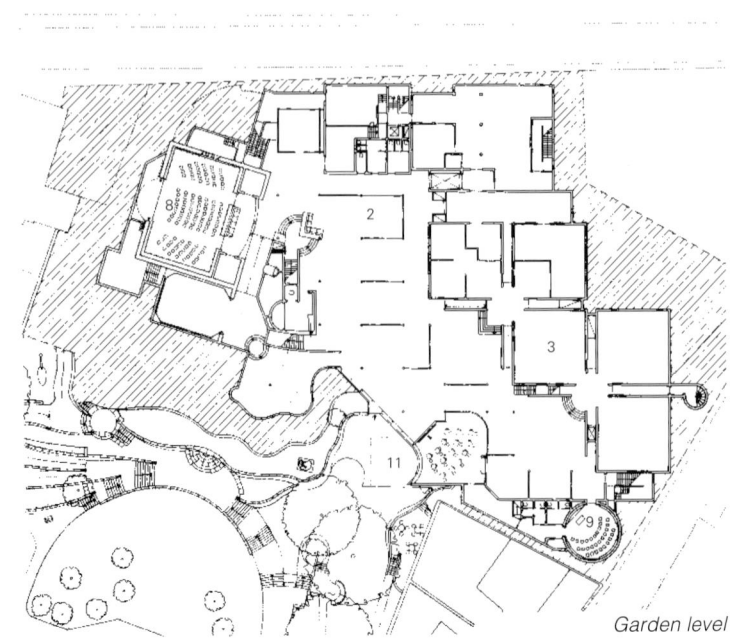

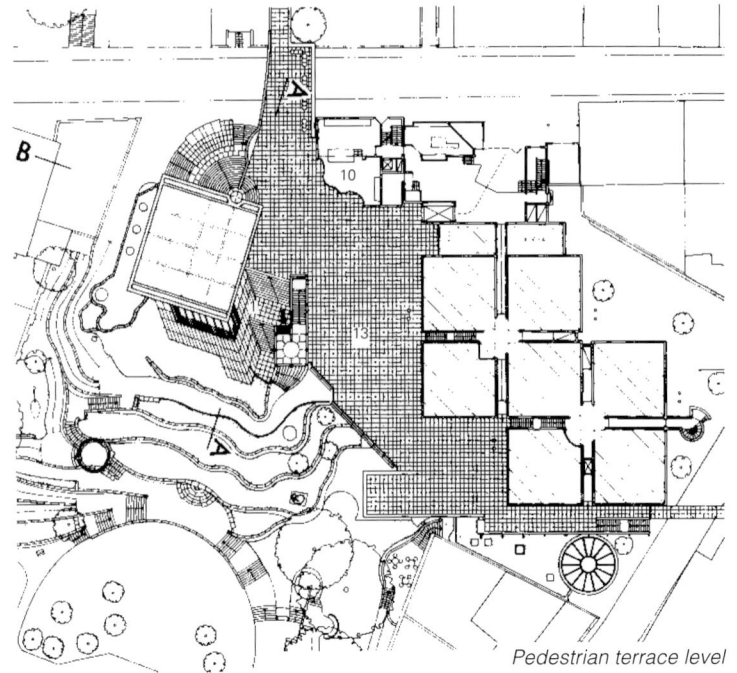

Garden level

Pedestrian terrace level

Overall view from garden 庭側全景

Mönchengladbach is a city filled with historical buildings, with its cathedral at the head of the list. This municipal museum was originally built as part of the city's urban planning, on top of a hill (Abteiberg = abbey hill) named after a monastery attached to the cathedral in the heart of the city. One of the largest in Germany at that time, this museum has required ten years from its conception to the opening.

Situated along the southern rise of Abteiberg, the museum is almost buried into the slope, making it difficult to grasp a full picture of it just looking from outside. Through a bridge across the hilltop on the north, the approach leads to a terrace paved with sandstone placed over the rooftop of the exhibition hall. From the terrace rises a tower. Opposite is the upper part of the exhibition hall finished with galvanized exterior that constitutes the western wall. Visitors make their way into the building from the main entrance in a cubic volume placed in a corner of this terrace. The cube accommodates a chrome pillar inside the white-marbled frame. Now the terrace is linked to a garden along the slope beneath, to form a pedestrian network. The main exhibition hall occupies the two levels below this terrace. Between these levels are arranged smaller exhibition rooms of various shapes, as in a labyrinth. Once again, there is an absence of visibility of a total picture, this time inside the museum.

Here, a multitude of architectural methods, elements and effects are combined to collide with each other in continuity. In such manner, the underground labyrinth has been made into a space providing pleasure and excitement that sometimes would contradict taboos. A sensuous place that cultivate our sensitivity in calmness. An architecture as a vector, showing way to the Contemporary Art of the time.

メンヘングラートバッハは聖堂を筆頭とする歴史的建造物の多い町である。町の中央に位置する、その聖堂に付属する修道院にちなんで付けられた名前の丘（アプタイベルク＝修道院の丘）に建つ都市計画の一部として建築された市立美術館。当時、その規模において、ドイツ有数の美術館であり、構想から開館まで10年を要した。

アプタイベルクの南側斜面に建てられたこの美術館はその外側から一見しても、斜面に埋め込まれるように配置されているため、全貌が把握できない配置である。アプローチは、北側、丘の頂上から架けられたブリッジを渡り、展示ホールの屋上に設けられた砂岩の敷き詰められたテラスに出る。テラスには学芸部のタワーがそびえ、その反対側に亜鉛引き外装の企画展示ホールの上部が西側壁面を形作る。入館者はそのテラスの一角にあるキューブのメイン・エントランスより建物に入っていく。キューブは白大理石のフレームにクロームの円柱が納められている。このテラスはその下の斜面の庭園と結びつけられて、ペデストリアン・ネットワークが作られている。主展示室はこのテラスの下二層分があてられ、それらのレベルの間に様々な形の小展示室が組み合わされて内部においてもその全貌が把握出来ないように迷宮化されている。

この美術館において様々な建築の手法や要素、その効果が連続的に組み合わされ、衝突させられることで、地下の迷宮空間は享楽的であり、時にタブーに触れるかのような興奮をもたらし、また、冷静に感性を研ぎ澄ます。そして、官能的なものに仕上げられている。現代美術の当時向かっていたベクトルを導く建築であった。

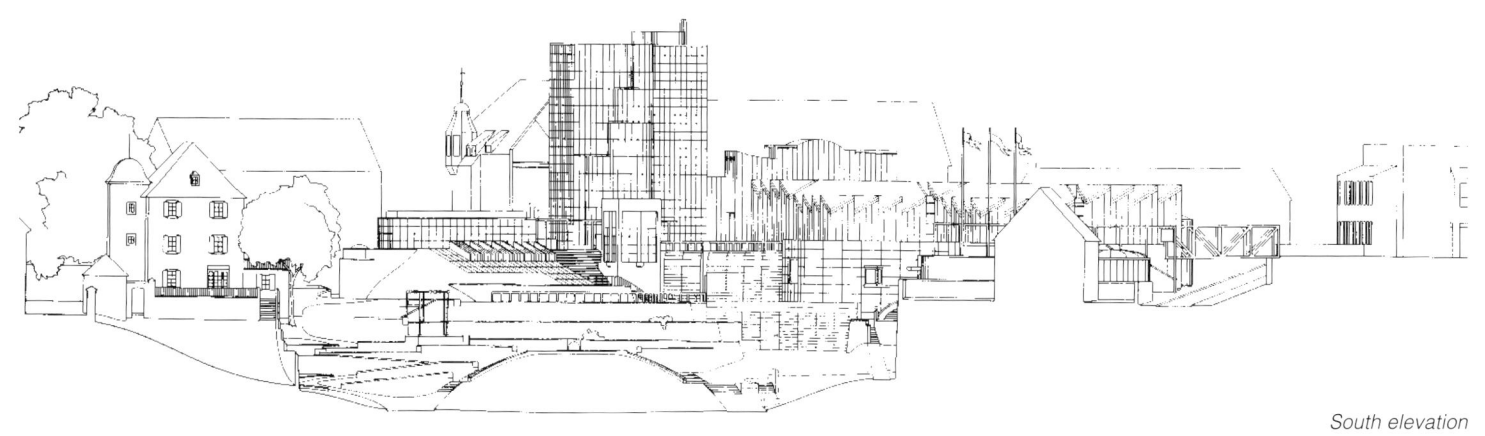

South elevation

Terrace: main entrance (left) and office tower　テラス：メイン・エントランス（左）と学芸部のタワー

Downward view of terrace　テラス見下ろし

Garden 庭園

Exhibition hall on Abteistrasse level　アプタイ通りレヴェルの展示ホール

Temporary exhibition hall　企画展示ホール

Exhibition room on Abteistrasse level
アプタイ通りレヴェルの展示室

Exhibition hall on garden level　庭園レヴェルの展示ホール

Exhibition room on Abteistrasse level　アプタイ通りレヴェルの展示室

Top-lit exhibition room　トップライトのある展示室

View of cafeteria from exhibition hall　展示ホールよりカフェテリアを見る

Top-lit exhibition room トップライトのある展示室 △▽

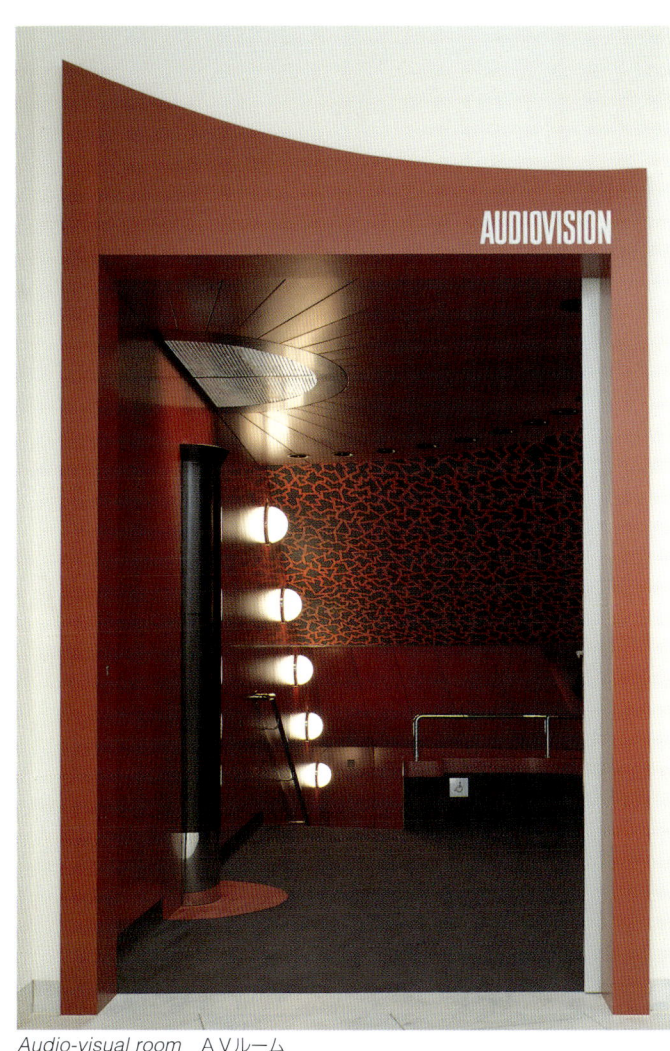

Audio-visual room ＡＶルーム

1974−78/1988−91 (Crescent Wing)
Norman Foster

SAINSBURY CENTRE FOR VISUAL ARTS
Norwich, U.K.

Overall view from south: Crescent Wing　南側全景：クレセント・ウィング

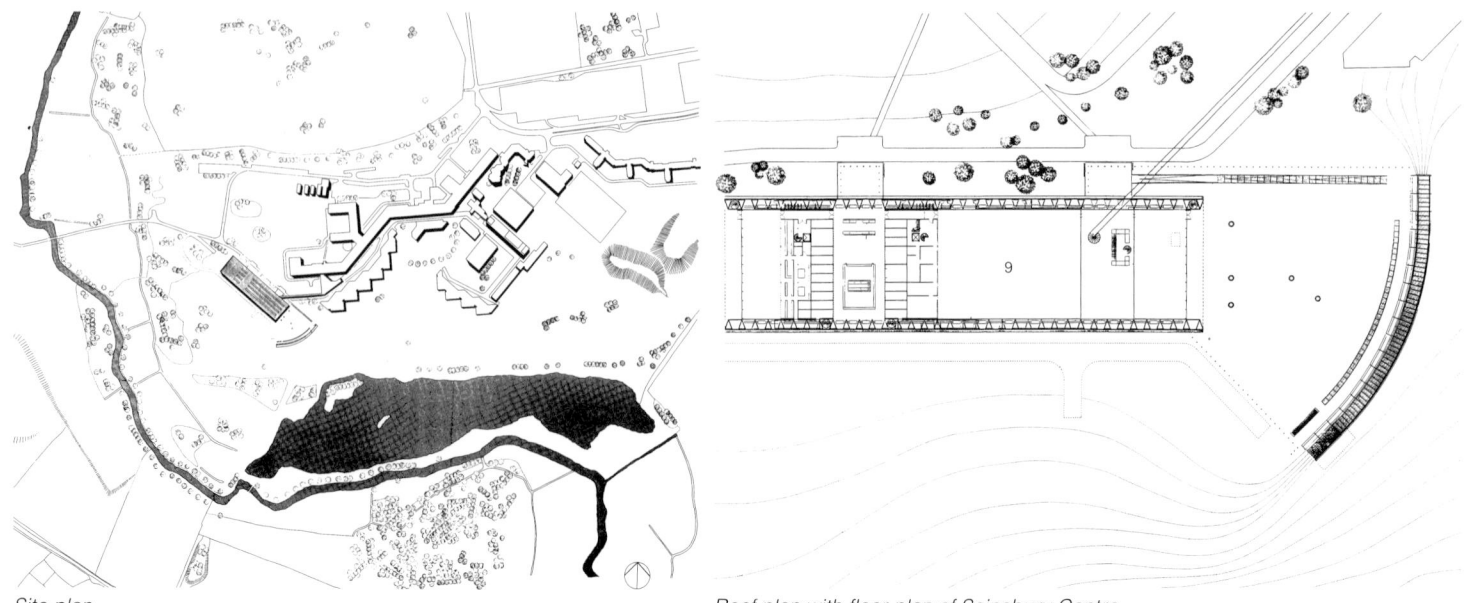

Site plan

Roof plan with floor plan of Sainsbury Centre

Sainsbury Centre, 1978 セインズベリー・センター, 1978

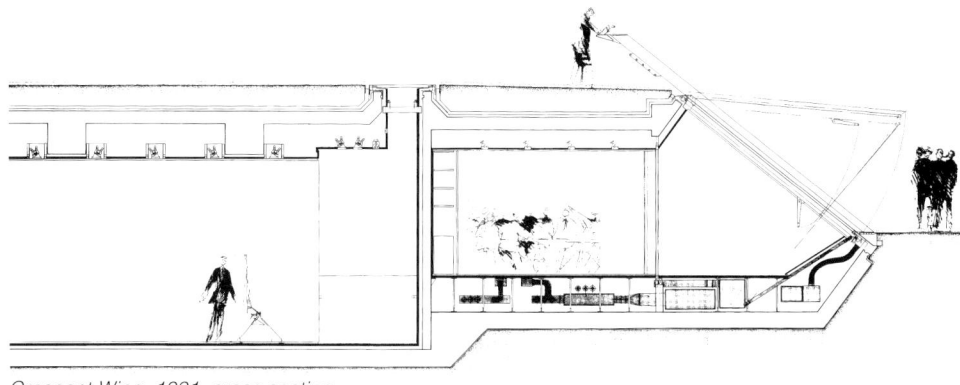

Crescent Wing, 1991: cross section

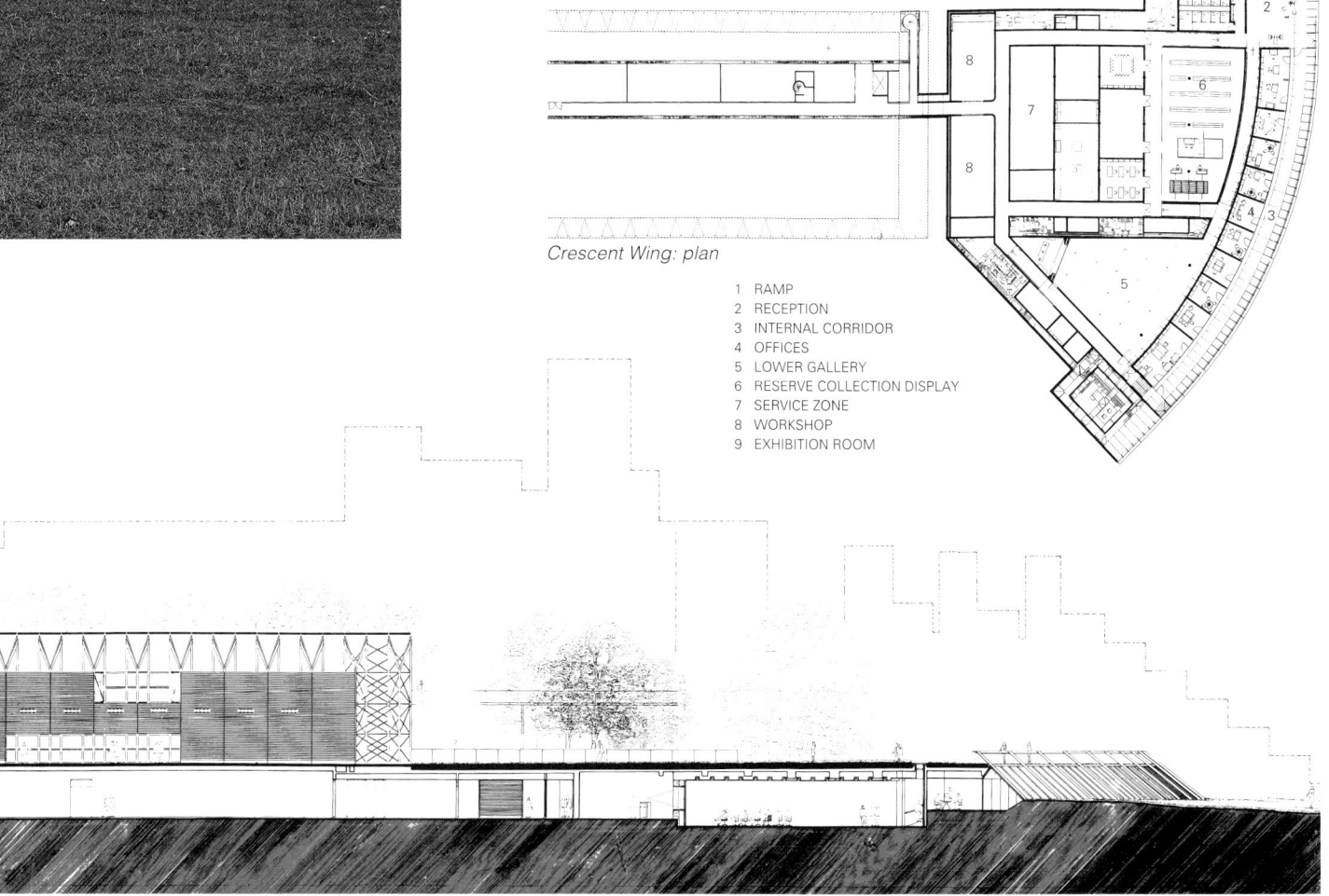

Crescent Wing: plan

1 RAMP
2 RECEPTION
3 INTERNAL CORRIDOR
4 OFFICES
5 LOWER GALLERY
6 RESERVE COLLECTION DISPLAY
7 SERVICE ZONE
8 WORKSHOP
9 EXHIBITION ROOM

Section

Interior of main wing　本館内部

Southwest elevation　南西面

Spiral staircase らせん階段

When Sir Robert and Lady Sainsbury donated their private art collection to the University of East Anglia, together with an endowment fund for a new building, it was decided to enlarge the brief to make the Sainsbury Centre an academic and social focus in the University. Accordingly, the new building encompasses not only the Sainsburys' collection of primitive and twentieth century art and a temporary exhibition space, but also a conservatory, restaurant, senior common room and the faculty of fine art. All these activities are grouped within a single, clear span structure, glazed at both ends, and lit from above by a controlled mixture of natural and artificial light. A basement spine provided the necessary storage and workshop facilities.

The building is divided cross-wise by bands of accommodation all unified by the ceiling—a complex layered arrangement of grilles, trusses and catwalks. Triangular towers and trusses house all services, toilets and ancillaries as well as providing a freeway for lighting installations and maintenance. The primary steel structure supports a flexible arrangement of solid or glazed cladding panels. The entire inner wall and ceiling lining is a tuneable system of perforated aluminium louvres. At each end, the steel structure is clearly articulated.

A major expansion of the Centre, the Crescent Wing, was commissioned by Sir Robert and Lady Sainsbury in 1991.

ロバート・セインズベリー卿夫妻が、自らが所有する美術品のコレクションを、新しい建物を建設するための基金と共にイースト・アングリア大学に寄贈した際、当初の構想は拡大され、大学内に於ける研究活動と交流の中心となるセインズベリー・センターをつくることが決定された。従って、この新しい建物には、プリミティヴ・アート及び20世紀美術から成るセインズベリー・コレクションの常設及び特別展示用のスペースばかりでなく、美術学部、レストラン、大学教員及び特別研究員の交流の場となるシニア・コモン・ルーム、そして学部が包摂されることになった。これらの活動領域は、単一のクリア・スパンによる建物内に統合されている。建物の両端はガラス張りで、自然光と人工光を混合した調整された光が上方から内部を照らす。建物の背骨に沿って広がる地階には、必要とされる収納庫とワークショップが設置された。

帯状に連なる調整装置は、建物を縦横に分割し、グリル、トラス、キャットウォークが複雑に重層する天井がそれを一体化する。両側面を構成する三角柱状のタワーと屋根トラスは、照明器具の設置やメンテナンスのために自由に入れる通路を提供すると共に、サービス、トイレ、補助施設を収める。鋼管による主構造は、壁パネルあるいはガラス・パネルの自在な配置を可能とする。内壁全体と天井には、調整可能なシステムである有孔アルミ製のルーバーが取り付けられている。両端部で、鋼管の構造体は明快に表現される。

センターには、セインズベリー卿夫妻からの依頼により、1991年、クレセント・ウィングが増築された。

Northeast side of main wing 本館の北東側

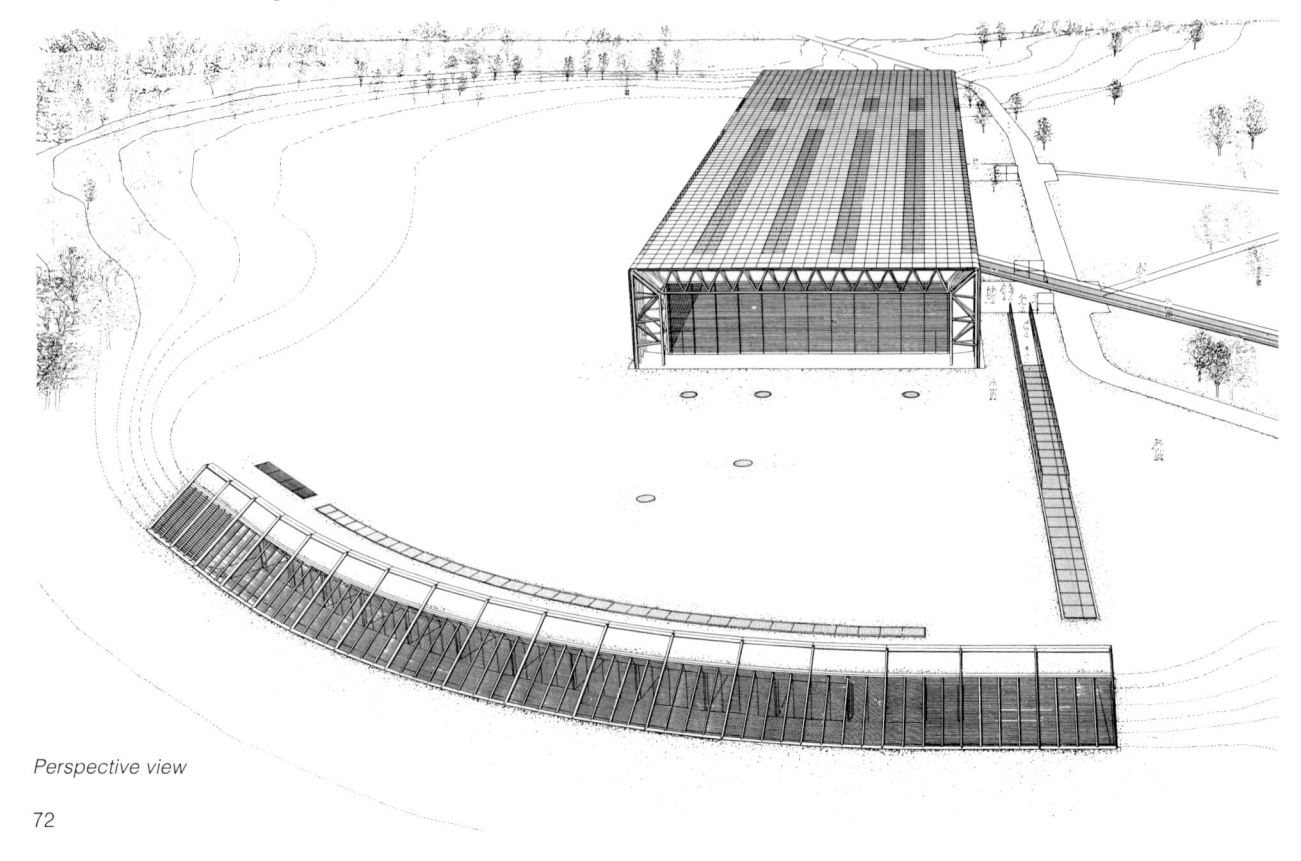

Perspective view

Glazed wall of Crescent Wing クレセント・ウィングのガラス壁

Crescent Wing: corridor クレセント・ウィング：廊下

Crescent Wing: exhibition room
クレセント・ウィング：展示室

Crescent Wing: exhibition room クレセント・ウィング：展示室

1977–84
JAMES STIRLING, MICHAEL WILFORD

STAATSGALERIE EXTENSION AND NEW CHAMBER THEATER
Stuttgart, Germany

Overall view 全景

This is an extension to an existing national museum, theater, library and conservatory, with extensive citations taken from Schinkel's plan for 'Altes Museum' that can be observed in the arrangement of a large, round patio in the center of the site.

In order to fit the building to the public road which crosses the site diagonally, the latter line of motion is raised to a higher position, pulled around the Sculpture Plaza and tugged down to the entrance terrace. It then secures access beneath the arch under the theater, and finally leads the pedestrians who came across this path into the museum. A 3-meter high terrace occupies the full width of the site along its longitudinal direction. It provides visitors with direct access to the front entrances of both museum and theater. This layout produces historical linkage with other public buildings in the line facing the mall.

Exhibition space inside the museum is distinctly partitioned into small sections, and was designed as a sequence of 'rooms'. Each of these rooms is given the right proportion and a flat ceiling of light-diffusing glass, so that even under natural light, no shadow is cast. All of these details constitute a preparation for a 'journey' through the exhibition in chronological order. Starting from the new annex, it would be a journey 'from the present to the past'; from the old building, a journey 'from the past to the present'.

Each space is composed of historical citations of architectural language and of modern textures of bright colors, glass or metals that are put together in a collage.

A piece of work representing architecture derived from the methods of Postmodernism, by request of preservation of historical context and revitalization of cultural programs.

既存の国立美術館、劇場、図書館、音楽学校への増築。シンケルの「アルテス・ムゼウム」のプランを積極的に引用している。敷地中央に大きな円形の中庭を設けている。

敷地内を斜めに横切る公道を建物にうまくかみ合わせるために、この動線を一旦高い位置まで持ち上げ、彫刻広場をまわして、玄関テラスまで降ろし、そこから劇場下のアーチをくぐる通路を確保し、さらにこの動線を利用する歩行者を美術館へ誘う。また、敷地の長手方向に沿って、3メートル高のテラスを敷地幅一杯にとり、美術館と劇場の正面玄関へは、このテラスから直接入るようにしている。この配置によって、モールに面して並んでいる、他の公共建築物との歴史的なつながりをあたえている。

美術館の展示室は、1部屋ごとにはっきりと仕切られ、適正なプロポーションを持った「部屋」のつながりとして計画され、各部屋は散光ガラス

のフラットな天井面をもち、自然光でも影を落とさないようにしている。それらの配置は、展示物の年代順の「旅」ができるようになっている。新館から出発すれば「現在から過去へ」、旧館から出発すれば「過去から現在へ」と時を下ることになる。

　歴史的に引用される建築言語と現代的な鮮やかな色彩やガラスや金属などのテクスチャーが、コラージュのように組み合わされて構成される各空間は、それらの対比の均衡が巧みに取られている。

　歴史的なコンテクストの保存と文化的なプログラムの活性という要請に対して、ポストモダニズムの手法によって導かれた建築の代表となる作品である。

View from entry ramp　エントランス・ランプより見る

Gallery level

Entry level

Canopy on entrance エントランスのキャノピー

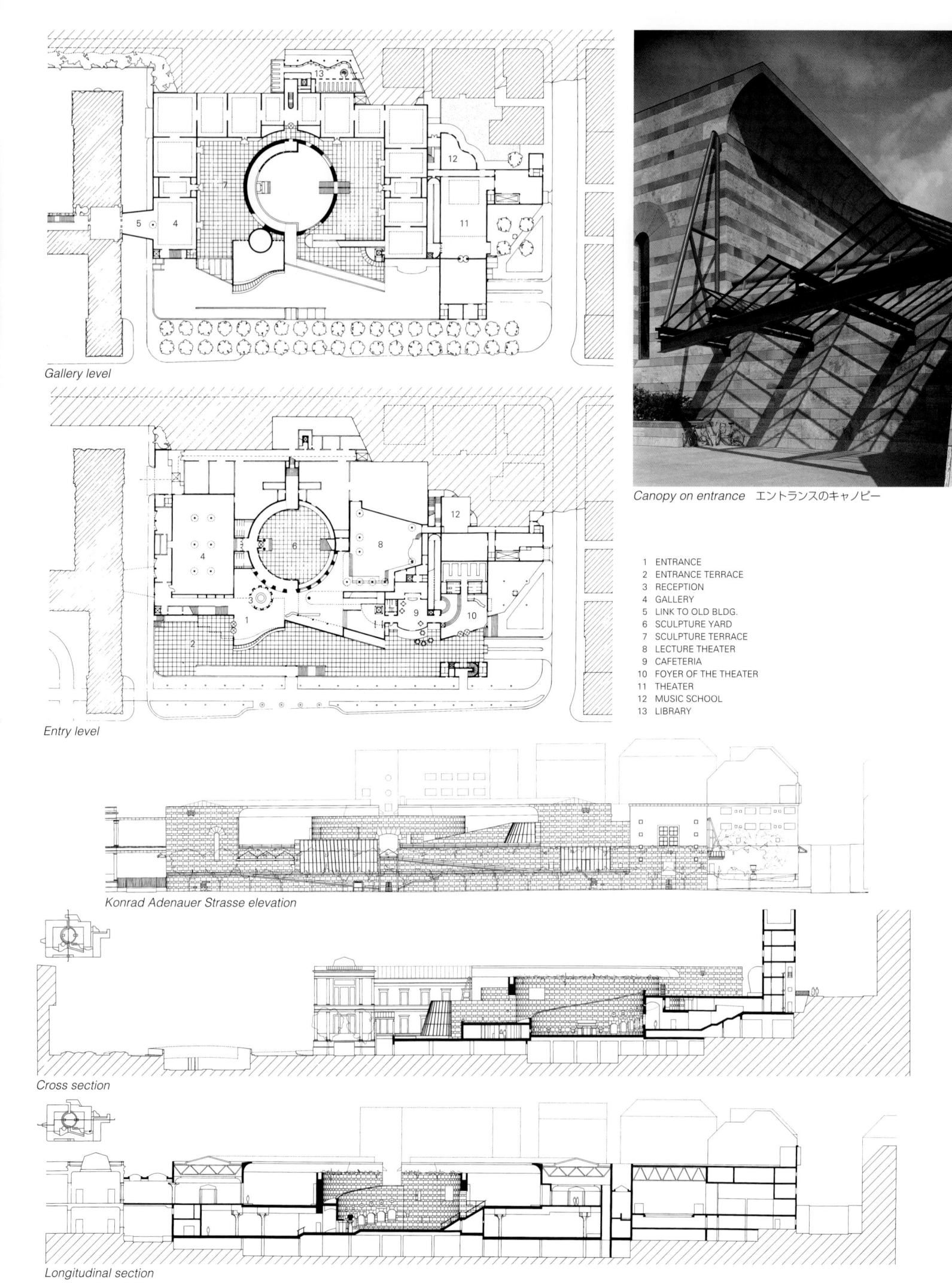

1. ENTRANCE
2. ENTRANCE TERRACE
3. RECEPTION
4. GALLERY
5. LINK TO OLD BLDG.
6. SCULPTURE YARD
7. SCULPTURE TERRACE
8. LECTURE THEATER
9. CAFETERIA
10. FOYER OF THE THEATER
11. THEATER
12. MUSIC SCHOOL
13. LIBRARY

Konrad Adenauer Strasse elevation

Cross section

Longitudinal section

Entrance terrace エントランス・テラス

Entrance to theater wing 劇場棟へのエントランス

Sculpture yard (encircled court)　彫刻庭園（円形中庭）

Sculpture terrace　彫刻テラス

Entrance　エントランス

Entrance hall　エントランス・ホール

Sculpture yard (encircled court) 彫刻庭園（円形中庭）

Open lift assembly エレベータ

Museum hall　美術館ホール

Lecture theater　講堂

Museum hall　美術館ホール

Gallery with flared column　朝顔型の柱のある展示室

81

Upper level gallery　上階の展示室 △▽▷

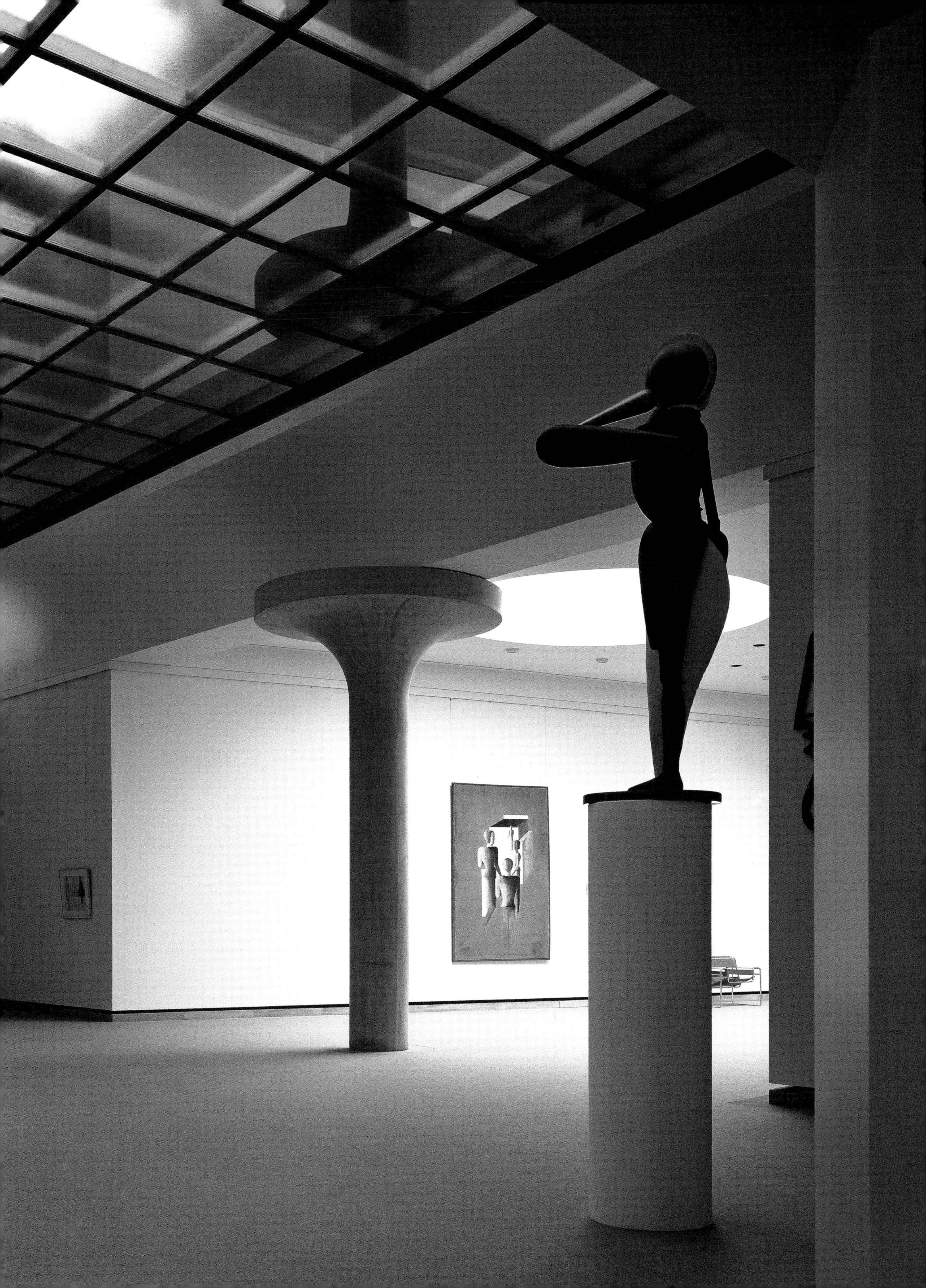

1979–84
O.M. UNGERS

GERMAN ARCHITECTURE MUSEUM
Frankfurt am Main, Germany

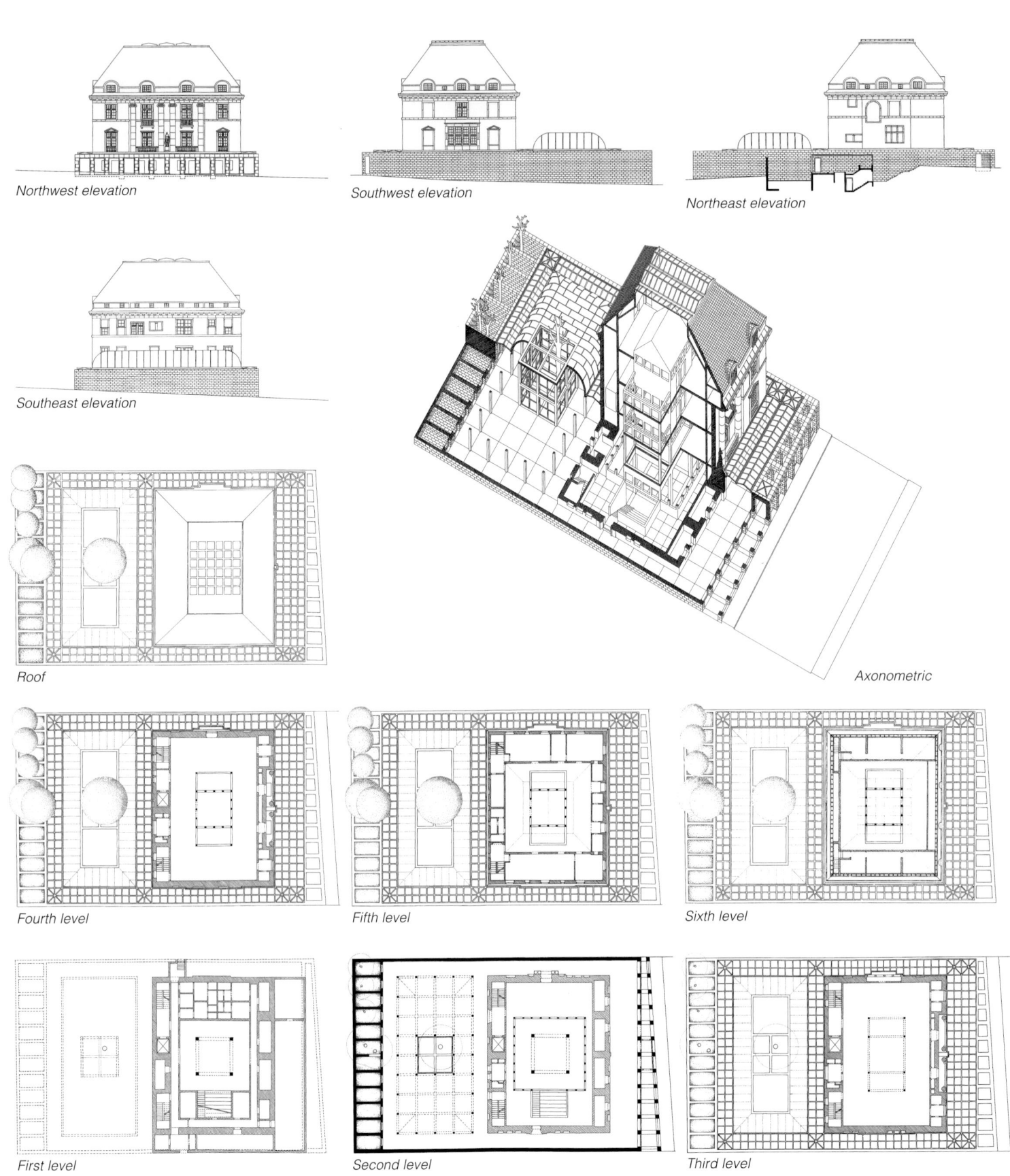

Northwest elevation

Southwest elevation

Northeast elevation

Southeast elevation

Roof

Axonometric

Fourth level

Fifth level

Sixth level

First level

Second level

Third level

The site is located on Schaumainkai, a street along the river Main that flows through the city of Frankfurt. It is a museum for architecture, conceived in line with the city's cultural policy of preserving a number of historical building standing along this street by turning them into museums. The original building assigned for this museum has used to be a comparatively small duplex house. Only the exterior was preserved, and reconstruction involved mainly the interior in order to create a space for architectural exhibitions.

Because of the modest size of the original building, the site was used in its entirety, up to the fences that mark the border of the premises, in order to meet the requirements of a museum. The old building itself has thus become an item of exhibition within the exhibition space, thereby taking on a double meaning. In this way, the existence of this original building of rather little importance has been heightened ironically to an icon of an architecture museum.

Floor structures from the old building were all removed, for they would not bear the load of the museum. A new grid structure was introduced inside the original walls.

The architectural theme of this museum is 'a house within a house'. Spatial layers generated by such nested structure accommodate the exhibition spaces. The outermost shell consists of thick fences of masonry. Then come the original walls made of stone and bricks, and the lattice walls of concrete inside the building. Finally, glass and steel define a transparent space of solid grid. Here, the overall theme is the relationship between each space, or the process of relating from outside to the inside—in another words, the space itself and the stages of its transformation.

敷地はフランクフルト市を流れるマイン河岸通りにあり、ここに建ち並ぶ一連の歴史的な建物を各種の美術館として利用することでそれらを保存するという市の文化政策に則った建築のための美術館である。この建築美術館にあてられた既存建築は比較的小規模の2家族用住宅であり、この外観を保存し、主に内部を改築することで建築関係の展示を目的とする空間を造り出している。

既存建物が小住宅であったため、敷地境界を形成する塀までの敷地全体をフルに利用して、要求される美術館の空間とした。こうすることで、既存の古い建物そのものが、展示空間中の展示物ともなる。つまり、展示空間であると同時に展示物でもあるという両義的な意味を与え、それほど重要な価値の無いこの建物の存在をアイロニカルに建築の美術館のアイコンのレベルにまで高めている。

古い建物の床の構造は美術館の荷重に耐えられないことからすべて撤去し、外壁のみが残され、グリッド状の新たな構造が内部に与えられた。

この美術館における建築的なテーマは「家の中の家」であり、この入れ子構造によって発生する空間の層が展示空間にあてられている。外郭は厚い石造の塀であり、次に石と煉瓦の既存建物の壁、そして内部のコンクリート造の格子壁があり、最後にガラスとスティールの透明な立体格子の空間を持つ。それぞれの空間の関係性、外部より内部に至る関係性＝空間とその変容の段階がここでのテーマとなっている。

Northwest facade 北西側ファサード

Gallery on ground level 1階のギャラリー

Entrance hall エントランス・ホール

Light court gallery　光庭廻りのギャラリー

Lecture hall　レクチャー・ホール

Great hall 中央ホール △▽

Skylight of central gallery 中央ギャラリーのスカイライト

1979–85
RICHARD MEIER

MUSEUM FOR DECORATIVE ARTS
Frankfurt am Main, Germany

View from street 街路より見る

1. ENTRY COURT
2. ENTRY FOYER
3. TEMPORARY EXHIBITION
4. CAFE/RESTAURANT
5. ADMINISTRATION
6. LIBRARY
7. COURTYARD
8. VILLA METZLER (existing)

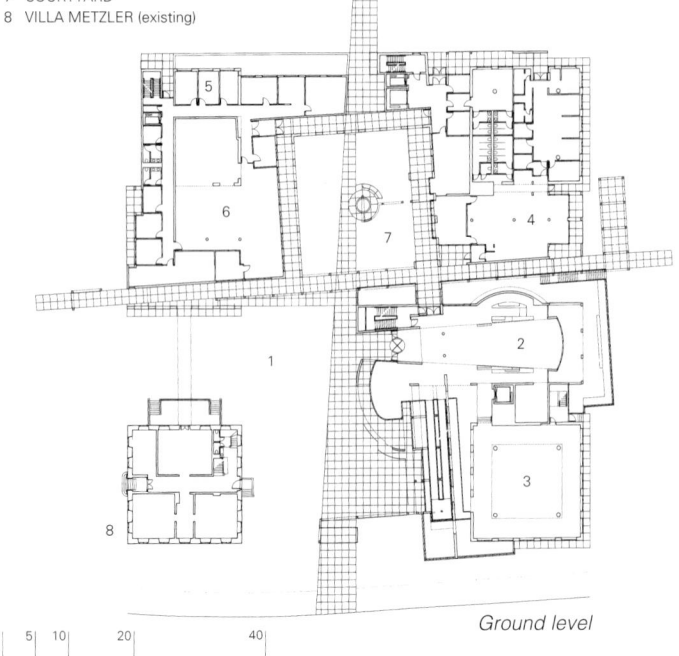

Ground level

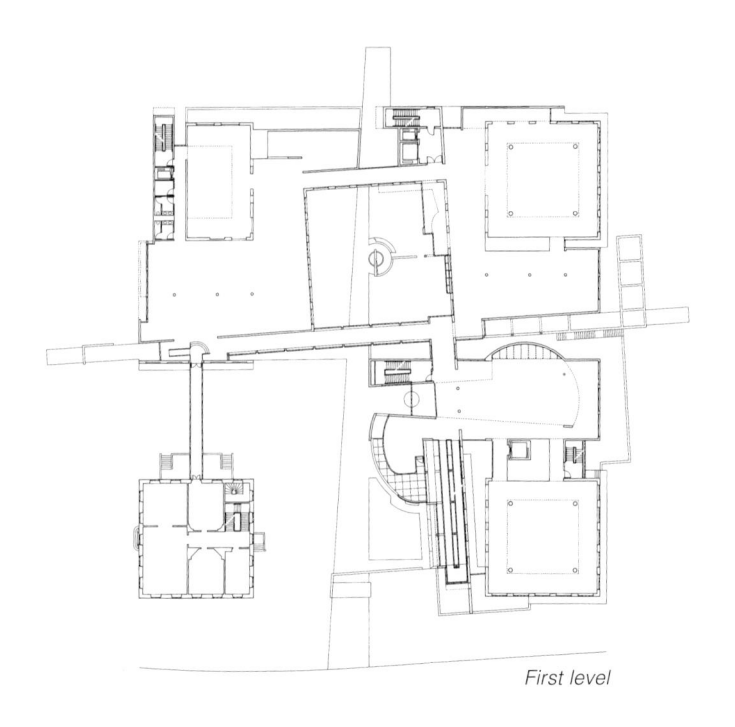

First level

Main entrance　メイン・エントランス

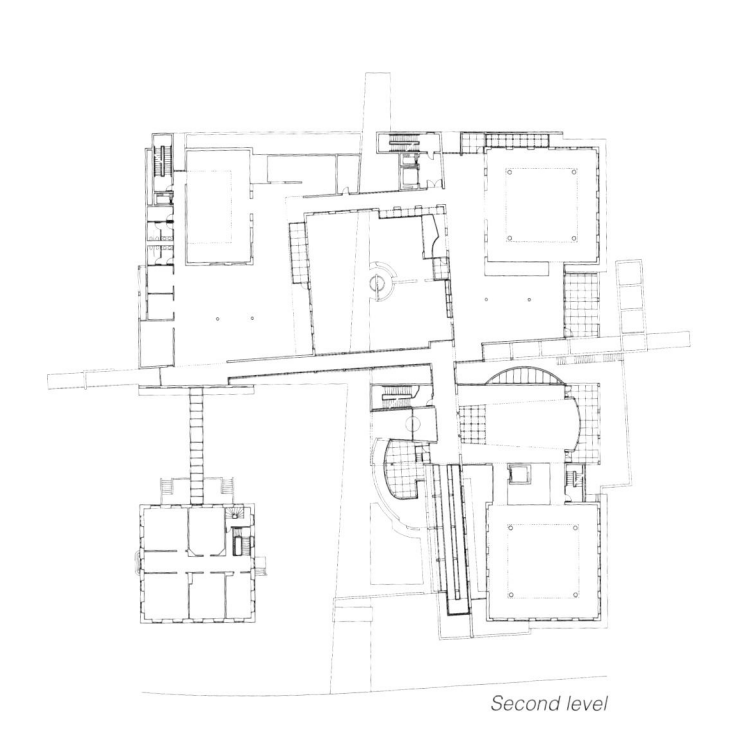

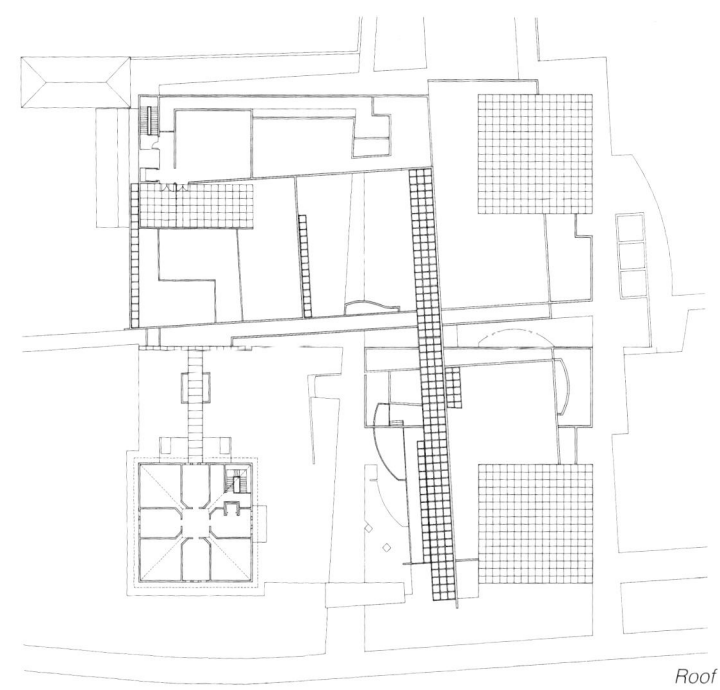

Second level

Roof

The Museum für Kunsthandwerk incorporates a new extension to the nineteenth-century Villa Metzler, existing and future museum buildings, a tree-filled park, and bank along the River Main.

The new museum houses Frankfurt's decorative arts treasures and forms a sympathetic and respectful extension of the Villa Metzler and a thoughtful twentieth-century complex, complementing the park while creating a lightness and elegance of its own.

Site Design

The design makes of the site a pedestrian link between two parts of the city, the residential community of Sachsenhausen to the south and the city center across the river, inviting all to take advantage of the museum and park while making a major contribution to the city's urban structure. The complex respects and reinforces pedestrian paths, preserves the site's existing tree silhouettes and frames and unifies the museum buildings, diminishing the separating effect of these frontal buildings along the Schaumainkai and river and eliminating the "no-man's-land" behind them.

Organization and Design of the Interior

The new building acknowledges its function of housing art and—in its circulation, lighting, installations, and spaces—contributes to the museum's educational role in the broadest sense by encouraging quiet contemplation of the collections, appreciation of the park and city and discovery of esthetic values of the collection and the architecture itself.

Four floors are organized into quadrants and differentiate public, semipublic, and private functions and secure and non-secure areas. The architecture invites entry from the plaza, the focal intersection of pedestrian ways, then imperceptibly guides visitors through a prescribed exhibit sequence on three floors. The first floor has public orientation areas, each function occupying one quadrant: entry hall and temporary display; restaurant; library and administration. Visitors begin with an introduction to masterpieces on temporary display. Wide ramps—interior extensions of the paths—are intended to draw them to the collection areas above and in the Villa. The simple architecture of the permanent collections frames and defers to exhibits, allowing objects to create environments of their own. The glazed, open entry hall, wide, light-filled ramps, connecting bridges, bay windows and two-story spaces give, by contrast, lively views of the park, city and architecture, new and old.

Porcelain, a main material of the collection, is used in a twentieth-century way in the design of the new building, whose white enameled metal facade panels allude to the Bavarian rococo furniture and fine Meissen characteristic of German decorative arts.

West elevation 西面

Entry foyer ホワイエ

View from park on west　西側公園より見る

Pergola　パーゴラ

装飾工芸美術館は、19世紀に建てられたヴィラ・メツラーへの新たな増築、既存の美術館、将来建設予定の美術館、樹木に覆われた公園、さらにマイン川の堤までを含む全体計画である。

新しい美術館には、ヴィッラ・メツラーに現在保管されているフランクフルト市所蔵の装飾美術品が収められる。建物のデザインは、ヴィッラに共鳴し、敬意を込めた増築であり、また、軽快で洗練された形をとりながら、公園を完璧なものに仕上げる、緻密に考え抜かれた20世紀の複合建築を意図している。

敷地計画
敷地の計画としては、南のザクセンハウゼン住居地区と、対岸のシティー・センターという当市の2地区を結ぶペデストリアン・リンクを構成し、都市機構に大きく貢献しながら、すべての人が美術館と公園を利用できるようにする。この複合施設は、ペデストリアン・パスを重視し、強調する。樹木はそのまま残し、美術館に陰影を刻み、枠どりをし、まとまりを与える。それにより、シャウマインカイン通りと河川に向いた建物の立面が分離している印象を押さえ、建物背後にひろがる「人気のない地帯」を消し去ってしまう。

構成と内部計画
新しい建物の構成にあたっては、美術品を収納する場という機能を尊重すること、サーキュレーション、照明、設備、空間そのすべてを、収集品を静かに観賞し、公園と市の真価を認め、収集品と建築それ自身の美しさを発見できるようなものにすることで、広い意味で美術館の教育的役割を果すよう意図する。

平面は4分割され、パブリック、セミ・パブリック、プライベートに機能区分され、監視を置くエリアと置かないエリアで構成する。プラザからの入口はペデストリアン・ウェイが交差する焦点で、ここから訪問者は、3平面にわたる、定められた展示のシークエンスへと、知らず知らずのうちに導かれてゆく。1階には、案内サービス部門がおかれ、機能別に、玄関ホールと特別展示場、レストラン、図書室と管理事務室が、それぞれひとつの象限を占める。訪問者はまず、特別展の作品観賞に始まり、広いランプ——室内にまで延長されたパスを通って、上階の展示場そしてヴィッラへと導かれる。常設展示品を収めるシンプルな建物は、展示品そのものが部屋の雰囲気を創り出すように、枠どり、展示を主体として構成する。ガラス張りのオープンな玄関ホール、広くて光に溢れたランプ、建物をつなぐブリッジ、ベイ・ウィンドウ、2層にわたる空間が、公園、都市と建築、新しいものと旧いものの生き生きとした眺めを、その際立った対比によって引き出す。

磁器が展示品の主なものだが、これを現代の手法で新しい建物のデザインに生かした。白いホーロー引きの金属質のファサード・パネルは、ドイツの装飾美術を代表するバイエルン・ロココの家具とマイセン磁器への思い入れである。

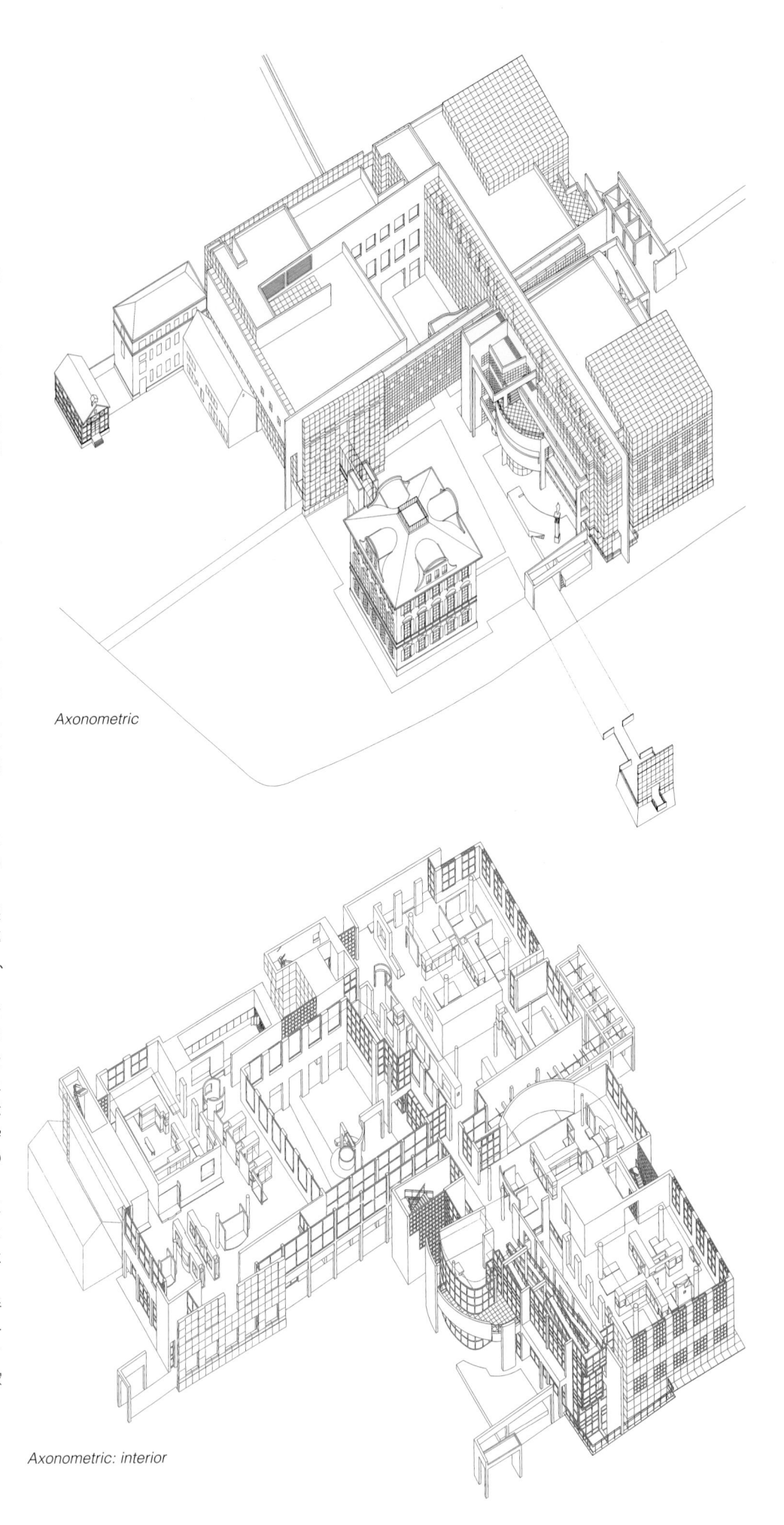

Axonometric

Axonometric: interior

Ramp ランプ ▷

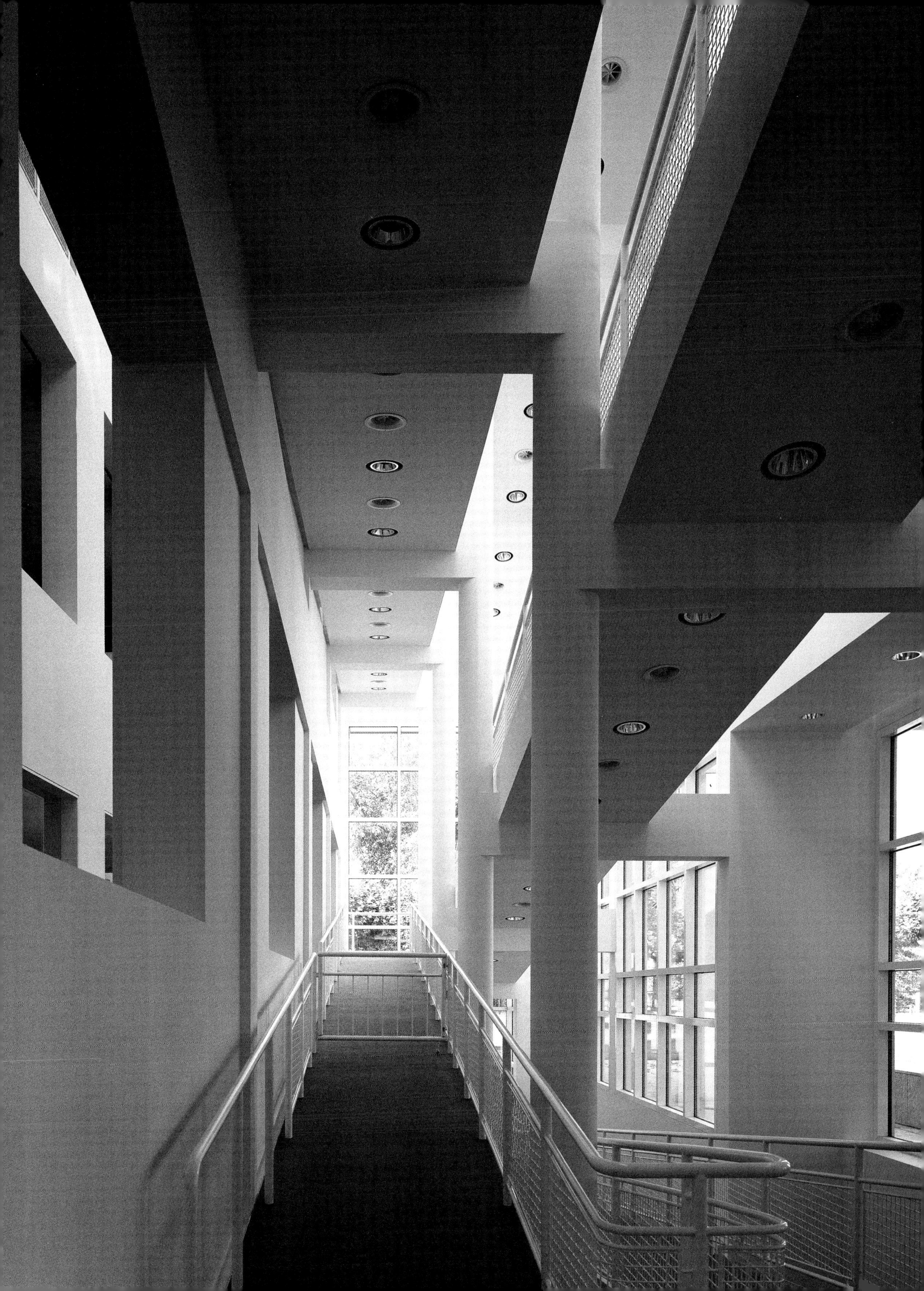

△▽ *Exhibition space*　展示室

Courtyard 中庭

Villa Metzler ヴィラ・メツラー

Ramp ランプ

Corridor on second floor 2階通路

1981–83
YOSHIO TANIGUCHI

KEN DOMON MUSEUM OF PHOTOGRAPHY
Yamagata, Japan

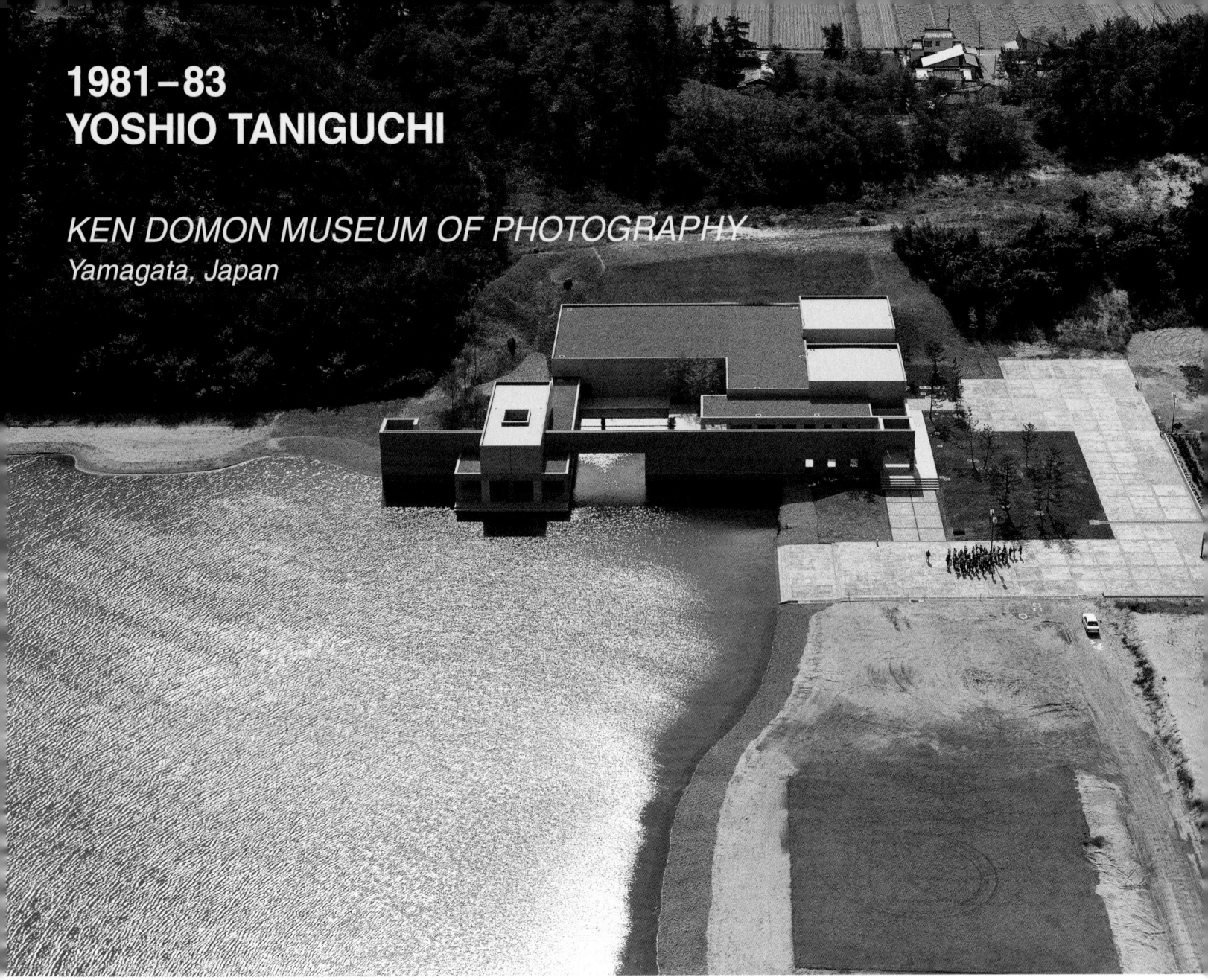

Aerial view 航空写真

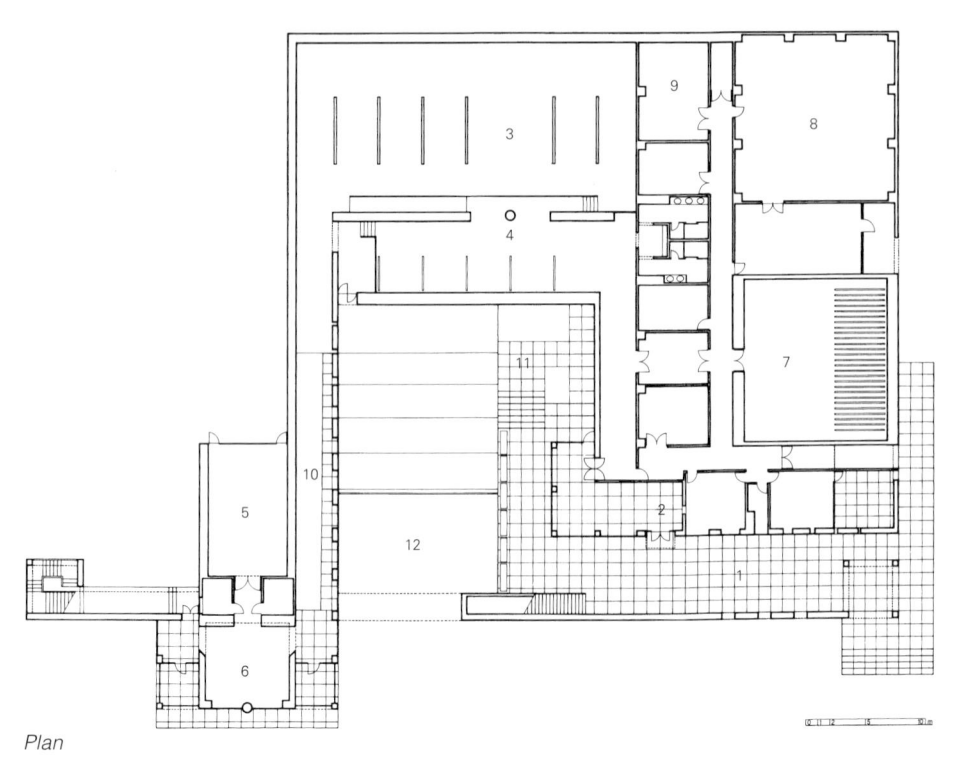

Plan

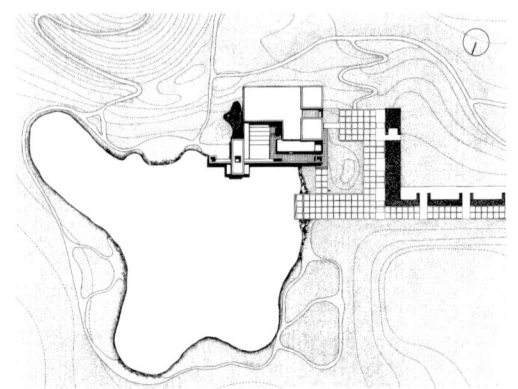

Site plan

1 APPROACH
2 ENTRANCE
3 MAIN EXHIBITION ROOM
4 PERIODICAL EXHIBITION ROOM
5 AUDIO-VISUAL ROOM
6 KEN DOMON MEMORIAL ROOM
7 STORAGE
8 MECHANICAL
9 ELECTRICAL
10 GALLERY
11 COURTYARD
12 POND

Night view 夜景

North elevation

Section

A museum dedicated to the photographer Ken Domon, built in his hometown Sakata City in Yamagata Prefecture and housing the complete collection of his works. The site is on the bank of Mogami River within Iimoriyama Park, in front of an artificial lake that takes advantage of the high waterlevel.

Every effort was made to keep the exterior of the building as plain and simple as possible: in harmony with the beauty and grandeur of the surrounding nature, and appropriate to offer itself as a background to Domon's art of photography. The exterior features exposed concrete and granite finishing. Exposed concrete is mainly used in the mountain side to express energy of the forms through its aspects of massiveness and integration. Granite finishing is used on the exterior facing the artificial lake, and along the main line of motion inside the building. As opposed to concrete, it delivers a feeling of lightheartedness, with details that consciously reveal the material is only a covering.

The interior is roughly divided into two spaces: one is for the exhibition, and the other is a lounge for taking rest. The former is a space enclosed within walls, away from natural light to protect the photographs on display, while the latter, Ken Domon Memorial Room, is a space filled with bright light, as if it were floating on the artificial pond. This pair of contrasting spaces was designed with the intention of providing the visitors with a rich museum experience, through their moments inside the two spaces and within the surrounding nature.

A huge wall sets toward the artificial pond, partitioning the inner exhibition space and the outer lounge giving to the lake. It is a clear expression of the counterpoint that exists between these two spaces, thereby attributing a strong symbolism to the entire museum.

写真家、土門拳の郷里である山形県酒田市に全作品を収めた美術館である。敷地は最上川の川岸、飯森山文化公園の中で、敷地前面には高い水位を利用した人工湖が作られている。

建物外観の特徴は、周囲の美しく雄大な自然と調和し、土門拳の写真芸術の背景としてふさわしいものとなるように極力簡素に仕上げられている。外装は、打放しコンクリートと花崗岩仕上げによる。打放しは主に山側に使用され、その重量感と一体感によって力強い造形的特徴を表現し、一方、花崗岩仕上げは、人工湖側の外部と室内の主要動線に使用されて、コンクリートとは反対に貼石であることを意識的に見せるディテールをもって軽快感を演出している。

内部は大きく二つの空間で構成されている。一つは展示のための空間であり、もう一つは休息のためのラウンジである。展示空間はその展示物である写真の保護のために自然光の入らない、壁に囲まれた空間であり、ラウンジである土門拳記念室は対照的に人工池に浮かべられたかのような、明るい陽光の入る空間となっている。来館者がこれらの対照的な空間を相互に利用することと、建物周囲の自然に触れ、楽しむことで、豊かな美術館体験が出来るように意図されている。

人工池に面して伸びる一枚の大壁は、内側の展示空間と外側の湖に張り出したラウンジの間におかれ、この二つの空間の対比を明快に表現するとともに美術館全体に強い象徴性を付加する。

North view　北より見る

Approach アプローチ

◁△ *Pond besides courtyard* 湧水の流れる中庭

△▽ Main exhibition room　展示室

Wall detail　壁のディテール

Garden, "Nagare"　視聴覚室前庭「流れ」

1981–86
ARATA ISOZAKI

MUSEUM OF CONTEMPORARY ART, LOS ANGELES
Los Angeles, California, U.S.A.

View from Grand Avenue　グランド・アヴェニューより見る

Sculpture court on left　左は彫刻庭園

View toward office wing オフィス棟を見る

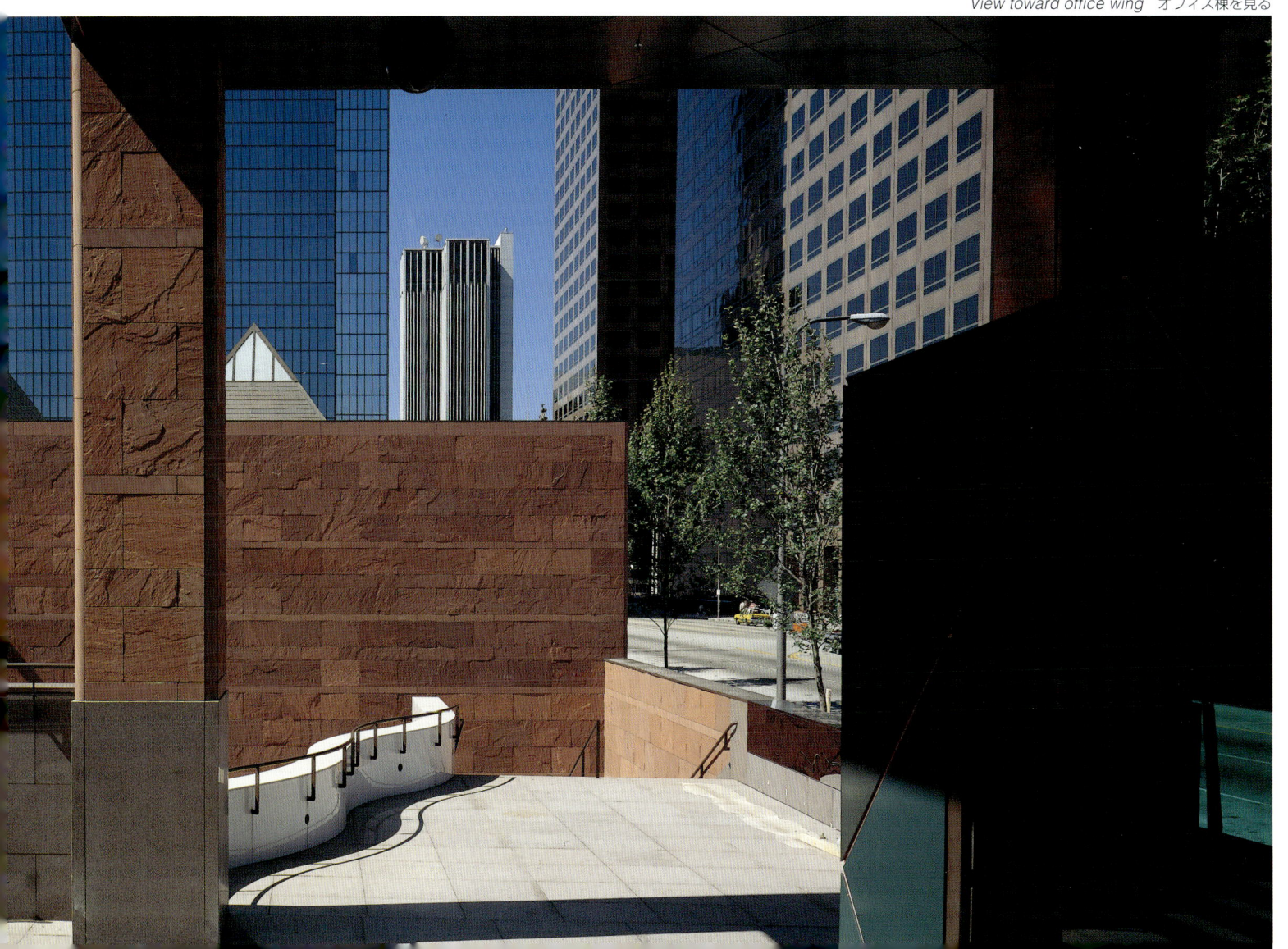

Site:

The Museum of Contemporary Art (MOCA) will be located at the center of the California Plaza mixed use development in the Bunker Hill section of downtown Los Angeles.

Although California Plaza will be realized in stages, at the completion of the project, MOCA will be bounded by an office tower on the north, on the south by a hotel, residential condominiums on the east and Grand Avenue on the west. The museum sits atop and partially within the parking structure of California Plaza.

This location presented several severe restrictions to both the planning and massing of the museum. Consideration of the visibility of the retail spaces at the Plaza level imposed height limitations, predetermined floor elevations at parking levels specified lower limits as well. Moreover, it was required that the dimensions of the museum's bays enable optimum use of the parking area below.

During the planning process, the actual location of the museum site was changed three times by the developer and Plaza architect. Before the final solution was reached, over thirty schemes on these different sites were proposed.

Brief:

Along with nearly 34,000 square feet of gallery space, the museum, program includes an auditorium, a library, cafeteria, bookstore, various offices and extensive service areas. These functions are separated by level and connected vertically.

The museum presents itself to the street as two structures bracketing a sculpture and entry court. Pyramids, cubes and a circular vault rest top walls of red Indian sandstone the base of which is red granite. Bands of honed finish sandstone alternate with larger pieces of rough, cleft finish to give a subtle pattern of horizontal striation to the wall.

On the north, the copper sheathed vaulted library bridges over the pedestrian's path to form a symbolic gateway to the museum. Beneath the cover of this gate is an aluminum clad cube from which tickets are purchased. A lift behind this cube facilitates, for the handicapped, the change in elevation between the Grand Avenue and Plaza levels.

On the south loom one large and two small pyramids. the lower portion of the large pyramid is copper. Its skylight illuminates the entrance gallery. The small pyramids are skylights for the next gallery.

Beyond the library, eight small pyramids atop a low wall light the north gallery. Two sets of twelve linear skylights are behind the south gallery's walls.

The sculpture court which overlooks the museum court below is the focus of the various facilities of the museum which open onto the Plaza level. On the north, at the base of the office block, are the bookstore and office lobby. Facing the sculpture court, the office walls are sandstone. On the opposite (north) side of the office block, square aluminum panels are placed in a diamond pattern. Offices have square punched windows.

At the south of the sculpture court is the entry for groups and handicapped persons. The elevator located here serves both the gallery and auditorium levels. The orientation room is equipped with audio-visual equipment for instruction of school tours and other groups. A stair leads directly to the galleries from this room.

From the sculpture court, the galleries are reached by descending the grand stair to the museum court. This sunken entry enables the museum to maximize ceiling height in the galleries and still conform to the exterior height limitations of California Plaza.

The museum court, entrance lobby and cafe are finished in the same materials and are intended to be perceived as an open, continuous space. Floors are granite and walls are white crystallized glass.

敷地：
ロスアンジェルス現代美術館（通称MOCA）は、ロスアンジェルスのダウンタウンのバンカー・ヒル地区を対象として行われる複合用途開発であるカリフォルニア・プラザの中のひとつの焦点となる位置に配される。

カリフォルニア・プラザの建設は数段階にわけて進められる予定であるが、計画全体の建設完了時には、MOCAは、北側を高層オフィス、南側をホテル、東側をコンドミニアムによって囲まれ、また西側ではグランド・アヴェニューに面することになる。美術館はカリフォルニア・プラザの地下駐車場の上に乗る形で、最下層のサービス階およびその上のギャラリー階の下半分は、パーキング・ストラクチャーに埋め込まれた形になっている。

こうした配置を強いられたために、美術館はその平面計画上、ならびにマッスの取扱い上、数多くの苛酷な制約条件を受けることになった。プラザ・レベルにある店舗用スペースをアヴェニュー側から見えやすくするために、美術館の建物には高さ制限が課され、駐車場のレベルはすでに決定済のために、地下深さも制限された。これに加えて構造スパンも下の駐車場の使用効率を最大化する値とすることが要求された。

プランニングの過程で、美術館の敷地はディベロッパーおよびプラザの建築家の要請で三度にわたって変更された。最終案に到るまでに、この異なる3つの敷地上に30を越える計画案が作られたのである。

概要：
プログラム中最も重きを置かれ、延べ34,000平方フィート（≒3,160m²）を占めるギャラリーは、ロスアンジェルス在住のアーティストたちからの強い要望に答えて、最大限の無柱空間を含む、大小高低さまざまな空間——ただしその仕上げはいずれも出来る限りニュートラルであることが要求された——を配し、展示のフレキシビリティに応じられるよう考慮した。またギャラリー諸室の性格付けは、トップライトの採光形式の違い（ピラミッド型または線型、一重または二重のグレージング）によって補われ、入場者は2つの螺旋状の動線に導かれながら、こうした諸空間が作るシークエンスの中を回遊することになる。他のプログラムとしては240席のオーディトリアム、カフェテリア、ブックストア、図書室、諸事務室、ならびに広大なサービスエリア（保管庫等）である。ゾーニングは主として階構成によって行なわれ、その間を大きな荷物用エレベーターを含む垂直動線がつないでいる。

外観上の構成は、2つの地上構造物およびその間にとられたスカルプチャー・コート、エントランス・コートから成っている。足もとに赤御影を回したインド産赤砂岩の壁の上には、ピラミッド、立方体、ヴォールトなどが置かれる。赤砂岩は磨きの細い帯と割肌の帯とが交互に配され、微かな水平縞のパターンを作っている。

北側のブロックに銅板葺きのヴォールト屋根をのせた図書室がペデストリアンの上に架け渡されて美術館への入口のシンボリックなゲートとなっている。その下にアルミの立方体のチケット・ブースが置かれる。プラザのレベル差をつなぐ身障者用リフトがその後ろに設けられる。

南ブロックには3つのピラミッド屋根が作られる。大きいピラミッドは下半分は銅板葺き、上部のトップライトはエントランス・ギャラリーへの採光となる。2つの小ピラミッドは次のギャラリーのトップライトである。

北側の大ギャラリーにも同様のトップライトが8個並べられている。これに対して南側の大ギャラリーには12本のリニアーなトップライトが配される。ミュゼアム・コートを下に望むスカルプチャー・コートは、ほぼプラザのレベルにあって美術館の諸施設がこれに直面する。北側、赤砂岩壁にパンチング窓のオフィス・ブロック（逆側はアルミのダイアモンド・パターンで仕上げられている）の足もとにはブックストアとオフィス・ロビーが置かれる。

また反対の南側には団体および身障者用入口が設けられ、ここのエレベーターはギャラリー階およびオーディトリアム階に通じる。またオリエンテーション・ルームがとられ、スクール・ツアーやその他の団体客のガイド用視聴覚設備が付けられている。この部屋からギャラリー階へは直通階段が通じる。

スカルプチャー・コートから幅広の屋外階段を降りて行くとミュゼアム・コートに導かれる。この半地下の導入はカリフォルニア・プラザの高さ制限内で、ギャラリーの天井高を最大限に取るための設定である。

ミュゼアム・コート、エントランス・ロビー、カフェは、床は赤御影、壁はネオパリエという同一の仕上げを施されることで、オープンな連続した空間であると捉えられるよう意図されている。

East elevation

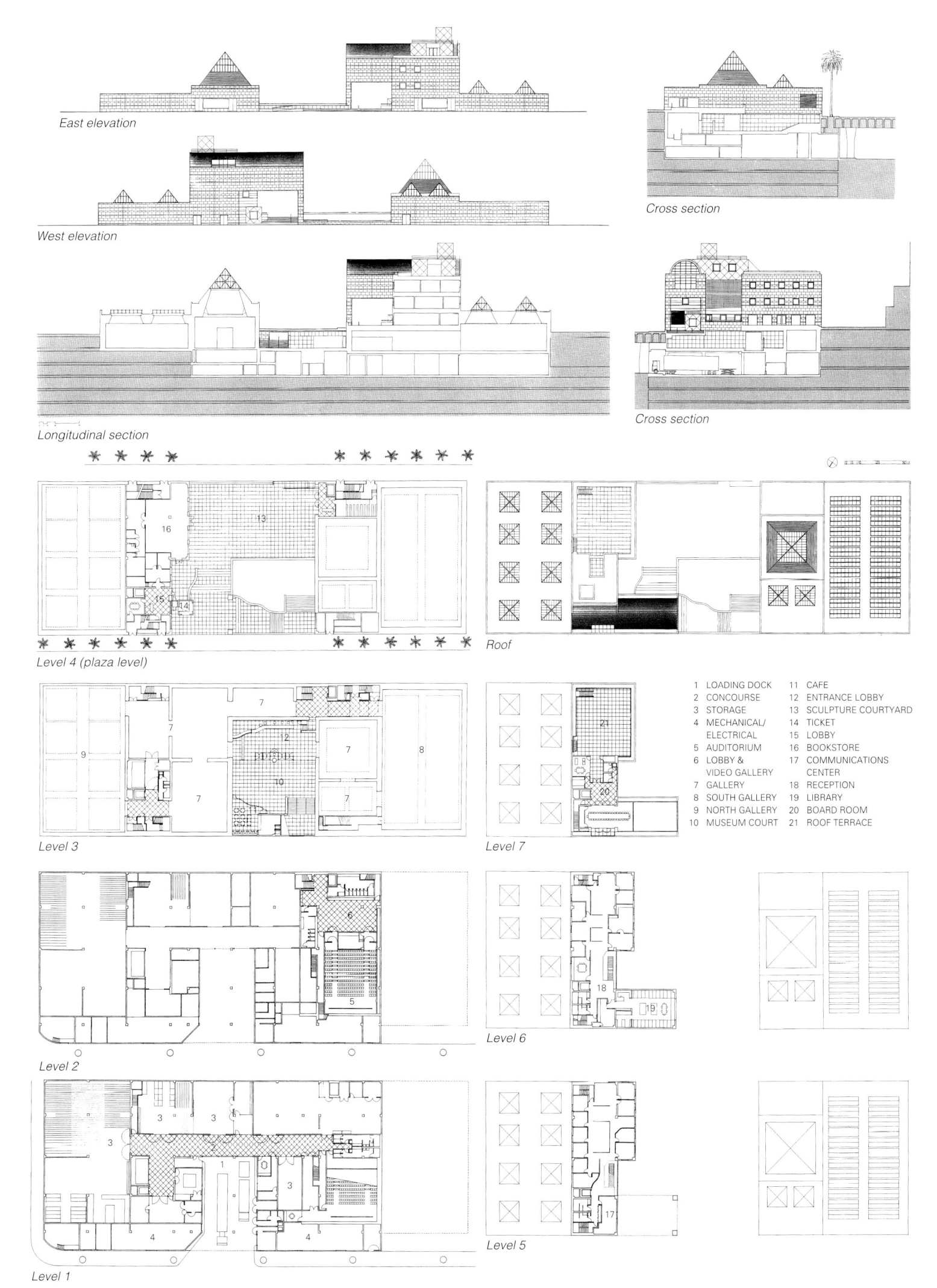

West elevation

Cross section

Longitudinal section

Cross section

Level 4 (plaza level)

Roof

Level 3

Level 7

1 LOADING DOCK	11 CAFE
2 CONCOURSE	12 ENTRANCE LOBBY
3 STORAGE	13 SCULPTURE COURTYARD
4 MECHANICAL/ ELECTRICAL	14 TICKET
5 AUDITORIUM	15 LOBBY
6 LOBBY & VIDEO GALLERY	16 BOOKSTORE
7 GALLERY	17 COMMUNICATIONS CENTER
8 SOUTH GALLERY	18 RECEPTION
9 NORTH GALLERY	19 LIBRARY
10 MUSEUM COURT	20 BOARD ROOM
	21 ROOF TERRACE

Level 2

Level 6

Level 1

Level 5

105

Exhibition room 展示室

Window of office　オフィスの窓

Exhibition room　展示室

107

South gallery　南展示室

North gallery　北展示室

Exhibition room 展示室

1981–86
RENZO PIANO

MENIL COLLECTION MUSEUM
Houston, Texas, U.S.A.

Overall view from east　東側全景

Entrance on north　北側エントランス

"Leaf" on south elevation　南面の "リーフ"

Entrance hall エントランス・ホール

Dominique de Menil charged Renzo Piano in 1981 with the design of a new museum in Houston for the Menil Collection, one of the most important collections of surrealist art and primitive African art in the world. The museum opened in April 1987.

The aim of the design was to create a space facilitating a direct and relaxed relationship between visitors and exhibited objects, through, the creation of a non-monumental and familiar environment in contact with nature.

The building fits into a 19th century green residential area in Houston, where, together with the other already existing buildings, it would form a sort of "Village Museum".

The solution of having natural lighting in the exhibition rooms gives the building its architectural character; the works of art displayed are not directly struck by sunlight, and this creates an ever-changing environment that reflects the natural conditions outside.

Accurate studies of solar angular conditions, the filtering of ultraviolet rays, multiple refraction, etc. was carried out with an appropriate "solar machine", in cooperation with Ove Arup and Partners. In addition to these studies, experiments were made with several structural materials that have resulted in an element designed as a "Leaf"(ferro cement and cast ductile iron structure truss) which is a device for modulating both artificial and natural light.

The basic idea in this museum is to arrange the actual exhibition rooms on the ground floor, and leave the storage rooms (Treasure House) well separated upstairs. The Treasure House is not totally isolated from the museum. It can be visited on guided tours to ensure that requirement humidity and temperature are met.

The objects are never all exhibited at one time. Only two hundred to three hundred objects at a time are brought down to the ground floor to be exhibited and the objects are rotated very often. This allows the works of art to be maintained in the best environmental conditions for preservation so that they can be enjoyed by visitors without suffering damage.

The logic of the building is related to nature: the platform protrudes from the building facade to provide pedestrian paths sheltered from sun and rain. The tropical gardens have been arranged in such a way that plants and trees may grow through the building, showing the importance of a true relationship between the building and the surrounding natural setting.

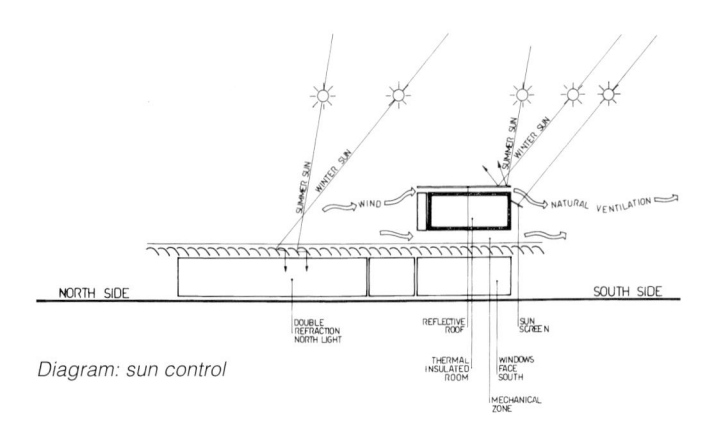

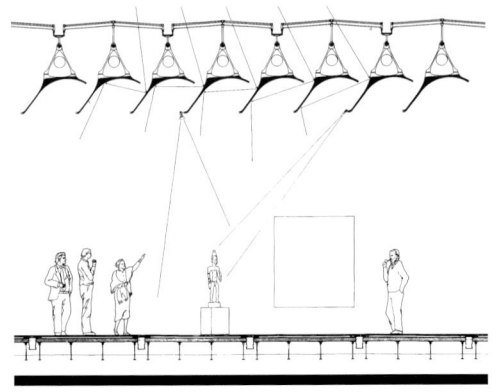

Diagram: sun control

Section: lighting

Exhibition space 展示室 △▽

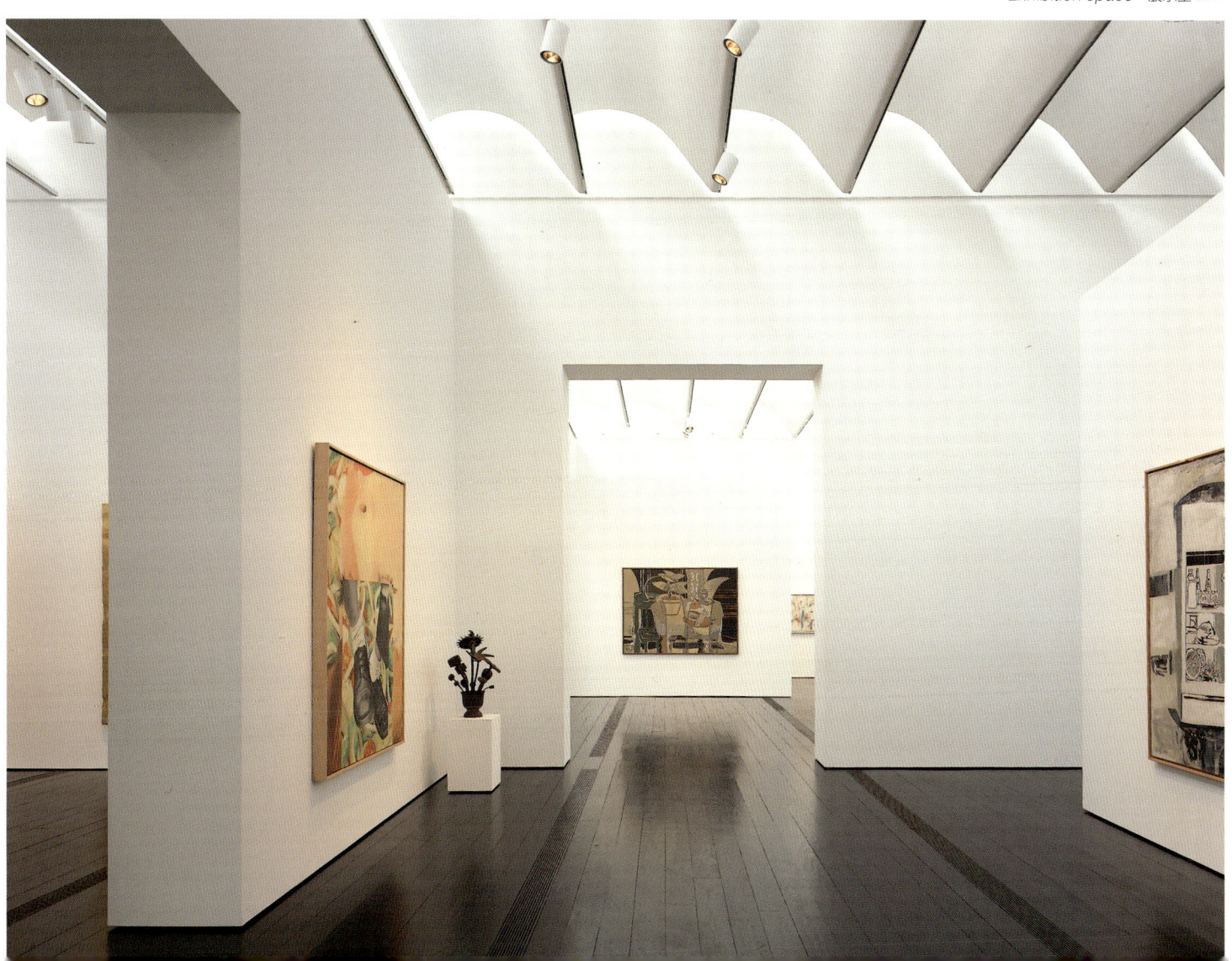

ドミニック・ド・メニルは、1981年、メニル・コレクションを展示するためにヒューストンに建てる、新しい美術館の設計をレンゾ・ピアノに依頼した。コレクションはシュールレアリスト美術とアフリカの原始美術では世界有数のものである。美術館は、1987年4月にオープンした。

デザインの意図は、モニュメンタルではなく、自然に親しみやすい環境をつくることによって、来館者と展示されている作品が直接的でリラックスした関係を持てるような空間をつくることである。

建物は、ヒューストンの19世紀からの緑の多い住宅地区にあり、既存の建物といっしょに、一種の"美術館村"を形成するだろう。

展示室を自然採光にしたことが、この建物に建築的性格を与えている。展示されている美術作品には直射光はあたらない。そして戸外の自然状況を反映して絶えず変化してゆく環境をつくりだしている。

オーヴ・アラップ社と共同して太陽光線の角度、紫外線の濾過、多重屈折などの正確な研究を行い、適切な"ソーラー・マシン"をつくりだした。これらの研究に加え、いくつかの構造材料について実験が行われ、人工照明および自然光の両方を調節する方法である、"リーフ"(フェロセメントとダクタイル鋳鉄のトラス構造の組み合わせ)として設計されたエレメントが生まれた。

この美術館に対する基本的な考えは、実際の展示場を1階に配置し、収納庫を上階に離して設置することである。収納庫は美術館から全面的に切り離すわけではない。湿度、温度の要求を確実に守るために、ガイド付で見学できる。

美術品は一度にすべてが展示されることはない。階下の展示室で展示される美術品は、一回に200から300点で、頻繁に展示替えが行われる。これによって、保存のための最善の環境に美術品を保管することができ、作品を傷めることなく来館者も鑑賞を楽しむことができる。

建物の設計論理は自然と関わっている。ファサードから突き出したプラットフォームは陽射しや雨から守られた歩行者通路を提供する。植物や樹木が建物を通して成長し、建物と自然環境が良い関係を保つことの大切さを示すように、熱帯性植物を植えた庭園が配置された。

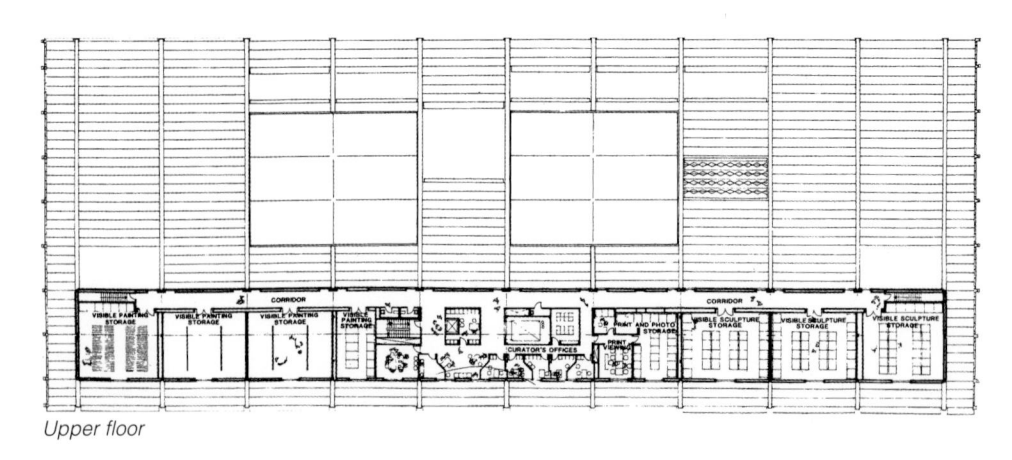

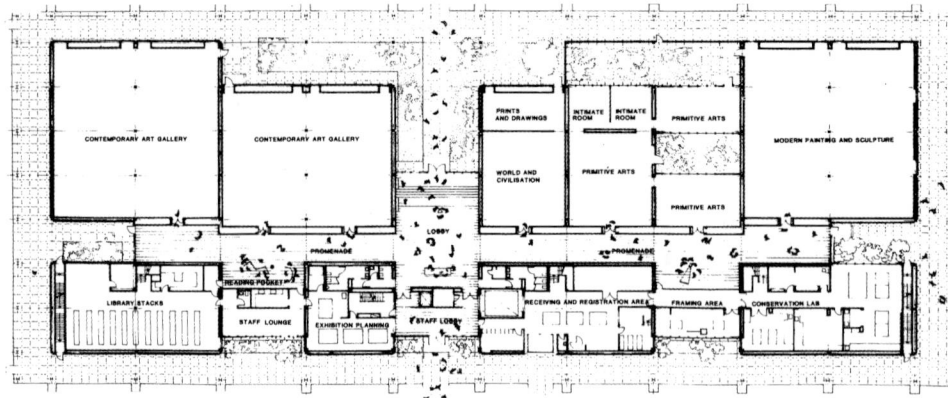

Upper floor

Ground floor

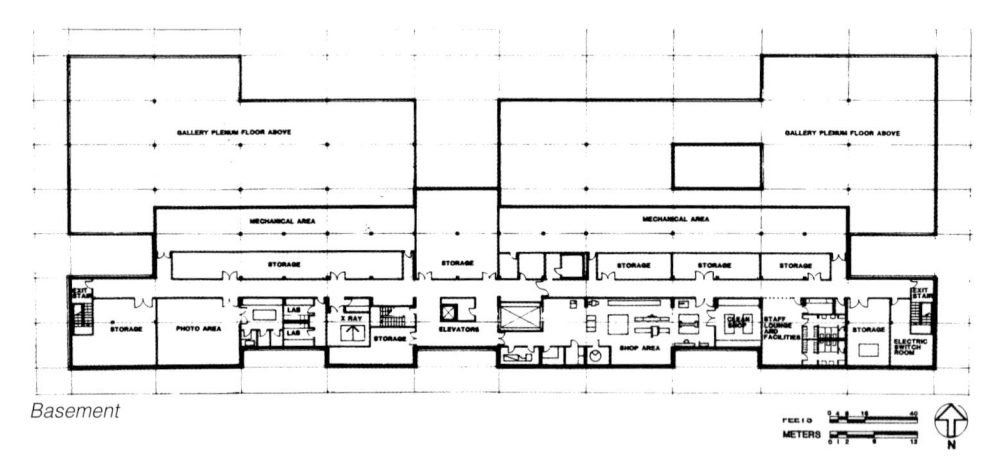

Basement

West elevation

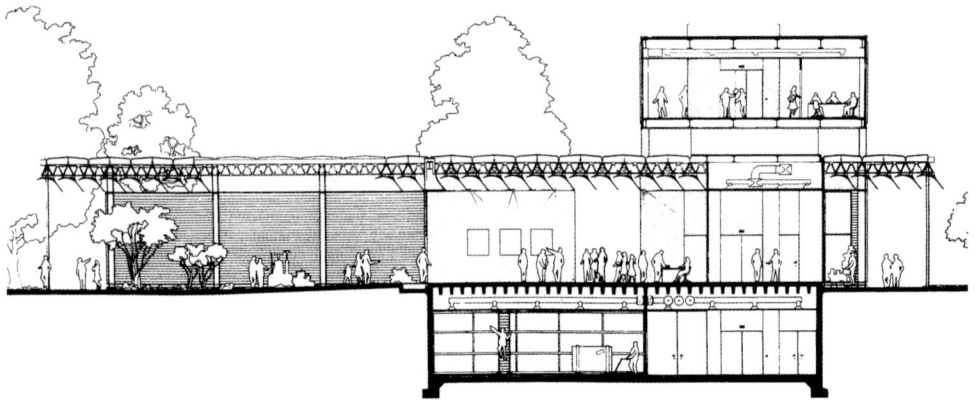

Cross section

Exhibition space 展示室 △▽

Corridor on upper floor 上階廊下

1981–87
JEAN NOUVEL + ARCHITECTURE STUDIO

ARAB WORLD INSTITUTE
Paris, France

North view 北より見る

The Arab World Institute may be referred to as a showcase, established by 20 Arab States and the French Government for the purpose of cultural exchange between Islamic and Western societies. Its programs include a museum for Arabic arts and cultures, space for temporary exhibitions, library, reference room, auditorium, restaurant, cafe, and workshop for children—it is in fact a cultural center open to all. The site is located within the urban fabric of traditional Paris, facing the river Seine on the opposite bank of the isle of Saint Louis. The building, entirely glazed, is composed of two volumes: the northern volume that curves along the adjacent Saint Germain Boulevard, and the southern volume that seems to complement a corner of the campus of Jussieu, a characteristic ensemble of university facilities specialized in sciences. A 3-meter wide passage runs between the two volumes along the northern volume's razor-sharp western edge, leading to the entrance.

The most distinctive feature in this building is probably the diaphragms that constitute its southern facade. They are made up of three types of metallic diaphragms different in size, operating like the iris of a camera lens, and are arranged to form geometric patterns typical of Islam. These devices are part of a computerized system controlling light penetration inside the building that reacts to changes in the intensity of sunlight. The strong sunshine of the Islamic world and the Arabesque pattern to block it off—here, the caprice of space and time created by these two elements is reproduced by means of technology, in the midst of Parisian streets, within a solid space of glass.

This is an 'Islamic architecture' translated into a hi-tech image—a metaphysical space where Islam meets the West, and History meets the Present.

Approach アプローチ

　アラブ世界研究所はアラブ諸国20カ国とフランス政府が設立し、イスラム文化と西洋社会の交流を目的としたショーケース的な研究所である。プログラムはアラブ美術・文明博物館、仮設展示のための空間、図書館、資料庫、オーディトリアム、レストラン、カフェ、子供のためのワークショップなどであり、文化センター的な性格をもつ、開かれた研究施設である。敷地はサン・ルイ島の対岸、パリの伝統的な都市ファブリックのなかにあり、セーヌ川に面し、前面に走るサンジェルマン大通りに対応してカーブする北側のヴォリュームと、特徴的なジュシュー大学科学学部のキャンパスの一角を補完するように配置された南側のヴォリュームによる構成。建物は全面ガラス張り。南北のヴォリュームの間に3mほどの通路が置かれ、北側ヴォリュームの、刃物のようにシャープに研がれた西端のエッジの脇を通りエントランスに至ることになる。

　この建物で最も特徴的なものは南側のファサードを構成するダイヤフラムであろう。大、中、小の3種類のカメラの絞り機能を応用した金属のダイヤフラムで、イスラム特有の幾何学パターンに似せて構成している、これらの絞りには、日照量に対して反応するコンピュータ・プログラムによって館内の明るさを調整するシステムが組み込まれている。イスラム世界の強い日差しとそれを遮るアラベスク模様が作る空間と時間の戯れを、パリの町中に建つソリッドなガラス空間の中、テクノロジーによって再現している。

　イスラムと西洋、歴史と現代の出会いをメタフィジカルに空間化した、ハイテクなイメージに翻訳された「イスラム建築」である。

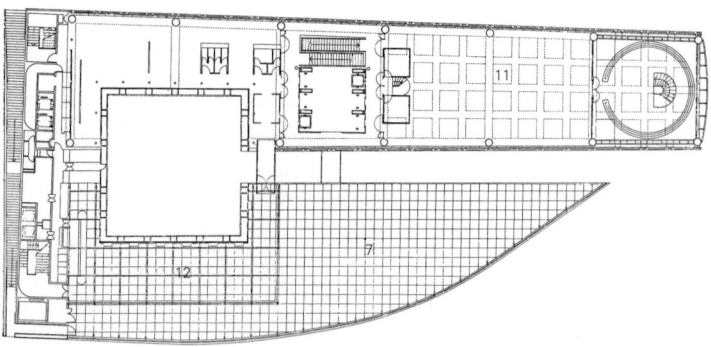

Ninth floor

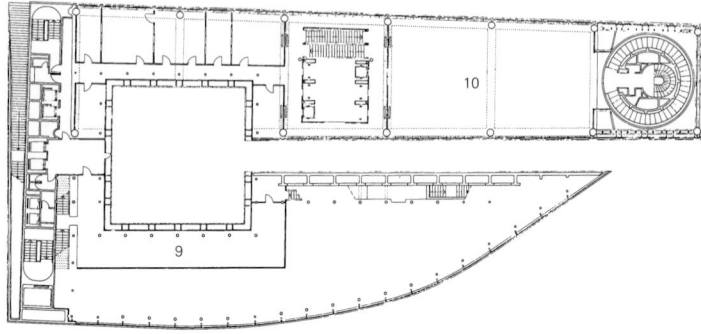

Fifth floor

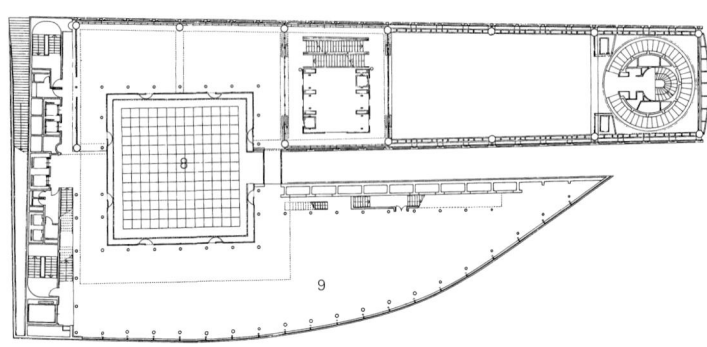

Fourth floor

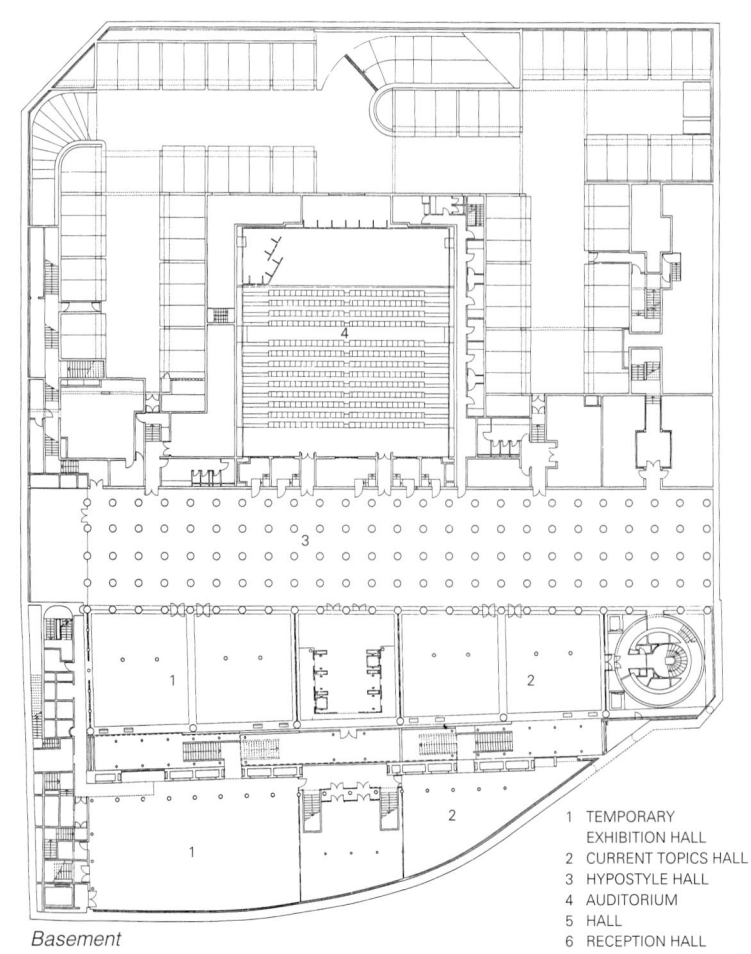

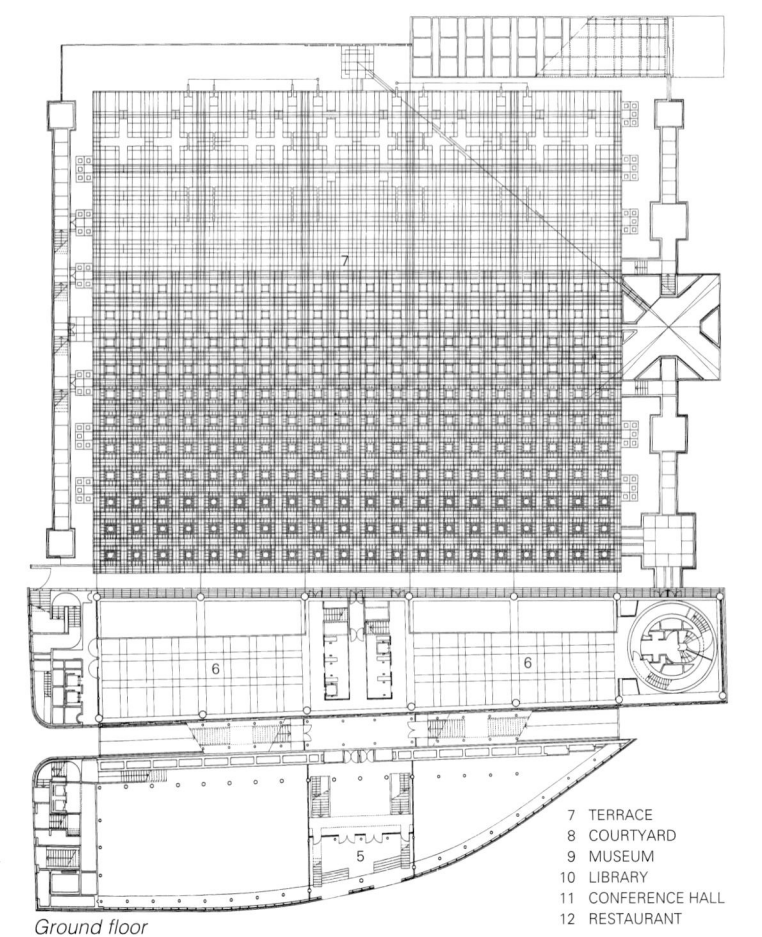

Southwest corner of south wing　南ウィングの南西隅部

Basement

Ground floor

1. TEMPORARY EXHIBITION HALL
2. CURRENT TOPICS HALL
3. HYPOSTYLE HALL
4. AUDITORIUM
5. HALL
6. RECEPTION HALL
7. TERRACE
8. COURTYARD
9. MUSEUM
10. LIBRARY
11. CONFERENCE HALL
12. RESTAURANT

Interior 内部

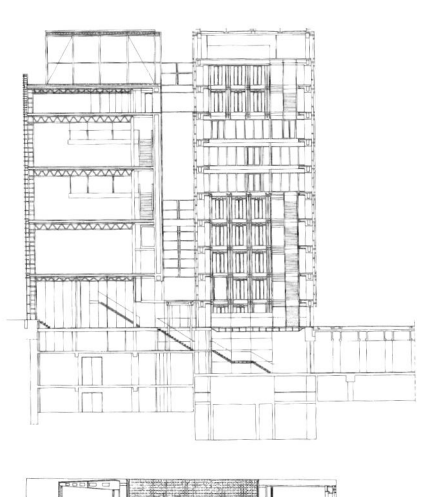

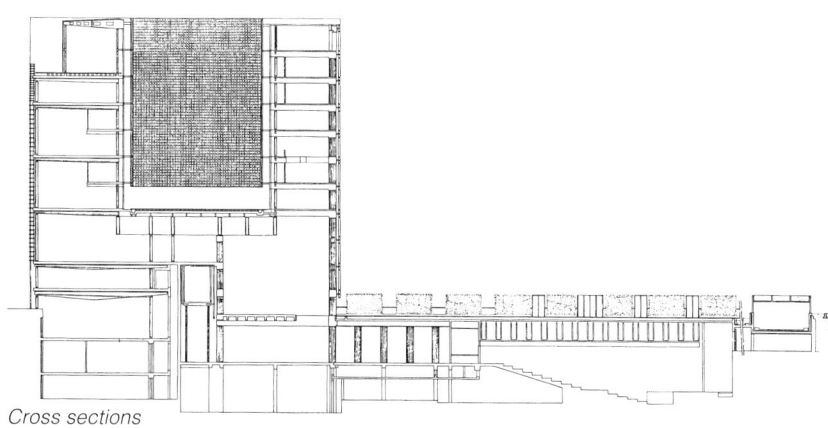

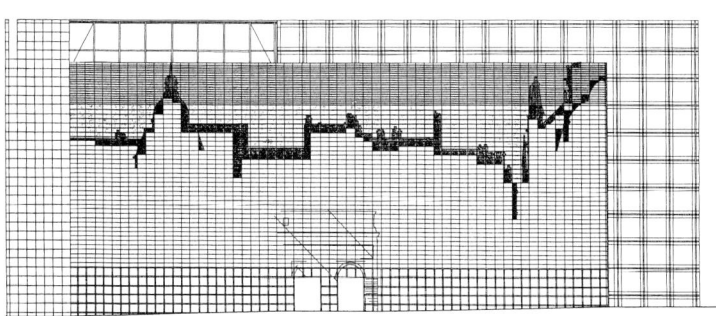

North elevation

Cross sections

Longitudinal section

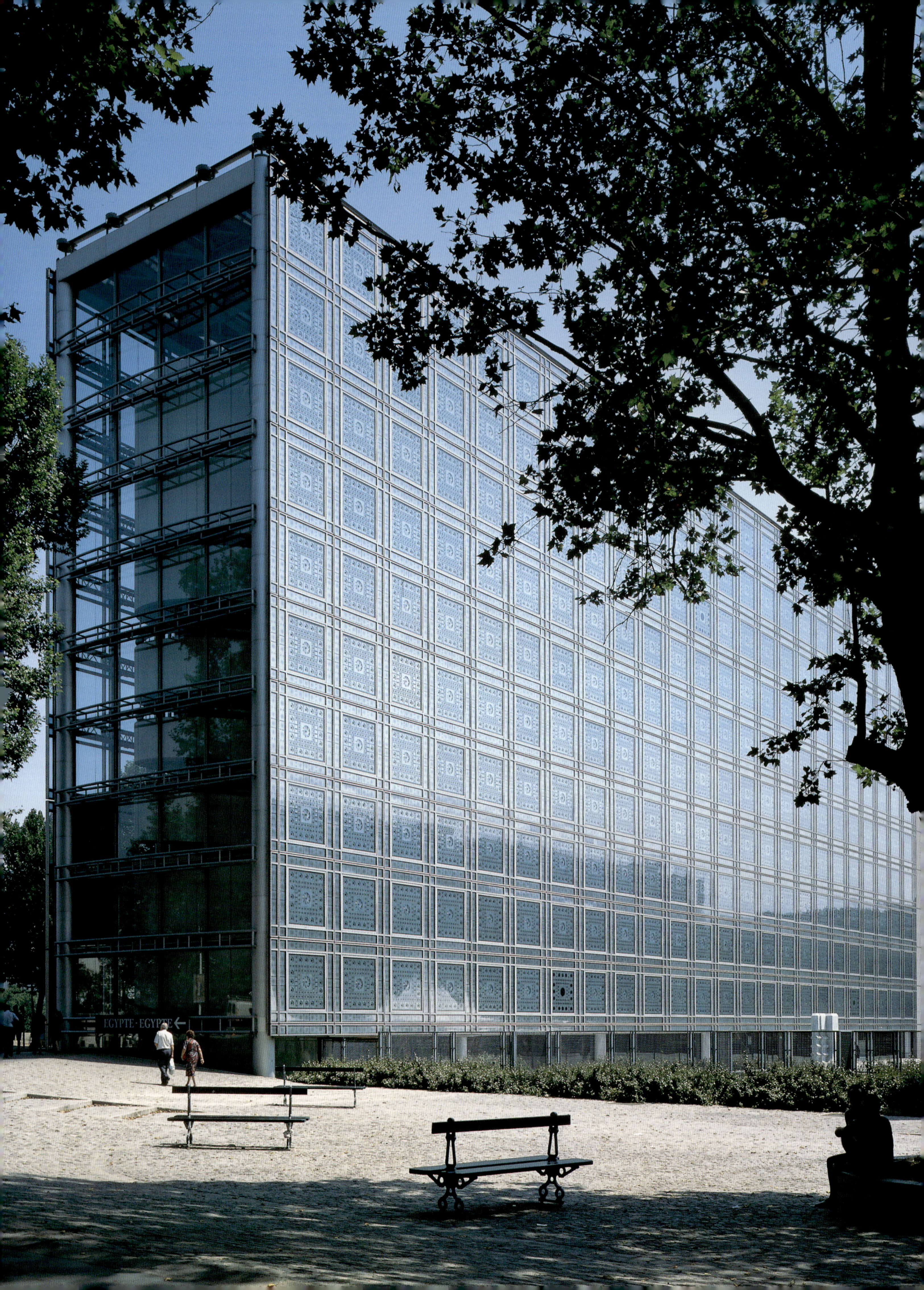
EGYPTE · EGYPTE

South wing: library　南ウィング：図書館

◁ *South wing*　南ウィング

Diaphragm　ダイヤフラム

1982-84
FRANK O. GEHRY

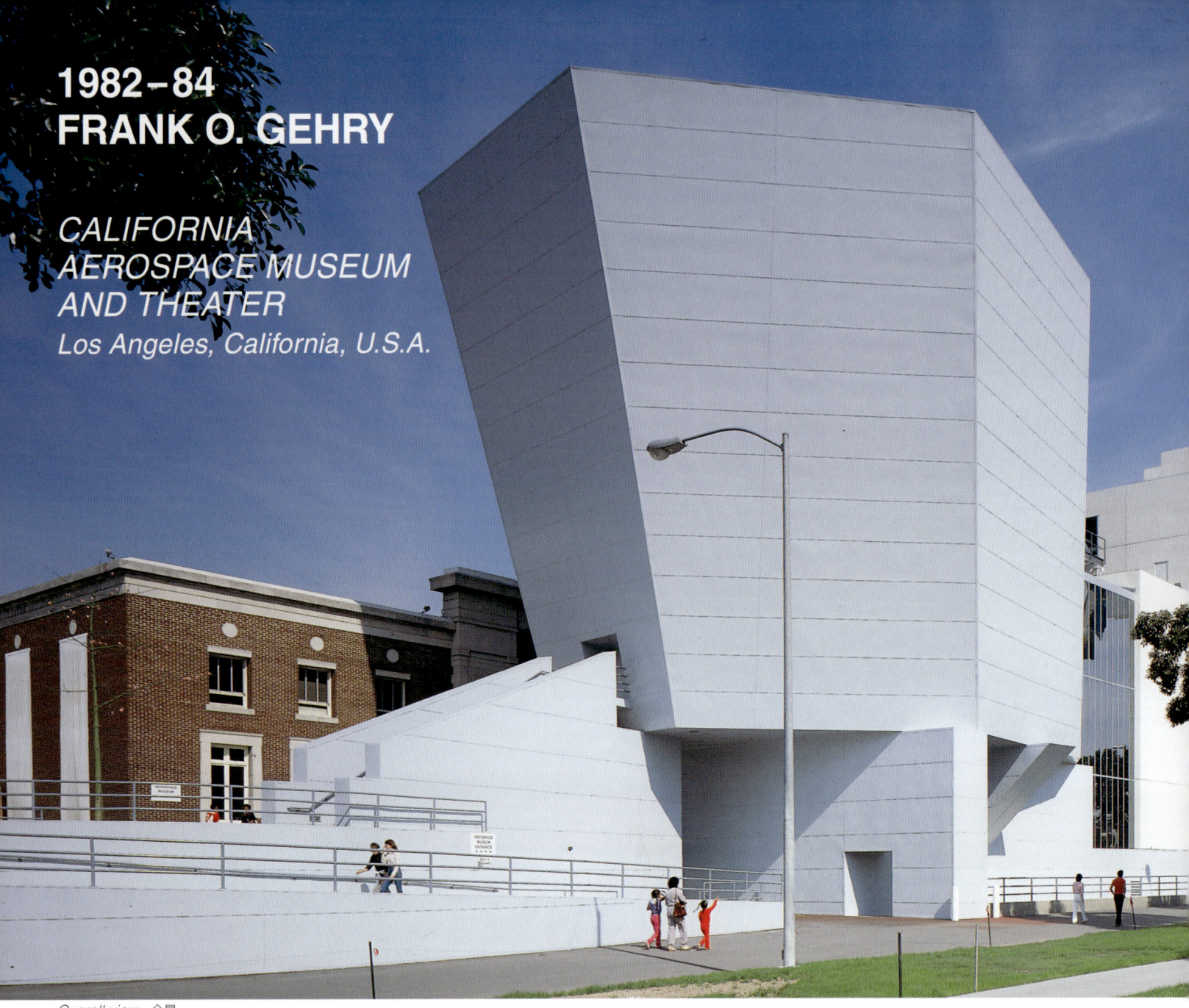

*CALIFORNIA
AEROSPACE MUSEUM
AND THEATER*
Los Angeles, California, U.S.A.

Overall view 全景

Main facade 正面

View from bridge　ブリッジより見る

Canopy for existing building　既存建物のキャノピー

Exposition Park has been a center of Natural History and Science Museums and is currently the site of new building construction which is scheduled for completion with the opening of the 1984 summer Olympics. The Aerospace Museum and Theater are two of these projects and are the beginning of a long term master plan to develop an Air and Space Museum complex.

The client asked that the museum building be designed as an exhibit to focus attention on the Aerospace Museum complex. Frank Gehry responded by developing the building as a set of sculptural objects when viewed from the exterior and as one continuous space from the interior.

The museum was designed to sit between an existing brick building, which in the future will be remodeled to house additional exhibition space, and a drive which is being developed as a pedestrian mall from which entrances to the park's museums will stem. To effectively develop the narrow site so that large-scale aerospace artifacts could be displayed, the building was designed with high open spaces which, in the western half of the structure, cantilever over the mall. The central part of the building contains three levels of viewing platforms.

The Aerospace Theater has been designed as a simple octagonal mass to sit in an area of the aerospace complex which will serve as an outdoor exhibit area. The theater will houses a large (50 by 70 foot) screen.

エキスポ公園は、自然科学博物館の中心を占めていたが、今は、1984年夏のオリンピックの開催に合わせて計画された新しい建物の敷地となっている。新しく計画されたのは、航空宇宙博物館と劇場で、将来、航空宇宙博物館複合体へと発展させていく長期的な全体計画の最初の建物となる。

クライアントは、この2つの建物のデザインが、航空宇宙博物館複合体へ焦点をあて注目を集める表現をとるように要望していた。フランク・ゲーリーは、外から見ると彫刻的な形の集まりであり、内部はひとつの連続空間という建物を考えることによってこれに応えた。

博物館は、既存の煉瓦造の建物と公園内の車道との間におさまるように設計されている。煉瓦造の建物は、将来、改造して展示スペースを収容する予定であるし、車道の方は、博物館複合体の入口となる歩行者モールとなるように整備が進められている。巨大な航空機などの展示ができるように、狭い敷地を効率よく使って、建物の西半分をモールの上にキャンチレバーで張り出させ、天井の高いオープン・スペースをつくった。建物の中央部には3層にわたる展望台がある。

航空宇宙劇場は、単純な八角形で、この複合体計画の戸外展示スペース用の敷地に建てられる。劇場には50×70フィートの大きな映写スクリーンが取り付けられる。

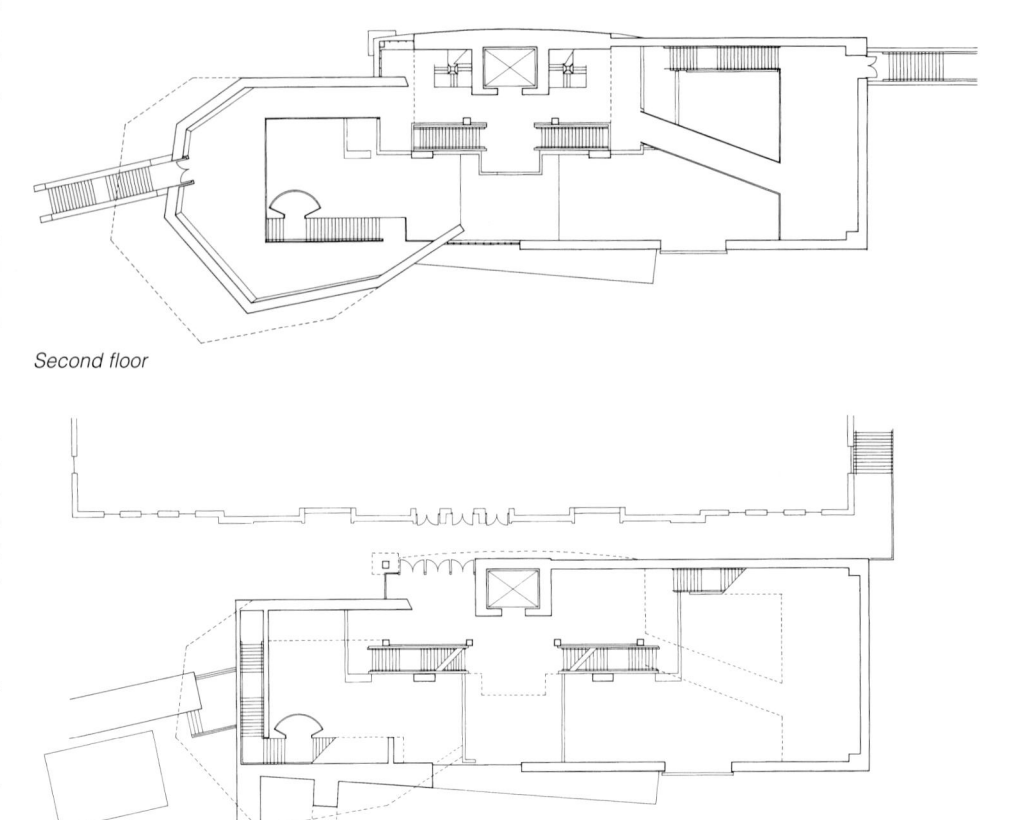

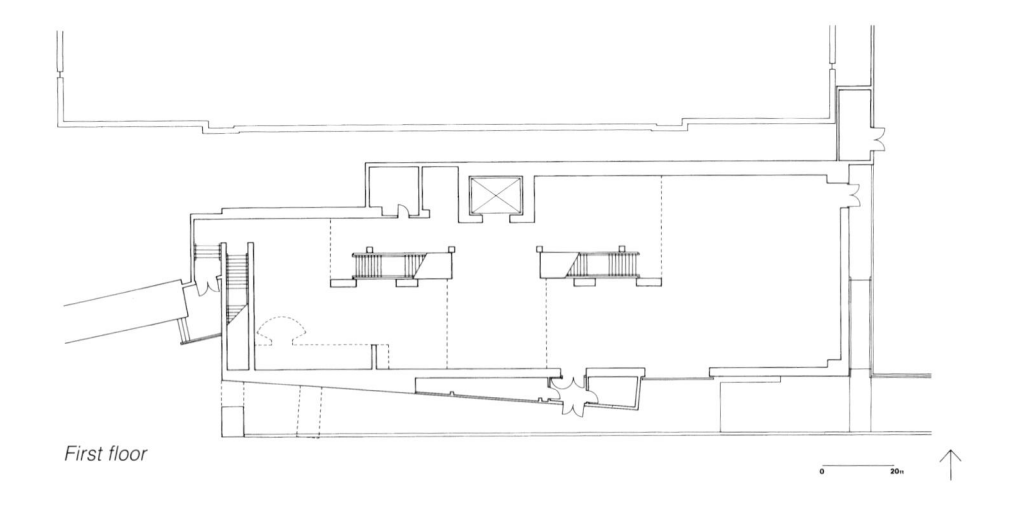

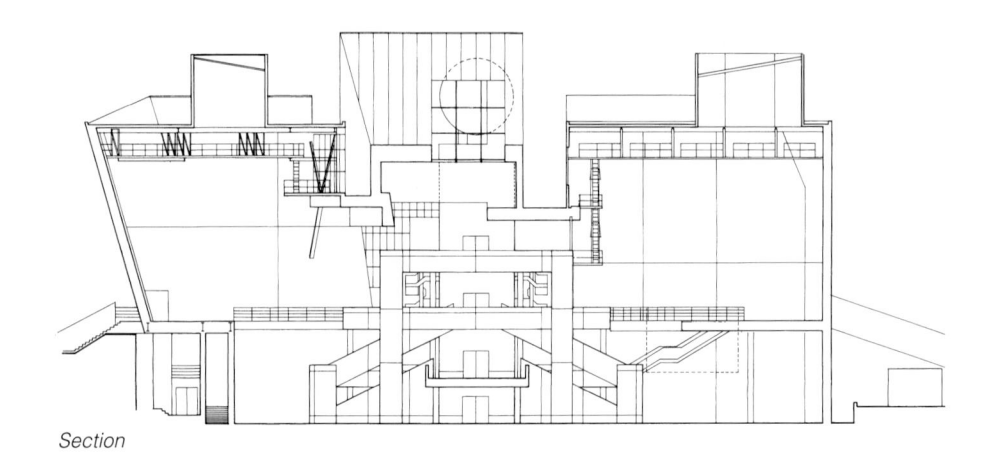

Second floor

Mazzanine of first floor

First floor

Section

Exhibition space on first floor　1階展示室

1982-90
GÜNTER BEHNISCH

GERMAN POSTAL MUSEUM
Frankfurt am Main, Germany

View toward entrance エントランス側外観

Garden on east 東側庭園

Exhibition space: view from basement　展示室：地階より見る

Basement: skylight　地階：スカイライト

On the south bank of the Main stand 19th century villas in what used to be a quiet and exclusive residential district. They are in marked contrast to the tall buildings in the commercial district across the river. Today, many of those villas have become museums, and the area has been transformed into a cultural district. The Museum of Decorative Art by Richard Meier, the Architecture Museum by O.M. Ungers, the Film Museum, and the Post Museum by Behnisch are scattered along the river.

This museum used to be housed in one of the villas, but the increasing size of the collection led in 1982 to the holding of a competition, which was won by Behnisch's proposal. He chose to preserve the villa as an office and library and designed a new building in a high-tech manner. The building, which has an essentially rectangular plan, features a four-story space wrapped in a curved glass screen that joins the exhibition spaces on different floors. The basement, which takes up the entire site, is the main exhibition room and provides access to the old building. The entrance hall, cafe and auditorium are on the first floor, and exhibition rooms are on the second and third floors. It has been made possible to see the garden from all parts of the museum through the glazing over the four-story space.

This museum, with its collection of material and equipment related to postal and communication services and covering everything from their origin to the most recent advances, is a superb and skillfully detailed example of contemporary high-tech.

フランクフルトのマイン河南岸には、対岸の高層ビルが建ち並ぶ商業地区とは対照的に、19世紀に建てられ、静かな高級住宅地を構成していたヴィラが並んでいる。今日ではその多くが美術館や博物館となり、文化地区へと変貌した。リチャード・マイヤー設計の装飾美術館、O・M・ウンガース設計の建築美術館、フィルム美術館、そしてベーニッシュの郵便・通信博物館等が河に沿って点在している。

この博物館は、以前はこれらのヴィラのひとつを利用していたが、収蔵品の増加に伴い、1982年にコンペが行われベーニッシュ案が入選した。彼は、ヴィラを事務所や図書室として残し、ハイテックな手法で新館を構成した。長方形プランをもつ新館には、庭に面して円筒形のガラス壁に覆われた、4層吹抜けの空間が置かれ各階の展示室を結んでいる。敷地全体に広がる地階は主展示室となり旧館と連絡している。1階はエントランスホール、カフェやオーディトリアム、2、3階には展示室を配置し、そのどこからも4層吹抜けのガラスの壁を通して、庭が見えるように配慮されている。

創生期から最先端までの、郵便・通信の資料、機材が展示された博物館は、ハイテックな現代建築としてみごとに表現されており、古いヴィラともよく均衡し、細部の納まりも巧みである。

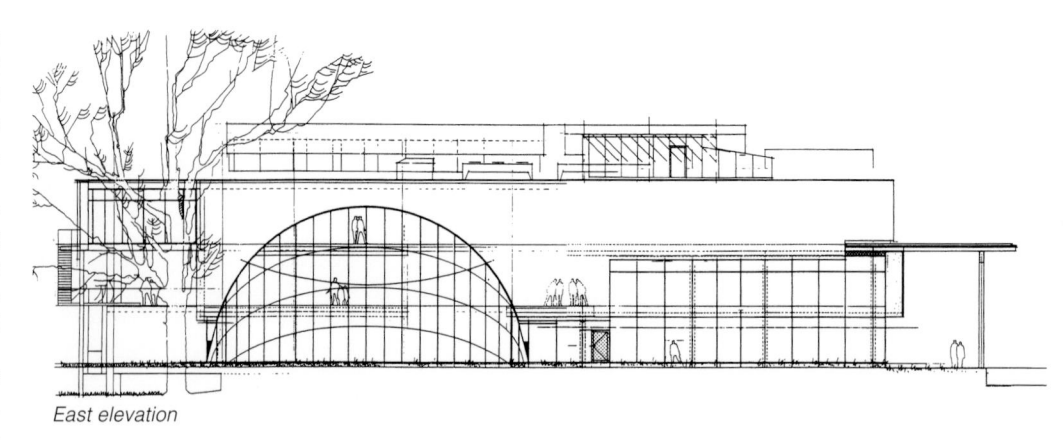

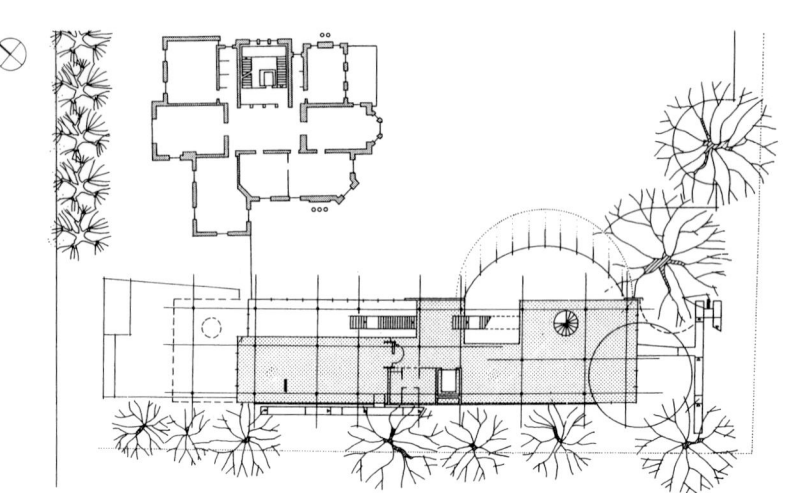

East elevation

Second floor

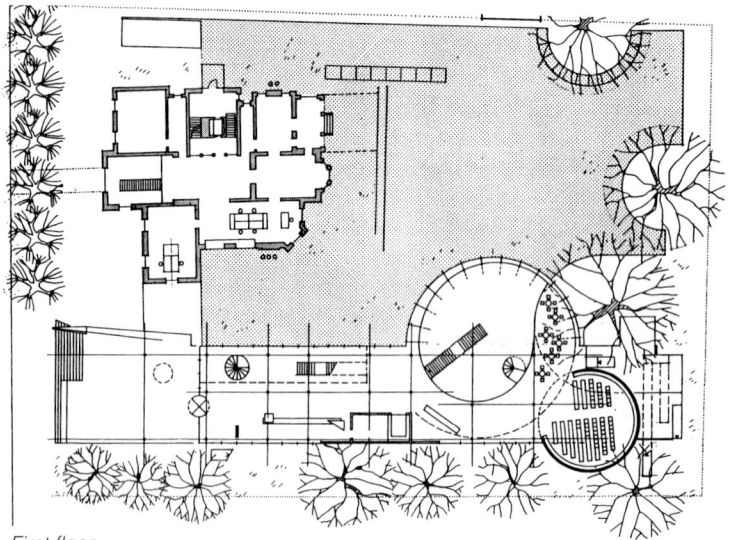

First floor

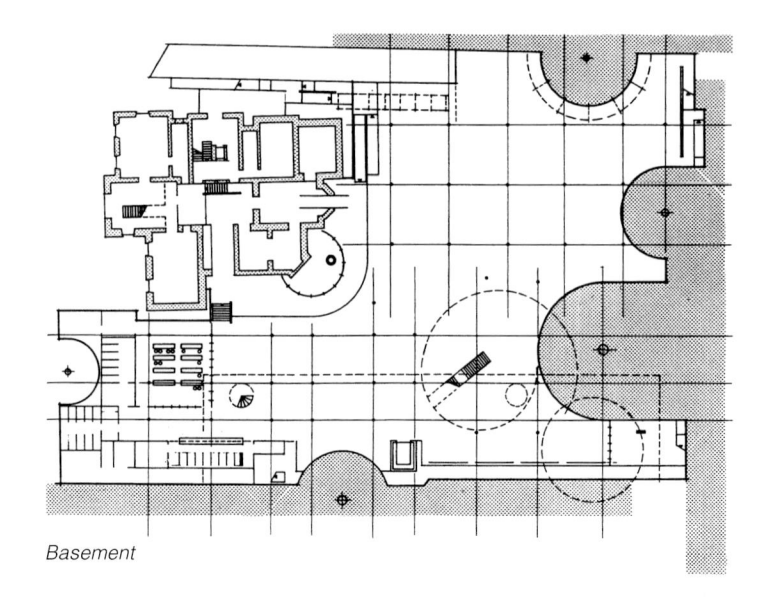

Basement

View from first floor 1階より見る

Staircase　階段

Staircase: view toward entrance　階段：エントランス方向を見る

Exhibition space on second floor　2階展示スペース

MicroScapes

Third floor　3階 △▽

1982–91
HANS HOLLEIN

MUSEUM FOR MODERN ART, FRANKFURT AM MAIN
Frankfurt am Main, Germany

View from east 東より見る

Northwest corner 北西隅部

North elevation 北面 △▽

View toward main entrance メイン・エントランスを見る

133

A program similar in size and scope to Mönchengladbach (Abteiberg Museum, 1982), the Frankfurt Museum for Modern Art is also in the historic heart of the city and determined by its compact, triangular site. Again it houses contemporary art, with a certain emphasis also on permanent installations—partly specifically done for the museum. The symmetry of the site—and the building—is overlaid by a diagonally asymmetrical path through the building, which consists of mainly three floors, one with a central toplit hall and a top-floor with skylights. While the program for the central hall called for a variety of uses, the specific spaces for the art and artists are reduced to the essential.

The outside building block had to keep a given cornice-height. Above it is a premeditated roofscape of skylights and spaces for mechanical equipment.

As with any public building in Frankfurt, this one is made of red sandstone and stucco, also for reasons of economy.

The competition was decided in 1983 but it took several years for the final decision to build to be reached. Again in the final phase of construction local political and administrative problems halted the course of construction and delayed the opening foreseen for the fail of 1990. It was finally opened in spring 1991.

規模、機能とも、ドイツ・メンヘングラートバッハ市のアプタイベルク美術館（1982）と同様なプログラムである。コンパクトな三角形の敷地で、同じように街の歴史地区の中心にある、現代美術を展示することも共通しているが、常設展示に力を入れ、いくつかの場所は、特別に作品に合わせて構成している。敷地と建物のもつ対称性に対し、建物内を非対称に貫く動線が斜めに重ねられている。建物は主に3つの階で構成されている。そのひとつの階にはトップライトのついた中央ホールがあり、最上階にはスカイライトがかかっている。中央ホールは多目的に使えることが求められている一方、美術品と作家のためのスペースは必要不可欠なだけの広さまでに縮小されている。

建物の外観は、既存の建物のコーニスの高さを保たねばならない。コーニスから上は、前もって考えていたスカイライトと機械設備スペースによる屋根景観として構成した。

フランクフルトの公共建築のいずれとも同様、この建物もまた、赤砂岩とスタッコ仕上であるが、その理由もまた同じく経済性からである。

競技設計は、1983年に行われたのだが、建設が最終的に決定されるまでに数年を要した。建設の最終段階で、またも、地方の政治上の問題から工事が中止され、最終的には1991年春にオープンした。

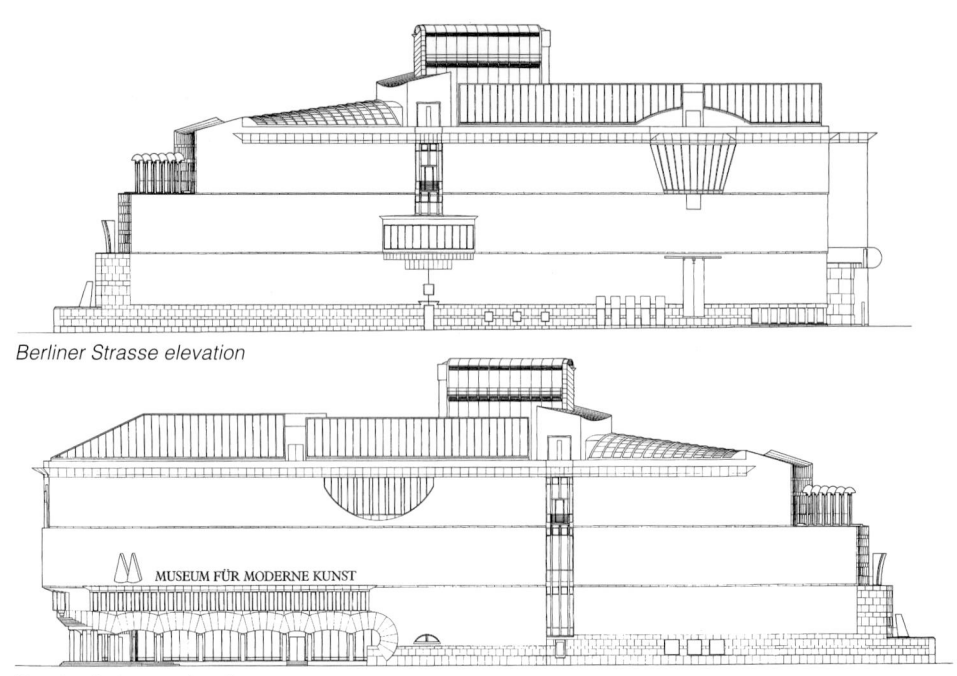

Berliner Strasse elevation

Braubachstrasse elevation

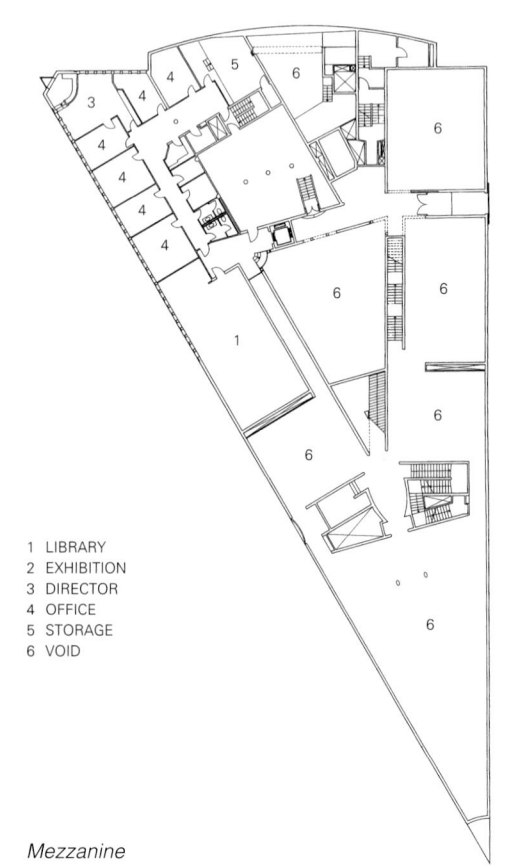

1 FOYER
2 LECTURE ROOM
3 STAGE
4 WORKSHOP
5 MECHANICAL

1 MAIN ENTRANCE
2 FOYER
3 CAFE
4 MAIN HALL
5 EXHIBITION ROOM
6 TEMPORARY EXHIBITION
7 SERVICE
8 STAFF ENTRANCE

1 LIBRARY
2 EXHIBITION
3 DIRECTOR
4 OFFICE
5 STORAGE
6 VOID

Basement

Level 1

Mezzanine

Entrance foyer　エントランス・ホワイエ

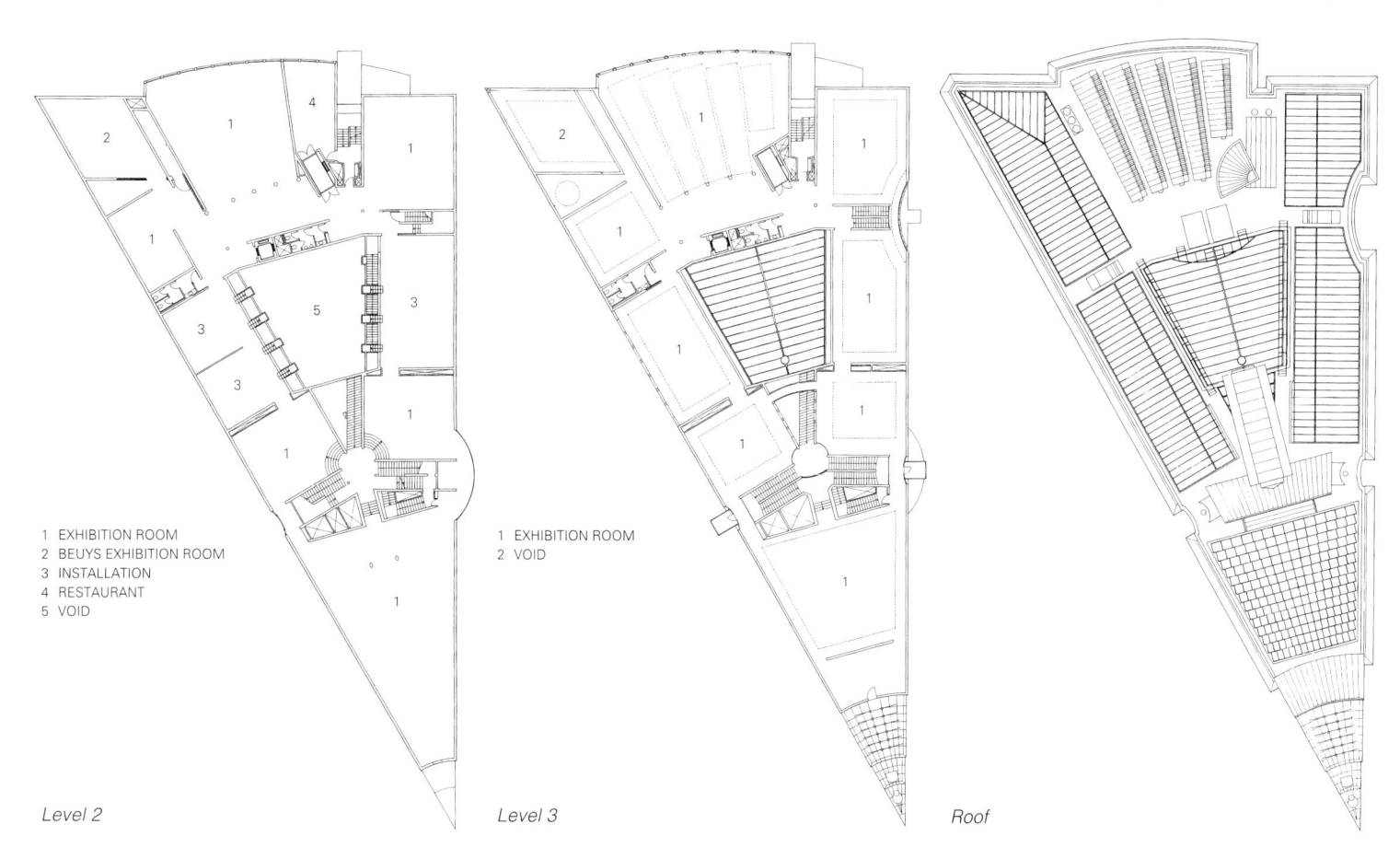

1 EXHIBITION ROOM
2 BEUYS EXHIBITION ROOM
3 INSTALLATION
4 RESTAURANT
5 VOID

1 EXHIBITION ROOM
2 VOID

Level 2　　　　　*Level 3*　　　　　*Roof*

Circulation area サーキュレーション・エリア

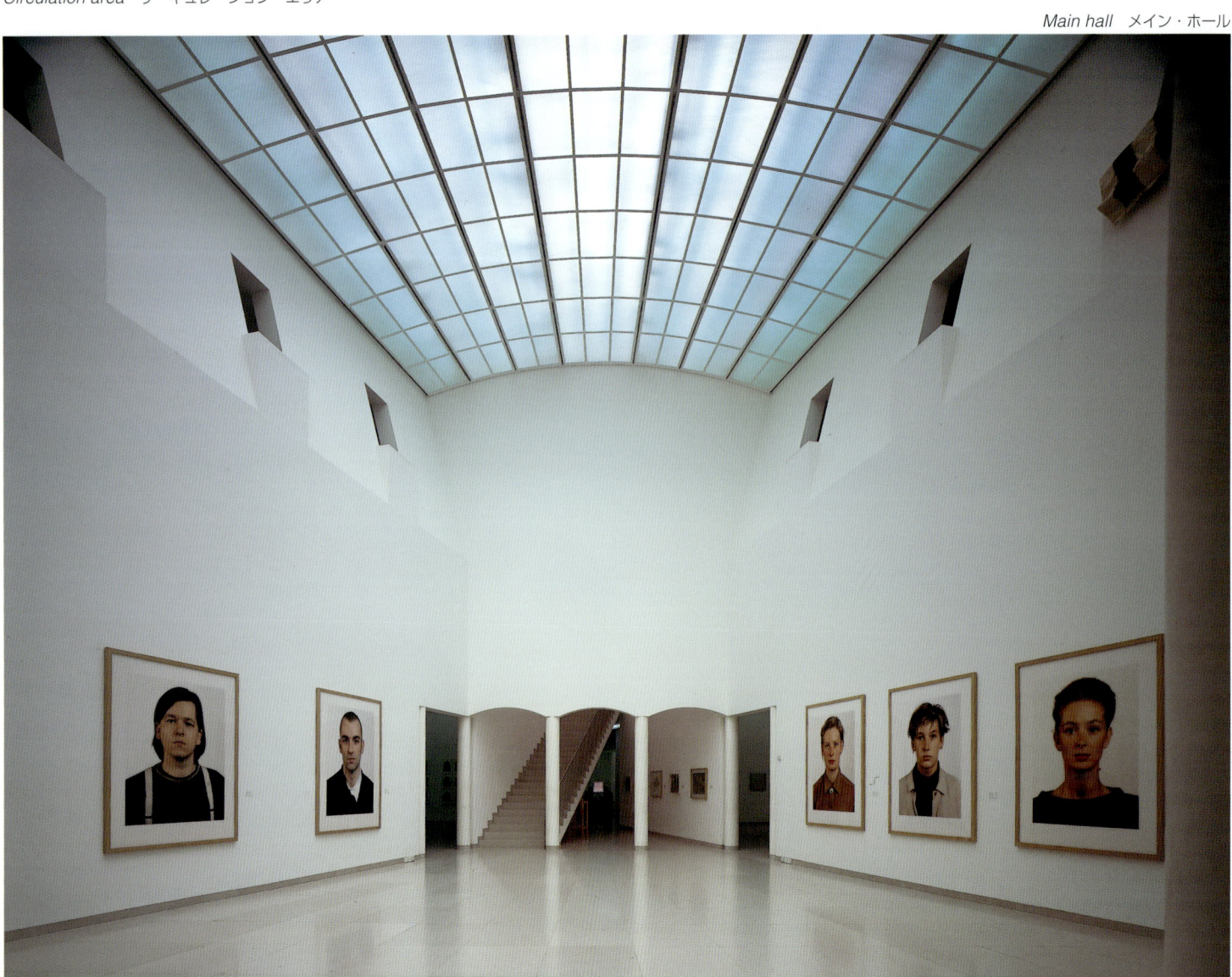

Main hall　メイン・ホール

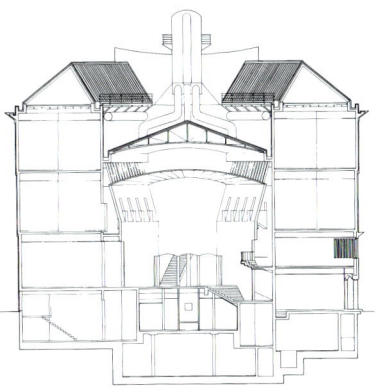

Cross section

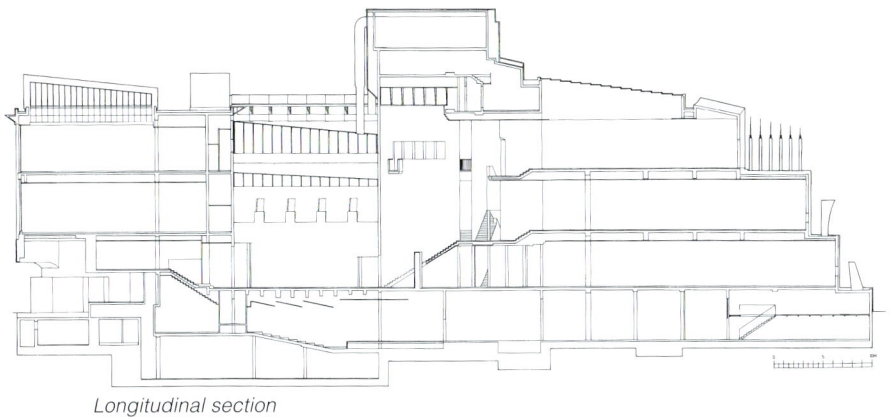

Longitudinal section

Main hall　メイン・ホール

Circulation area　サーキュレーション・エリア

Exhibition room on level 1　1階展示室

Exhibition room on level 2　2階展示室

Exhibiton room on level 3　3階展示室

Beuys exhibition room　ヨゼフ・ボイス展示室

Exhibition room on level 3　3階展示室

1983–86
FUMIHIKO MAKI

NATIONAL MUSEUM OF MODERN ART, KYOTO
Kyoto, Japan

Overall view from southeast 南東より見る

South elevation 南面

Main entrance　メイン・エントランス△▽

Situated in the northeastern part of Kyoto City, Okazaki Park is known as Japan's first public park in a modern sense. Major urban cultural facilities including this National Museum of Modern Art, Kyoto are gathered inside this park. The museum site occupies one of Kyoto's best scenic area, facing the huge, vermilion-lacquered torii (shrine gateway) which is a symbol of the park, as well as the Biwako Canal. As the museum houses the national collection of 20th-century Western and Japanese fine arts, its design primarily focuses on attributing serenity worthy of this scenic zone to the architectural presence, along with the expression of contemporarity that is, a sense of the times. Horizontality is emphasized among the eaves in an attempt to create a harmony with the surrounding environment. At the same time, verticality is emphasized by placing transparent shafts in four corners, as a manifestation of stateliness proper to public buildings of significant importance. The exterior consists basically of pale gray granite cast inside precast concrete boards that would last through the times and match the scenic landscape. In addition to this, 4 types of material—transparent glass, translucent glass screen with effects similar to traditional shoji screen and aluminium with a touch of gray—are applied to where each of them would be most effective in forming a delicate gradation on the surface layer, thereby producing an exterior fit for Okazaki Park.

Inside, the ground-level entrance hall leads to a quadruple-height space in the center of the building, around which are arranged a number of rooms for various purposes. The ground floor accommodates the entrance, information counter/museum shop, tearoom, exhibition lobby, auditorium, and administrative office. The director's room, reception room, and curators' office are found on the second floor. The toplit central stairwell guides the flow of space to climb up to the temporary exhibition rooms on the third floor. Part of the permanent exhibition rooms on the fourth floor is designed to share the same flow of space.

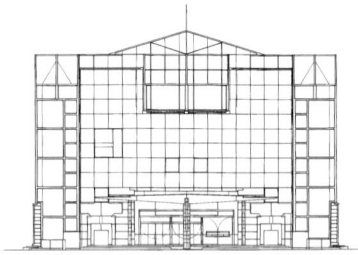

Atrium of entrance hall エントランス・ホールのアトリウム

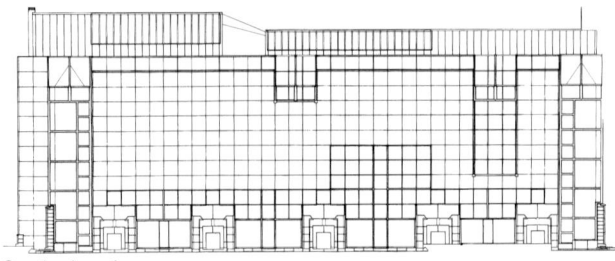

East elevation

South elevation

1 ENTRANCE
2 ENTRANCE HALL
3 GALLERY
4 AUDITORIUM
5 SPECIAL EXHIBITION
6 PERMANENT EXHIBITION
7 OFFICE
8 LOUNGE
9 CAFETERIA
10 SHOP

京都国立近代美術館が計画された岡崎公園は、京都の東北に位置し、日本における最初の近代的な意味での公園として知られている。主要な都市文化施設はこの公園内に集中している。美術館の敷地は、公園のシンボルとしての朱塗りの大鳥居に面するとともに、琵琶湖疏水にも面している、京都でも有数の景勝地である。当美術館は、20世紀の西洋および日本美術国家コレクションを収蔵する美術館であるため、その近代という時代性の表現とともに、風致地区にふさわしい静寂な雰囲気をもつ建築の在り方が、設計の重要なポイントとして考えられている。そこで、軒の水平線を強調して、周辺環境と調和させるとともに、4つのコーナー部分に透明なシャフトを配置し、その垂直性によって時代性を強調し、かつ、重要な公共建築物としての荘重さを表現しようとしている。外装材料としては、風致地区の景観に調和し、かつ長い年月にも耐えうるよう、淡いグレーの花崗岩を打ち込んだPC版を基本とし、透明ガラス、障子のような効果をもつ半透明のガラススクリーン、グレーに発色するアルミの4種類のマチエールを使い分け、微妙な表層のグラデーションを構成し、岡崎公園にふさわしい外観をつくり出そうとしている。

一方内部は、1階のエントランスホールを介して4階までの吹抜けが建物の中心に位置し、そのまわりにさまざまなスペースが設けられている。1階は、エントランス、受付、売店、喫茶室、展示ロビー、講堂、庶務課事務室が中心となり、館長室、応接室、学芸課事務室は2階に位置している。そして、トップライトをもった吹抜けの中の中央階段を通じて3階企画展示室へ空間は流れ、また4階の常設展示室の一部からもこの空間を感じられるように計画されている。

Entrance hall エントランス・ホール

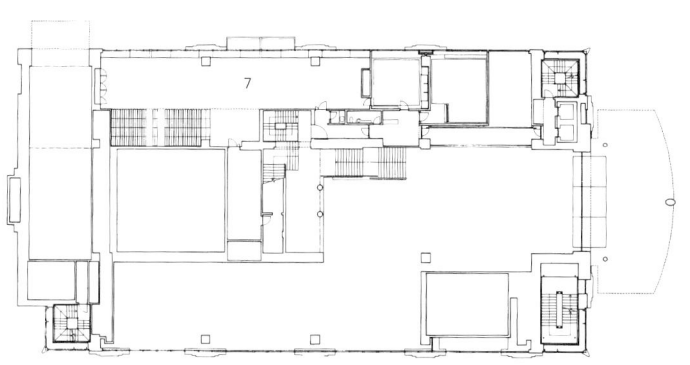

Second floor

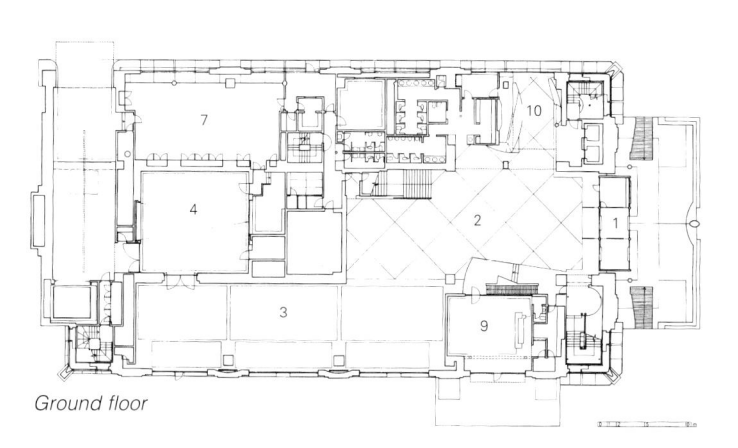

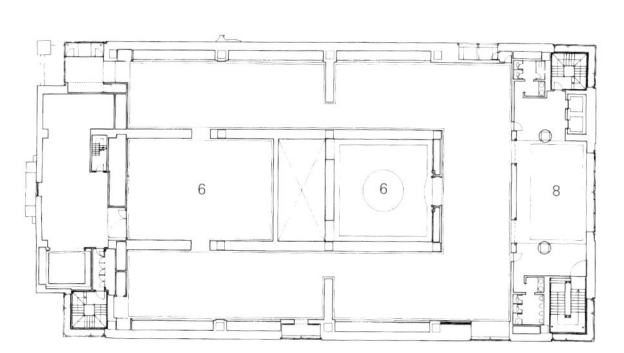

Fourth floor

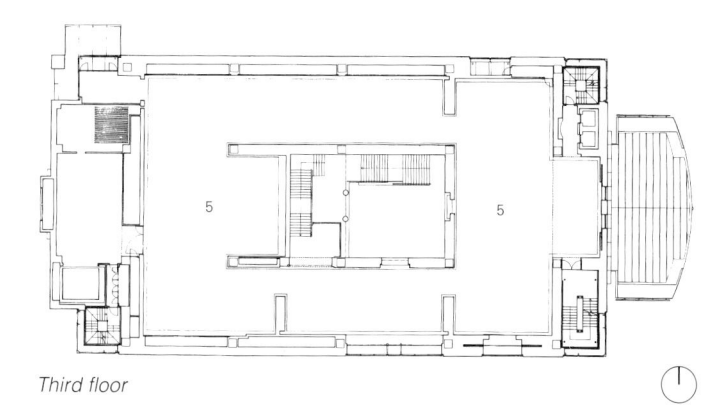

Ground floor

Third floor

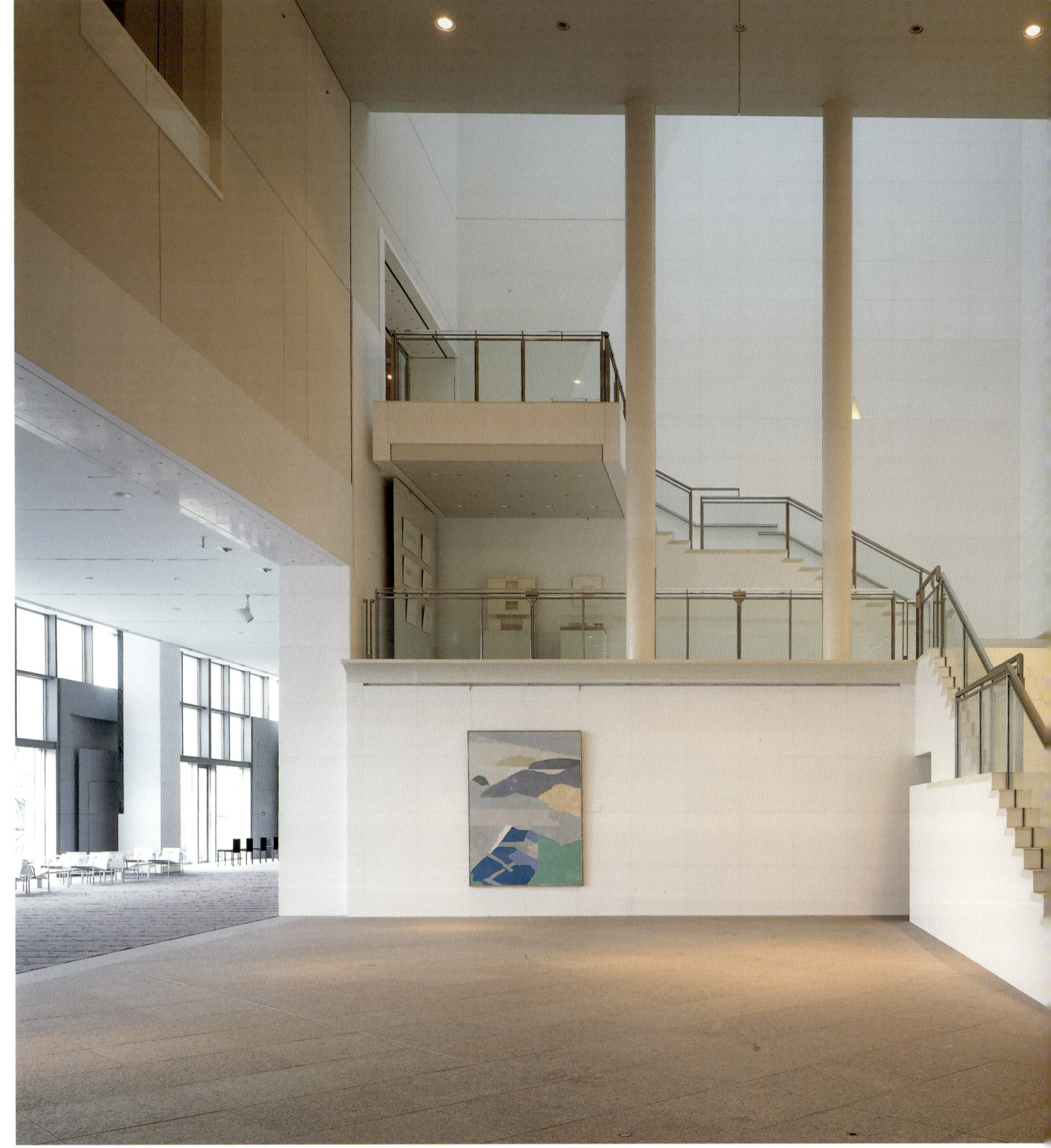

Entrance hall: staircase on west　エントランス・ホール：西側の階段

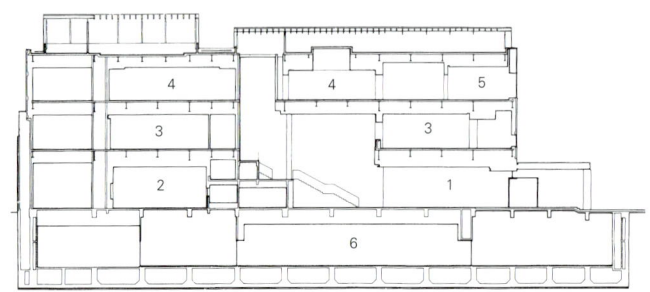

Longitudinal section

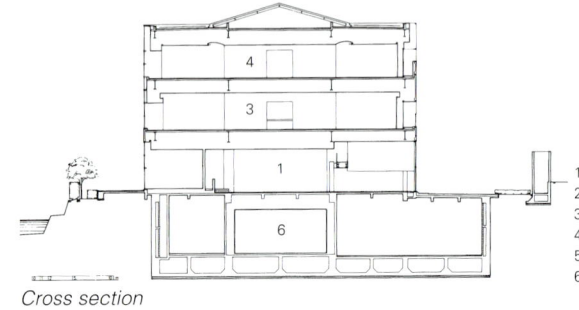

Cross section

1 ENTRANCE HALL
2 AUDITORIUM
3 SPECIAL EXHIBITION
4 PERMANENT EXHIBITION
5 LOUNGE
6 STORAGE

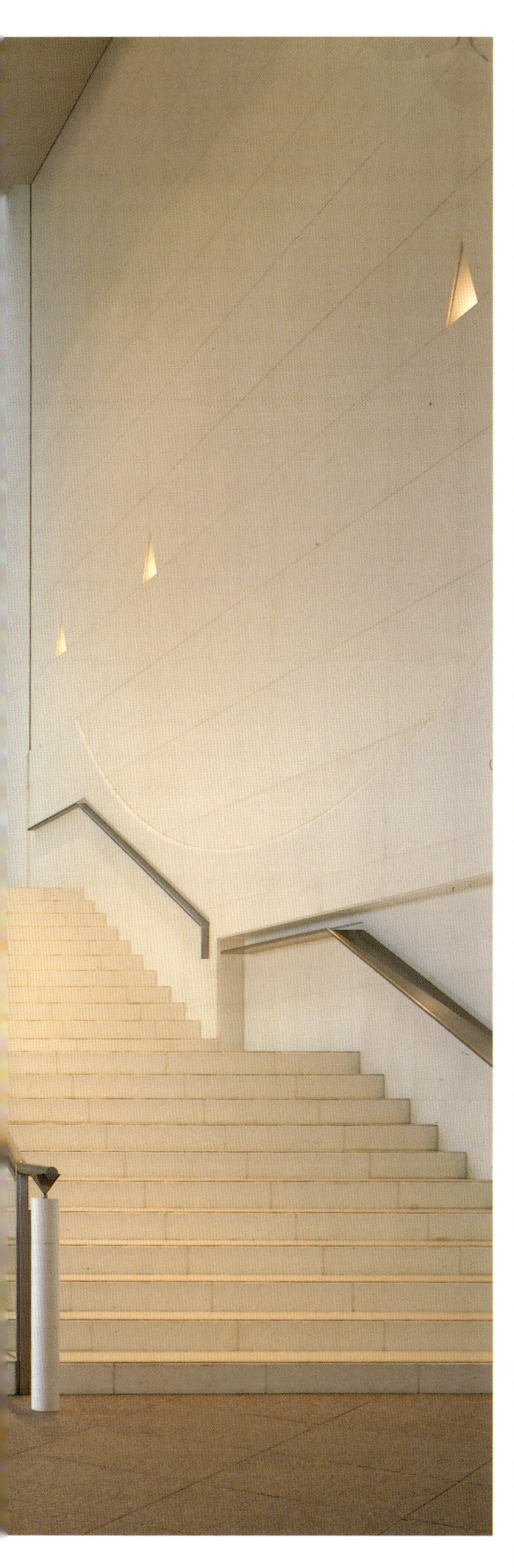

Museum shop ミュージアム・ショップ

View toward gallery on ground floor 1階展示室方向を見る

Gallery on ground floor: wall detail 1階展示室：壁面のディテール

Entrance hall: view of staircase from south　エントランス・ホール：南より階段を見る

Cafeteria　カフェテリア

Exhibition room on fourth floor　4階展示室

Staircase　階段室

Exhibition room on fourth floor　4階展示室

147

1986–88
HIROSHI HARA

IIDA CITY MUSEUM
Nagano, Japan

Overall view from south   南側全景

Aerial view 航空写真

View from north 北側外観

Iida is located on a river-terrace in the midst of a valley between two 3,000-meter mountain ranges and happens to be my hometown. The art museum is sited on top of the terrace where a castle used to stand. The museum focuses on the work of Shunso Hishida, an important figure in Japanese art history and a native of Iida.

Because of their age and delicate materials these paintings require special ventilation and illumination. Even exposure to artificial light has to be quite limited. Thus in spite of the modest scale of the exhibition rooms below grade, a three-tier air-conditioning system was employed.

Since this is a municipal building it must serve as a community center as well as a museum. Our design had to provide facilities for creative activities and local exhibitions in addition to being a center for ethnological and regional studies. These latter are accommodated in relatively informal spaces, including an exhibit area, research rooms, and a small auditorium.

The double-height lobby may be used as an informal exhibition space and serves to unify all the other spaces. This is covered by a steel-truss roof structure formed in the image of the Southern Alps. The formal exhibition-area occupies much of the lower level but is just one of several museum display areas.

Exterior stairs are located at both ends of the building, with access to the roof top. This open-air space along with a partial reconstruction of the castle, the rebuilt study of Kunio Yanagida (an ethnologist who worked extensively in the area), the home of a local poet Kounosuke Hinatsu, and an adjacent shrine, all help transform the entire site into a park.

Hiroshi Hara

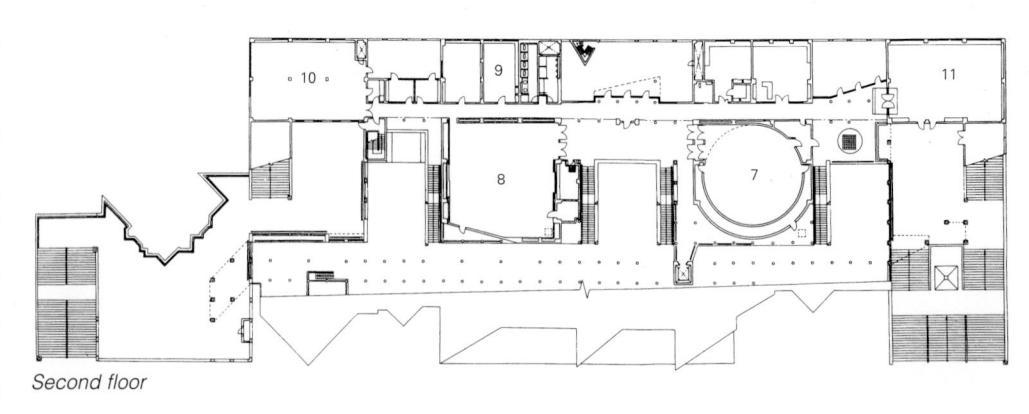

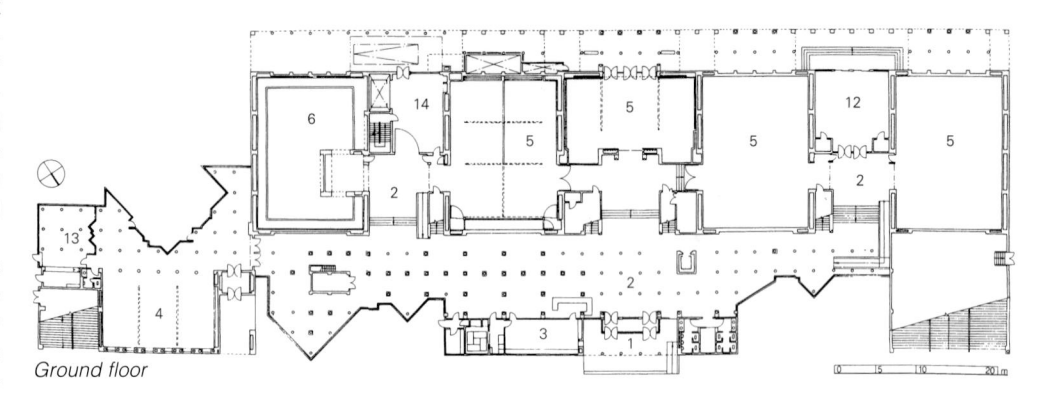

Second floor

Ground floor

West elevation

East elevation

1 ENTRANCE
2 MAIN LOBBY
3 ADMINISTRATION
4 "CITIZENS' GALLERY"
5 EXHIBITION ROOM
6 SHUNSO MEMORIAL ROOM
7 PLANETARIUM
8 LECTURE HALL
9 CURATORS' ROOM
10 LABORATORY
11 WORKSHOP
12 STUDY ROOM
13 CAFE
14 UNPACKING

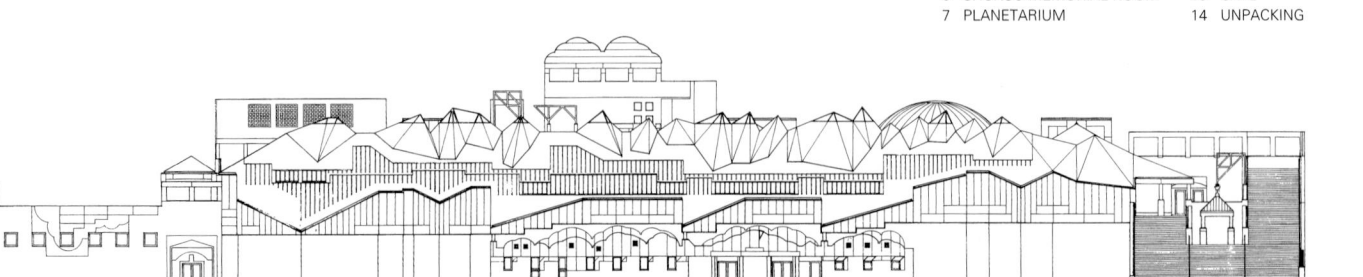

North elevation

South elevation

View from north　北より見る

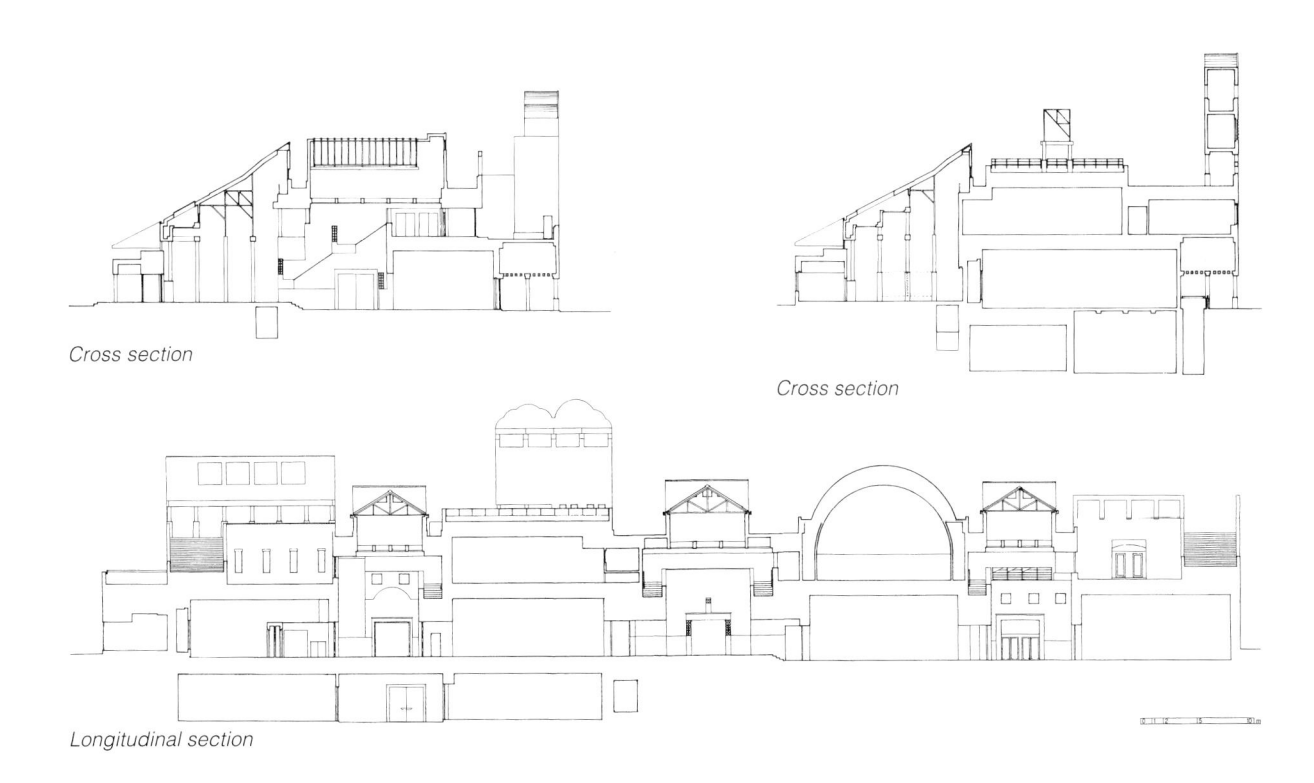

Cross section

Cross section

Longitudinal section

　飯田市は、3,000メートル級のふたつの山脈にはさまれた谷間の段丘の上にあり、私の郷里である。敷地は、段丘の先端部に位置する城趾である。この地の出身である日本絵画史上重要な位置を占める菱田春草の作品の展示が核となっている。
　日本画は、画材の繊細さ故に、自然光はもちろんのこと、自然状態の空気にも触れることはできない。照明器具の光にも、年間数日さらすことが許される程度の厳密さを要する。したがって、この美術館は小規模であるにもかかわらず、地下に3段階に空調した収蔵庫を設け、展示室は完全に密閉化して均質空間とすると同時に十全な管理ができるサービス動線を用意している。
　一方、地域の美術博物館の在り方からすれば、収蔵展示機能とは別に、市民の創作・発表活動、あるいは民族学研究、あるいは地域研究などの活動の中心的な場となることが重要である。したがって、フォーマルな展示室とは別に、インフォーマルな展示室、研究室、小講堂などが、市民活動領域として用意してある。
　インフォーマルな展示空間を兼ねつつ、全体を統合するのがロビーで、この部分には、南アルプスの山脈を抽象化した形態の屋根を架けてある。この屋根は、鉄骨のトラスで支えられている。
　空間の組み立てとしては、フォーマルであると同時に均質空間でもある展示室群を基壇として、均質空間を多様な空間のひとつの構成要素とするように計画した。
　建物両端部に屋外階段を設けて、屋上が常時市民に開放されること、遺構の一部を保存・復元したこと、谷に橋を架けて飛び地をつなぎそこに飯田と関係の深かった民俗学者柳田国男の書斎の移築、この地の出身の詩人日夏耿之介の自宅の再現をはかることなどによって、隣接する神社をふくめて、敷地全体の公園化をはかっている。　　　　　　（原広司）

Main lobby　メイン・ロビー

Main lobby: entrance on left　メイン・ロビー：左はエントランス ▷

Roof terrace　ルーフ・テラス

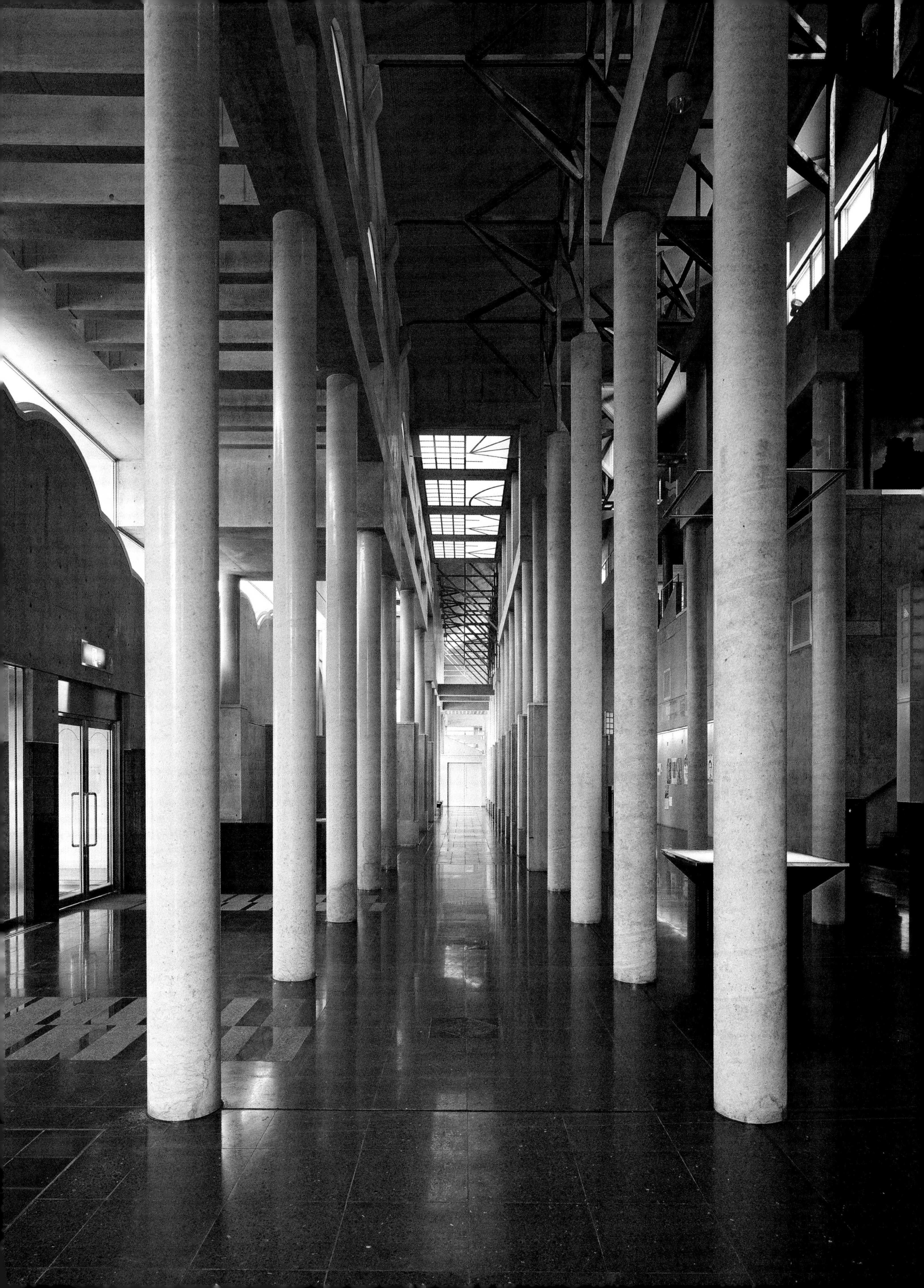

Study room　学習室

Skylight of main lobby　メイン・ロビーのスカイライト

South lobby　市民ロビー

View toward main lobby　メイン・ロビー方向を見る

Alcove 美術ロビー

View toward exhibition room 展示室を見る

1987–92
HENRI CIRIANI

HISTORICAL MUSEUM OF WORLD WAR
Péronne, France

Historically, this former stronghold of the northern front was a backdrop for the junction of the French and British troops. Nowadays, Péronne lies near the northern motorway, seventy minutes away from Paris.

The museum does not spring from a collection of war objects but from the notion that the First World War marked a major disruption in the course of history. Indeed the museum purports to evoke what the Somme region was, where soldiers of every nation battled and often died.

The competition brief was clear in emphasizing not only the absurdity of the conflict but also the stubborn faith of the belligerent parties. This was structured chronologically in periods running from before 1914 to after 1918 which were meant to appear as historical gaps.

Our proposal developed around this idea of the gaps, the periods of the different exhibition halls are separated by in-between vertical open spaces which also serve as lighting devices. A central portrait gallery where the relation of the individual to the whole is defined functions as a central core. Here it will be possible for visitors to ring for different kinds of portraits of people, famous or unknown, living or dead. Gathering around this central core are the halls containing the different historical periods. The helix figure was used as most appropriate both symbolically and functionally for it not only creates close views but it brings in natural light.

The new museum, barely attached to Péronne's old castle (where Louis XI was held prisoner), tries to establish a respectful relationship with the latter; it shares its simplicity and height and completes its figure, giving the solid mass an elegant west elevation which addresses the landscape and creates a cultural promenade under pilotis along the lakeside.

Finally, the building's pure white volumes prefigure the radiant image of a monument to peace. Lightly but firmly standing on the ground, we shall see a series of blank volumes united by their calm horizontality.

The exterior surfaces are white concrete punctuated by a pattern of white marble cylindrical juts whose role it is to anchor shadows onto the facade, welcoming rainmarks and moss, and also representing the importance of the sum of individuals in this world conflict.
Henri Ciriani

Elevation

1 CHATEAU ENTRANCE
2 CHATEAU COURTYARD
3 RESTAURANT
4 WORKSHOP
5 CAFETERIA
6 HALL
7 LIBRARY
8 MEETING ROOM
9 ADMINISTRATION
10 SERVICE YARD
11 STORAGE
12 ENTRANCE
13 ENTRANCE HALL
14 TICKET OFFICE
15 GALLERY
16 SHOP
17 "THE BREACH"
18 RECEPTION AREA
19 EXHIBIT/BEFORE THE WAR
20 EXHIBIT/CENTRAL SPACE
21 EXHIBIT/1914-1916
22 EXHIBIT/1916-1918
23 EXHIBIT/AFTER THE WAR
24 AUDIO-VISUAL ROOM

Garden level

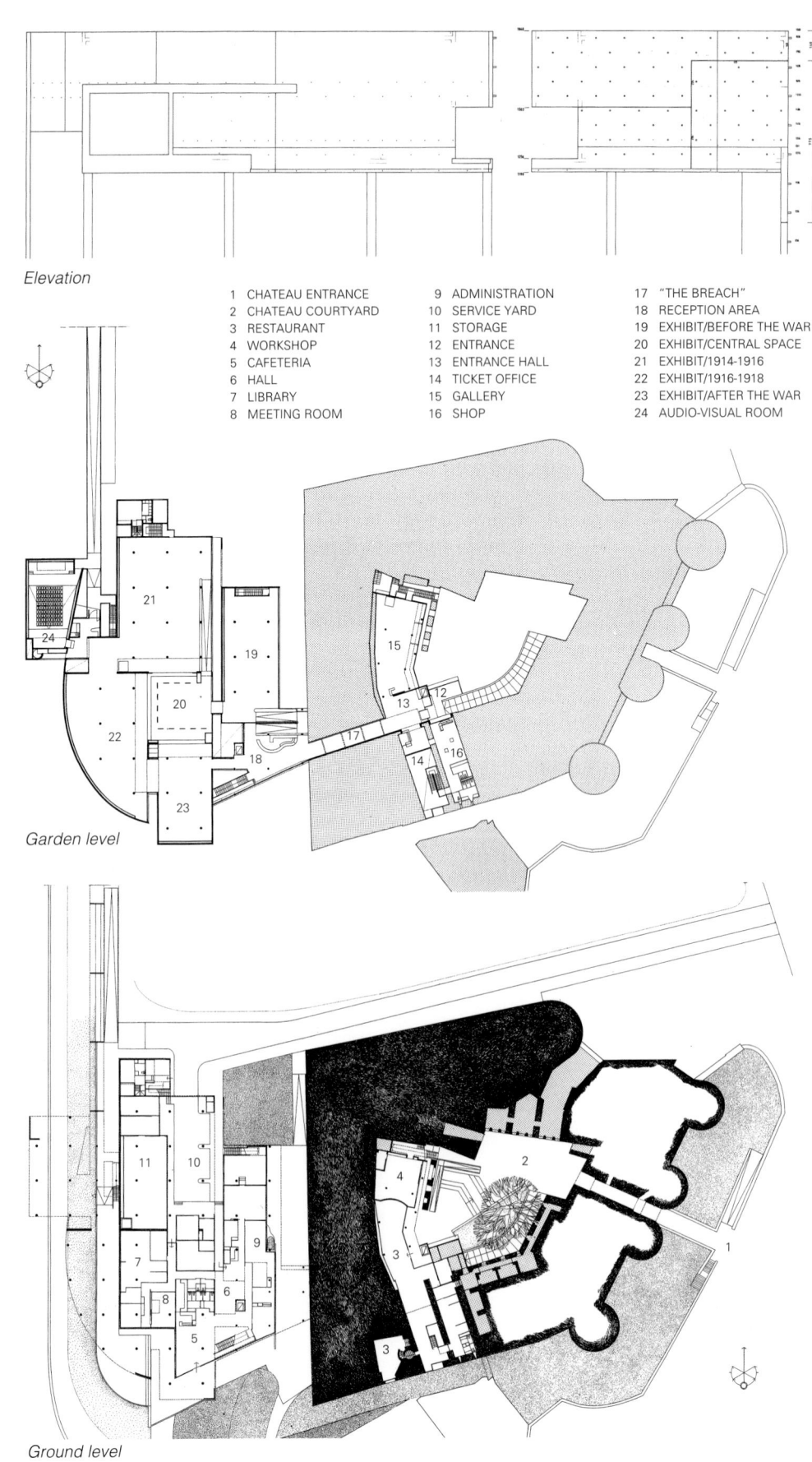

Ground level

West view 西より見る

North view from walkway 北側歩道より見る

歴史的には、この北の前線にある以前の塔は、フランスとイギリスの軍隊の出会いの場の背景となったものである。現在、ペロンヌはパリから車で70分、北行する自動車道の近くに位置している。

この記念館は戦争に関する記念品をおさめるのではなく、第一次世界大戦が歴史の上で大きな破壊をもたらしたことを記録するものである。事実、この記念館は各国の兵士達が戦い、多く戦死した場所であるソンム県の過去の姿を呼び覚まし表明するのである。

コンペの概要は、戦争の不条理だけでなく、交戦国軍隊の不屈の信念をも強調することをはっきりとうたっていた。展示は、歴史の断絶を意味する1914年以前から1918年以降の時代を年代的に構成することになる。

我々の案は、この、時代の断絶をテーマに展開させている——時代で異なる展示ホールは、採光の面でも働いている垂直にのびたオープン・スペースを間にはさんで分けられている。個人と全体との関わりを表す中央のポートレート・ギャラリーは中央コアの機能を果たしている。ここで人々は、有名無名、死んだ者、生きている者達のさまざまな肖像に取り囲まれる。中央コアのまわりにそれぞれ異なる時代の記録を収めたホールが集まっている。展示を近くから眺められることと、自然採光の面から、象徴的にも機能的にも最も適切であるので、螺旋形を用いた。

記念館はペロンヌの古い城（ルイ11世が捕囚されていた）の隣に建て、城に敬意をはらったつながりが生まれるようにする。その簡潔さを共にし、同じ高さとし、ソリッドな量塊に優雅な西側立面——景観に開かれ、湖沿いのピロティの下にプロムナードをもつ——を与えることで、完結させている。

最後に、建物の純粋な白いヴォリュームは平和の瞬間の輝くようなイメージを予示する。軽快に、しかし揺ぎなく大地に立ち、静かな水平性でむすばれた開口のないヴォリュームの連なりを私達は見ることになるだろう。

建物の外側は、コンクリートの白い壁で、そこに、白大理石で円柱形の突出が付けられている。これは、ファサードに日の影を落とし、雨の跡や苔を喜んで受け入れる役目を果たし、また、この世界大戦に巻き込まれた人間の夥しさのもつ重みを表現してもいる。
（アンリ・シリアニ）

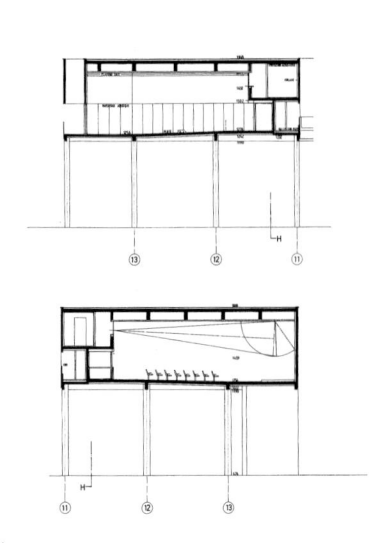

Sections

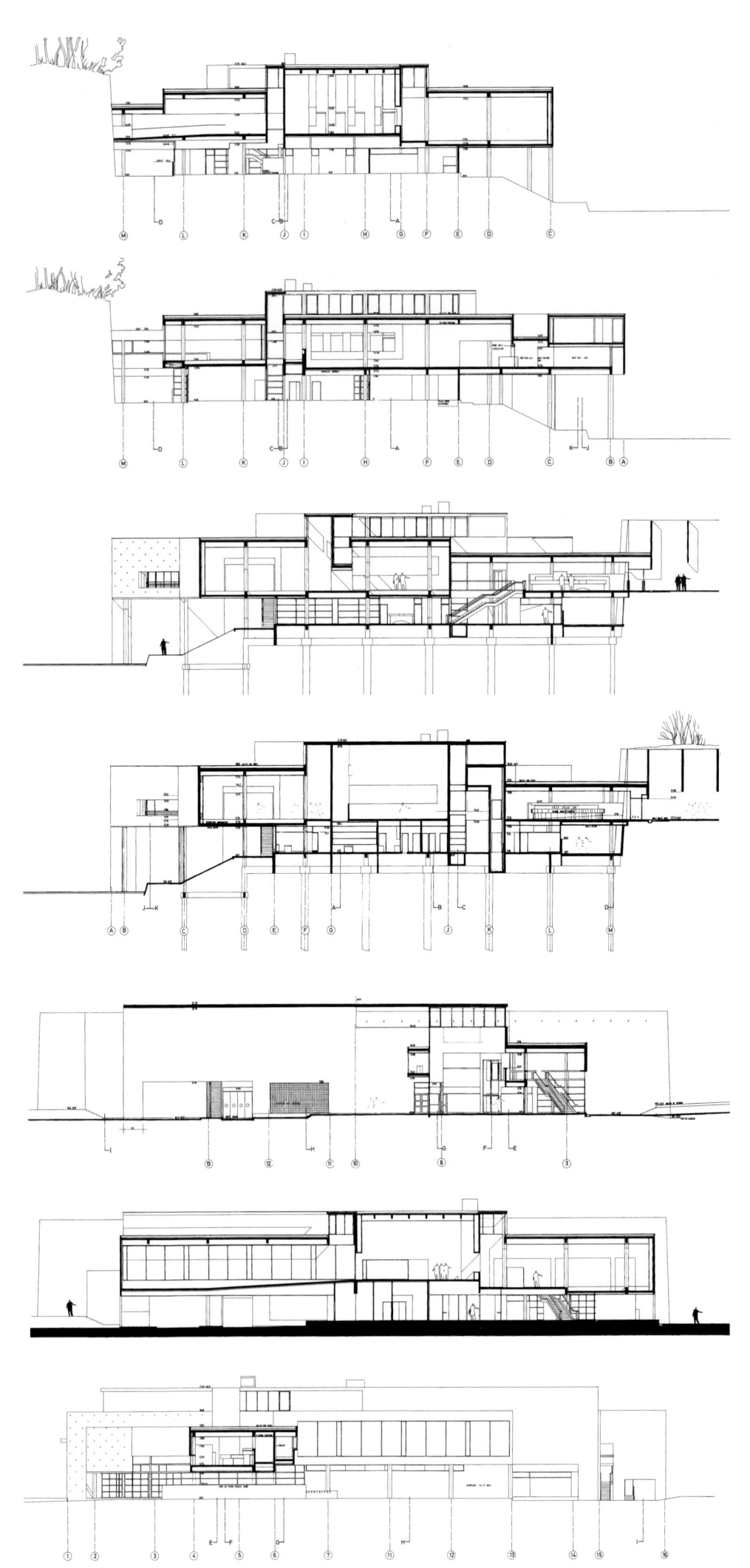

South view　南側外観

North view: service yard　建物北側：サービスヤード

Hall ホール

Exhibition room: 1916-1918　展示室：1916–1918

Reception レセプション

Main entrance メイン・エントランス

Circulation space 連絡通路

Central exhibition room 中央の展示室

1987–95
RICHARD MEIER

MUSEUM OF CONTEMPORARY ART, BARCELONA
Barcelona, Spain

Overall view from southeast

Plaça del Angels

Located in the area of the Casa de la Caritat, the Museum creates a dialogue between the quarter's historic urban fabric and the contemporary art within. The labyrinthine nature of the site's existing paths and routes is reflected in the building's organization, most notably in the main entry, which is paralleled by a pedestrian passageway between the museum's rear garden, and a plaza in front of the Museum. This paseo joins a pedestrian network running throughout the old city. The gentle fold of this circulation path emphasizes the centrifugal movement of the cylindrical lobby and describes a fifth facade, connecting the geometries of the Museum to an urban context characterized by skewed intersections and the domes of ancient churches.

The main entry is reached via a ramp running parallel to the facade. Once past this portico, visitors enter a cylindrical reception area overlooking the paseo, a circle interweaving the squares of the Museum's geometry with the rectilinear blocks of the city. From the entry lobby, visitors ascend a ramp vertically unfolded within a triple-height hall. Extensively glazed and affording broad views of the Plaza, this transparent volume serves to orient the visitor, mediating between the Museum's most public facade and the more closed volumes of the galleries. The louvered glass wall of the ramp also helps to filter natural light entering from the south.

The principal galleries are large, open spaces that have been designed to allow for both traveling exhibitions and the presentation of large works of art. In order to enter the main galleries visitors must cross over full-height light "slots", complete with glass-lensed floors. The louvered skylights above the main galleries illuminate the art below while describing the space as a kind of internal courtyard.

Main entrance　メイン・エントランス

Night view　夜景

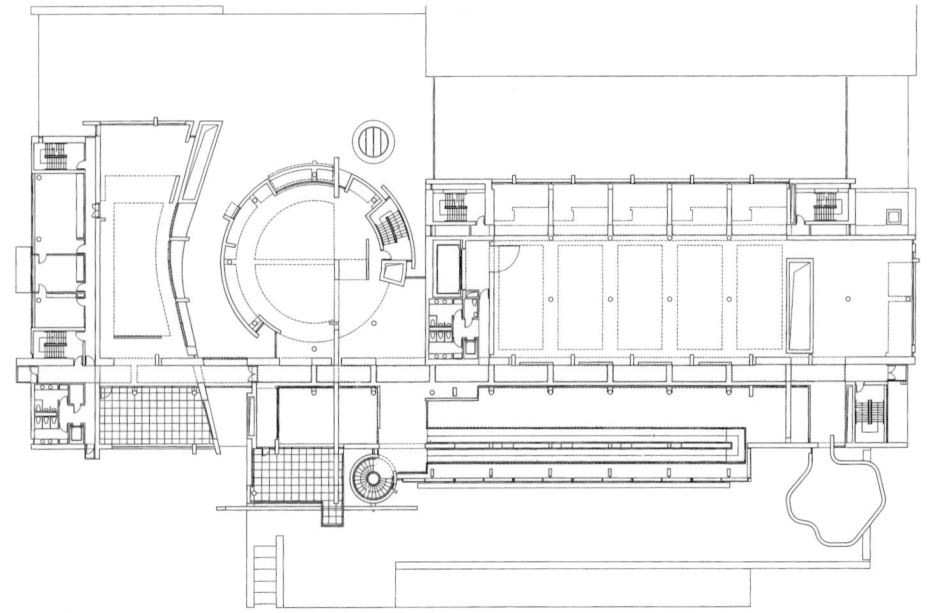

First floor

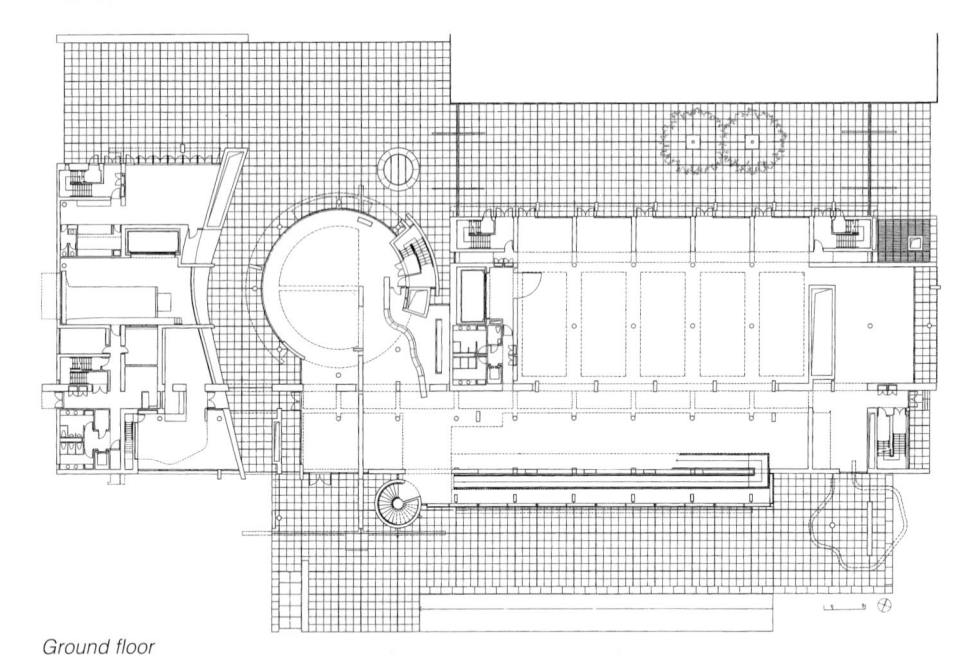

Ground floor

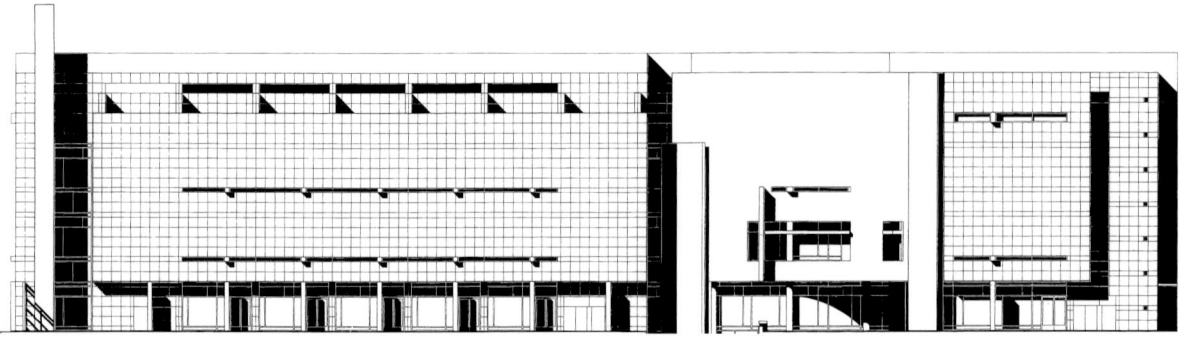

North elevation

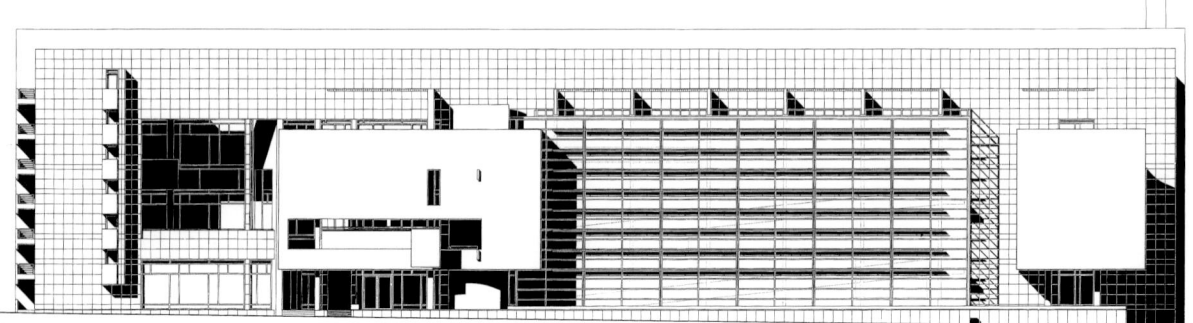

South elevation

バルセロナ市内のカサ・デ・ラ・カリタ地区に建つこの美術館は、旧市街の都市ファブリックと美術館が内包する現代美術の間に対話を引き起こしてくれる。敷地に以前からあった本道や小道の迷路のような性格は、建物の内部編成に投影されているのだが、なかでもそれが顕著なのはメイン・エントランスの中、美術館の裏庭と正面広場の間に並行して走る歩行者通路である。このプロムナードは、旧市街を貫く歩行路のネットワークに合流している。緩やかに折り返して行くこのサーキュレーション・パスは、円筒形のロビーの遠心的な動きを強化し、5番目のファサードとなって、美術館を構成するジオメトリーを、斜めに交差する街路や古い教会のドームに特徴づけられた都市の文脈に結び付ける。

メイン・エントリーにはファサードと平行に走るランプを通って行く。ポルティコを過ぎ、プロムナードを見渡す円筒形のレセプション・エリアに入る。その円形は、美術館を組み立てている方形を都市の直線的なブロックと織り合わせる。エントリー・ロビーから3層吹き抜けたホールの中、垂直に展開するランプを上って行く。豊かなガラス面から広場を大きく見渡せるこの透明なヴォリュームは、美術館の最もパブリックなファサードと閉ざされたギャラリーの間にあり、来館者はそこで自分の位置を見定めることができる。ランプのガラス壁にはルーバーが付き、南から入る自然光を和らげる。

メイン・ギャラリーは、広く開放的な空間で、巡回展や大型の芸術作品の展示のどちらにも対応可能である。これらのギャラリーに入るためには、ガラス・レンズの床から建物の高さいっぱいに伸びる光の"スロット"を横切らなければならない。メイン・ギャラリーのルーバーを備えたスカイライトは、下の芸術作品を照らす一方で、この空間を一種の屋内にあるコートヤードのように見せている。

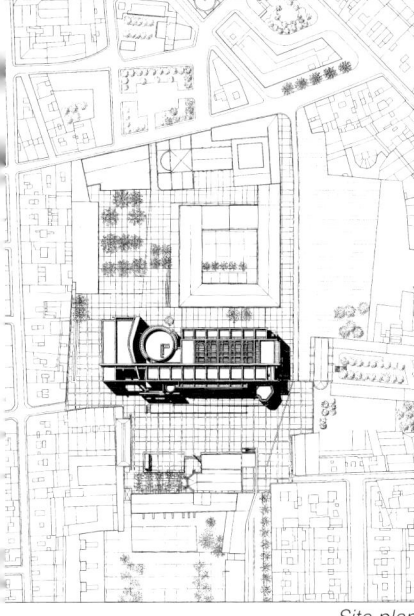

Site plan

North elevation 北面

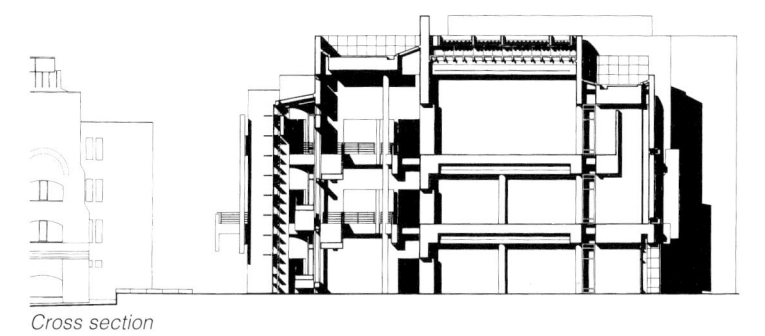

Cross section

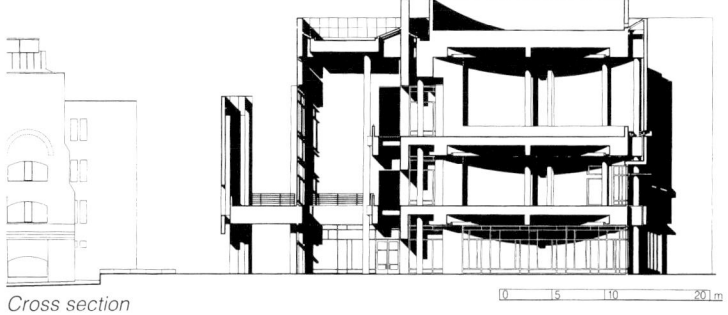

Cross section

165

Reception レセプション

Gallery on first floor 2階展示室

Ramp ランプ ▷

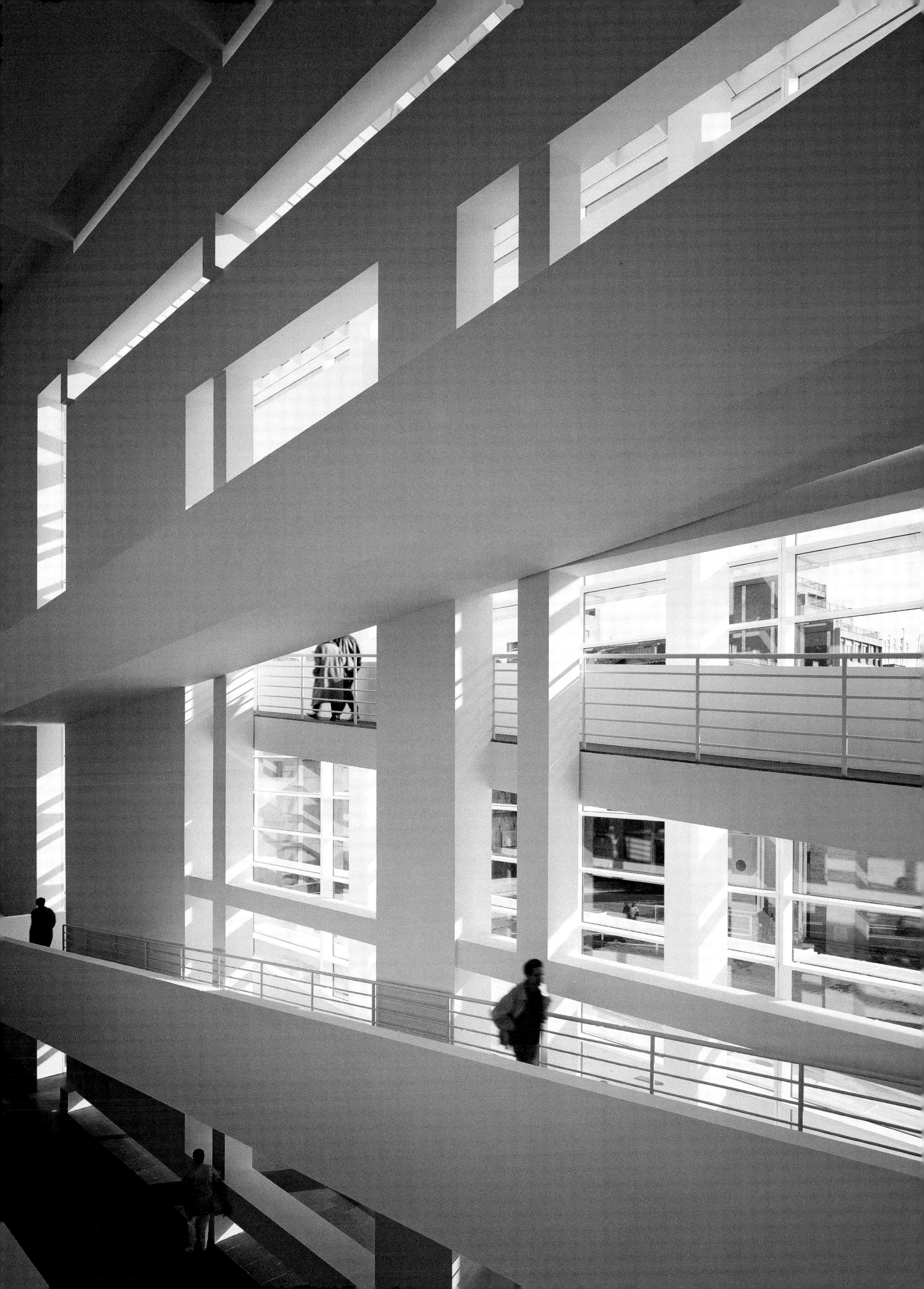

Gallery on first floor　2階展示室

Cylindrical gallery on second floor　3階円筒形展示室

168

Special exhibition gallery　特別展示室

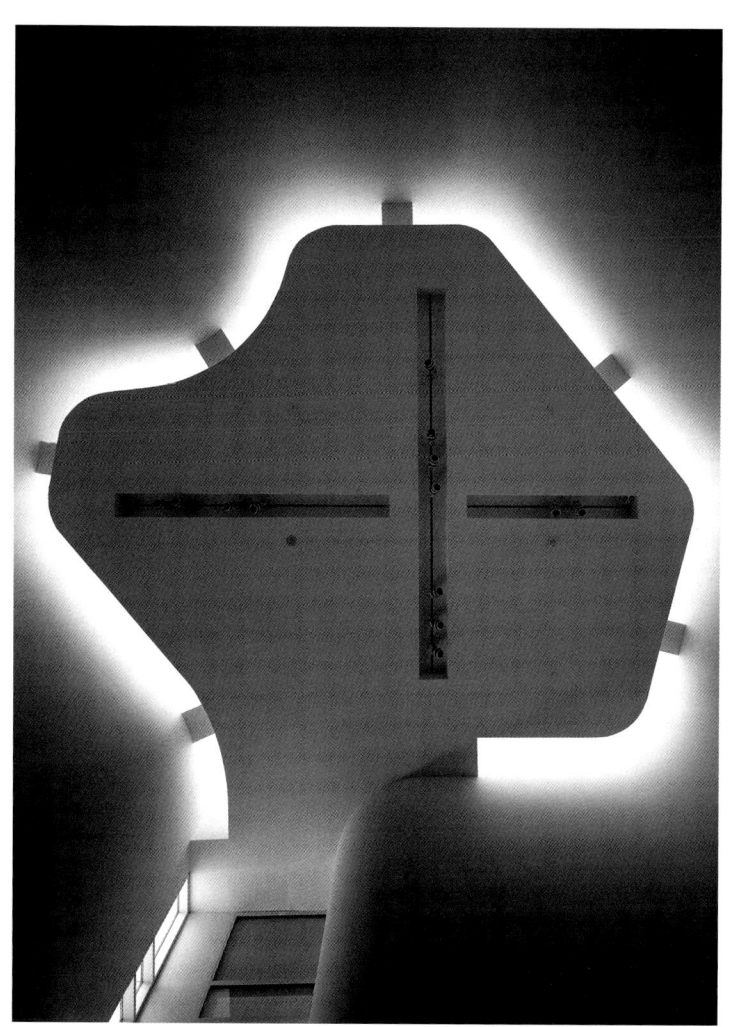

Skylight　スカイライト

Gallery on second floor　3階展示室

1988–91
TOYO ITO

YATSUSHIRO MUNICIPAL MUSEUM
Kumamoto, Japan

Overall view from northeast 北東側全景

Night view 夜景

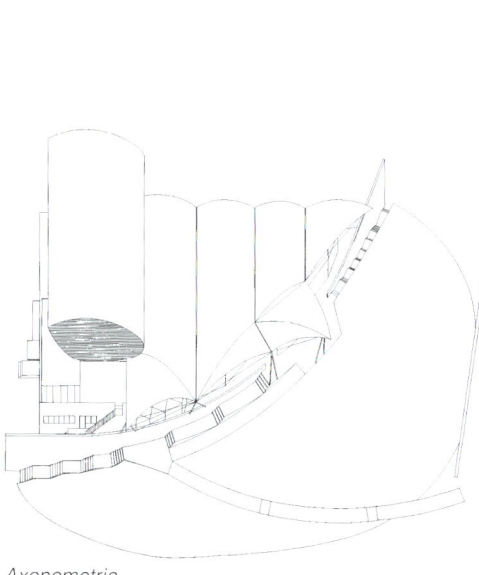

Axonometric

Northwest view　北西より見る

171

Night view from east　東側夜景

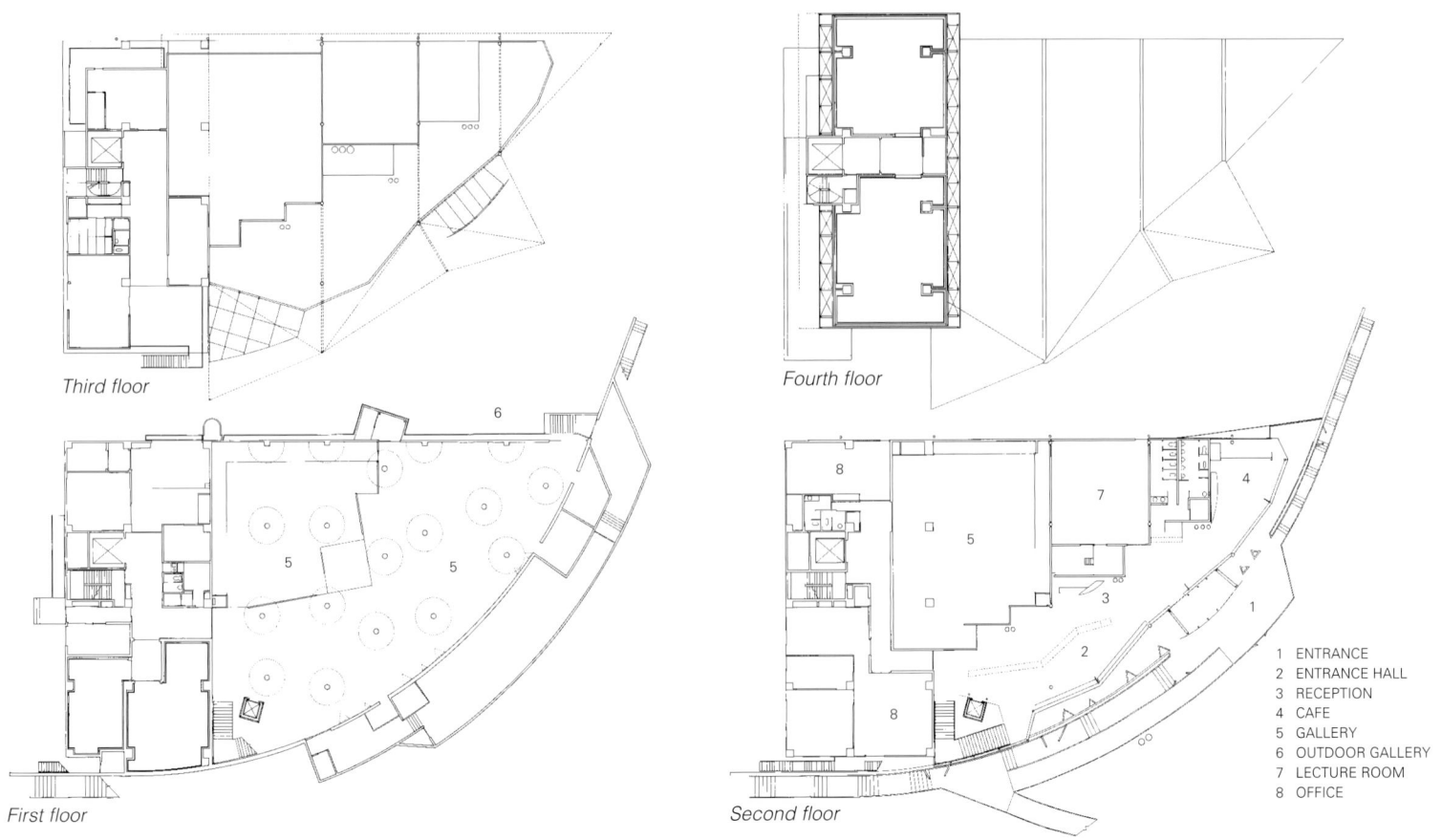

Third floor

Fourth floor

First floor

Second floor

1. ENTRANCE
2. ENTRANCE HALL
3. RECEPTION
4. CAFE
5. GALLERY
6. OUTDOOR GALLERY
7. LECTURE ROOM
8. OFFICE

Entrance エントランス

A facility opened in autumn '91, exhibiting a collection of historical folk material of Yatsushiro City in Kumamoto Prefecture. Land in this city is extremely flat, as it was reclaimed for the most part. The site is near the remains of a castle in the city center. Across the road in the front are the traditional Japanese garden and a tasteful wooden tea-hut. Upon planning, utmost priority was given to the harmony with this magnificent environment.

With this in mind, a volume of four layers was set back, and the ground level near the approach was raised to bury a layer accommodating the largest space for permanent exhibition. Looking from the front, the museum looks as if it were built on top of a small hill. This grassy hill is open to public.

The main entrance is found on the second level, welcoming the visitors walking up the gently curving slope of the approach, floating on the hill. Roofed by a rhythmical sequence of vaults, the second level features the entrance hall, a coffee shop, lecture room and special exhibition room, with glass windows of maximum surface area offering a panoramic view from the hilltop.

On the ground level is the permanent exhibition space, with random pillars supporting beamless boards and walls of great curvature

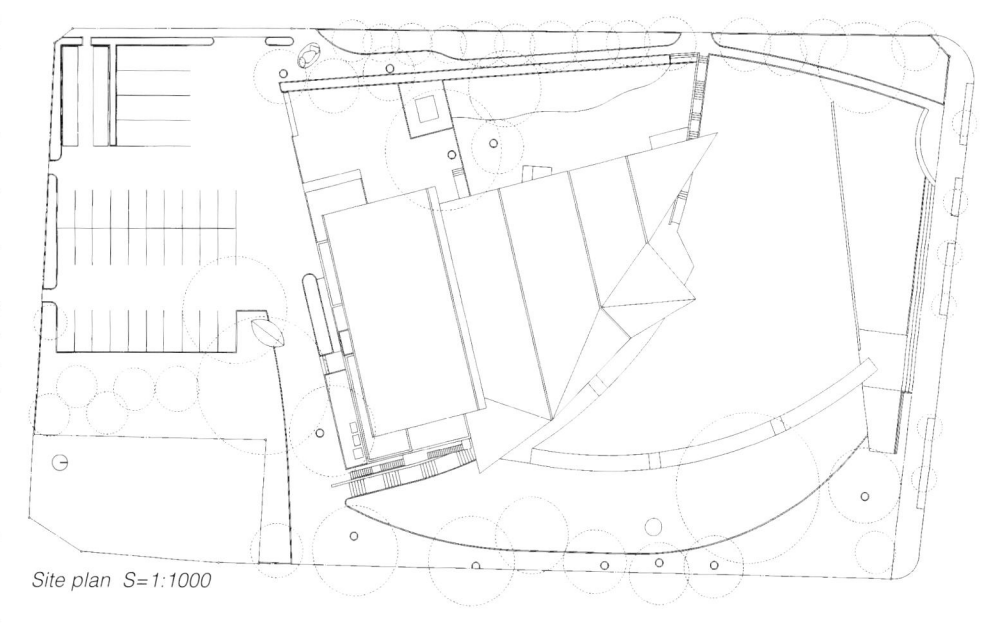

Site plan S=1:1000

that constitute a space where visitors have the feeling of walking through a clump of trees. The repository floats as a cylinder covered in aluminium and stainless steel panels, and presents itself as a symbol of its function as the building's warehouse.
Toyo Ito

△▽ *Entrance hall* エントランス・ホール

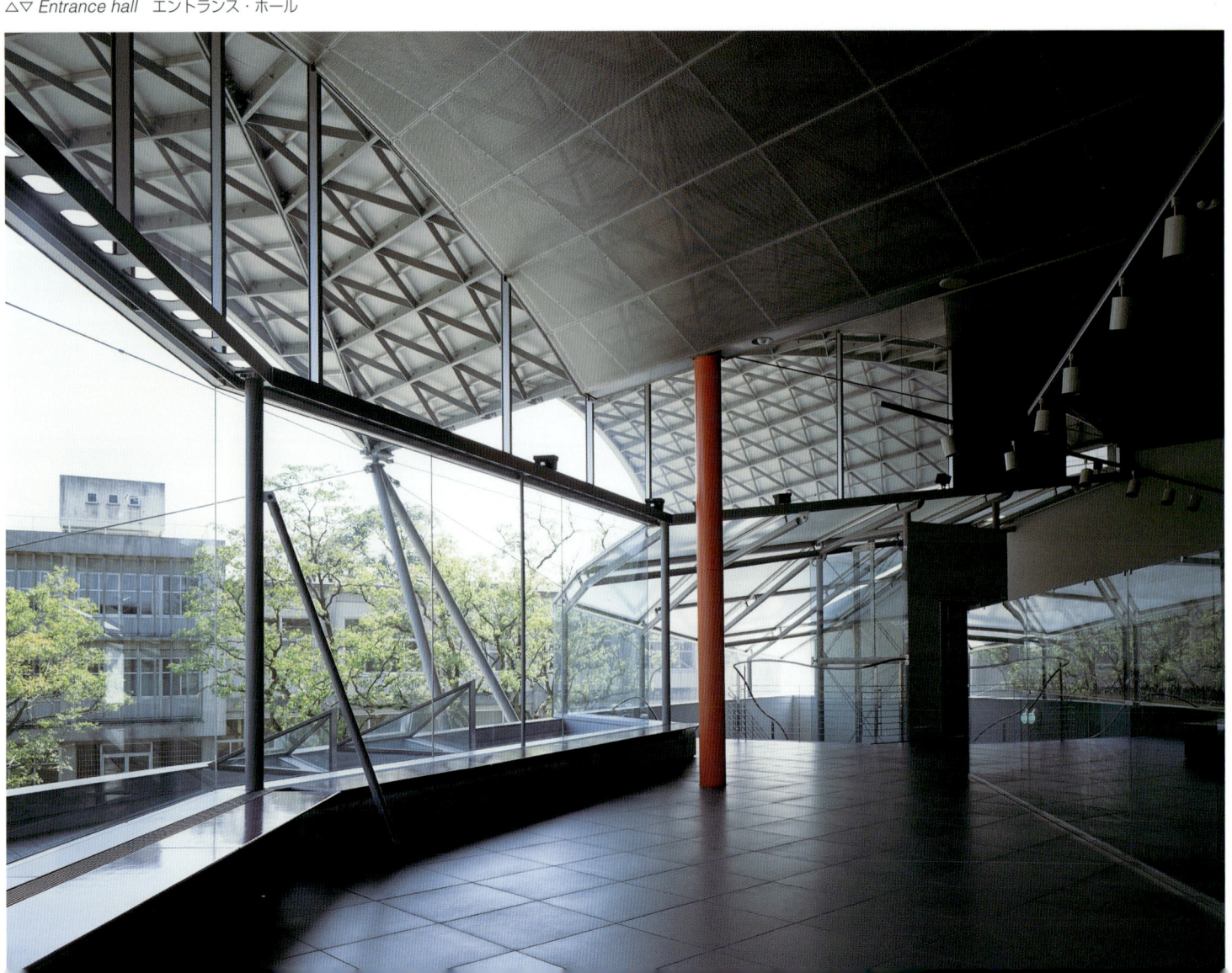

Staircase　階段室

Entrance　エントランス

Cafe　カフェ

Lower gallery on second floor 2階展示室

Curved wall with ceiling lights 湾曲した壁面と照明

熊本県八代市に91年秋オープンした市の歴史民俗資料を中心として展示する施設である。八代市の土地は、大半が干拓によって作られたために、きわめて平坦である。敷地は市の中心に位置する城址の近くで、前面道路を挟んだ向かいには伝統的な日本庭園や瀟洒な木造の茶室などがある。設計に際しては、特にこの環境との調和が最大の課題であった。

この課題を解決するため、4層のヴォリュームを後方へ向かってセットバックさせ、さらにアプローチ側には1層分の土盛りをして、最も大きなグラウンド・レベルの常設展示スペースは、地下に置かれたかのように処理されている。したがって、建築は前面からは、あたかも小さな丘の上に建てられているかの如くに見える。この小さな丘は、芝生に覆われ市民に開放されている。

メインエントランスは2階に置かれ、来場者は丘の上に浮かびながら緩やかにカーブするスロープを歩いてアプローチする。軽快なリズムで連続するヴォールト屋根に覆われた2階にはエントランスホール、コーヒーショップ、レクチャールーム、特別展示室などが置かれ、可能な限りガラス面を大きくして丘の上からのヴューを楽しめるよう配慮された。

グラウンド・レベルの常設展示スペースは、無梁板を支えるランダムな柱と大きく湾曲する壁面によって構成され、木立の間を散策するようなスペースが形成されている。また、収蔵庫はアルミ及びステンレスパネルに覆われたシリンダーとして宙に浮かび、この建築の蔵としての機能を象徴的に表現する。　　　　　　　　（伊東豊雄）

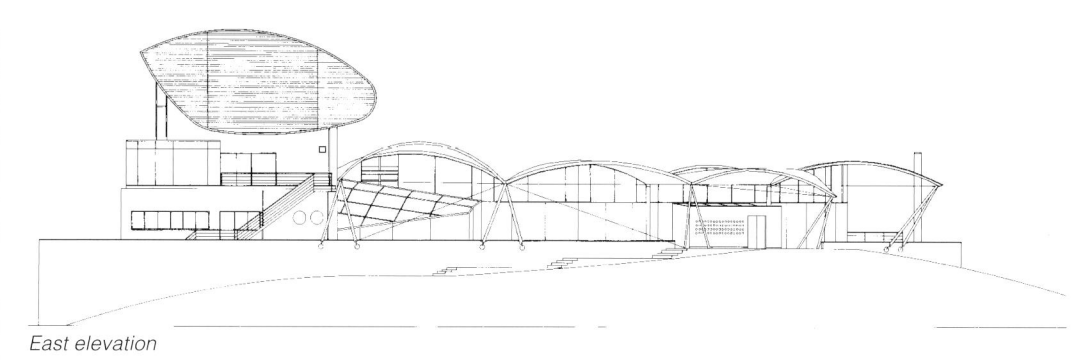

East elevation

North elevation

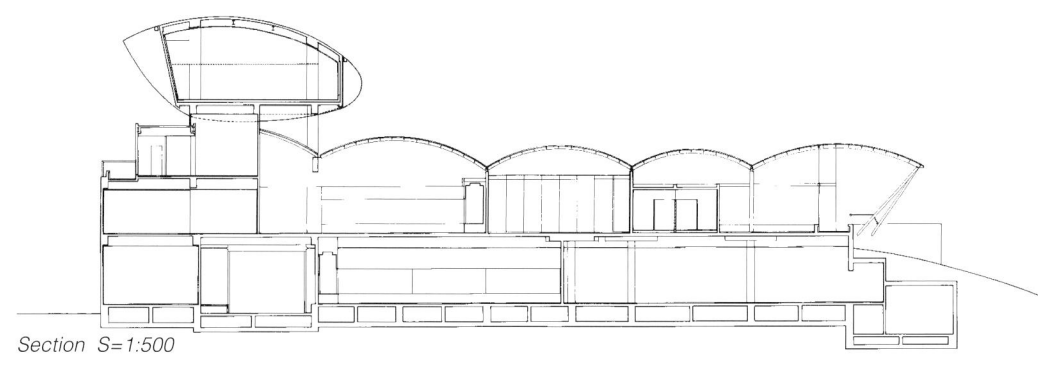

Section S=1:500

1988–92
TADAO ANDO

NAOSHIMA CONTEMPORARY ART MUSEUM
Kagawa, Japan

Stepped plaza　階段状のプラザ

◁ *Aerial view: Museum and Annex (1995)*　航空写真：美術館とアネックス（1995）

Ramp　ランプ

179

Naoshima is a small island in the Inland Sea of Japan. This art museum complex is sited on a promontory overlooking a quiet beach, at the southern tip of the island. While backed by hills, the site is exposed to the ocean on three sides, and enjoys a view of distant Shikoku. The museum is designed to receive, visitors directly upon their arrival by boat. Coming ashore via a newly constructed wharf, visitors are greeted by a stepped plaza which functions as the entrance to the facility. The plaza also houses a museum annex below the ground. It is only while mounting the plaza steps that visitors first observe—above—the stone rubble wall of the museum perimeter. A national park of spectacular beauty encompasses the site, therefore more than half of the volume of the building is buried underground in order that its scale not intrude on these surroundings. After ascending a mild slope, visitors arrive at the complex of buildings—and are made aware of the museum's existence for the first time.

Upon entering the museum, visitors are led directly into the gallery—a large subterranean space, two levels high, 50 meters long, and 8 meters wide. After passing through the gallery, they are received into the main lobby, a cylindrical volume—20 meters in diameter, with a ceiling height of 10 meters—which can accommodate temporary exhibitions and performances, and which connects the main gallery to an hotel and an exterior stepped terrace. The gallery, the hotel, and the stepped terrace all open—on their west sides—towards the ocean, and draw the tranquil ocean scenery of commuting boats, and the light of the setting sun deep into their interior spaces.

A stroll path circles the museum complex, its progress marked by plazas offering dramatic views of the ocean. As a result, the spectacular surroundings are made part of the museum and its grounds, and a rich environment is created where visitors, benumbed by city living, might feel their natural sensitivities return, as they partake in art and nature.

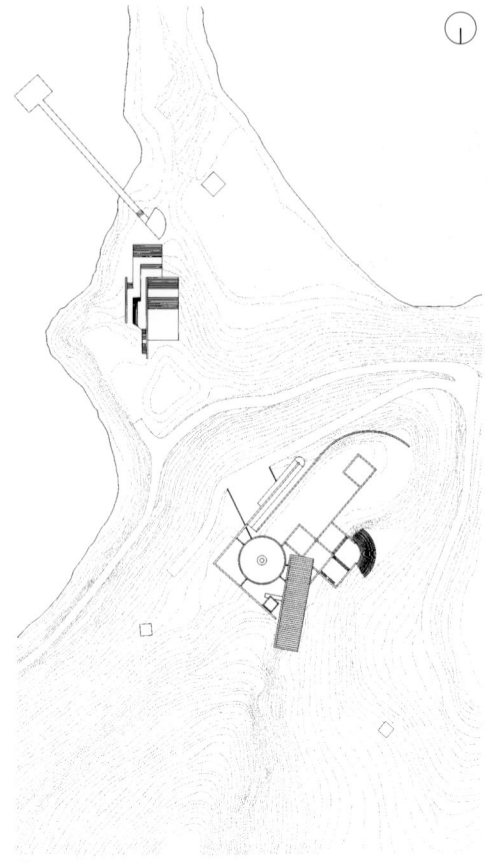

Site plan

First floor

Third floor

Basement

Second floor

1 ENTRANCE LOBBY
2 GALLERY
3 VOID
4 ATELIER
5 TERRACE
6 RESTAURANT
7 COURT
8 SUNKEN COURT
9 LIBRARY
10 LECTURE ROOM
11 CAFE
12 GUEST ROOM
13 ROOF TERRACE

直島は瀬戸内海に浮かぶ小島である。敷地は島の南端の海に突き出した小さな岬の丘の上にある。三方を海に開き、後ろに山をしたがえて、遠くには四国を望むことができる。この美術館へは、船から直接アプローチできるように計画した。新設された桟橋を上るとすぐ段状の広場へと導かれる。この広場は美術館の入口の役割を果たし、地下には美術館の別室が設けられている。広場を上るにつれ、本館の石積の壁が見えはじめる。国立公園に指定された美しい周辺環境を壊さないよう建物を低く抑え、建物のヴォリュームの半分以上を地下に埋設した。緩やかな坂を上って本館に辿り着くまで、隠されたギャラリーの存在を人々は知らない。

アプローチのスロープを上りエントランスに入ると、ギャラリーへと導かれる。このギャラリーは長さ50m、幅8mの2層分の高さをもつ地中の大空間である。さらに進むと円筒形のメインロビーに至る。このロビーは直径20m、天井高10mであり、ホテル棟、ギャラリー、段状テラスをつなぐ。ホテル棟、ギャラリー、段状テラスは西側を海に開かれ、行き交う船、沈む夕日など遙かな海の景色が建物内に導かれる。

美術館の周辺には散策路を巡らせ、ところどころに海を見渡すステージを設けるなど、周辺一帯をひとつの美術館エリアとしている。人々は、このような豊かな環境の中で自然と芸術を楽しみ、都会の生活で失われがちな感性を取り戻すだろう。

Sunken court サンクン・コート ▷

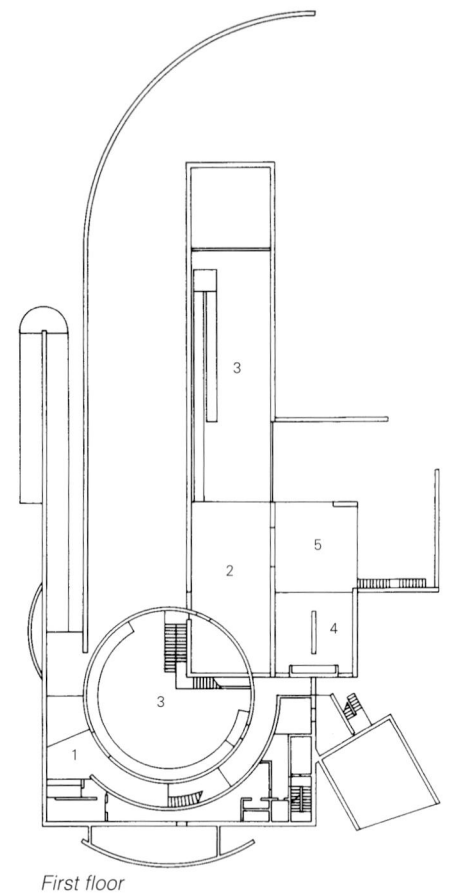

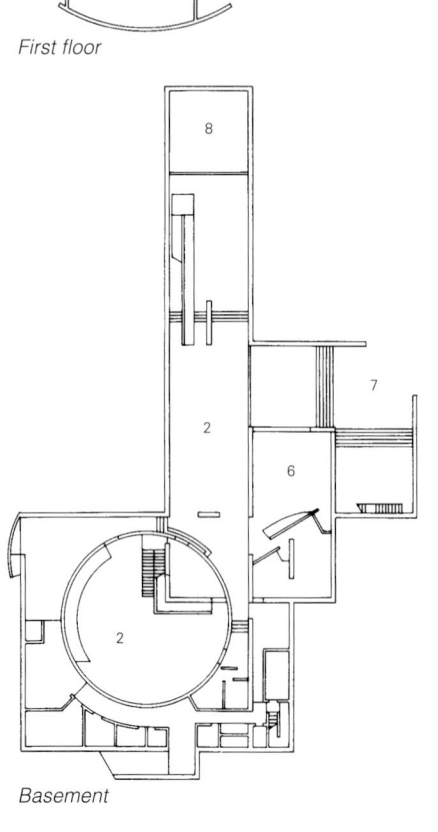

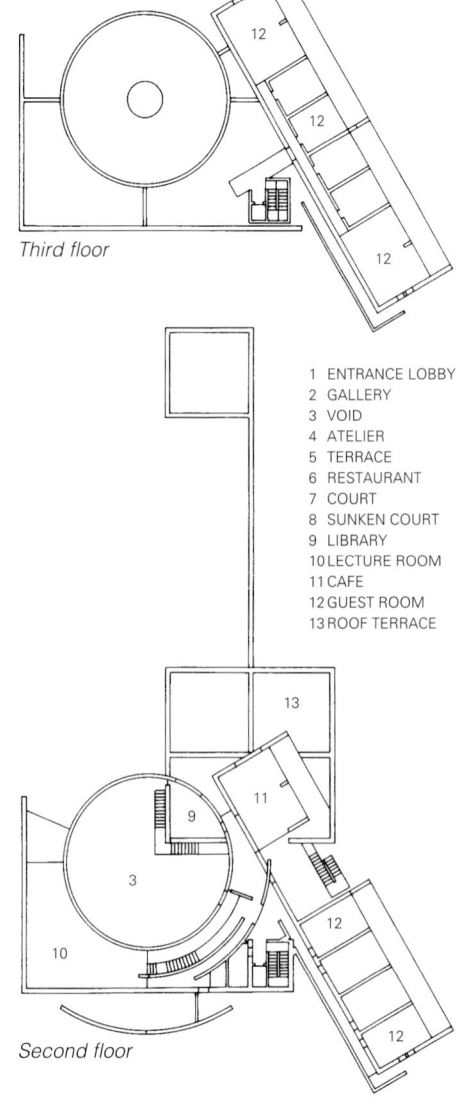

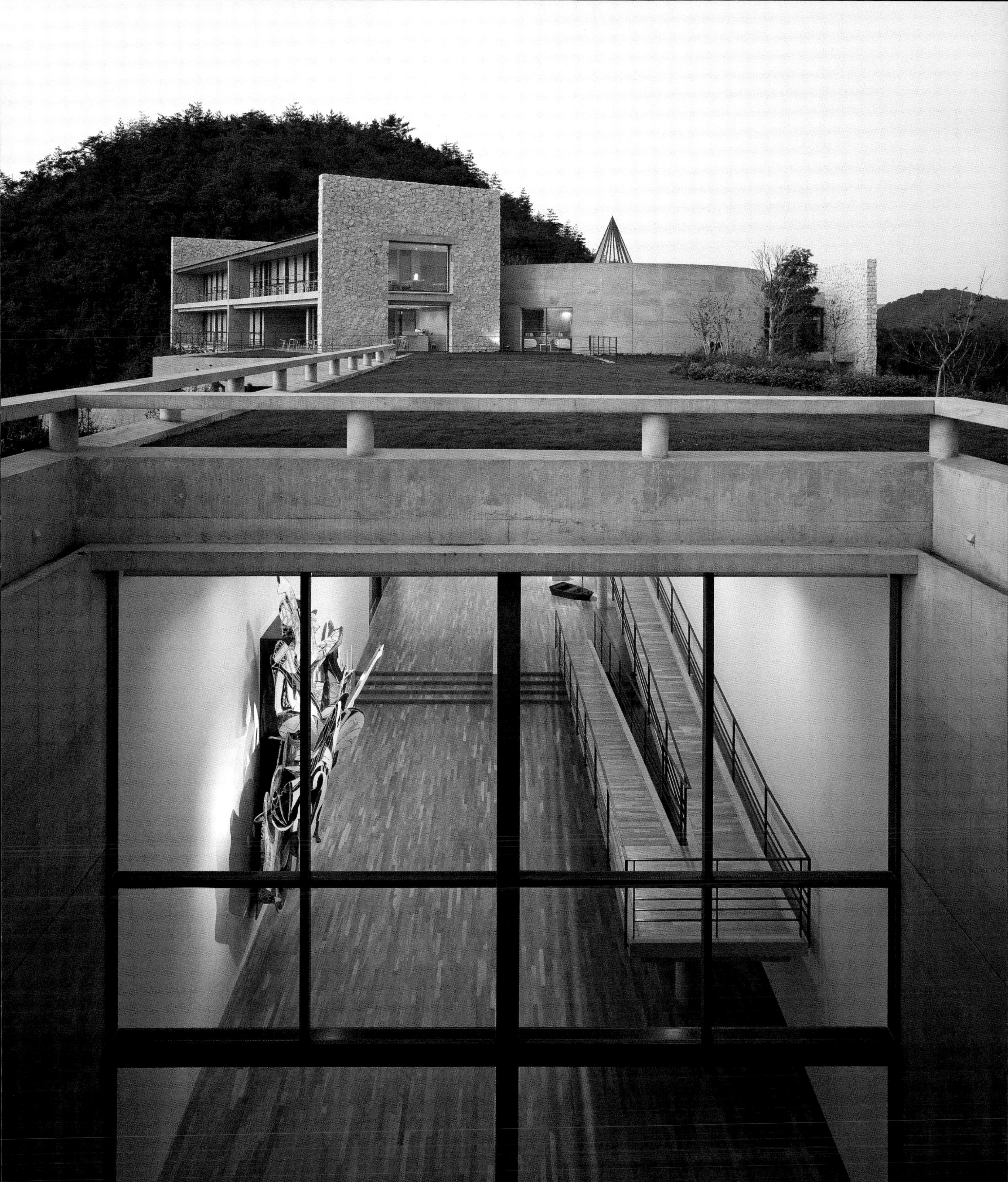

View toward gallery from court　コートよりギャラリー方向を見る

Gallery　ギャラリー

View of gallery from sunken court　サンクン・コートよりギャラリーを見る

Court　コート

Cylindrical gallery　円筒形ギャラリー

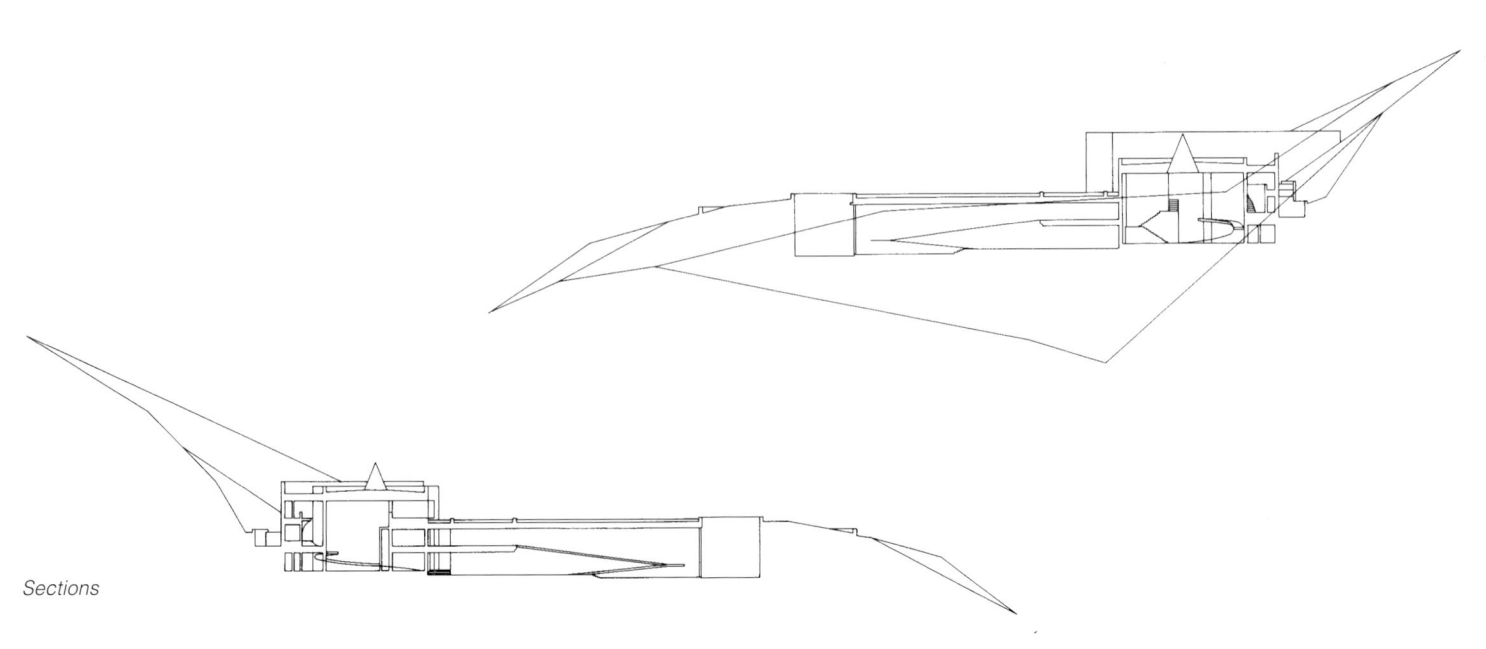

Sections

184

Cylindrical gallery　円筒形ギャラリー

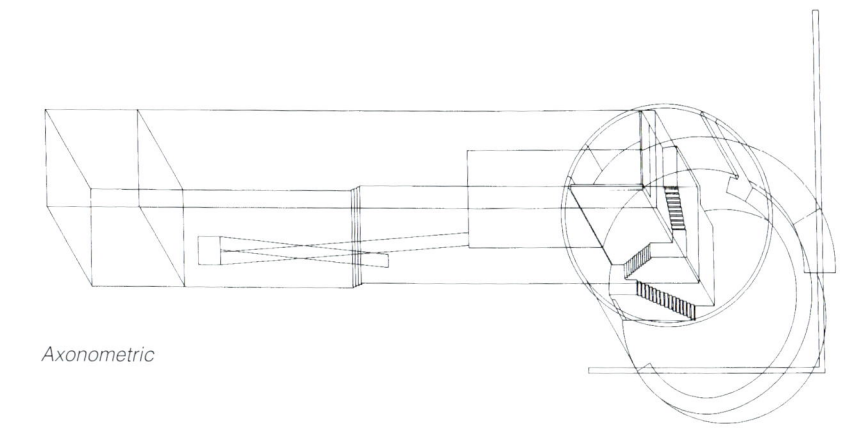

Axonometric

1988–93
JO COENEN

NETHERLANDS ARCHITECTURE INSTITUTE
Rotterdam, The Netherlands

Netherlands Architecture Institute (NAI), an independent foundation, provides an exemplary architectural forum for private designers across the globe.

The NAI achieves an architectural unity through fragments that work as a whole to provide a provocative museum experience. The ensemble marks the Institute's position in the city as it attends to the immediate site demands at the northern end of the Museum park's north-south development axis.

The program components link not only to function effectively, but also merge in function, making necessary spatial overlaps. Its principal components, museum (exhibition hall), archive, auditorium, and administration are housed in four distinct building forms, each legible on the exterior by its primary finish.

The central hall is entered from either a broad concrete ramp from the north road or through the park's entrance over a narrow timber walkway spanning the reflecting pool. The two entrances form an enjoyable urban route through and into the hall which links visitors via a wooden bridge to all important spaces of the Institute.

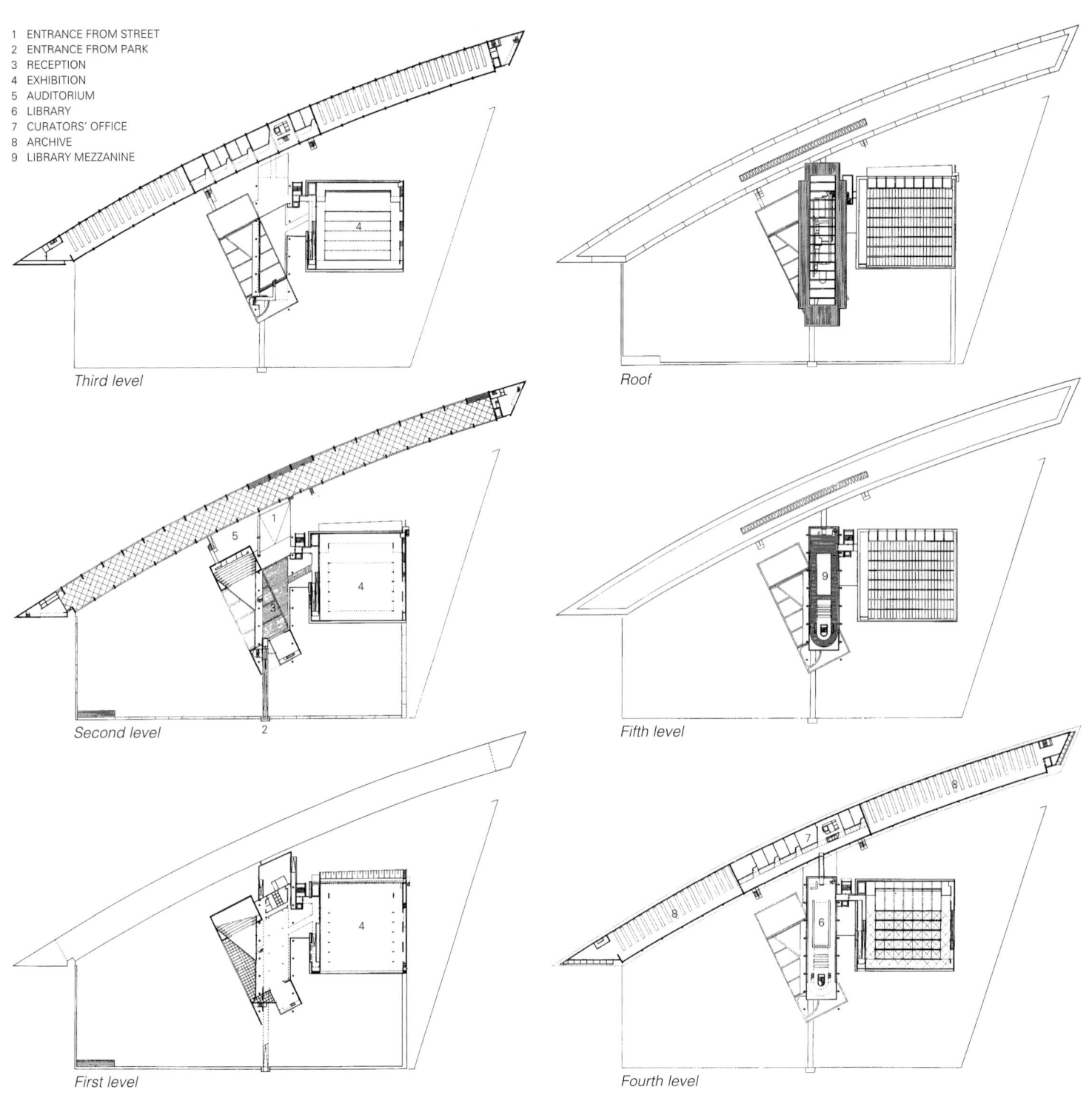

1 ENTRANCE FROM STREET
2 ENTRANCE FROM PARK
3 RECEPTION
4 EXHIBITION
5 AUDITORIUM
6 LIBRARY
7 CURATORS' OFFICE
8 ARCHIVE
9 LIBRARY MEZZANINE

Third level

Roof

Second level

Fifth level

First level

Fourth level

The central administration hall, enclosed in glass on a visible concrete frame, rises under a steel pergola construction serving as a key urban landmark. Its upper levels of offices and public library have views over Rotterdam.

Off this hall is the museum, clad in a dark red baked brick; its levels of exhibit space are connected by a perimeter stairwell as well as by visual connections between floors.

The skewed auditorium, primarily of glass and wood, intersects the main hall from the opposite side. Bending from the north, the long gently curved archive in coated steel plate sits atop a concrete arcade.

オランダ建築協会（NAI）は、世界各国の建築家に建築フォーラムの場を提供する。

ミュージアム・パークの持つ南北軸の北端という敷地条件に留意し、ロッテルダムのなかでのこの建物の位置づけを象徴するように考えている。

プログラムを構成する各要素は、空間的重層をつくりながら、効果的に機能するばかりでなく、機能そのもののなかに同化吸収されるように連結されている。その主要な構成要素、ミュージアム（展示ホール）、資料棟、オーディトリアム、本部オフィスは、その主要な仕上材料によって外部から識別できる、4つの異なった形態の建物に分散して置かれている。

中央ホールへは2方向から入ることができる。一つは、北側の道路から広いコンクリートの斜路を通って。一つは、公園側の入口を抜け、リフレクティングプールにかかる狭い木の歩路を越えて。2つの入口は互いに通り抜けでき、来館者を木製のブリッジを経て建物のすべての主要空間とつないでいるホールへ導く、楽しい都市的な道筋を構成している。

打放しのコンクリートフレームをガラスで囲んだ中央の本部オフィス・ホールは、都市のランドマークの役割を果たしているスティールのパーゴラの下に建ち上がっている。その上階のオフィスと図書室からはロッテルダム市街が見晴らせる。

このホールの隣は、暗赤色に焼いた煉瓦で被覆されたミュージアムである。ミュージアムの各階は、周辺部の階段室によって、また吹抜けや透視的な床材の構成による視覚的な見通しによって結ばれている。

主にガラスと木で構成されているオーディトリアムは、オフィス棟の反対側から斜めにメイン・ホールに切り込んでくる。暗赤色に塗られた波型鋼板に包まれた、北側から、長く、緩やかにカーブしていく資料棟はコンクリートのアーケードの上に据えられている。

View from southeast 南東より見る

Approach by bridge ブリッジによるアプローチ

Archive wing 資料棟

Entrance hall エントランス・ホール

Archive wing 資料棟

Exhibition hall 展示ホール

Library 図書室

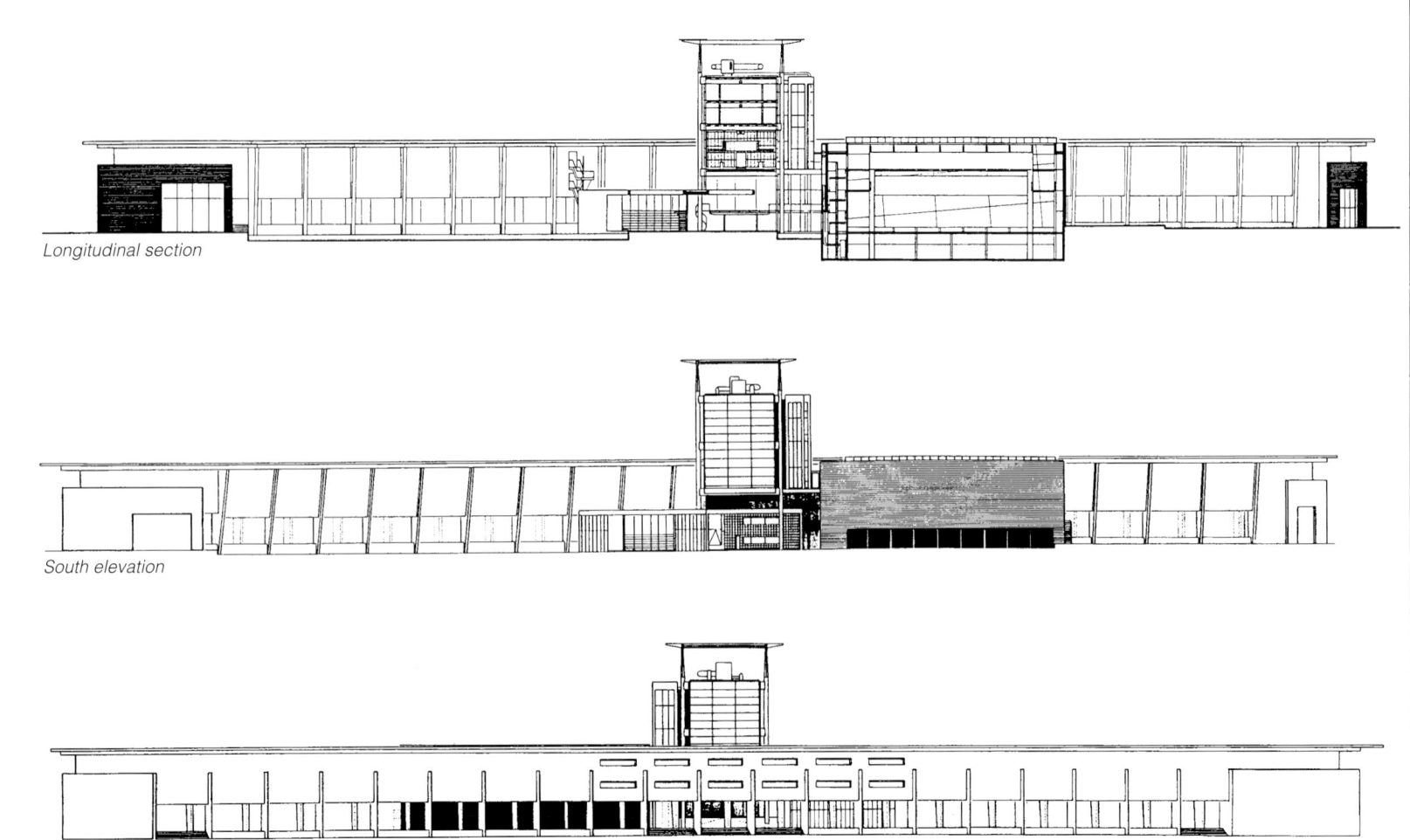

Longitudinal section

South elevation

North elevation

Library 図書室

Mezzanine of library 図書室中2階

Office 事務室

1988–93
FUMIHIKO MAKI

CENTER FOR ARTS YERBA BUENA GARDENS
San Francisco, California, U.S.A.

View from southwest 南西より見る

View toward main entrance メイン・エントランス方向を見る

Southwest elevation 南西面

Southwest elevation: forum on right　南西面：右はフォーラム

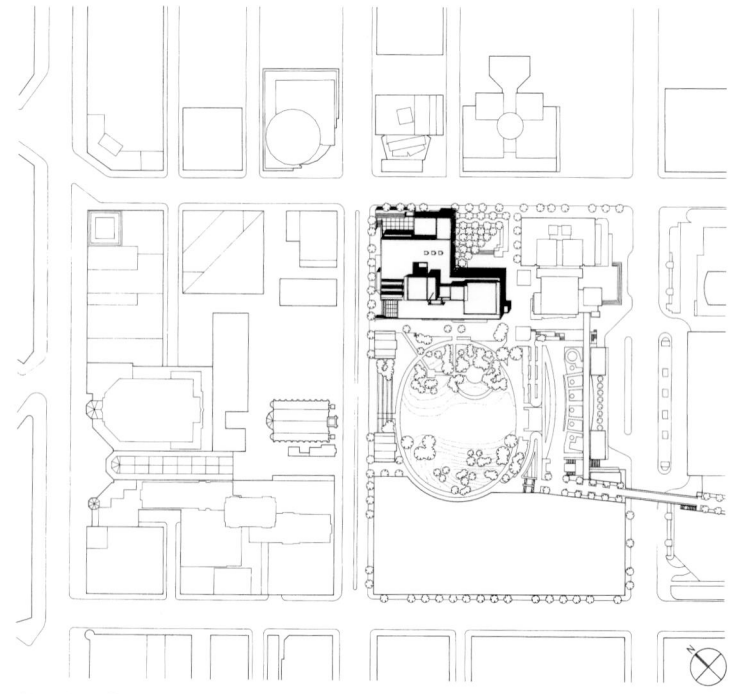

Site plan S=1:5000

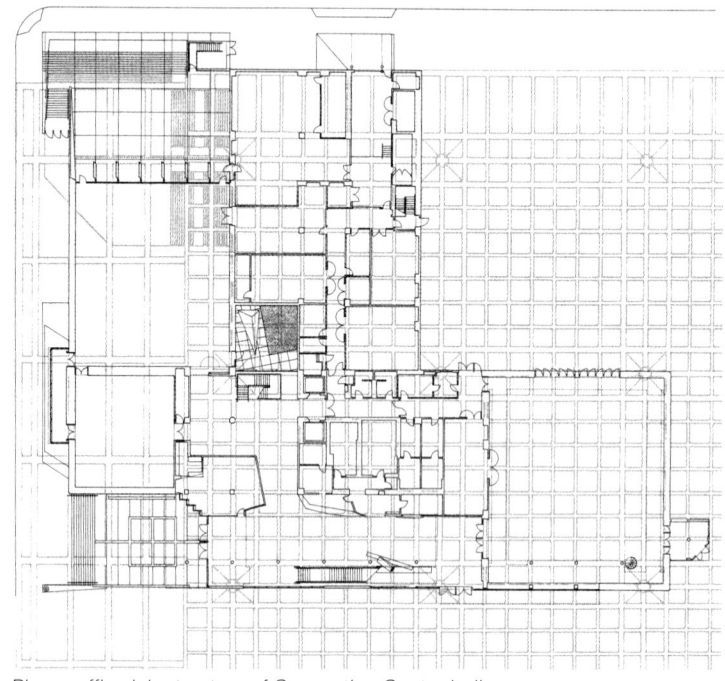

Plan: waffle slab structure of Convention Center bellow

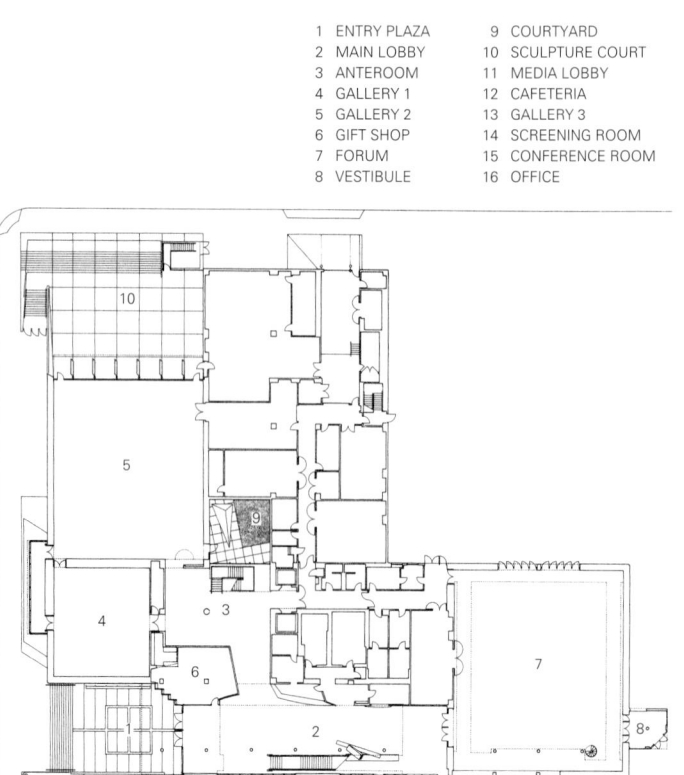

1	ENTRY PLAZA	9	COURTYARD
2	MAIN LOBBY	10	SCULPTURE COURT
3	ANTEROOM	11	MEDIA LOBBY
4	GALLERY 1	12	CAFETERIA
5	GALLERY 2	13	GALLERY 3
6	GIFT SHOP	14	SCREENING ROOM
7	FORUM	15	CONFERENCE ROOM
8	VESTIBULE	16	OFFICE

Ground floor S=1:1000

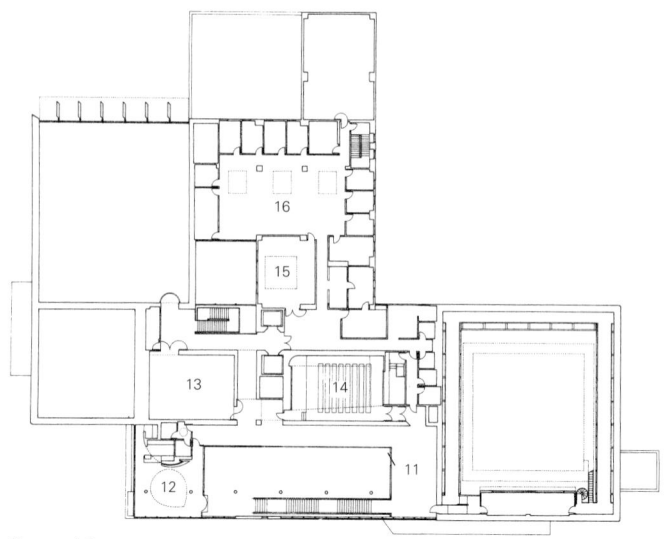

Second floor

The L-shaped site is located on the south of Market Street in downtown San Francisco. Facing the intersection of Mission and Third Streets, it is a gate to the Esplanade Gardens.

The building accommodates facilities for two types of art—visual and performing. Functions for each of them assembled here are reciprocal yet independent. The main program includes 3 galleries, a media screening room and a multi-purpose forum. Each room is given its own size, proportion, finishing and lighting different from the others, to provide visitors with new experiences each time they step into another room. The casual disposition of the program is also expressed in the planning, in which activities inside the building are linked with the surrounding public spaces. The two layers of the primary space adjacent to the domains of highly public nature (Mission Street and the Esplanade Gardens) are interconnected by means of pedestrian hallways inside the double-height lobby. Although each room is self-contained, a series of sequenced spaces is created by controlling the lines of vision toward the outside or the neighboring rooms.

The low silhouette of the building that displays an emphasis on horizontality, is finished with lustrous materials to express lightness. Corrugated aluminium—categorized among industrial commodities—, flat aluminium panels, glass and granite are introduced along with sophisticated details, so as to contribute the brand-new feeling expressed in this project.

サンフランシスコのダウンタウン、マーケット・ストリートの南側に位置するL字型の敷地は、ミッション・ストリートとサード・ストリートの交差点に面した、中央庭園へのゲートとなる位置にある。

ヴィジュアル・アートとパフォーミング・アートの両方を収容するため、この建物には、相互関係を持ちながらそれぞれに独立した機能が集められた。主要プログラムは、3つの展示室、映写室、そして多目的に活用できるフォーラムである。内部を移動するうちに常に新しい経験が得られるよう、寸法、プロポーション、仕上げ、採光はそれぞれの部屋によって異なるものとなっている。プログラムのカジュアルな性格は、周囲の公共空間と建物内部のアクティビティを連続させるプランニングにも表現されている。公共性の高い領域（ミッション・ストリートとエスプラナード・ガーデン）に沿う、2層の主要空間は、吹抜けのロビーの中の歩行者通路によって結びつけられる。個々の部屋は完結しているが、外部や隣接する部屋への視線をコントロールすることで、空間のシークエンスが生み出されている。

水平性の強い建物の低いシルエットは、光る材料で仕上げられ、軽快さを表現している。工業製品であるコルゲート・アルミ、フラットなアルミパネル、ガラス、そして御影石などが洗練されたディテールと共に用いられることによって、この場所の新しい感覚を表現している。

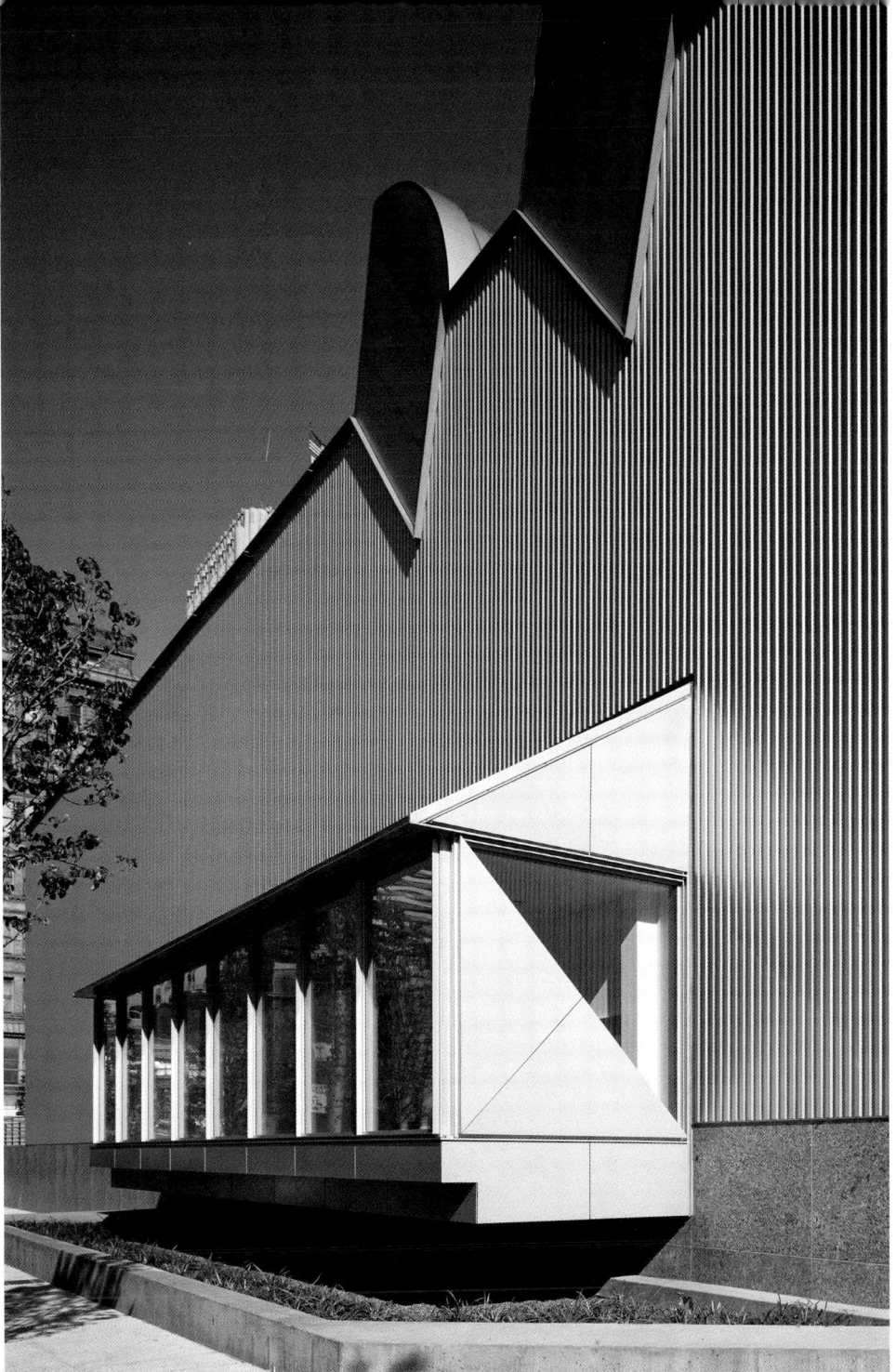

Northwest elevation 北西面

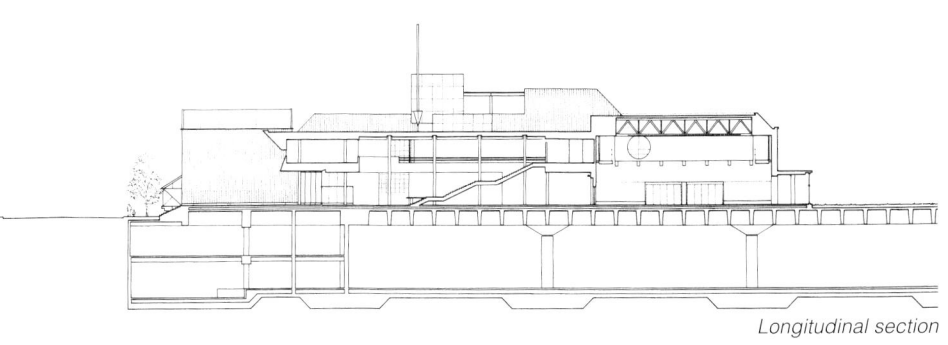

Longitudinal section

Main lobby　メイン・ロビー

Anteroom アンテルーム

Main lobby メイン・ロビー

Gallery 2 展示室 2

1989–91
SVERRE FEHN

GLACIER MUSEUM
Fjaerland, Balestrand, Norway

The concept of a glacier as a physical element has been very much present during the planning of the Glacier Museum. This enormous mass of ice and snow lies like a bandage round vast areas of land. Lying in the content of this mass are secrets of the past in the transparent invisibility of the glacier. The glacier has something animal in its essence, in its slow gliding movement which makes its great imprints on the crust of the earth's surface, and in the fiction's wet waste running out towards the sea and forming new areas of land.

The situation of the Glacier Museum is on the last projection of the Josstedal glacier—a delta which runs out of Fjaerland fjord, part of the Sogne fjord complex. The whole of Fjaerland with its fjord lies like a floor in a natural space, with the mountainsides as gigantic walls. In this space with the plain as a plinth, the museum rises like an instrument in which visitors become the focal point in the total panorama and provides the peace to sense its own dimension.

A traditional museum works to visualize lost objects. Today we feel it necessary for museums to make visible the invisible. Our future is dependent on conditions in our old-fashioned sky. The atmosphere we have breathed through the centuries hides its data in the ice masses of the glacier, and in the alpine mountains of ice which at a few degrees shift in temperature would flood the fertile plains of the earth.

As the ferry slowly moves along Fjaerland fjord, you look behind you, and on the lush bright green plain the Glacier Museum lies like a huge pale grey stone. I have always wondered where the great moss-covered giant stones come from in the Nordic landscape.

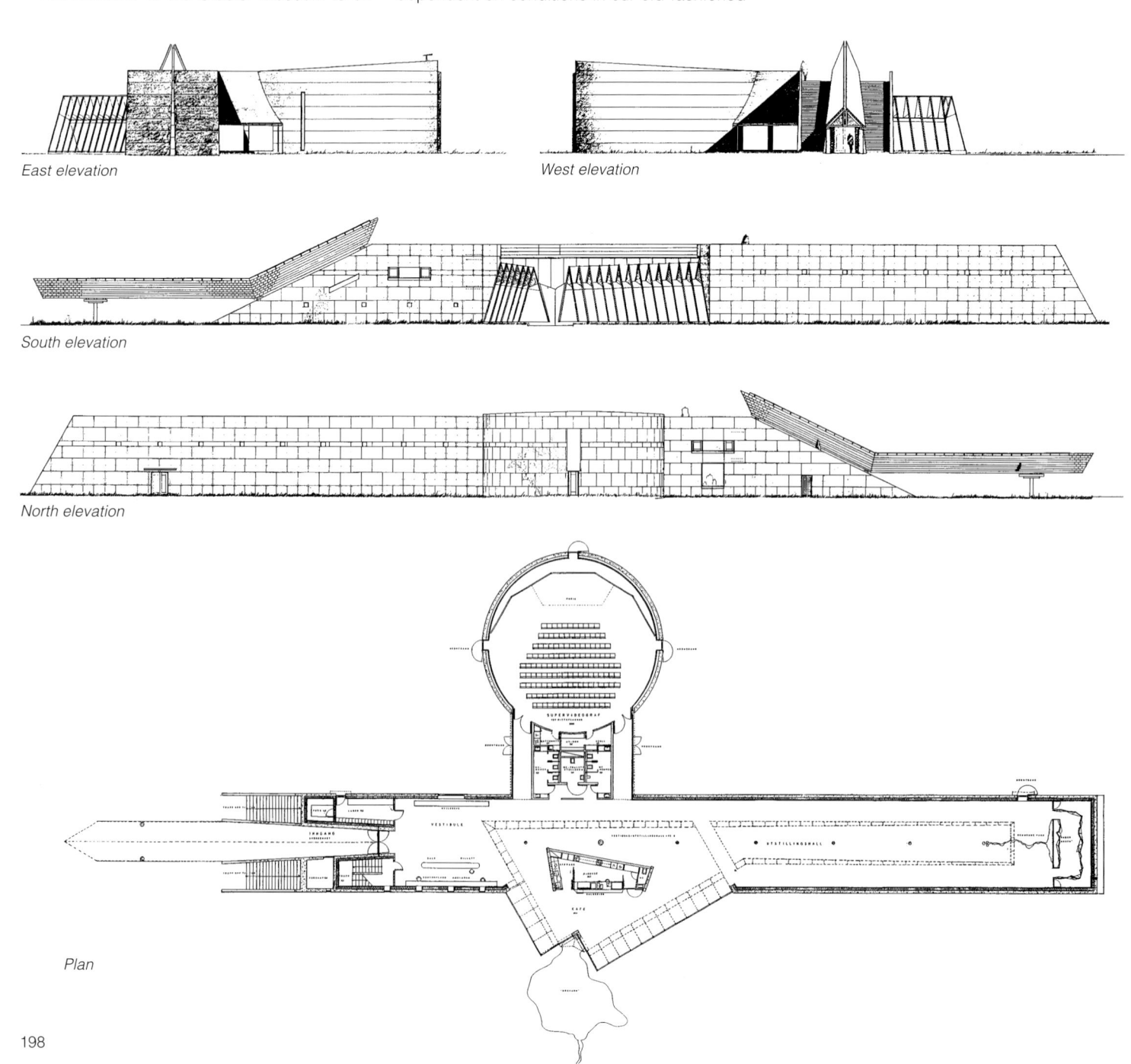

East elevation

West elevation

South elevation

North elevation

Plan

View toward main entrance メイン・エントランス方向を見る

North view 北より見る

South view 南より見る

　自然界のエレメントとしての氷河というコンセプトは、この氷河博物館を計画している間ずっと、非常に重要な存在であり続けた。氷と雪の巨大な塊は、この土地の広大な領域に包帯を巻いたように横たわっている。塊のなかにあるのは過去の秘密である。氷河はその本質のなかに何か動物的なものを持っている。地表の地殻の上に巨大な跡をつけて行く、そのゆっくりと滑って行く動きのなかに、そして、海へ向かって流れ出て行き、新しい土地を形成する、摩擦が削り出す岩と氷の塊のなかに。

　氷河博物館のある場所は、ヨーステダール氷河の先端――ファールランド・フィヨルドから流出したデルタであり、ソグネ・フィヨルド・コンプレックスの一部である。ファールランド全体は、そのフィヨルドと共に、山側が巨大な壁になった、自然空間のなかの床のように広がっている。基盤としての平面を伴ったこの空間のなかに、博物館は一つの楽器のように立ち上がる。そのなかで来館者は、パノラマ全体の焦点となり、そのディメンションを感じ取る。

　従来の博物館は、失われた事物を見せるものであった。今日、われわれは、博物館は、見えないものを見えるものにする必要があると感じている。

われわれの未来は、昔ながらの天空の状況に依存している。何世紀にも亘ってわれわれが吸ってきた大気は、氷河の氷の塊のなかにそのデータを隠している。氷に包まれた高い山々は、気温が数度変われば、地球の豊かな平原を洪水で覆うだろう。

　ファールランド・フィヨルドに沿ってゆっくりとフェリーが進むにつれて後ろを振り返ると、明るい緑色の茂みの上に氷河博物館が薄い灰色をした巨大な石のように横たわっている。苔に覆われたこの巨大な石が、どこからノルディックの風景のなかに来たのだろうかと、私はいつも不思議に思う。

Cafeteria カフェテリア

Skylight スカイライト

View toward cafeteria カフェテリアを見る

View from main entrance メイン・エントランスより見る

Main entrance メイン・エントランス

201

1989-91
RICARDO LEGORRETA

MARCO MUSEUM OF CONTEMPORARY ART, MONTERREY
Monterrey, Mexico

View from northwest 北西より見る

Entrance lobby エントランス・ロビー

Entrance lobby エントランス・ロビー

Located in the main corner of Monterrey's Marcoplaza and next to the Cathedral and Municipal palace, the museum has been integrated to the urban landscape and is inspired by the traditional plan of Mexican houses, where a central courtyard is surrounded by a series of arcades that subsequently give access to galleries. The pedestrian access is directed through a small plaza where a giant dove by Juan Soriano offers a nostalgic homage to Luis Barragan's sculpture.

From this plaza and through discrete door, one can access the vestibule which with its great height, color and light serves as a link to the auditorium, cafeteria and museum shop. After experiencing an sculptoric lattice, one arrives to a magnificent patio that besides being both a central element and distributor of galleries, is used for concerts, dinners and other meetings.

Daily, just about every 15 minutes the central courtyard is covered by a 2 inch flow of water which energizes and refreshes the environment.

The art exhibition takes place in a different galleries of different proportions, forms and heights. Strategically situated windows provide sources of natural light and keep the visitors in touch with the city and the central patio.

This criteria offers surroundings more in tune with daily life and makes the museum a cultural center as well an occasional visit by the local citizens of Monterrey.

The materials and in tense colors complement the informal and elegant character of the building.

モンテレー市にあるマルコプラザの中心的な一角を占め、大聖堂や市庁舎と隣り合って建つこの美術館は、周囲の都市景観に溶け込んでいるが、そのプランは、メキシコの伝統的な住宅からヒントを得たもので、中央のコートヤードを取り囲む回廊から各ギャラリーへ進む構成となっている。来館者はフアン・ソリアーノ作の巨大な鳩がルイス・バラガンの彫刻への郷愁的なオマージュを捧げている小さなプラザを通って中へ入る。

このプラザから、奥のドアを抜けると前室である。その高く吹き抜けた空間、色彩、光が、オーディトリアム、カフェテリア、ショップへの連結役を果たしている。彫刻的な格子組みの構成を楽しみながら進むと、壮大なパティオに出る。パティオは建物の中心的な要素であり、各ギャラリーへの起点であるばかりでなく、コンサート、夕食会その他の集会の場としても利用できる。

毎日、ほぼ15分ごとに、コート中央は2インチの高さまで水が満たされ、周囲の空間を活気づけ、リフレッシュさせる。

美術品が展示される各ギャラリーは、それぞれプロポーション、形態、天井の高さが異なっている。計算して設置された開口からは、自然光が入り、そこから市街風景や中央のパティオが見え、周囲との親近感が保たれる。

これによって、日常生活と同調した雰囲気が生まれ、美術館は、文化センターであると同時に、モンテレーの地域住民が折りにふれて訪れるような場所となっている。

使われている材料と強い色彩が、この建物の親しみやすく、しかも格調のある性格を一層引き立てる。

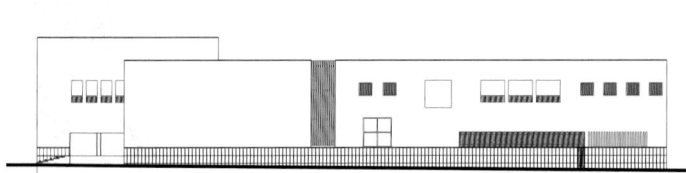

West elevation

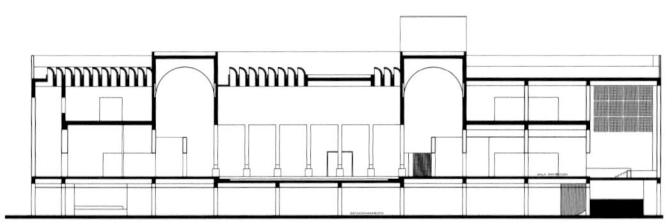

North elevation

Section

Section

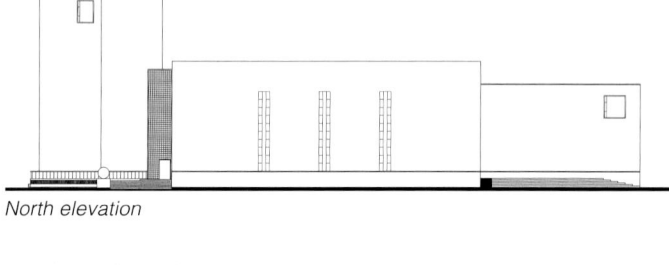

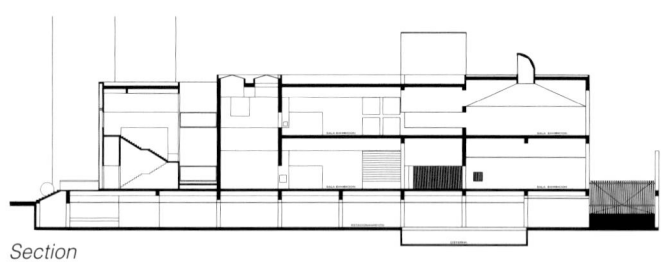

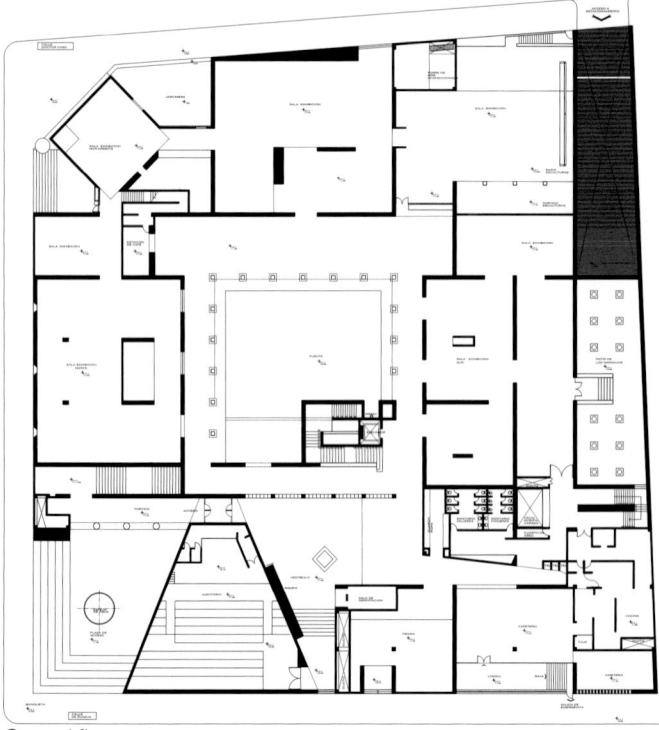

Ground floor

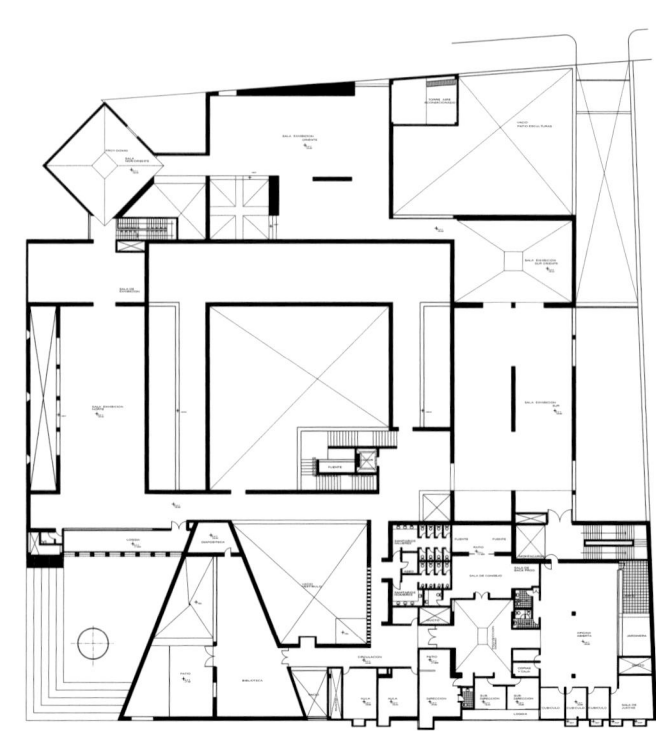

Second floor

Water court　水のコート △▽

Water court: view toward west　水のコート：西を見る

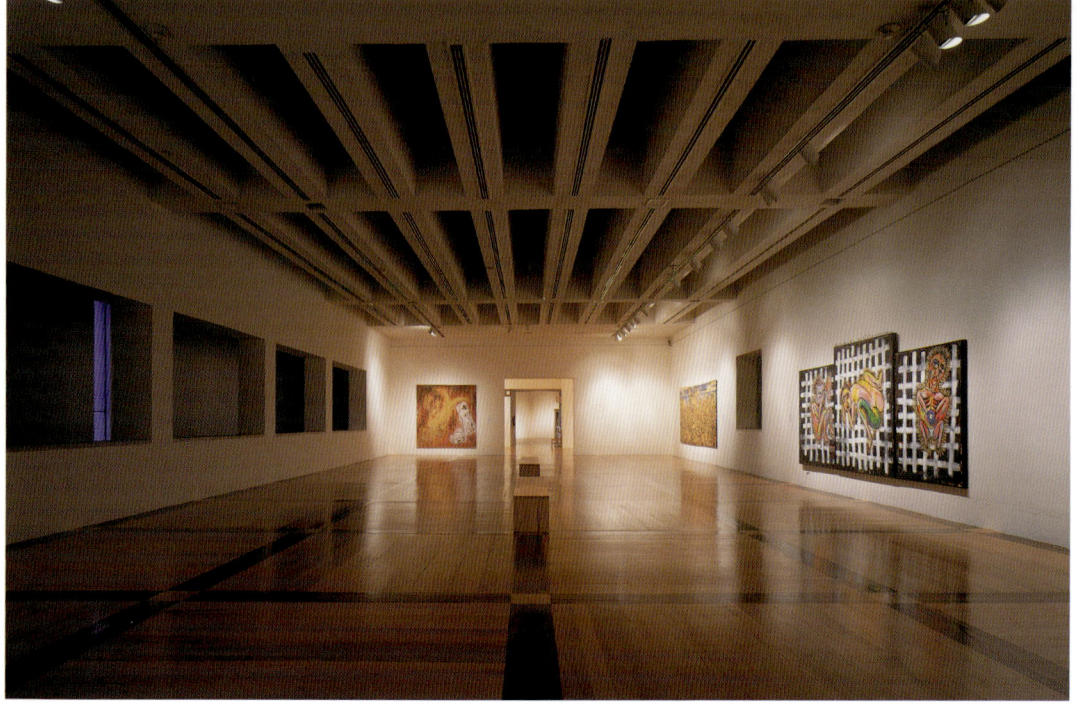

Exhibition room on second floor　2階展示室

Exhibition room on northeast　北東側展示室

Skylight　スカイライト

Court flooded every 20 minutes　20分毎に水が注がれるコート

1989–97
PETER ZUMTHOR

ART MUSEUM, BREGENZ
Bregenz, Austria.

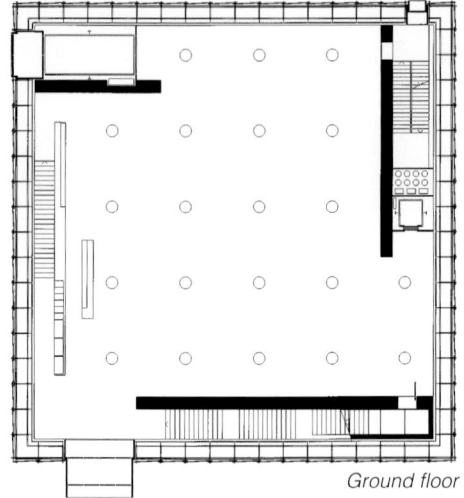

Ground floor

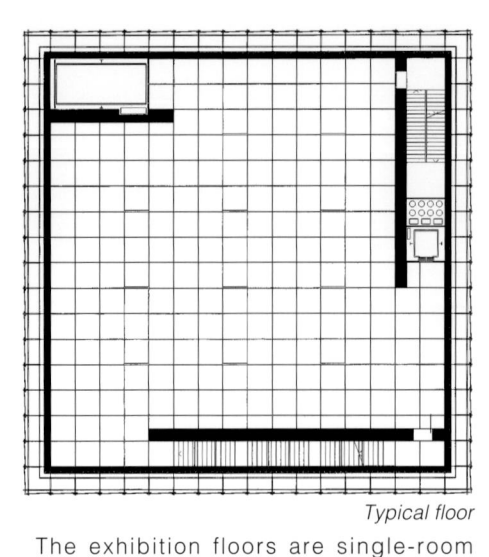

Typical floor

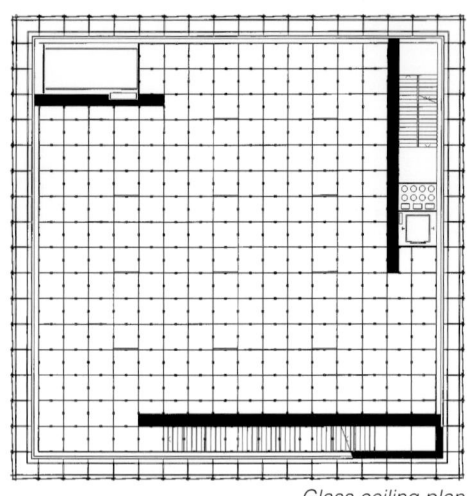

Glass ceiling plan

Bregenz, Austria is a town with a lake, adjacent to German and Swiss borders. The museum site faces the downtown and the Lake Constance across the street. The building is given a symbolic design as it is defined to become the cultural core of the town. Covered with frosted glass, this abstracted volume has in fact become a new landmark within the town's historical urban context.

External walls feature a dual structure: translucent glass skin is fixed onto the structural body that is the concrete walls. It does not wrap them up completely, as some space is left between the glass shingles. Glass units are uniform in size. They are supported by simple, metal structural details. The sequence of these units makes up the outer walls.

The exhibition floors are single-room spaces of identical size, same size to the entrance hall on the first floor. Each slab is supported by vertical bearing walls, along which stairways are arranged on the outside. A layer of space is secured above the ceilings of galleries and stairways for lighting purposes. Natural light from the outside and artificial light distributed inside illuminate the exhibition space below. A minimal space of high flexibility, with concrete walls, frosted glass ceilings and cold colorings.

As the images of the glass envelope and of the concrete box inside change according to time and weather, the building puts on a multitude of expressions. During daytime, the quiet glitter of frosted glass that absorbs sunlight and the concrete in the background make a beautiful contrast of textures. After sundown, the building turns into an urban lantern when the cold artificial light escapes from the inner dual ceiling to cast light patterns onto the glass cortex outside.

オーストリアのブレゲンツはドイツ、スイスの国境が接している、湖の町である。美術館の敷地は、この町の中心街、ボーデン湖に道路を隔てて面している。町の文化的な中心となるように、建物はシンボリックな意匠が与えられている。曇りガラスによる外装によって、抽象化されたヴォリュームは歴史的な町並みの中で新しい町のシンボルとなった。

建物の外壁は二重構造になっている。構造体であるコンクリート壁の上にトランスルーセントのガラスの外皮が完全に閉じるのではなく、ガラス板相互に隙間を持たせて設置されている。ガラス・ユニットは単一寸法であり、簡単な金物のディテールで支持され、これらの繰り返しによって外壁を構成している。

展示室は1階のエントランス・ホールと同様の、各階とも同じ大きさのプランを持つ一室空間で、垂直に通る耐力壁が各スラブを支える。階段室はこの耐力壁の外側に沿って配置されている。各展示室と階段室はその天井裏に光のための空間がほぼ一層分ずつ取られ、外周からの自然光や内部に配置される人工光によってその下の展示空間を照らし出す。コンクリートの壁に曇りガラスの天井、自由度の高い、寒色系でまとめられたミニマルな空間である。

ガラスの外皮とその内側のコンクリートの箱の、それぞれの見え方は天候や時間によって変化し、建物は様々な表情を見せる。昼間は陽光を吸収してしっとりと光る曇りガラスと背後のコンクリートの組み合わせの質感の対比が美しい。また、夜間には、内側の二重の天井から外側に向けて漏れ出る冷たい人工光が、外皮のガラスにパターンを映し出し、都市のランタンとなる。

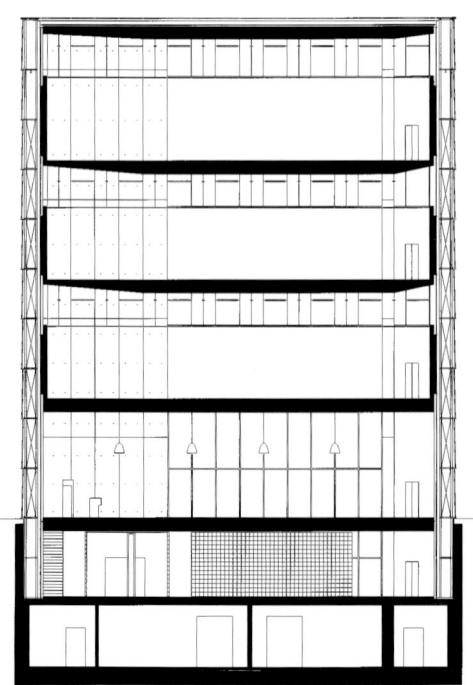

Section: floors

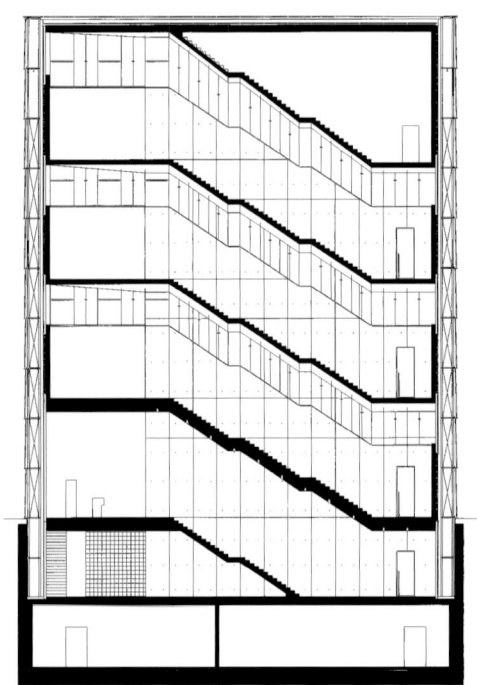

Section: staircase

Overall view 全景

△▽ Ground floor: reception   1階：レセプション

Staircase　階段室

Wall detail　壁面のディテール

Exhibition room　展示室

1989–98
DANIEL LIBESKIND

BERLIN MUSEUM WITH JEWISH MUSEUM
Berlin, Germany

View from south 南より見る

South end of building: old museum on right 建物南端：右は旧館

Courtyard コートヤード ▷

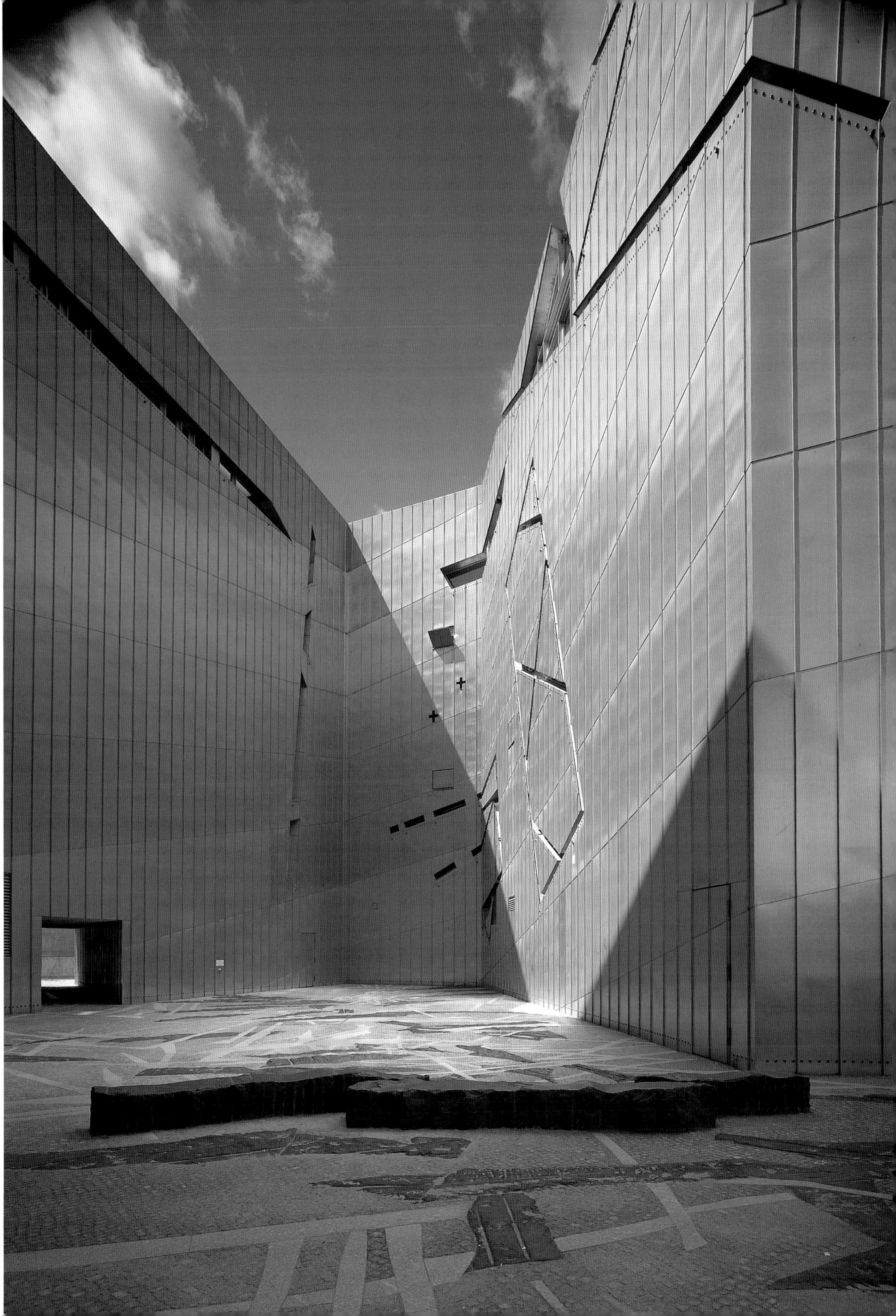

The Berlin Museum with the Jewish Museum won first prize in an international competition held in 1989.

The design of the new Museum is one which seeks to show the integration of the history of Berlin with the history of its Jewish citizens; a history which proved to be fatally intertwined. There were three fundamental aspects of the program which were addressed, namely: the inability to speak about Berlin's history without speaking about its Jewish history; the need to architecturally and physically incorporate the absence of Jewish life in Berlin after the Holocaust; and on an urban level to bring light across the once divided city which connects places and memory.

The new Museum is entered through the old Baroque building. The visitor descends underground whereupon an intersection of three "roads" occurs. The first "roads" is a short one, ending in an acute angled dead-end Holocaust Tower, wherein the final signatures of the deported and murdered Jews will reside. The second "roads" leads to the E.T.A. Hoffmann garden; a garden of pillars representing the emigration and exile of Jews abroad. The final "roads" is longest, displaying the remaining religious artifacts of Jewish community and leading to the gallery spaces above, via a main stair.

Slicing through the building, is the void; an impenetrable structure traversable by void bridges which criss-cross from one gallery to another. The visitors are oriented around this absent space: a space which addresses the eradication of Jewish life in Berlin. The Museum exhibition galleries will display the collection of the history of Berlin and its Jewish population in all cultural and artistic areas from the past to the future.

The scheme is a dramatic departure from the traditional Museum as it tackles the cultural issue of the German-Jewish relationship without simulated representation and sentimentality.

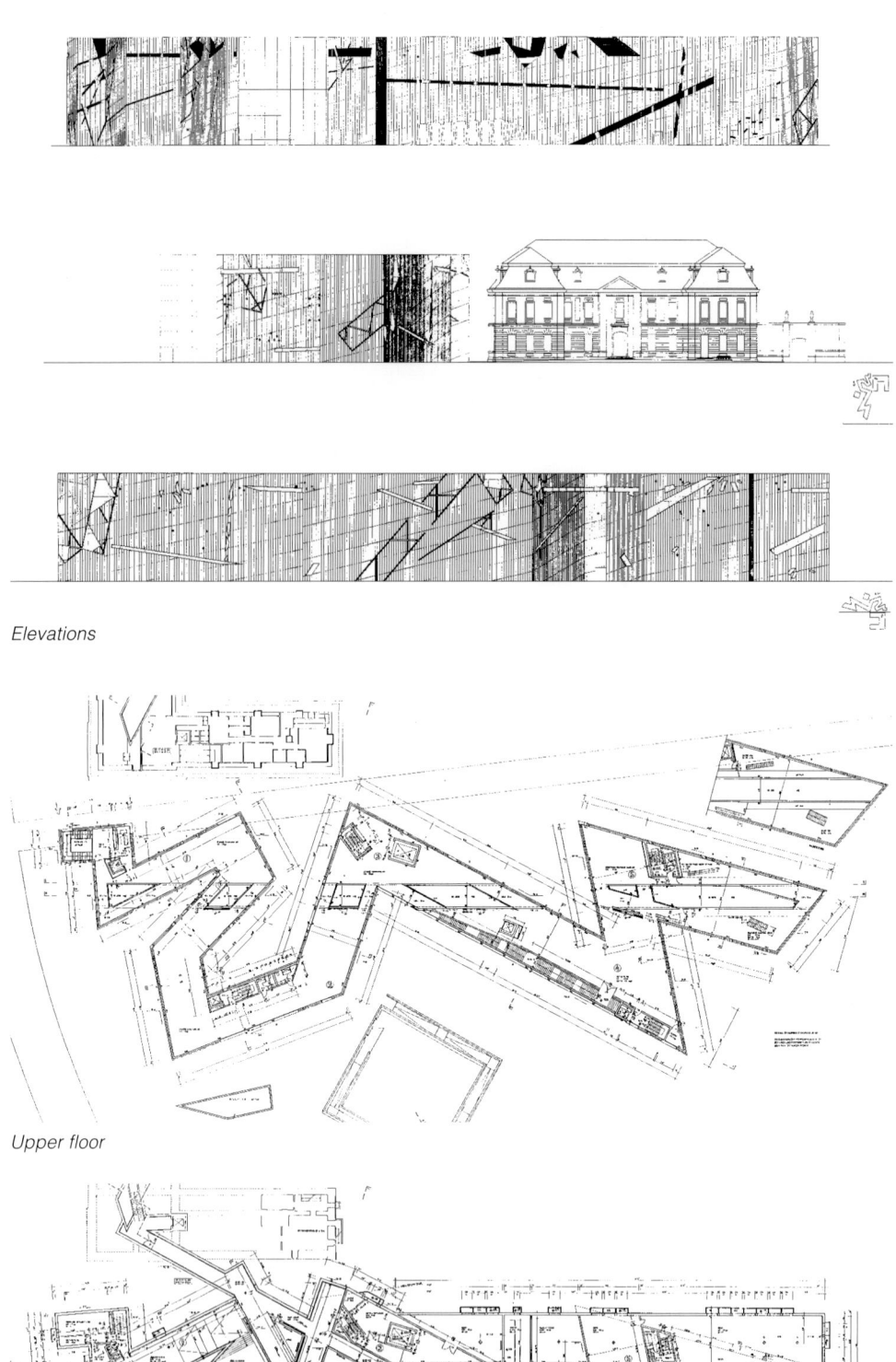

Elevations

Upper floor

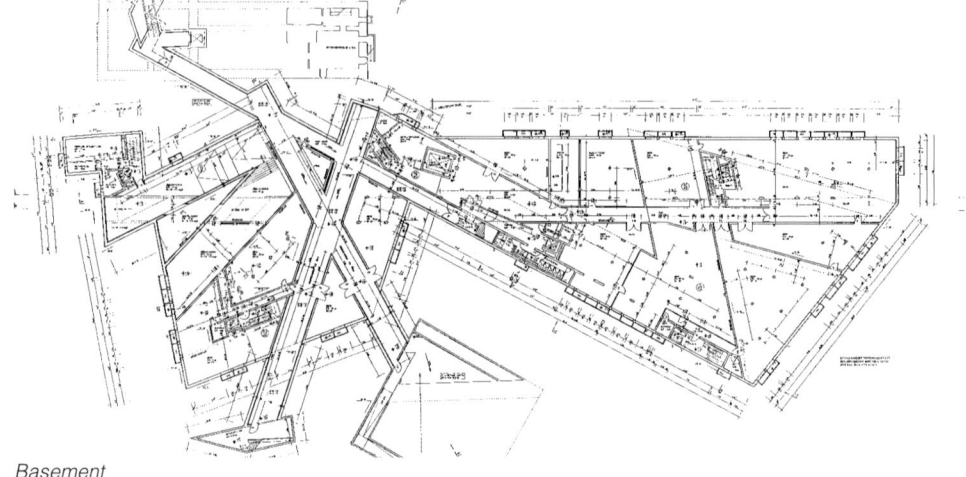

Basement

ベルリン美術館に対するユダヤ人博物館の増築計画は、1989年に行われた国際設計競技で1等に当選したものである。

新しい博物館に対するデザインは、ユダヤ市民の歴史とベルリンの歴史を統合して見せるにはどうしたらよいかを探求するものであった。それは、運命的な交錯を示す歴史である。プログラムには3つの基本的な局面が提示されていた。すなわち、ユダヤ人の歴史を語らずしてベルリンの歴史を語ることはできないということ。ホロコースト後のベルリンにおけるユダヤ人の生命の不在を、建築的にも物理的にもひとつに合体させることの必要性。そして、都市のレベルにおいては、かつて分割されていた街を横断する、場所と記憶をつなぐ啓示的な光をもたらすこと。

新しい博物館へは、旧棟のバロック建築を経由して入る。来館者は、3つの「道」が交差する地下に降りる。第1の「道」は短く、行き止まりに鋭角に設置されたホロコースト・タワーがあり、そのなかには、追放され殺害されたユダヤ人の最後の署名が備えられることになろう。第2の「道」はE・T・A・ホフマン庭園へ導く。そこは柱の並ぶ庭園で、海外へのユダヤ人の移住と亡命を表現する。最後の道が最も長く、ユダヤ人コミュニティに残されていた宗教関係の品物が展示され、主要階段によって、その上にあるギャラリーへと導かれる。

建物の端から端までを切り進むヴォイド空間。入り込むことの出来ないこの構築物は、一方のギャラリーからもう一方へ架かる十字に交差したヴォイド・ブリッジによって横断する。来館者は、この空虚な空間の周囲を進む。それはベルリンにおけるユダヤ人生命の根絶を表現する虚の空間である。博物館のギャラリーには、ベルリンとそのユダヤ市民の、過去から未来にわたる、あらゆる文化及び芸術領域に及ぶ歴史を展示することになるだろう。

このデザインは、ゲルマンとユダヤとの関係における文化的な問題に、欺瞞や感傷を持ち込むことなく取り組み、伝統的なミュージアム建築からの大胆な飛翔を試みたものである。

Great stairs 大階段

Void ヴォイド

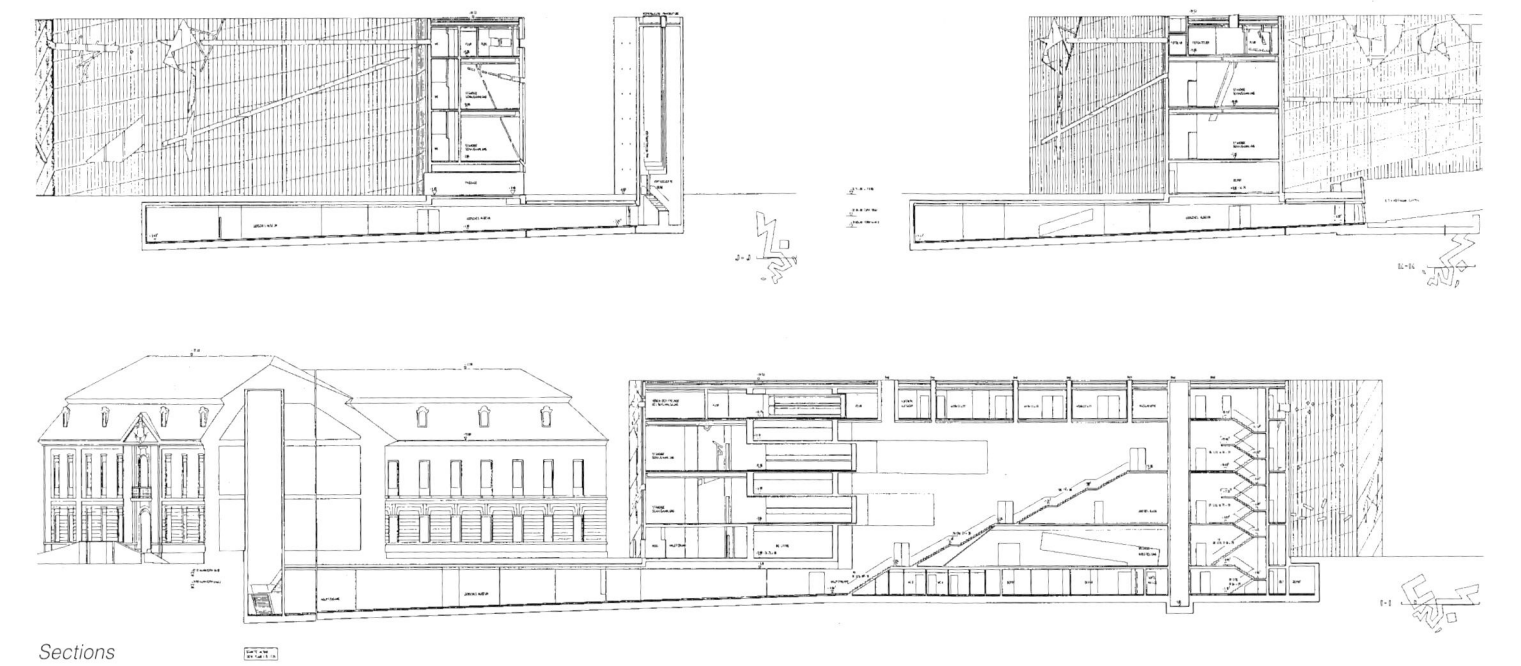

Sections

Staircase 階段室

Basement 地階

Gallery 展示室

1990-96
TOD WILLIAMS BILLIE TSIEN

PHOENIX ART MUSEUM
Phoenix, Arizona, U.S.A.

Overall view from Central Avenue　セントラル・アヴェニューから見る

View toward main entrance　メイン・エントランス方向を見る

Central Avenue elevation　セントラル・アヴェニュー側立面

View toward main entrance　メイン・エントランス方向を見る

The program consists of the renovation of the existing 90,000 square foot museum and the extension for another 50,000 square feet.

The newly added section built along the adjacent Central Avenue accommodates comparatively larger spaces such as the gallery for travelling exhibitions or a lecture hall featuring 294 seats, whereas the renovated section houses a cluster of smaller galleries. The new 9,100 square foot Cummings Great Hall is a double-height space for large-scaled contemporary painting and sculpture, and can serve for special events such as opening receptions.

As visitors make their way into the museum, they are provided with fresh spatial experiences. For example, the newly built double-height gallery spaces are linked by ramps, and the building divided at the entrance is interconnected by the bridge on the second floor, thereby producing a variety among the lines of circulation.

The outer wall facing Central Avenue has almost no openings in order to confront the heavy traffic volume outside. It is composed of 110 units of 12-foot wide, 11-inch thick, 30-ton precast concrete panels using an aggregate of green quartz and white sand. Elaborately designed vertical gaps and glass shingles jutting out of this elevation add some rhythm to the lengthiness of the wall itself.

90,000平方フィートの既存建物の改造と50,000平方フィートの増築による美術館。

敷地前面を走るセントラル・アヴェニューに沿って建てられた新築部分に企画展示のためのギャラリーや294席を持つレクチャー・ホールなどの比較的大きな空間群を配置し、改造された既存部分には小スケールのギャラリー群を配置している。新築部分の9,100平方フィートのカミングス大ホールは大スケールの現代美術絵画や彫刻作品に対応する2層吹抜けの空間で、オープニング・レセプションなどの特別なイベントにも使用される。

館内を通る動線は多様な変化と特色を持ち、新鮮な空間体験を来館者に与える。たとえば、新築部分の2層分の展示空間はランプによって結ばれ、エントランスで分節された建物は2階に架かるブリッジによって結ばれ、動線に変化を与えている。

セントラル・アヴェニュー側の外壁は、交通量に対抗するためにほとんど開口部を持たない。この外壁は12フィート幅、11インチ厚、約30トンの、骨材に緑色の石英と白砂を混ぜたプレキャスト・コンクリート・パネルによる。このパネル・ユニット約110枚によって構成されている。このエレベーションは垂直に入れられた溝や突き出されたガラス板の意匠によってその長さにリズムを与えている。

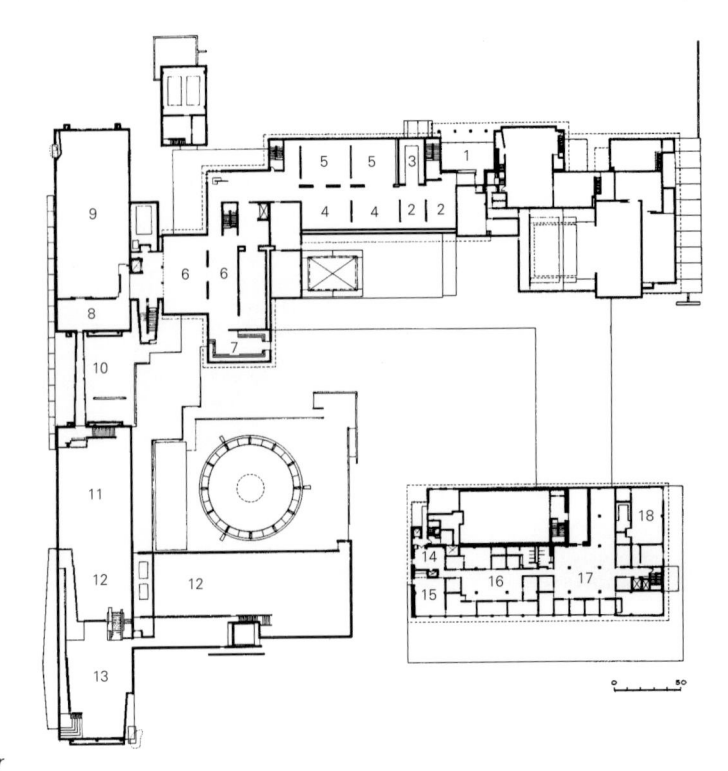

Second floor

1. DECORATIVE ARTS GALLERY
2. PRE-17TH C. ART GALLERY
3. COSTUME GALLERY
4. 18TH C. ART GALLERY
5. 19TH C. ART GALLERY
6. WESTERN ART GALLERY
7. THRONE MINIATURE ROOM
8. GRAPHIC GALLERY MEZZANINE
9. CHANGING EXHIBITS GALLERY
10. BRIDGE
11. GREAT HALL BELOW
12. 20TH C.ART GALLERY BELOW
13. CONTEMPORARY ART GALLERY
14. RECEPTION
15. CONFERENCE ROOM
16. ADMINISTRATION OFFICE
17. CURATORIAL STAFF
18. BOARD ROOM

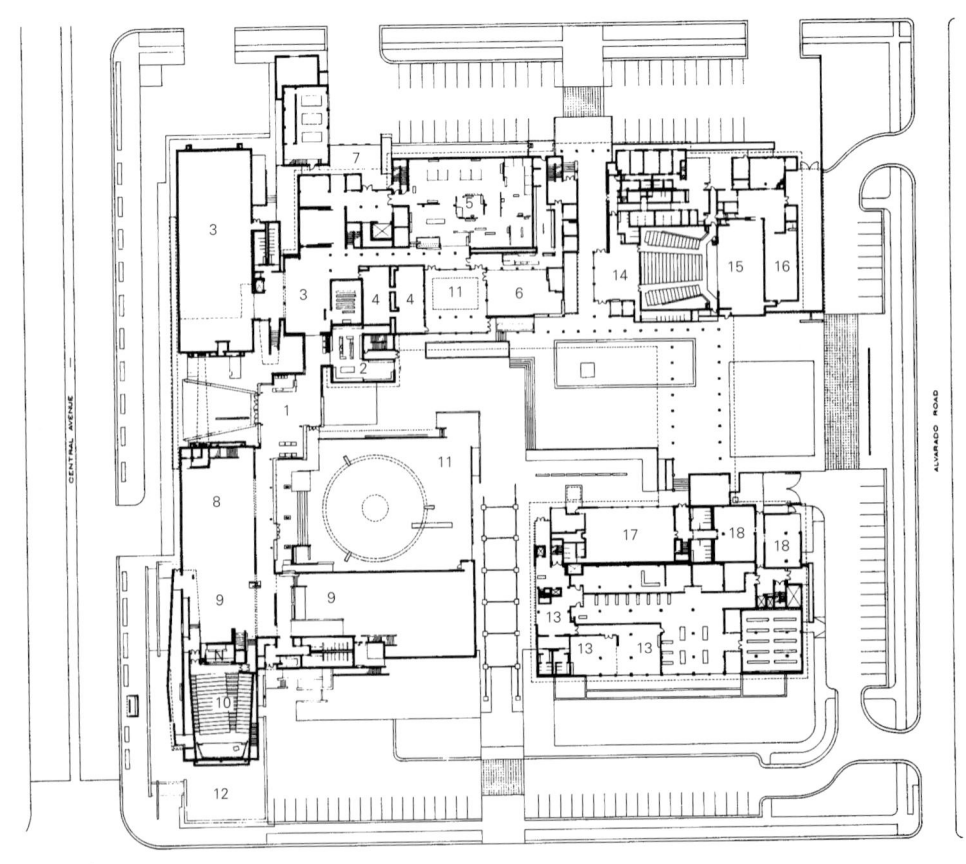

Ground floor

MUSEUM LEGEND
1. ENTRY LOBBY
2. STORE
3. CHANGING EXHIBITION GALLERY
4. ART ATTACK GALLERY
5. ASIAN ART GALLERY
6. RESTAURANT
7. LOADING DOCK
8. GREAT HALL
9. 20TH C. ART GALLERY
10. LECTURE HALL
11. OUTDOOR COURTYARD
12. PUBLIC SCULPTURE COURT
13. EDUCATION STUDIO

THEATER LEGEND
14. ENTRY LOBBY
15. AUDITORIUM/STAGE
16. WORKSHOP
17. THEATER
18. REHEARSAL ROOM

Courtyard 中庭

△ *View toward entrance lobby from east* 東よりエントランス・ロビーを見る　　　　*Entrance lobby* エントランス・ロビー ▽

Great hall 大ホール

223

Corridor at southwest corner　南西部の廊下

Corridor　廊下

View toward contemporary art gallery on second floor　2階現代美術展示室を見る

Gallery 展示室

Lecture room 講堂

225

1991–94
TADAO ANDO

SUNTORY MUSEUM + PLAZA
Osaka, Japan

Aerial view 航空写真

View from southwest　南西より見る

View from west　西より見る

Nanko (south port) of Osaka Bay has been an area of waterfront development over the past years. The project consisted of a museum on a site adjacent to an aquarium formerly built as part of such development. Osaka was once called a city of water, with its countless canals running throughout the city similar to those in Venice. They were the source of this city's charms in terms of both function and environment. In recent years, the importance of water is again brought to appreciation. Osaka is no exception and the city is reconsidering its shorelines and riverbeds. Unfortunately, superficial, fancy projects are in fashion, and the fundamental relationships between man and water remain ruptured. Here, it was required that an authentic, vital man-water relation be established.

My answer was to consider a plan for not only the museum but also for the waterfront plaza which originally belongs to Osaka City, as and integrated part of the museum. A hotel facility was scheduled to be constructed to the south of the museum site: the two buildings were to be built together on an artificial foundation of reclaimed land concealing a two-level parking area. Thus, the total planning had to include the museum, the hotel, and the sea itself in respective.

The building consists of a massive, reversed conic drum (48 meters in diameter at its highest elevation) in the center and two rectangular cubes arranged to form a 22.5-degree angle. The cube on the south accommodates the gallery, the one on the north the restaurants. Within the huge drum is a 32-meter diameter sphere, containing an IMAX theater. Visitors moving between the exhibition spaces, restaurants, and IMAX theater, will enjoy spectacular views over Osaka Bay.

Evening view: theater 夕景：劇場

The broad waterfront plaza—100 meters wide and 40 meters deep—leads to the sea as a series of steps and slopes. If a museum were a theater of Art and Man, this seaside plaza must be a theater of Man and sea as Nature. This theater is a meeting place of sea scent, ebb and flow of the tide, sun setting into the sea, and people gathering there to communicate with each other. In the center is an amphitheater. Its stairs are all regarded as seats and various types of stages are possible. Five monumental pillars are aligned along the water's edge, and are echoed by the breakwater 70 meters from shore—as evidence of my intentions, and to reinforce the continuity of the plaza with the ocean.

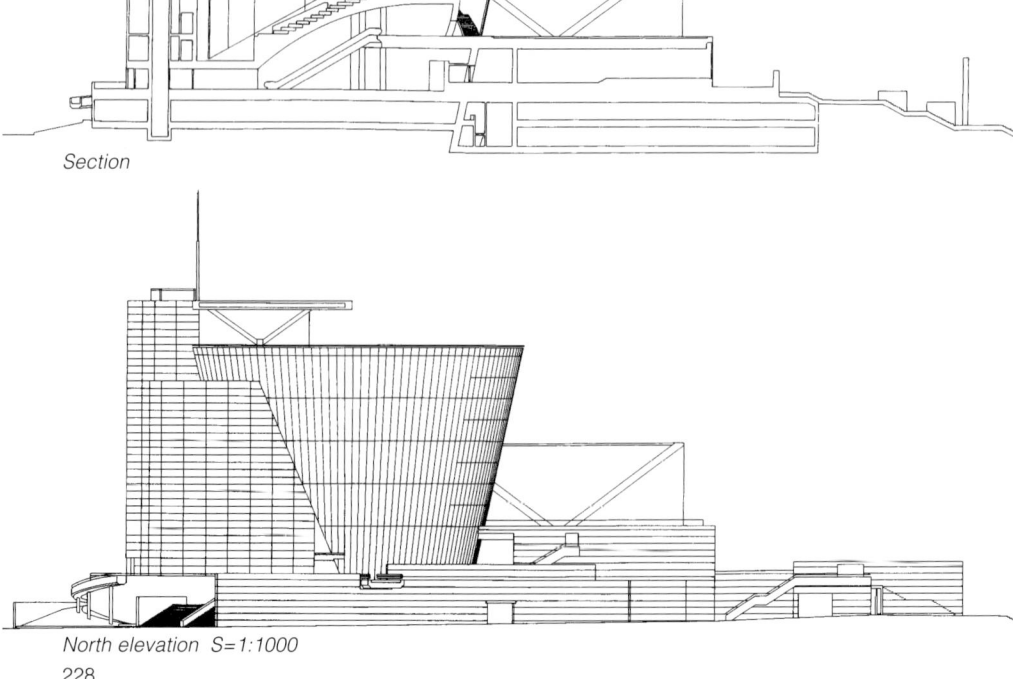

Section

North elevation S=1:1000

Sixth floor

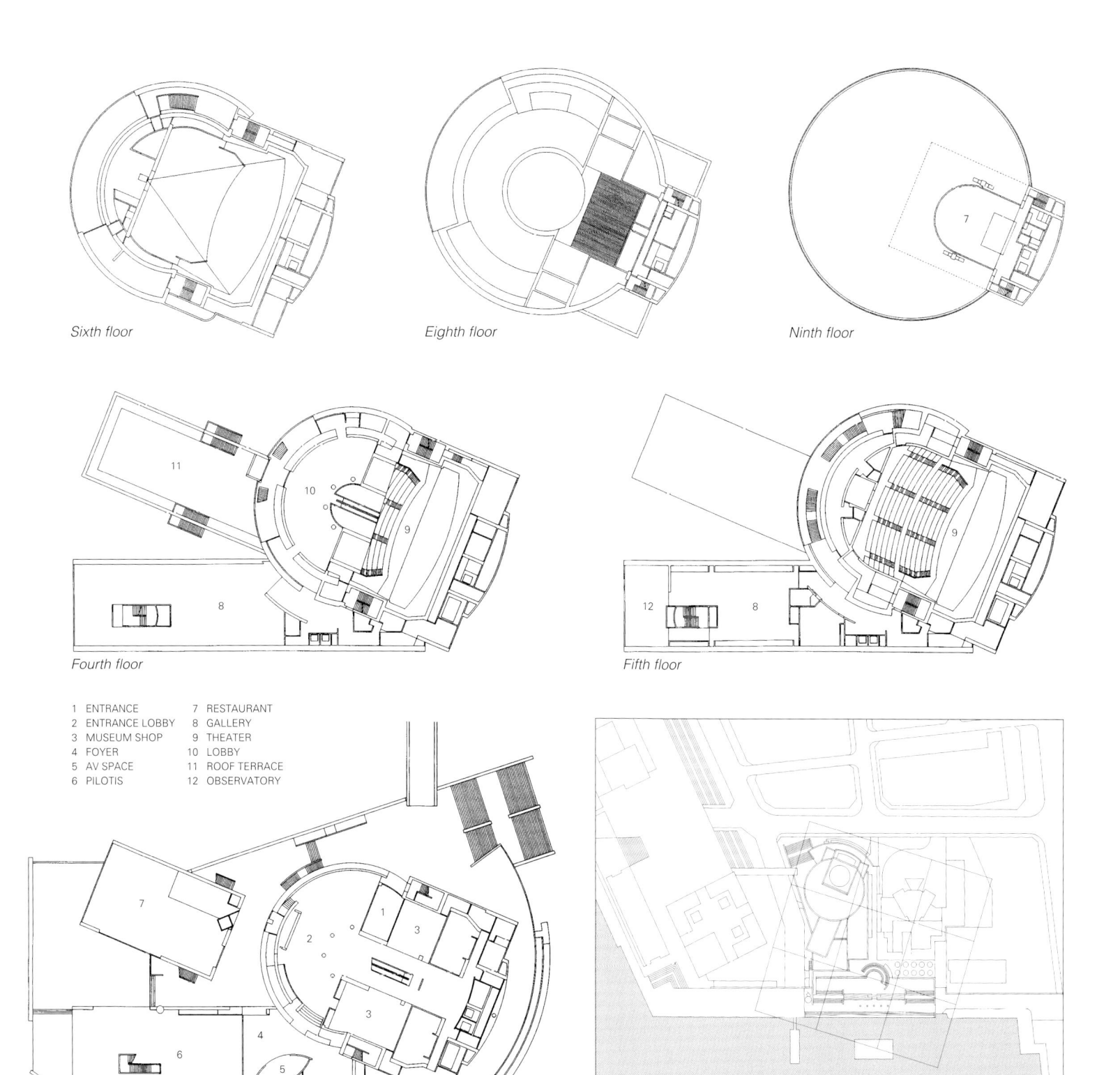

Eighth floor

Ninth floor

Fourth floor

Fifth floor

1 ENTRANCE
2 ENTRANCE LOBBY
3 MUSEUM SHOP
4 FOYER
5 AV SPACE
6 PILOTIS
7 RESTAURANT
8 GALLERY
9 THEATER
10 LOBBY
11 ROOF TERRACE
12 OBSERVATORY

Second floor S=1:1000

Site plan S=1:4000

大阪南港ではウォーターフロントの開発がここ数年の間進められてきた。計画は、この一環として既存の水族館に隣接する敷地に美術館を建設するものである。大阪はかつて水の都と呼ばれ、ヴェネツィアをしのぐほどの水路が縦横に走っていた。それは、機能的であると同時に環境的にも、この街を魅力的なものにしていた。近年、水への視点が再度問い直され、この大阪でも海岸、河川敷等、都市の見直しが進められている。しかし、表面的でファッショナブルな計画はあちこちに立てられているが、人と水の基本的な関係は断絶されたままである。ここでは、真の、人と水との生き生きとした関わりを確立することが求められた。

そのため計画では、美術館の敷地だけに留まらず、大阪市の管轄である海辺の広場を美術館と一体のものとして考えた。またこの美術館の南側の敷地にはホテルの建設が予定されていた。この両建物は2層分の駐車場を収めた人工地盤上に共に建てられることになる。したがって美術館、ホテル、海上全体を視野に入れて全体計画がなされた。

建物は、巨大な逆円錐状のドラム（頂部の直径48m）を中心に、二つの直方体が22.5度の角度で組み合わされている。二つの直方体は南側が展示室、北側がレストランに充てられている。そしてこの巨大なドラムの中に、直径32mの球からなるアイマックス・シアターが内包されている。展示室、レストラン、アイマックス・シアター、それらを取り囲む通路など、様々なところから海辺の景観を楽しむことができるよう計画されている。

海辺の広場は幅100m、奥行き40mの巨大な広場であって、スロープ、階段で海に向かって連続してゆく。私は、美術館が芸術と人間の劇場とするならば、この海辺の広場は自然としての海と人間の劇場であると考えた。この劇場では海の匂い、潮の満ち干、海に沈む太陽、そしてそこで語り合う人間が交錯する。中央には、円形劇場が設けられている。ここでは階段はすべて客席と考えられ、様々な舞台を設定することができる。海岸に配された5本のコンクリートのモニュメンタルな柱は、海岸線から70m離れた防波堤にも意思の痕跡として反復され、この広場から海への連続性を強化している。

"Mermaid Plaza" "マーメイド・プラザ"

Foyer ホワイエ

Observatory 展望ギャラリー △▽

1991–94
BALKRISHNA V. DOSHI

HUSSAIN-DOSHI GUFA MUSEUM
Ahmedabad, India

Essentially an art gallery exhibiting paintings and sculptures of noted artist M. F. Hussain, the Hussain-Doshi Gufa in Ahmedabad is located on a campus of the Centre for Environmental Planning and Technology, while becoming a metaphor, balancing the adjunct science and architecture education institutions.

As a human intervention and interpretation of a natural form the basic plan organization evolves out of the familiar module of an ellipse intersected with circles. The spaces formed within are however contiguous and amorphous through inclined planes of domes, curvilinear planes of walls, undulating floors and non-rectilinear leaning columns. A footprint of 280 square meters nearly doubles its surface area for paintings through convoluting planes. The shells, domes and skylight protrusion of various sizes and shapes float on a part-buried space and earth mounds to become an inherent ingredient of the natural landscape. Bent edges and eaves gutters extending over ground further accentuate this feeling and anchor the object to the ground. Projecting skylights and skin cutouts not only illuminate the spaces within but create mythic shafts and spots of light reminiscent of the galaxy and stars.

Buried spaces, earth mounds, raised volumes and china mosaic finish renders the architecture energy conscious, cutting down its energy intake, in an otherwise harsh, hot, dry climate. Material resources are further optimized through its shell-like forms and ferrocement construction techniques. A simple wire-mesh and mortarlined floor in a form of natural sag of cloth, evolved through scale-model studies, eliminates the need of any kind of foundation, as the basic form is continuous and efficient in optimizing the stresses and its distribution. Similar economy of material is achieved through roof shells in a form guided by computer designs which resolve stresses to a minimum, requiring only an inch-thick ferrocement shell without any form work. The construction is carried out with simple hand tools and by semi- and unskilled workers on site.
Yatin Pandya

Sections

Roof

1 ENTRANCE
2 GALLERY SPACE
3 PANTRY
4 TOILET
5 AMPHITHEATER

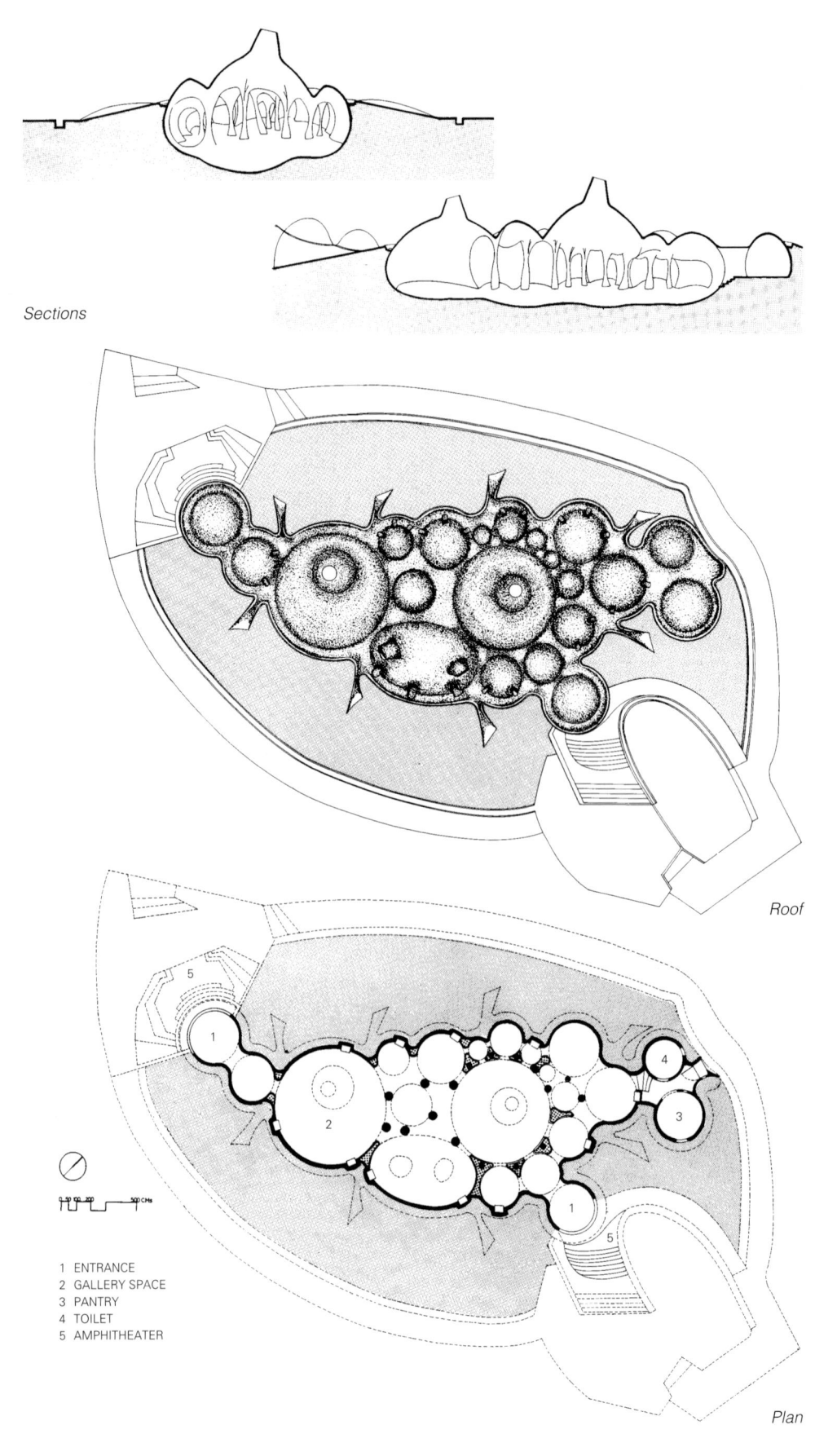

Plan

View from northwest 北西より見る

Exhibition gallery 展示ギャラリー

Skylight スカイライト

Exhibition gallery 展示ギャラリー

Working area ワークエリア

Entrance　エントランス

Exhibiton gallery　展示ギャラリー

著名なアーティストM・F・フセインの絵画や彫刻の展示ギャラリーを主体とする、アーメダバードのフセイン・ドーシ美術館は、環境計画／技術センターのキャンパス内に位置し、付属する科学と建築の教育機関との均衡をとりながらひとつのメタファーを構成している。

基本的な平面構成は、自然の形態への人間の介在と解釈として、交叉する円と楕円の見慣れたモデュールから展開させている。しかしドームの傾斜する面、曲線を描く壁面、波打つ床、そして直線的には構成されていない柱などによってつくりだされる内部空間は連続的かつ不定形である。

280平方メートルのプランは、湾曲する壁面によって、絵画のためのスペースを倍増させている。さまざまな寸法や形態のシェル、ドーム、突起するスカイライトが、一部地中に埋もれた空間や土の塚の上を浮遊し自然の風景の中の本来の一要素となる。湾曲したエッジや地上に伸びる庇の溝は建物を地上に繋ぎ留め、自然の中の一要素であるという感覚をさらに強める。突起したスカイライト、表皮に穿たれた孔は内部を明るくするばかりでなく、神話的な光の束や星雲や星を想わせる水玉模様をつくりだす。

地中に埋められた空間、土の塚、盛り上げられたヴォリューム、そして磁器のモザイク仕上げは、さもなくば厳しく暑い乾燥した風土の中で、熱吸収量を抑えるという、省エネルギー建築を意識したものである。材料の総量は、シェル状の形態と鉄筋コンクリートの採用によって効率の良いものとなった。縮尺模型によるスタディから導き出された、布が自然に弛んだ形に、ワイヤーメッシュとモルタルで簡単に敷かれた床はどんな種類の基礎も必要としない。平面の基本形は連続性をもっているので、効率よく荷重を分散することができるからである。同様に、荷重を最小限にする、コンピューターデザインで導かれた形態の屋根は、材料を節約でき、型枠なしの1インチ厚の鉄筋コンクリートのシェルだけでつくることができる。工事は単純な道具で現地の半熟練工および未熟練工によって行われた。　　　　　（ヤティン・パンディヤ）

1991–94
ARATA ISOZAKI

NAGI MUSEUM OF CONTEMPORARY ART/NAGI TOWN LIBRARY
Okayama, Japan

Overall view 全景

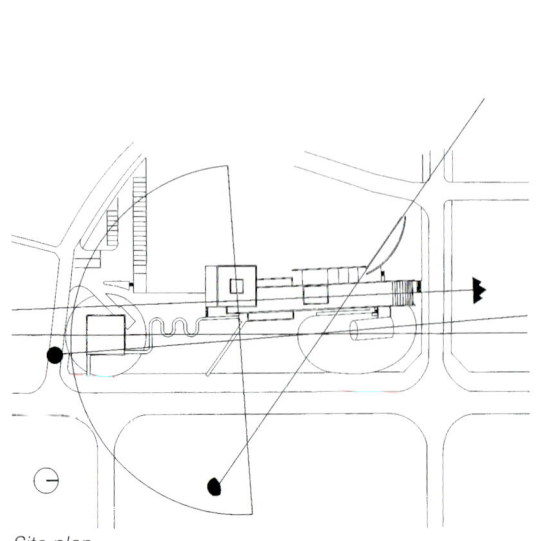

Site plan

"Sun" (middle) and "Moon" (right)　"太陽"（中央）と"月"（右）

View from pond 池より見る

Aiko Miyawaki: "Earth" 宮脇愛子："大地"

237

This Nagi Museum of Contemporary Art is a complete departure from conventional museums. It is specifically created to accommodate works that are considered the hardest to exhibit and to collect. This museum commissions this type of work from artists and builds a structure to house them individually. Here three site-specific works were selected: Shusaku Arakawa's work, "A Place that Creates those who Observe", a three-dimensional conceptual piece, stored in a cylindrical space; Kazuo Okazaki's "Eaves", the largest piece of a series, installed on the wall of a semi-circular space; and Aiko Miyawaki's "Utsurohi" which invites spectators to the inside of the stainless wire arches installed in a space that extends from the interior to an outdoor pool. These spaces are also connected to community facilities such as a library. The shapes of these three pieces can suggest the sun, the moon and the earth. The central axis orients toward Nagi Mountain which iconically dominates this area. The architectural entity becomes a mythical composition.

In the nineteenth century, the first generation of museums were built to accommodate collections and to exhibit them. The second generation exhibited two- and three-dimensional works on the walls and floors of simple abstract spaces. With the emergence of site-specific works in the sixties, a new type of museum is now in demand. This Nagi MOCA is a prototype.
Arata Isozaki

この奈義現代美術館は、通常の美術館とはまったく違った成り立ちをしている。すなわち、今日の美術館が、収蔵し展示することが不可能と思われるタイプの作品を、あらかじめ注文制作し、それを個別に覆う建物を連結したものである。この際、特定の場所もしくは空間の構築と切り離し得ない作品がとりわけ選ばれている。荒川修作の作品は"見る者がつくられる場"という概念の立体的構築物で、円筒形状の空間に収められる。岡崎和郎の作品は、"庇"と呼ばれる一連のもののうち最大のスケールをもつが、半月状の空間のひとつの壁にとりつけられる。宮脇愛子の作品"うつろひ"は、弧を描くステンレスワイヤーの群のなかに観客を招きいれるもので、室内から室外の水面へと連続するひろがりをもった空間が用意される。これらの諸室に図書館などのコミュニティ施設が連結されている。この3つの作品はその形態から、太陽、月、大地を暗示すると読むこともできるが、中央を貫く軸が、この土地を象徴的に支配している奈義山頂に向けられており、全体の建物が神話的構成をなしてもいる。

古いコレクションの収蔵と公開を目的とした19世紀に成立した第1世代、立体と平面の作品を壁と床に展示する抽象的均質空間をもつ第2世代に対して、このような特定の作家による特定の場所に限定して構想された作品に対応するものが1960年以降の現代美術にとって特に求められており、それを第3世代の美術館と呼べるだろうが、このNAGI-MOCAはその典型的な範例となっている。
（磯崎新）

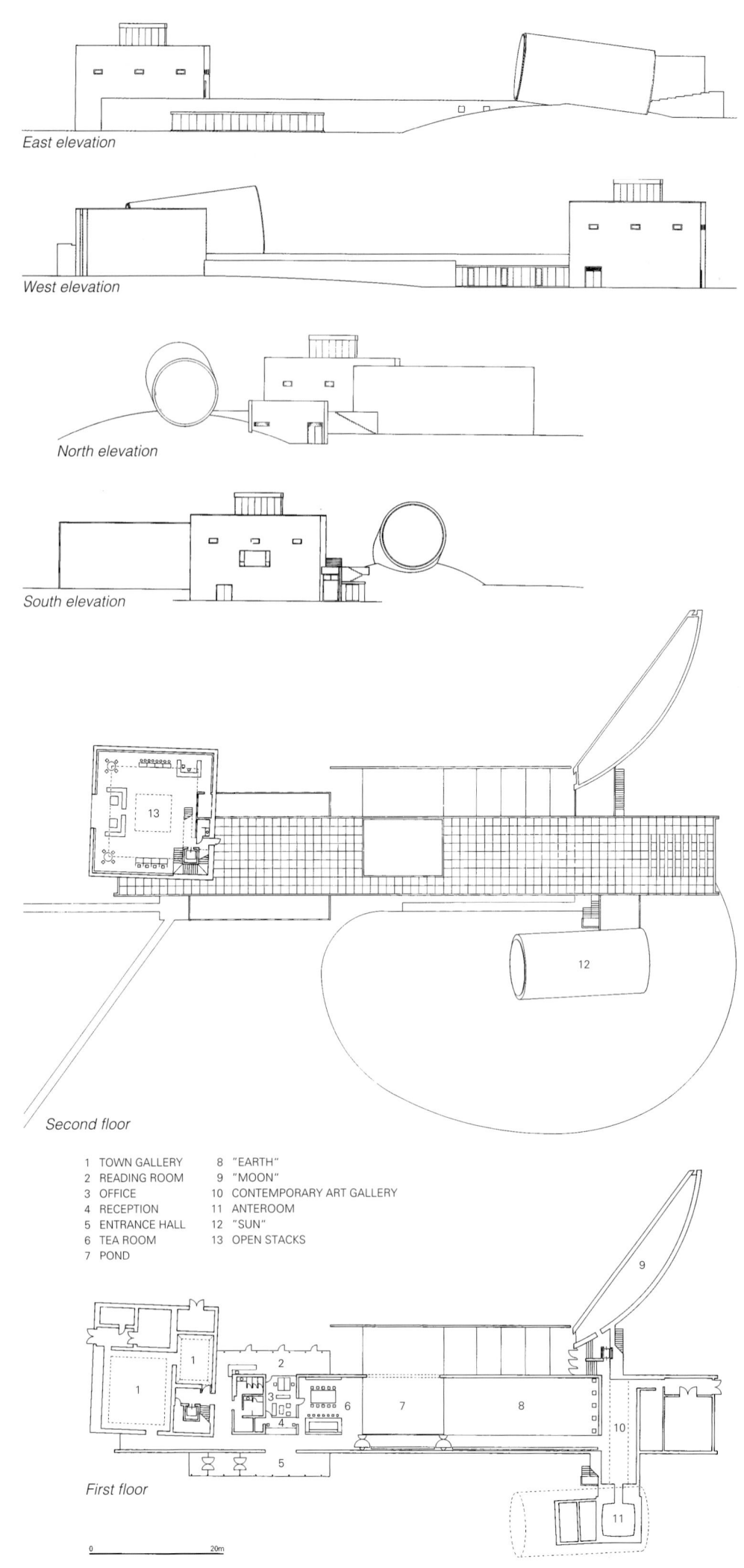

East elevation

West elevation

North elevation

South elevation

Second floor

1 TOWN GALLERY
2 READING ROOM
3 OFFICE
4 RECEPTION
5 ENTRANCE HALL
6 TEA ROOM
7 POND
8 "EARTH"
9 "MOON"
10 CONTEMPORARY ART GALLERY
11 ANTEROOM
12 "SUN"
13 OPEN STACKS

First floor

Entrance hall　エントランス・ホール

Library　図書館

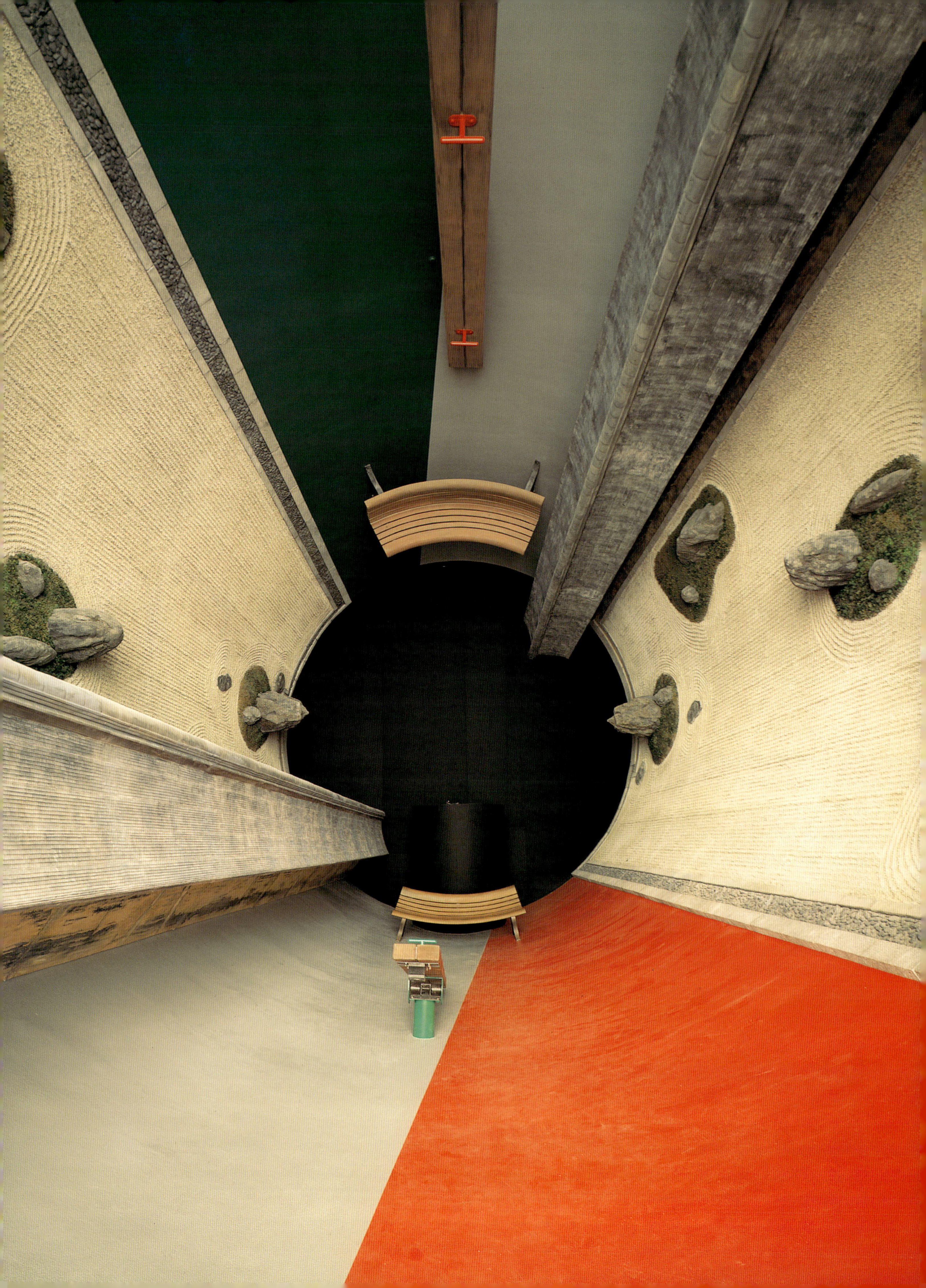

◁ *Shusaku Arakawa: "Sun"*　荒川修作："太陽"

Kazuo Okazaki: "Moon"　岡崎和郎："月"

1991–94
JEAN NOUVEL

CARTIER FOUNDATION
Paris, France

Overall view 全景

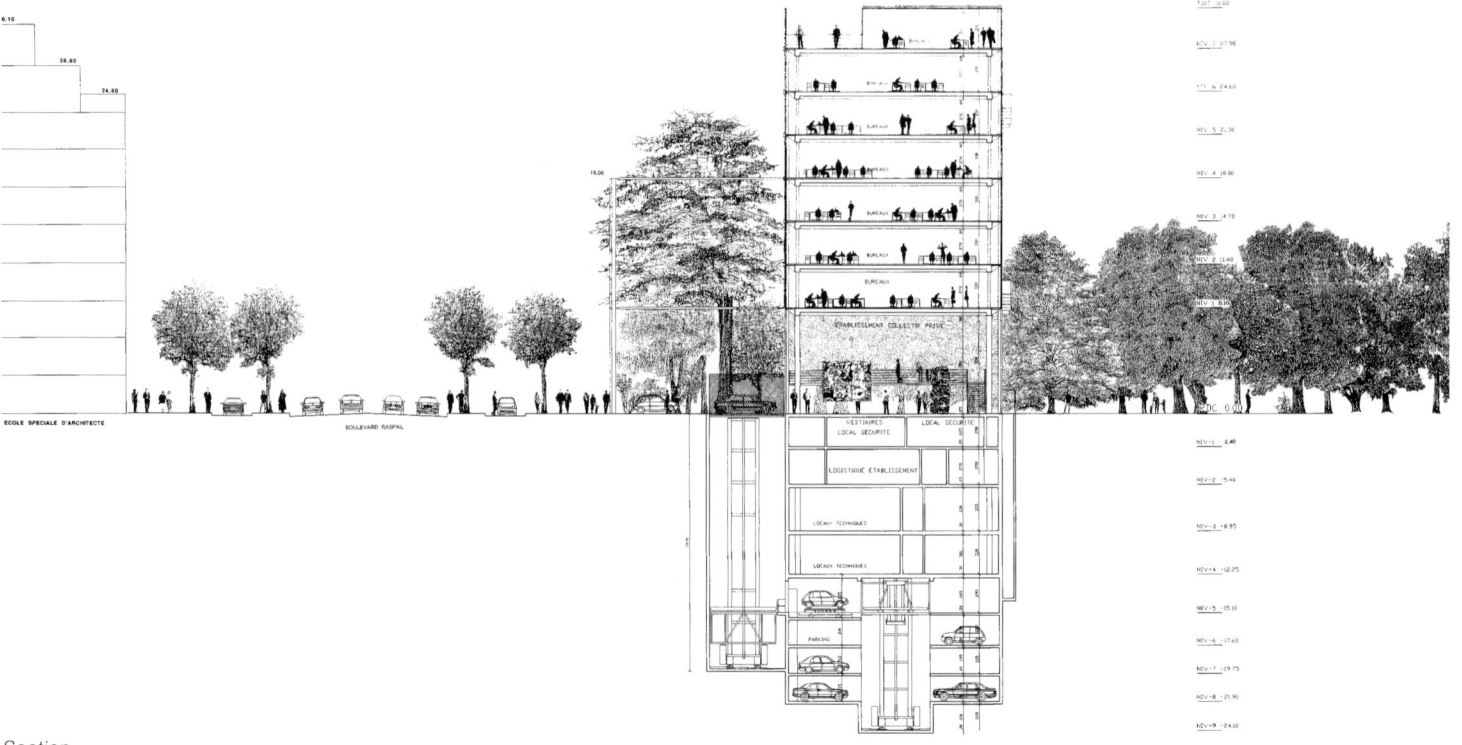

Section

Layer of glazed walls ガラス壁のレイヤー

Program
4,000 square meters of offices for Cartier France. 1,600 square meters for the Cartier Foundation for Contemporary Art, including exhibition space. 800 square meters of technical premises (123 parking places). 4,000 square meters of garden.

Feature
A superstructure which equals the substructure (16 Levels, eight of which are underground). An automated parking garage. Eight-meter high sliding glass doors at the garden level.

Materials
A Light architecture of fine steel netting and glass which required: 650 tons of steel. 5,000 square meters of glass panes.

Lighting
The building establishes subtle and direct exchanges with the neighborhood, boulevard and park, through the versatile play of transparency, reflection and refraction. which provides the site with both aesthetic and sensorial dimensions, whether it be the exhibition galleries at the ground and lower levels, or the office spaces on the upper floors.

Office area layout
Following a strict pattern which repeats on each of the seven upper levels, the offices are comfortably insulated from sound and open to outside light. The layout aims at giving the areas maximum lightness and fluidity while concealing the heaviness and the opaqueness of the volumes. For instance, the partitions are made of glass frosted in gradations, framed with thin metallic structures which are echoed in the geometry of the encased carpets. The ceilings offer the uninterrupted surface of a fine metallic net punctuated by diffused lighting. The desks themselves, whose very thin tops are lacquered with gray epoxy, conform to the minimal geometry which, in turn, agrees with strict parallelepipedic shapes of the filing cabinets. This conception evidences a will for uniformity which legitimizes diversity solely through the expression of individuals and their movements, to the exclusion of referenced furnishing designs.

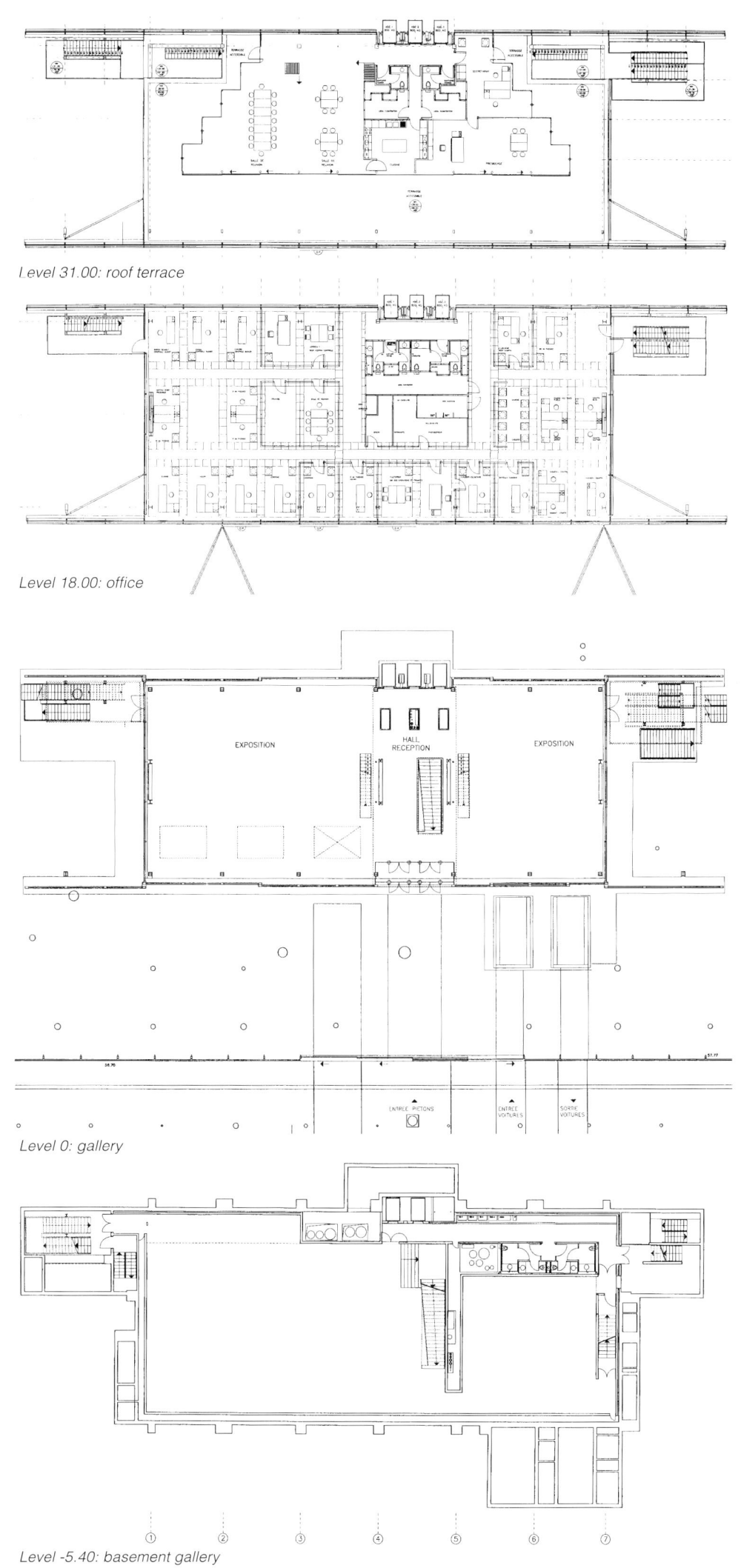

Level 31.00: roof terrace

Level 18.00: office

Level 0: gallery

Level -5.40: basement gallery

243

Gallery　ギャラリー

Night view　夜景

プログラム

カルティエ・フランス社のオフィス：4,000m²。カルティエ現代芸術財団（展示空間も含め）：1,600m²。機械室（123台収容の駐車場を含む）：800m²。庭園：4,000m²。

特徴

サブストラクチャーと同等のスーパーストラクチャー（16階建てのうち8層は地下）。自動制御の駐車場。庭園階にある8mのガラス引戸。

材料

ファイン・スティールの網とガラスによる軽量の建築には、スティール650トン、ガラス板の総面積5,000m²を必要とした。

照明

建物は、透明性、反射、屈折のめまぐるしい変化によって、近隣、大通り、公園と微妙で直接的な交換をつくりだし、これによって、1階および低層階の展示ギャラリーであろうと上階のオフィス空間であろうと、美的で感覚中枢的なディメンションが生まれる。

オフィス・レイアウト

地上7層に反復されている厳格なパターンに従って、オフィスは心地よく防音され、外光に開放されている。レイアウトの意図は、建物のこの部分の重さと不透明さを隠しながら、このエリアに最大限の明るさと流動性を与えることである。たとえば、カーペットの縁取りの幾何学に呼応させて、細いメタリックな枠組みをとり、グラデーションをつけたすりガラスの間仕切り。天井は、拡散光の強調する薄いメタル・ネットで一面覆われている。事務机の非常に薄い甲板は灰色のエポキシにラッカー仕上げで、ミニマルな幾何学に対応させ、ファイリング・キャビネットの厳格な台形に合わせている。このコンセプトには、関連する家具デザインは除外して、個人とその動きの表現を通してのみ多様性を正当化しようという同質性への意志が明らかである。

Gallery　ギャラリー

Roof terrace　屋上テラス

Reception　レセプション

1991–95
YOSHIO TANIGUCHI

TOYOTA MUNICIPAL MUSEUM OF ART
Aichi, Japan

Approach アプローチ

The program consists of galleries for the permanent collection of modern/contemporary arts and temporary exhibitions, galleries devoted to the lacquer artist Setsuro Takahashi, art library, lecture hall, restaurant and museum shop.

The place has once served as an elementary school with a distinguished history. A section of a castle that was originally built in 1782 has been restored and now stands right next to the museum. The site itself overlooks an urban scenery that has newly developed since Toyota Motor Corporation has established its factory in this city. The museum's choice of location was made as a clear demonstration of the flow of time that exists within the site's past and present, affording both the western view to the new city and the eastern historic landscape. Various functions are distributed onto three levels by taking advantage of the vertical interval of the site. The lowest level accommodates administrative offices and the loading, the upper level the main entrance for museum visitors, and the top level a garden.

The overall building is composed of the 3 volumes that make up the museum—permanent exhibition space, temporary exhibition

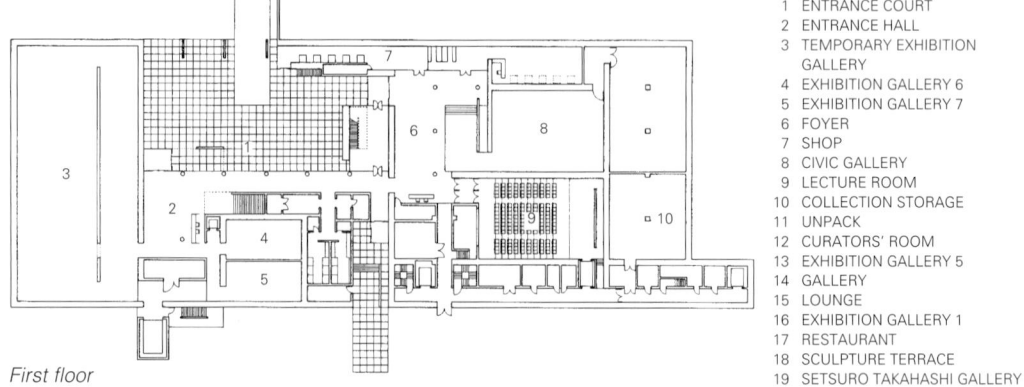

1 ENTRANCE COURT
2 ENTRANCE HALL
3 TEMPORARY EXHIBITION GALLERY
4 EXHIBITION GALLERY 6
5 EXHIBITION GALLERY 7
6 FOYER
7 SHOP
8 CIVIC GALLERY
9 LECTURE ROOM
10 COLLECTION STORAGE
11 UNPACK
12 CURATORS' ROOM
13 EXHIBITION GALLERY 5
14 GALLERY
15 LOUNGE
16 EXHIBITION GALLERY 1
17 RESTAURANT
18 SCULPTURE TERRACE
19 SETSURO TAKAHASHI GALLERY
20 EXHIBITION GALLERY 2
21 EXHIBITION GALLERY 3
22 EXHIBITION GALLERY 4

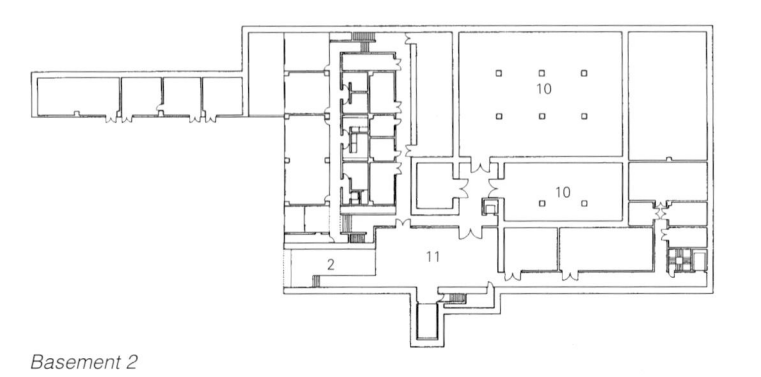

First floor

Basement 2

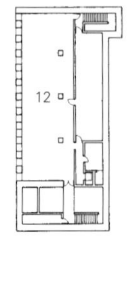

Basement 1

近代および現代美術を展示する常設の展示室と、企画展示室、漆工芸家の高橋節郎氏のための展示室と、美術図書室、講堂、レストラン、ミュージアムショップなどから構成される。

敷地はかつて歴史ある小学校が建っていた場所であり、隣地には1782年に築城された城の一部が復元されて建っている。また一方で敷地はトヨタ自動車がこの市に工場を建設して以来、新しく発展した市街地を眼下に見下ろす場所にある。美術館は、この敷地の過去と現在という時の流れを顕在化するため、西側の新しい都市への景観と、東側の歴史的景観が同時に望める場所を選んで配置された。敷地の3つの高低差を利用して、立体的な機能配分を行っている。一番低いレベルには事務管理関係の諸室と搬入口を置き、中間のレベルには来館者のための正面入口、そして一番高いレベルは庭園として整備している。

建築外観はこの美術館を構成する3つのヴォリューム——常設展示室、企画展示室、高橋節郎館と、それらを結ぶ回廊によって構成される。これら3つの展示空間は、収蔵庫、機械室、事務管理室などをそれらの下層で共有する。中央の半透明のガラスで覆われた白いヴォリュームは、常設展示室である。昼間は半透明ガラスを通る自然光により、内部を均質に明るくする。夜は反対に内部からの光によって建物は庭園に浮かび上がることになる。西洋や日本の近代美術は、このガラスの箱の内部をさらに区画した中に展示される。

建物の両端部の緑の石で覆われたヴォリュームは、企画展示室と高橋節郎館である。企画展示室はスカイライトから自然光が入る無柱の大空間であり、高橋節郎館は特に漆の展示に必要な機能と意匠を備えた展示空間となっている。

美術館周囲の庭園設計は、ピーター・ウォーカーとの協同による。

Entrance court エントランス・コート

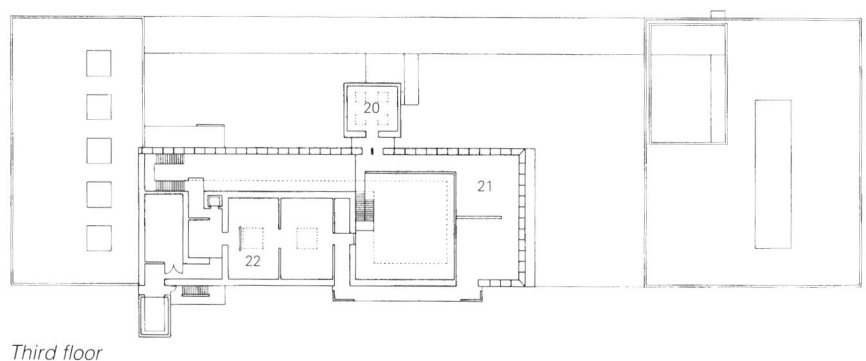

Third floor

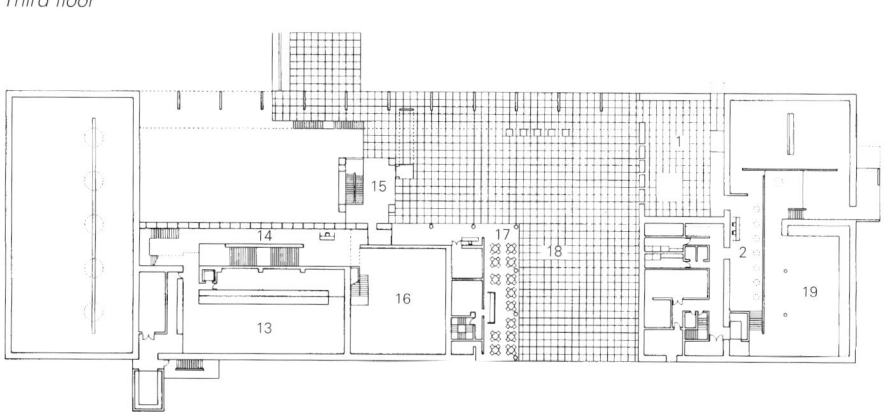

Second floor

space, and Setsuro Takahashi Gallery, and of the corridors that link them. The 3 exhibition spaces share the storage, machine room and administrative offices in the lower layer. The white volume in the center covered with semi-transparent glass houses the permanent exhibition. Inside, natural light passing through the translucent glass provides a homogeneous lighting during the day. In night time, the building is illuminated by light coming from the inside, and floats in the garden. The interior of this glass box is partitioned to display Western and Japanese modern arts and crafts.

Covered with green stone, the volumes at both ends of the building are the temporary exhibition space and Setsuro Takahashi Gallery respectively. The former is a columnless space of large size filled with natural light from the skylight, and the latter is a special gallery equipped with functions and designs required for exhibition of lacquer works.

Planning of the garden around the museum was realized in collaboration with Peter Walker.

Evening view 夕景

Overall view from west 西側全景

Sculpture terrace 彫刻テラス

Entrance court エントランス・コート

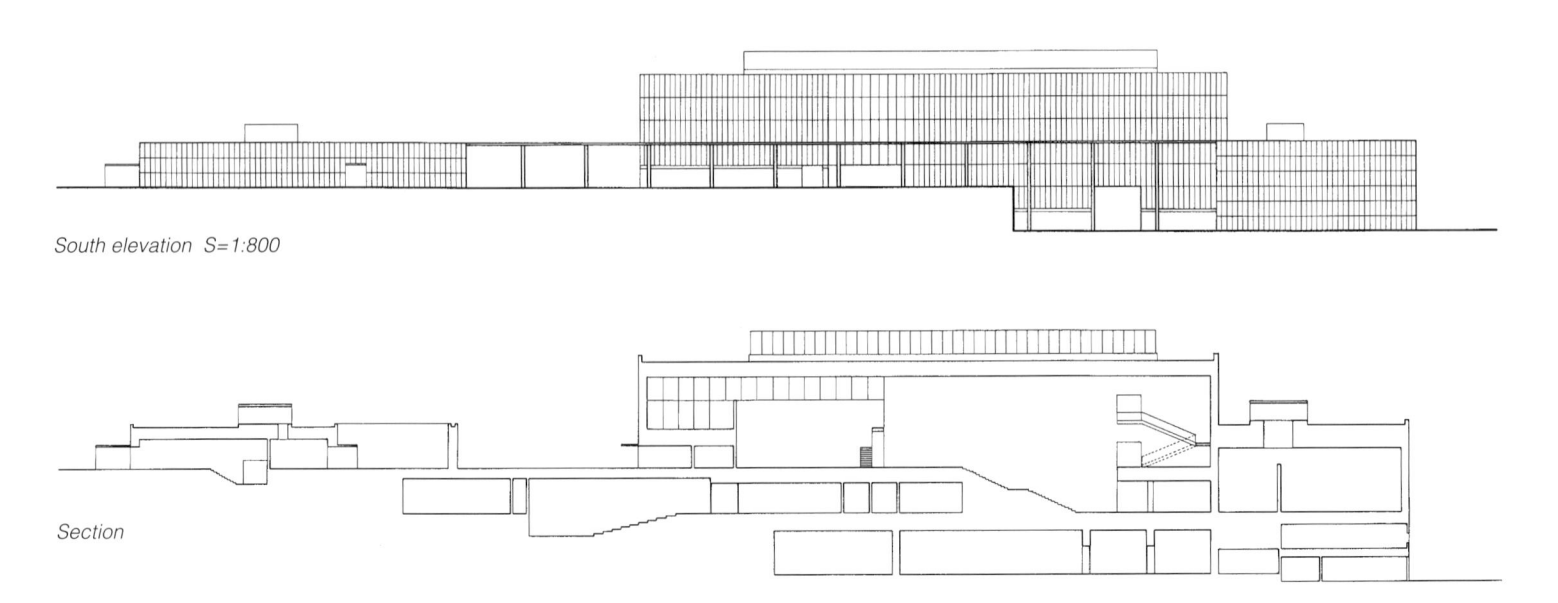

South elevation S=1:800

Section

Entrance court　エントランス・コート

Restaurant　レストラン △▽

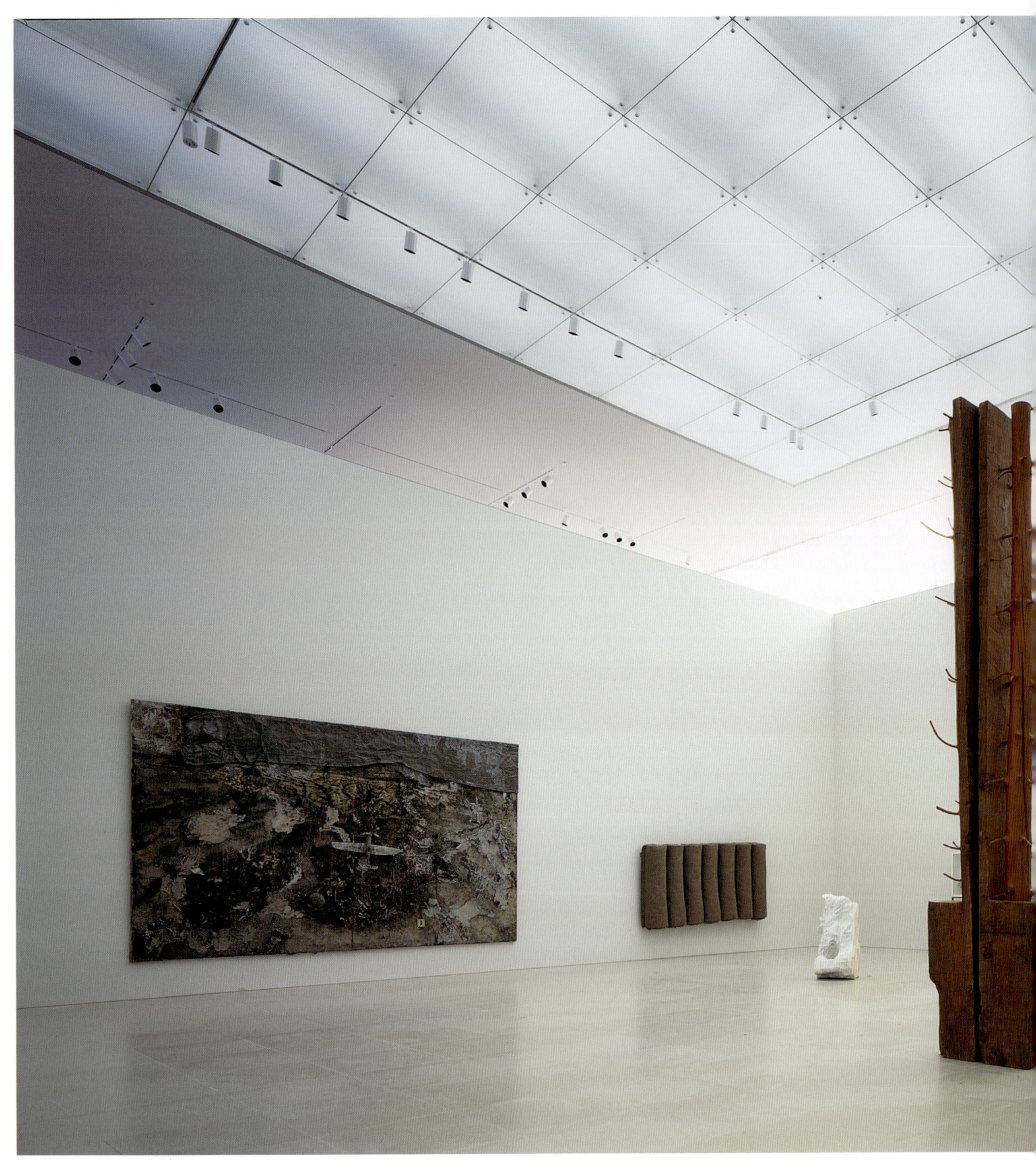

Exhibition gallery 1　展示室1

Exhibition gallery 1: view from exhibition gallery 4 展示室1：展示室4より見る

Gallery ギャラリー

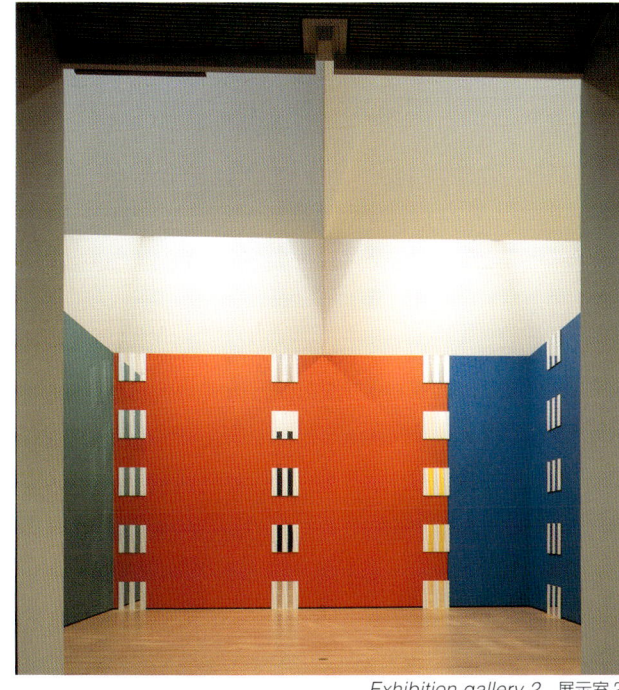

Exhibition gallery 2 展示室2

Entrance court of Setsuro Takahashi Gallery 高橋節郎展示室エントランス・コート

Setsuro Takahashi Gallery 高橋節郎館

Temporary exhibition gallery 企画展示室

Entrance hall of Setsuro Takahashi Gallery 高橋節郎館エントランス・ホール

Setsuro Takahashi Gallery 高橋節郎館展示室

1991–96
OSCAR NIEMEYER

MUSEUM OF CONTEMPORARY ART, RIO DE JANEIRO
Rio de Janeiro, Brazil

Aerial view 航空写真

North view 北より見る

A museum for Brazilian contemporary art from the 1960s up to the 90s, sited on a seaside cliff in the town of Niteròi, a suburb of Rio de Janeiro.

The building is in concrete, finished with white paint. There is dynamism in its shape, widening upward from the prop in the center like a 'champagne glass'. This particular form which is basically a combination of two curves, is a product of Niemeyer's idea rather than structural reasons.

His original architectural style is ever present in this museum: a style of modeling that relies solely on one's sensitivity, free from conventional architectural language. The building's unique silhouette is painted white in order to diminish the characteristic texture of concrete, thereby creating a sense of volume that is in a way unrealistic. Its bold and yet delicate form is a creation of Neimeyer's exceptional sensitivity. As a beautiful lyric poem, the architecture stands among the grandeur of natural landscape and yet emanates its own presence, touching the hearts of all those who visit.

An upward, curving slope leads to the entrance level. The exhibition space is a double-height single volume with high flexibility. Windows along the periphery of the lower level give to a spectacular panorama of the surrounding nature. Office, projection room and restaurant are accommodated in the space below the exhibition level.

ブラジルの60—90年代までの現代美術のための美術館。敷地は、リオ・デ・ジャネイロ郊外の町、ニテロイの、真下に海を望む崖の上である。

建物はコンクリート造で、その外観は白ペンキで仕上げられている。「シャンパン・グラス」の様な、中央の支柱から上にいくにしたがって広がる、ダイナミックな形態である。この形は力学的なカーブというよりも、ニーマイヤーのデザインから生まれたものであり、基本的に2つのカーブの組み合わせによって作られている。

因習的な建築言語に縛られることのない、自らの感性を頼りにした自由な造形による独自の建築スタイルがこの美術館でも発揮されている。この独特のシルエットは白く塗られることでコンクリートの素材感を削がれ、ある種の非現実的な量感を生み出している。その大胆かつ繊細なフォルムは類い希なニーマイヤーの感性の創出であり、美しい叙情詩の建築は壮大な自然の景観の中にあっても、存在感を十分に発散し、訪れる人々に感動を与える。

カーブを描いて上がっていく斜路によってエントランスのあるレベルに到達する。展示空間は2層分で中央に吹抜けを持つ、自由度の高い一室空間である。下層レベルの外周の窓からは壮大な自然のパノラマを鑑賞することが出来る。展示レベルの下にはオフィス、映写室、レストランのためのスペースが置かれる。

View from ramp 斜路より見る

Pool プール

Lower level

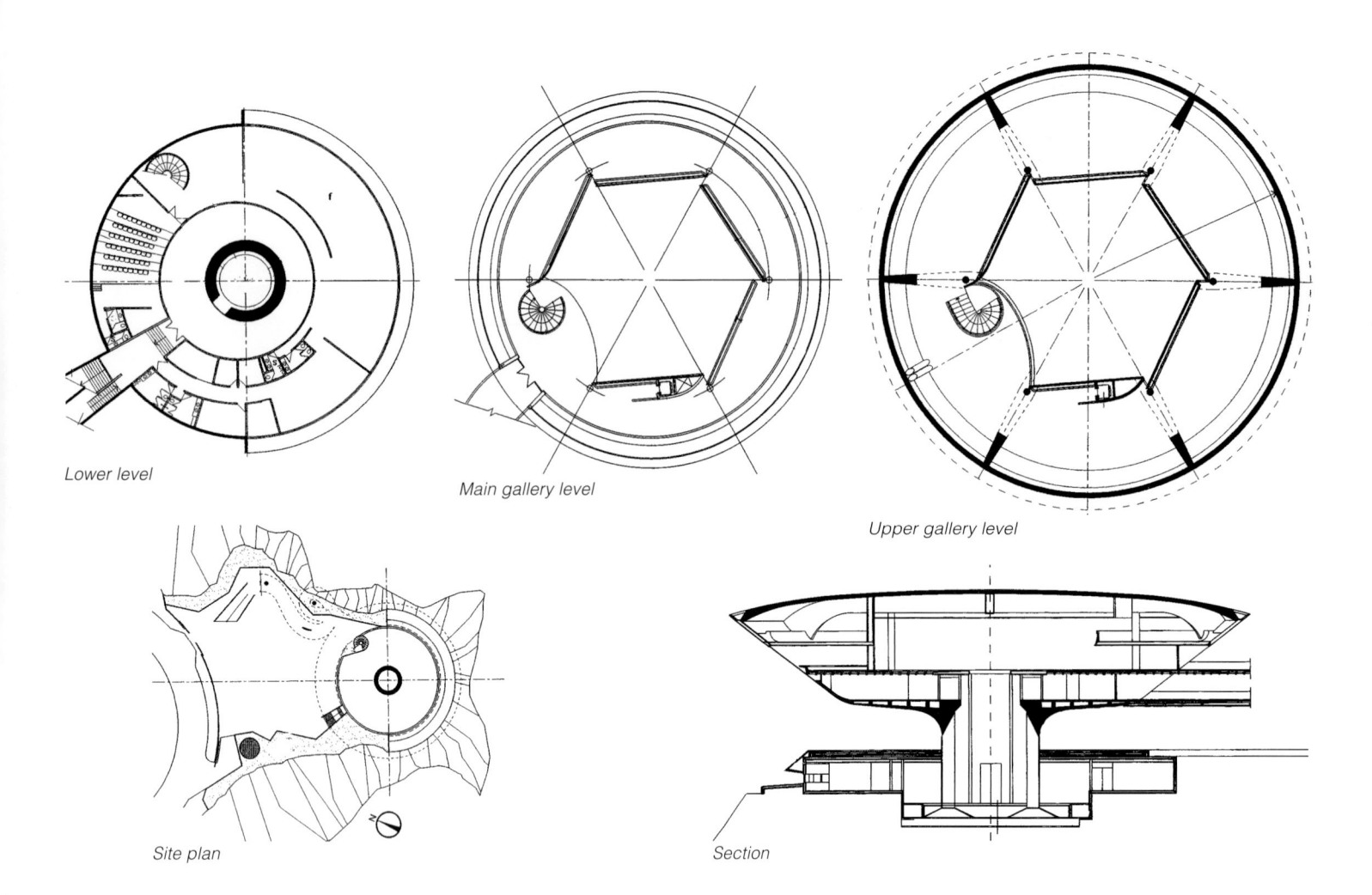

Main gallery level

Upper gallery level

Site plan

Section

▽ Main gallery　メイン・ギャラリー

View from gallery ギャラリーからの眺め △

1991–97
FRANK O. GEHRY

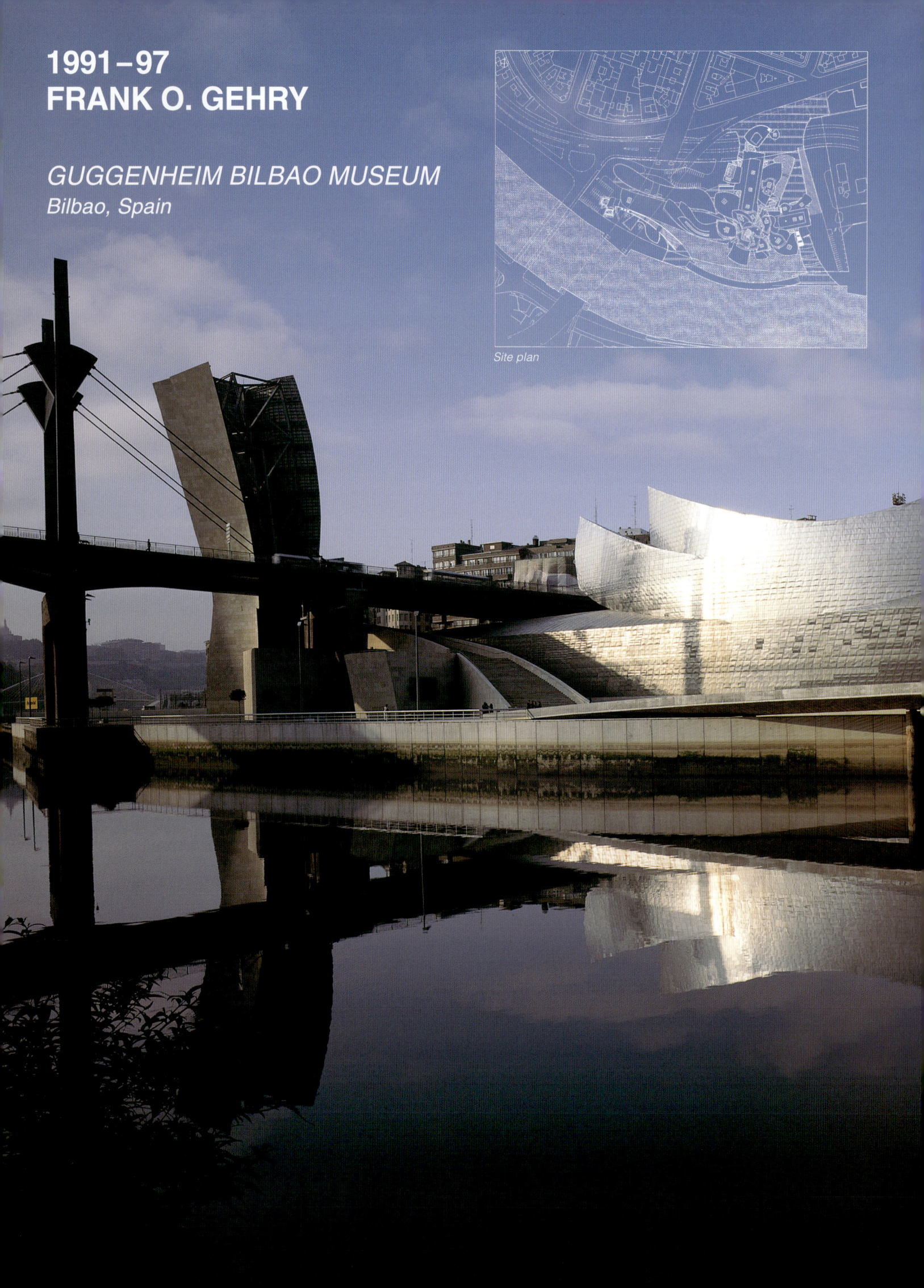

GUGGENHEIM BILBAO MUSEUM
Bilbao, Spain

Site plan

View from north 北より見る

The Museo Guggenheim Bilbao is the result of a unique collaboration between the Basque Country Administration, which finances and owns the project, and the Solomon R. Guggenheim Foundation which will operate the Museum and provide the core art collection. The Museum represents the first step in the redevelopment of the former trade and warehouse district along the south bank of the Nervion River. Directly accessible from the business and historic districts of the city, the Museum marks the center of a cultural triangle formed by the Museo de Bellas Artes, the University, and the Old Town Hall. A public plaza located at the entrance of the Museum encourages pedestrian traffic between the Museum and the Museo de Bellas Artes, and between the Old City and the River Front. The Puente de la Salve Bridge, which connects the 19th-century city center with outlying areas, passes over the site at its eastern edge, lending to the Museum the significance of being a gateway to the city.

The main entrance to the Museum is through a large central atrium, where a system of curvilinear bridges, glass elevators and stair towers connects the exhibition galleries concentrically on three levels. A sculptural roof form rises from the central atrium, flooding it with light through glazed openings. The unprecedented scale of the central atrium, rising to a height of more than 50 meters above the river, is an invitation to monumental site-specific installations and special Museum events.

The Guggenheim Foundation required gallery spaces to exhibit a permanent collection, a temporary collection, and a collection of selected living artists. In response to this requirement, three distinct types of exhibition space were designed. The permanent collection will be housed in two sets of three consecutively-arranged square galleries, stacked at each of the second and third levels of the Museum. The temporary collection will be housed in a dramatic elongated rectangular gallery that extends to the east, passing beneath the Puente de la Salve Bridge and terminating in a tower on its far side. The collection of selected living artists will be housed in a series of curvilinear galleries placed throughout the Museum, allowing the work to be viewed in relation to the permanent and temporary collections.

The major exterior materials of the Museum are Spanish limestone and titanium panels, with the rectangular shapes of the building clad in limestone and the more sculptural shapes of the building clad in titanium. Large glazed curtain walls provide views of the river and the surrounding city.

The design of the Museo Guggenheim Bilbao is influenced by the scale and the texture of the city of Bilbao, and it recalls the historic building materials of the River Front, thus demonstrating a thoughtful response to the historic, economic, and cultural traditions of the area.

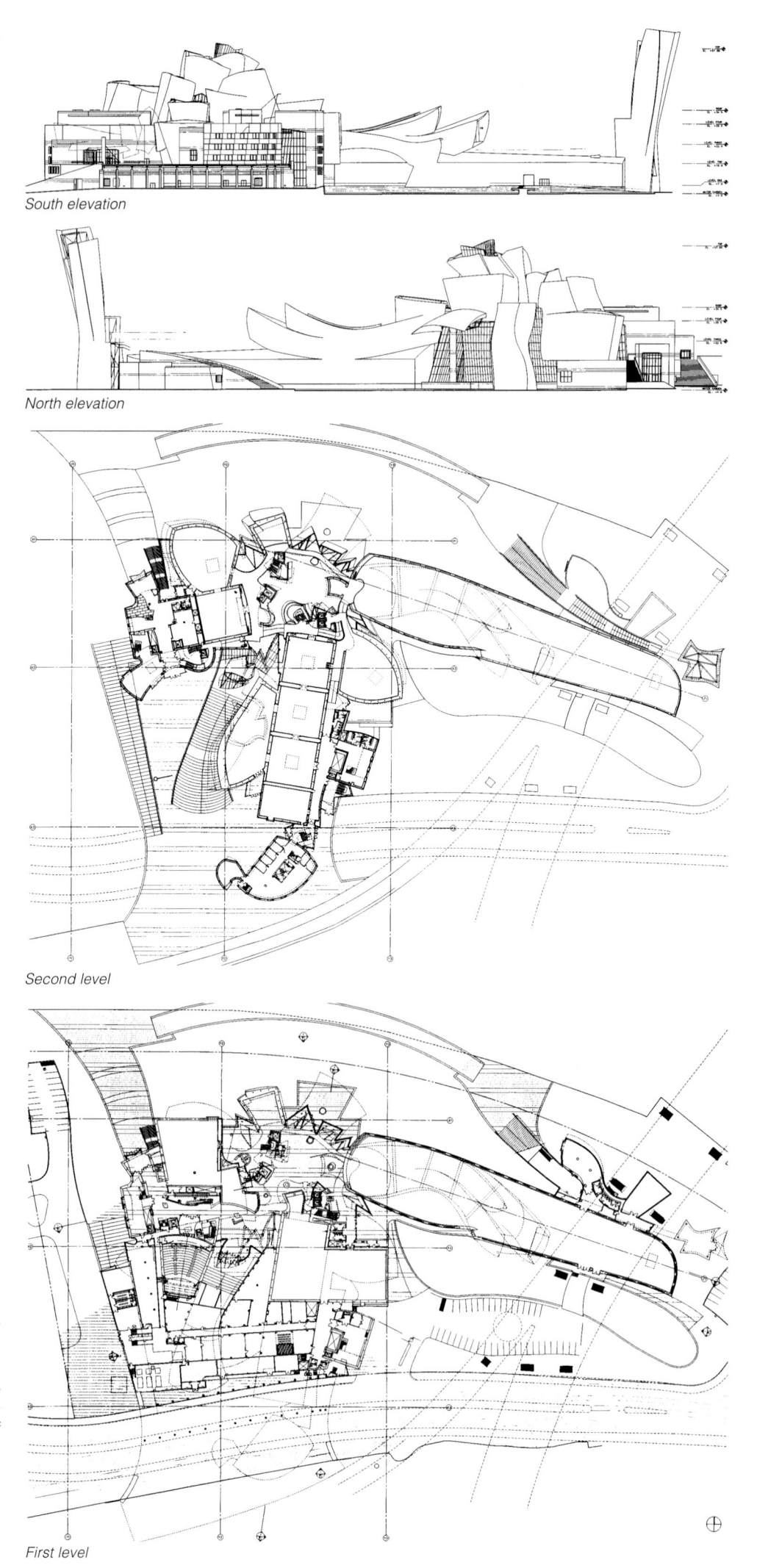

South elevation

North elevation

Second level

First level

ビルバオ・グッゲンハイム美術館は、建物の工費を負担しオーナーとなるバスク地方政府と、美術館の運営を担当し、中心となる展示作品を提供するソロモン・R・グッゲンハイム財団の間のユニークな協力関係によって実現した。美術館は、ネルビオン川の南堤に沿ったかつての商業倉庫街を再開発するための第一歩となる。街のビジネス及び歴史地区から直接行けるこの美術館は、ムセオ・デ・ベジャス・アルテス、大学、旧市庁舎の形成する文化トライアングルの中心を構成する。美術館入口前の公共広場は、この美術館とムセオ・デ・ベジャス・アルテスの間、そして旧市街とリヴァー・フロントの間の歩行者の往来を促進させる。19世紀の中心街を外側に広がる地区と結ぶプエンテ・デ・ラ・サルベ橋が、敷地の東端を横切り、この美術館に市内への門の意味を与えている。

美術館へのメイン・エントランスは中央の大アトリウムを経由して行く。ここでは、湾曲するブリッジ、ガラスのエレベータ、階段塔がこの中心を共有して3層に展開する展示ギャラリーを連絡している。彫刻的な屋根の形は、中央アトリウムから立ち上がり、ガラスの填められた開口を通して、アトリウムを光で満たしている。川面から50メートル以上の高さを持つ中央アトリウムのかつて類を見ないスケールは、途方もない大きさのサイト・スペシフィックなインスタレーションや特別なイベントを誘発するだろう。

グッゲンハイム財団は、常設展、企画展、現在活躍中の芸術家のなかから選んだ作品のためのギャラリーを要求した。この要求に答えて、それぞれに明確に異なった性格を持つ3つのギャラリーを設計した。常設展示のためのギャラリーは、連続する3つの四角いギャラリー二組で構成され、美術館の2階と3階に重ねられている。企画展は、東に向かってプエンテ・デ・ラ・サルベ橋の下を過ぎて終端にあるタワーの所まで長く引き伸ばされた長方形のドラマチックなギャラリーで行われる。活躍中のアーティストの作品は、美術館全体に配置された曲線で囲まれたギャラリーで展示される。これによって、常設展や企画展の作品との関係のなかでそれらの作品を観賞出来る。

建物の外壁に使われている主要な材料はスペイン産の石灰石とチタンのパネルで、矩形の部分は石灰石、彫刻的な形態の部分にはチタンを用いている。ガラスの大カーテンウォールからは、川や街の景色が見晴らせる。

ビルバオ・グッゲンハイムのデザインはビルバオの街のスケールやテクスチュアからの影響を受けており、リバー・フロントの古い建物の材料を思い出させる。これによって、リバー・フロント地区の歴史・経済・文化的伝統に応答している。

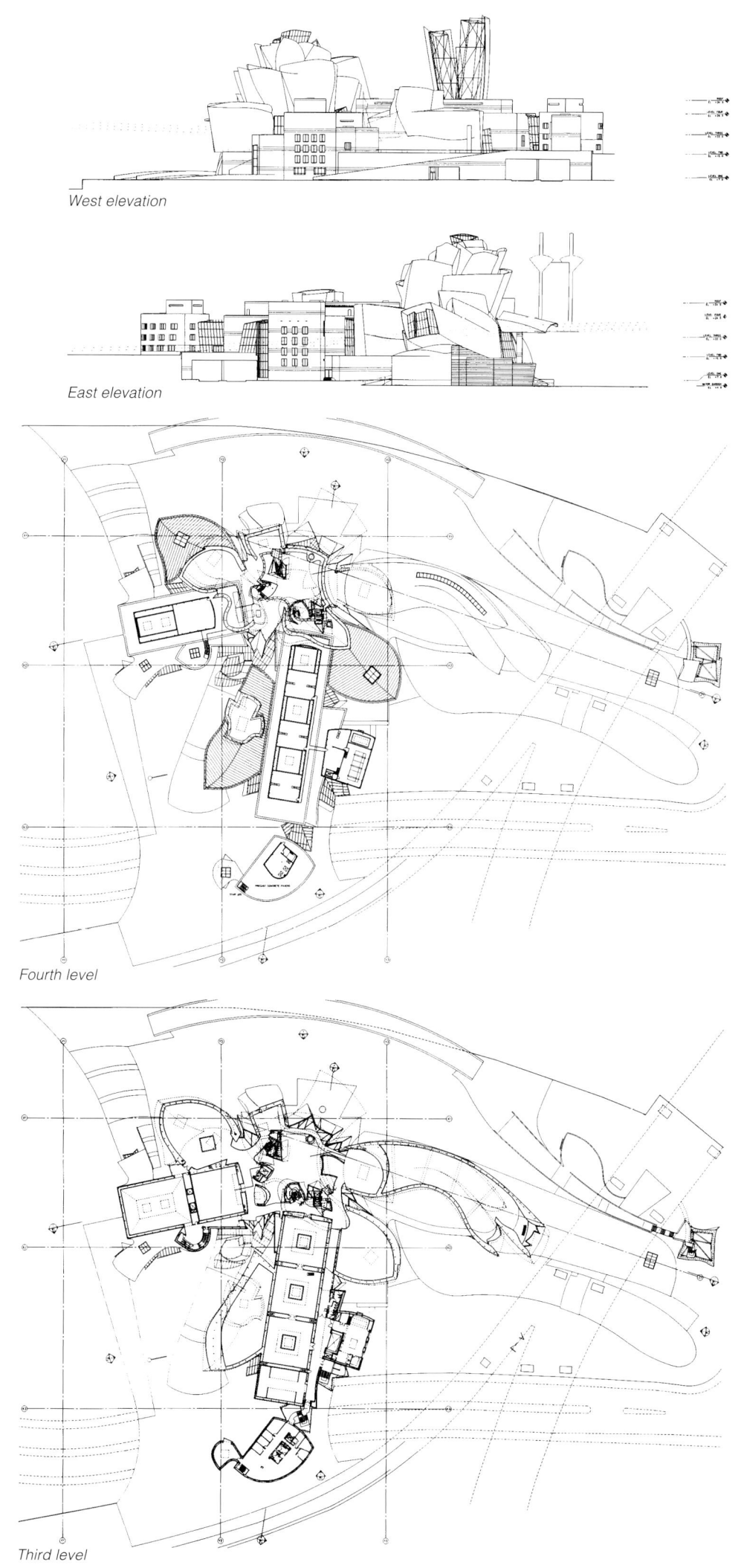

West elevation

East elevation

Fourth level

Third level

Main entrance　メイン・エントランス

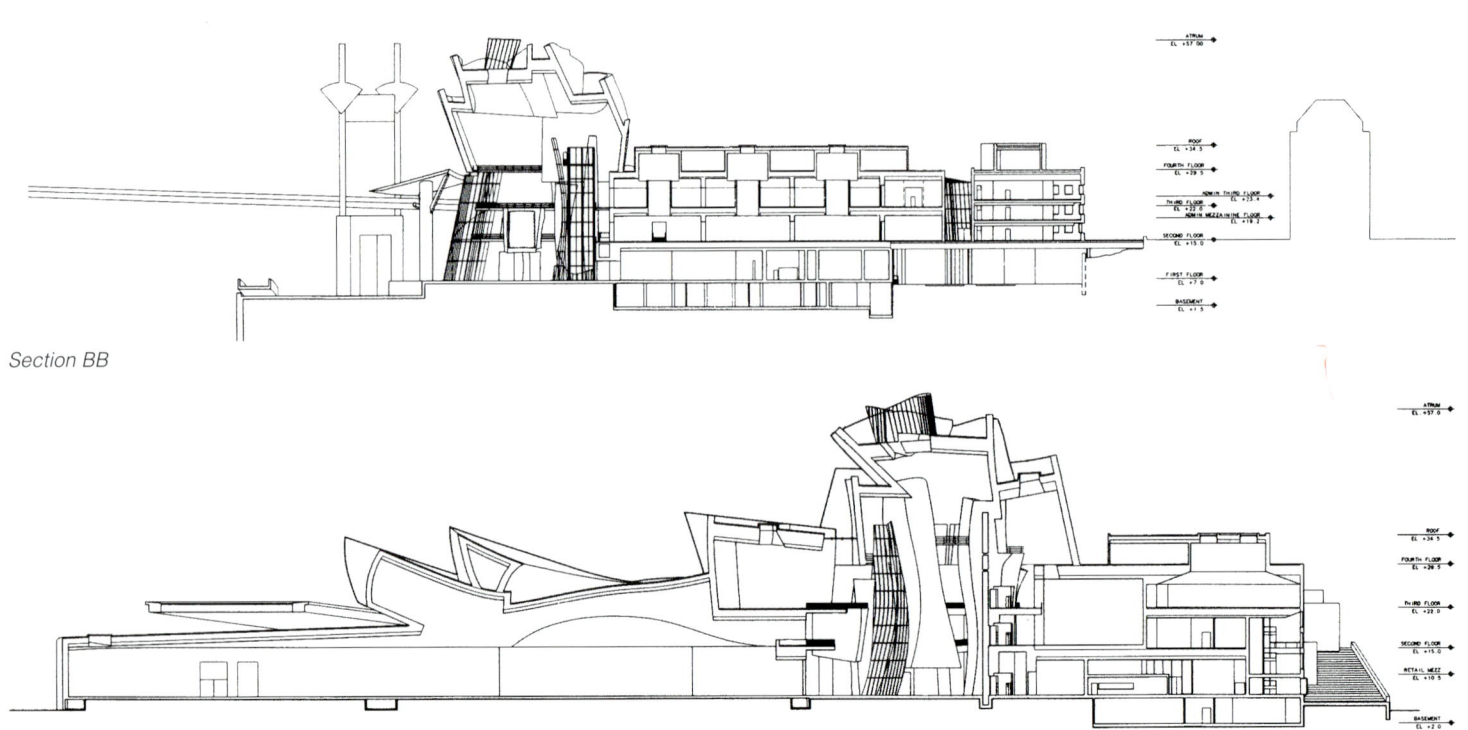

Section BB

Section AA

North elevation 北面

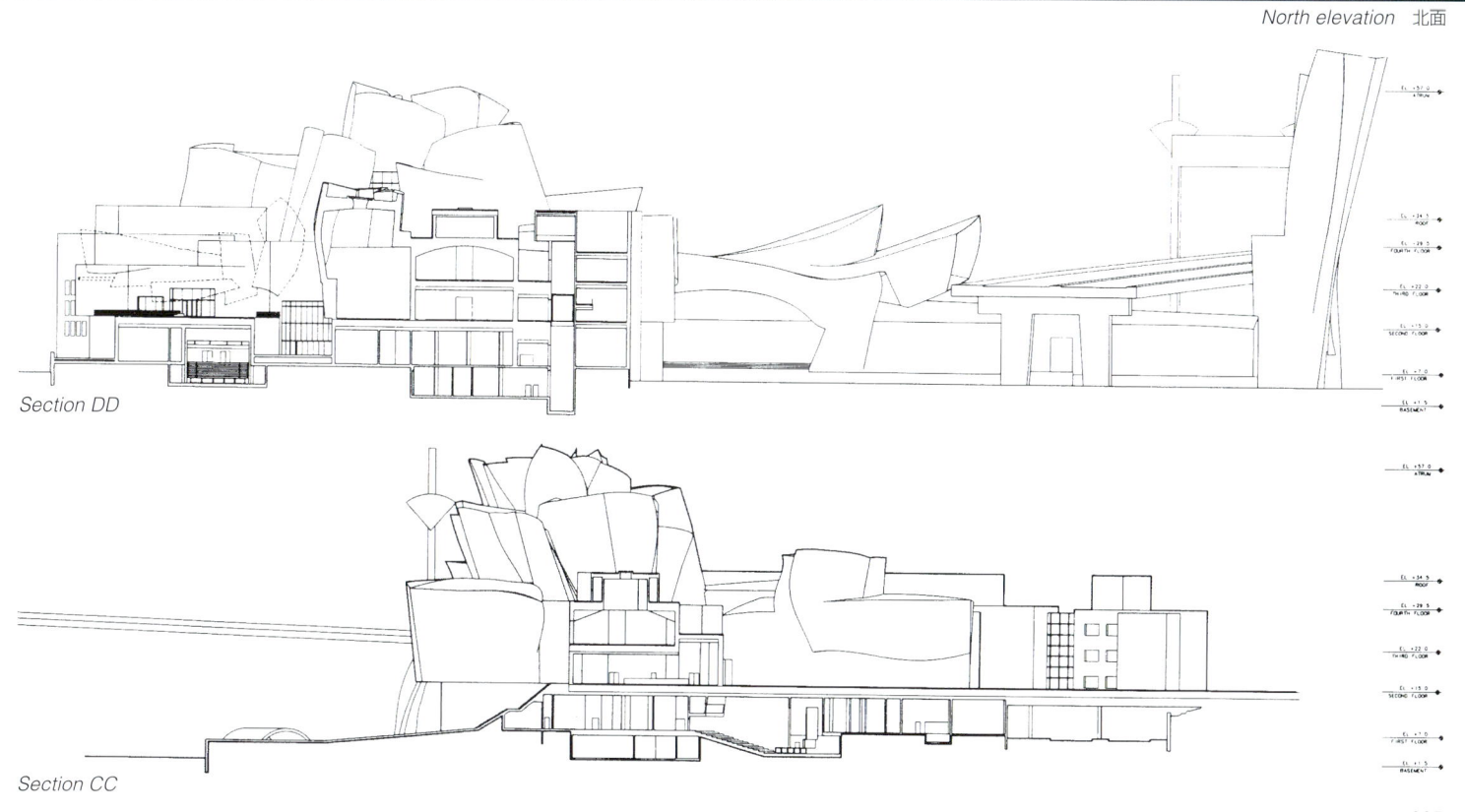

Section DD

Section CC

265

Atrium: view toward north　アトリウム：北を見る

Atrium: view toward east　アトリウム：東を見る ▷

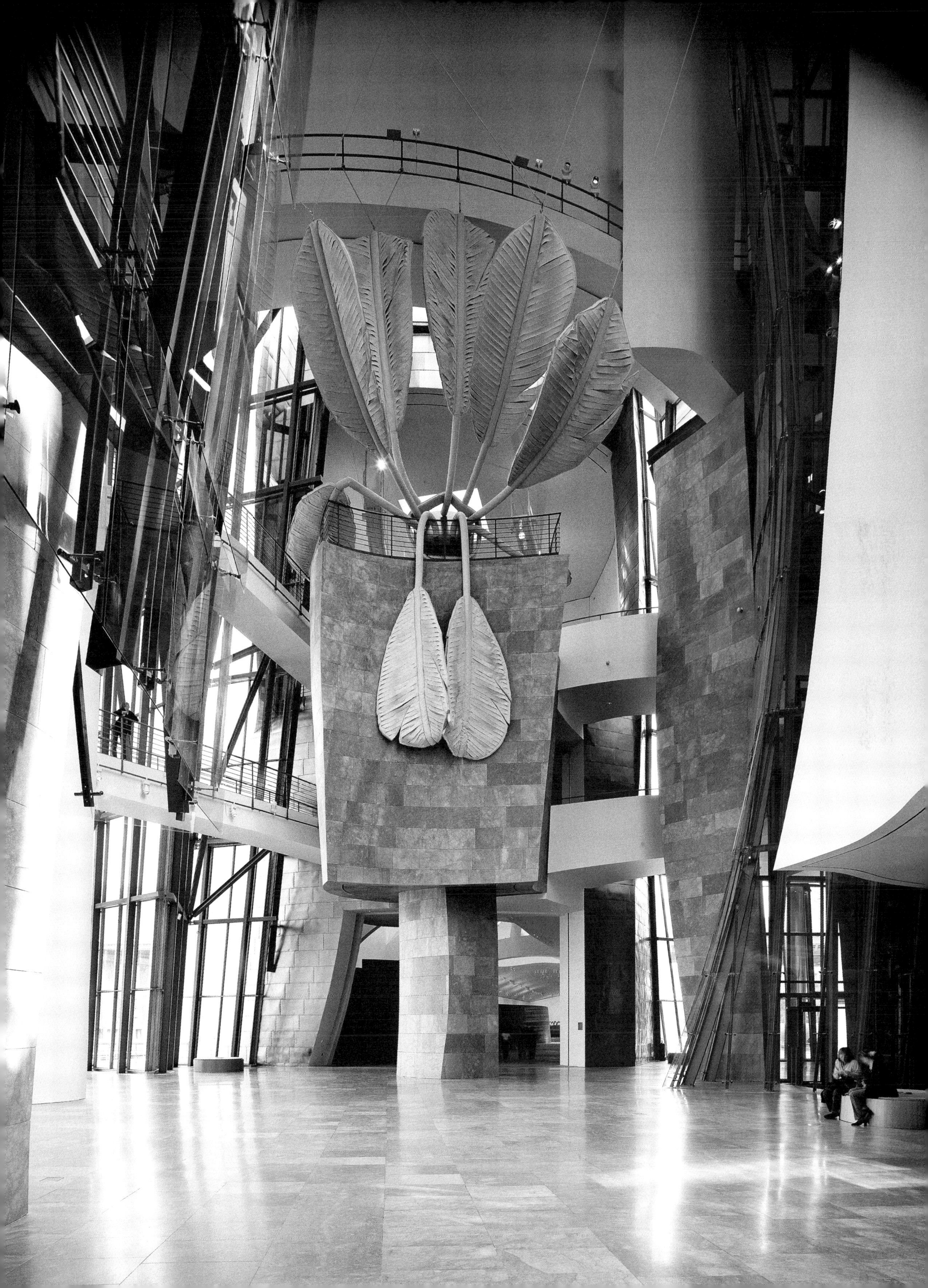

Gallery 104　104展示室

Atrium: upward view アトリウム：見上げ

Atrium: downward view アトリウム：見下ろし

Bridge on third level　3階ブリッジ

Third level　3階

Gallery 304　304展示室

Gallery 209　209展示室

Gallery 304　304展示室 ▷

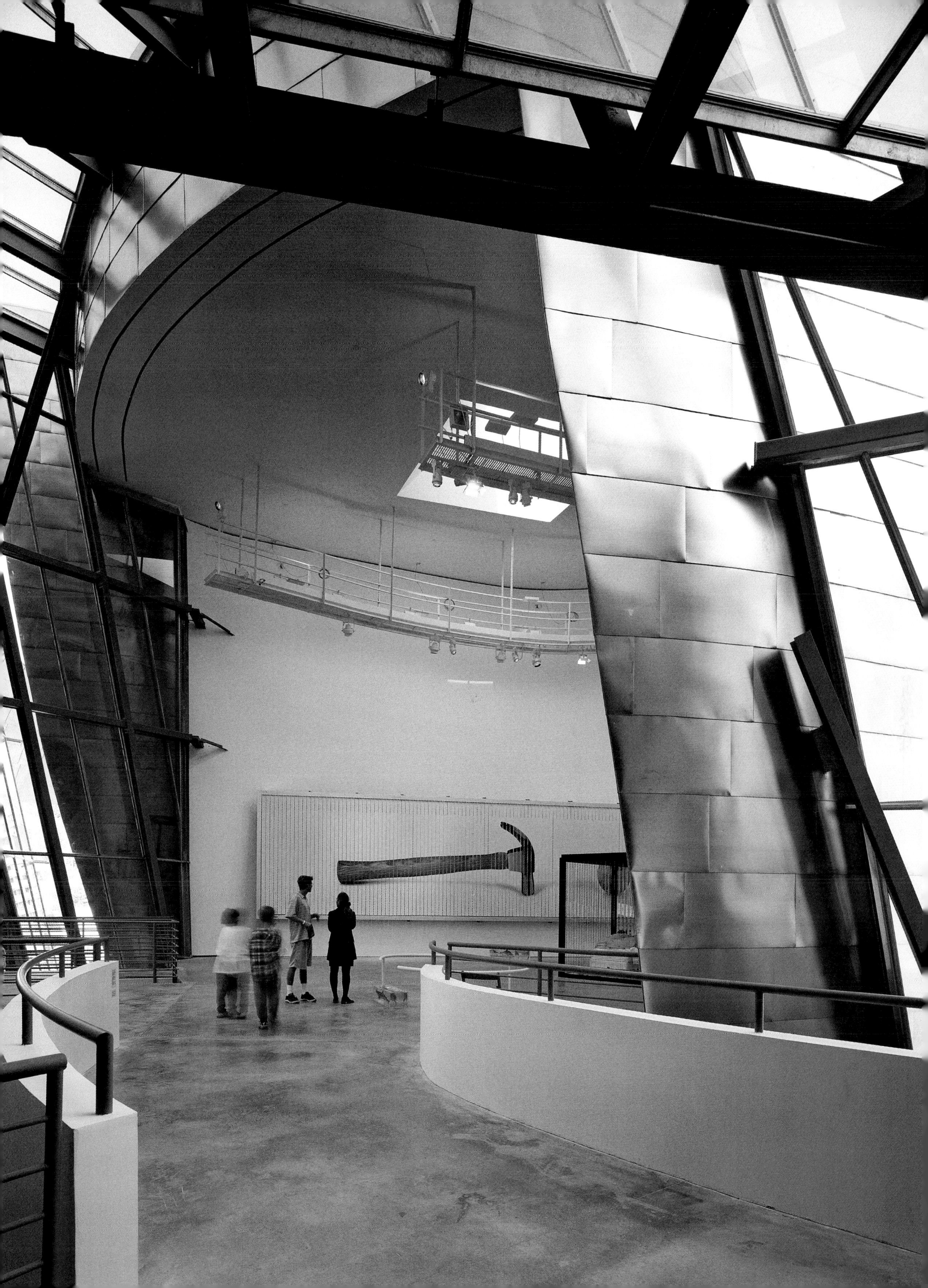

1991–99
ÁLVARO SIZA

CONTEMPORARY ART MUSEUM OF OPORTO
Oporto, Portugal

Overall view from north　北側全景

Entrance court　エントランス・コート

Entrance hall　エントランス・ホール

Site
The project for the new Museum of Contemporary Art of Oporto is being built in the Quinta de Serralves, a property comprising a large house surrounded by gardens, woods and meadows, which was commissioned by the Count of Vizela in the 1930's to serve as his private house. The Museum develops a new nucleus. autonomous and independent from the existing ones, that will absorb most of the functions now performed in the main house.

Shape
A longitudinal axis, set in an approximately north/south direction, serves as the frame for the development of the project. This axis takes the direction of the pre-existing paths of the vegetable garden.

In a morphological description of the building, we have a main body from which two asymmetrical wings are generated southward, creating between them a courtyard, and an L-shaped volume set to the North, creating between itself and the central body another courtyard, in the area of public access to the building.

The volume of the building is defined by vertical surfaces covered with stone or stucco; the top of these walls keep a constant level, while the bottom accompanies the variations of the changing ground.

Museum
The public access to the Museum's grounds is made at the highest level of the terrain through an opening in the existing wall that surrounds the property. This opening gives access to a patio where also converge the staircase and elevator coming from the subterranean car park, and paths coming from different gardens. A gallery leads to a large courtyard that gives access to the interior of the museum and, through an independent entrance, to the auditorium foyer.

Next to the Museum's entrance is placed a reception and information desk. From this space there is a passage to a square atrium with double height and a roof light, This atrium is centred on the longitudinal and transversal axes that define the building. The positioning of openings in this and adjacent rooms prolongs visually the axiallity to the outside in all cardinal directions.

Besides functioning as the geometrical generator and centre of the building, this main hall constitutes a distribution space from which the public may have access to the different facilities the Museum has to offer:
On the entrance floor—Exhibition Rooms, Book shop and Gift shop
On the upper floor—Cafeteria and Esplanade
On the lower floor—Library and Auditorium

The exhibition area is divided into several rooms, with different features of scale, proportion, light, and types of openings. These rooms are connected by a large, U-shaped gallery. The exhibition space occupies most of the entrance level, extending to the lower floor in one of the wings.

The doors that connect the different rooms can be used to create different routes or organize separate exhibitions simultaneously.

敷地
ポルト現代美術館の敷地は、庭園、林、小川に囲まれた大邸宅のあるキンタ・デ・セラルヴェスのなかにある。この屋敷は、1930年代にヴィゼーラ伯爵の私邸として建設が始まった。美術館は、母屋でこれまで行われてきた機能の大半を吸収し、独立した新しい中心を構成する。

形態
ほぼ南北に置かれた長手方向の軸線は、建物構成を展開するためのフレームの役割を果たす。この軸線は野菜畑を通っていた道の方位に合わせている。

建物の形態構成を説明すると、主屋から2本のウィングが非対称に南に向かって延び、その間にコートヤードが生まれ、L形のヴォリュームが北側に置かれて、主屋との間に、建物への一般のア

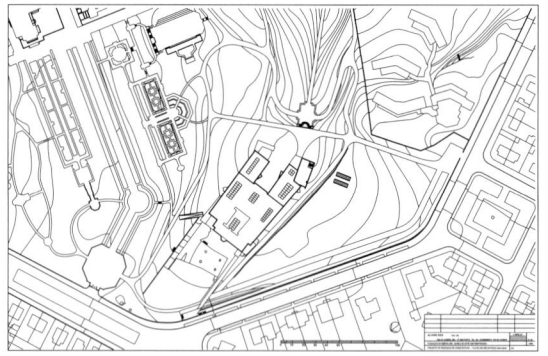

1 SERVICE ENTRANCE
2 STORAGE
3 GALLERY
4 LIBRARY
5 AUDITORIUM
6 OFFICE
7 FOYER
8 ENTRANCE
9 PATIO
10 SHOP
11 HALL
12 ADMINISTRATION
13 CAFETERIA
14 TERRACE
15 PARKING

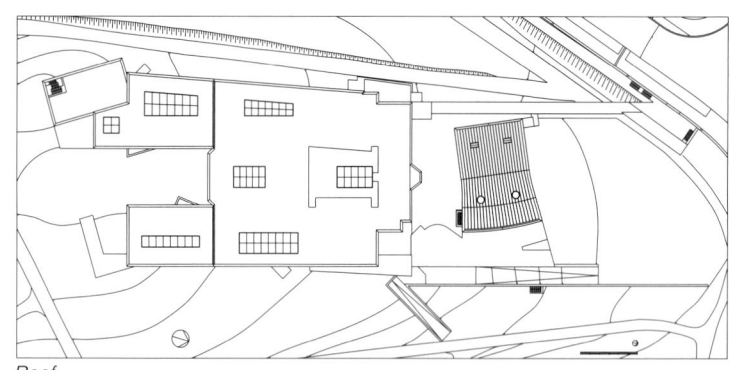

Site plan

Roof

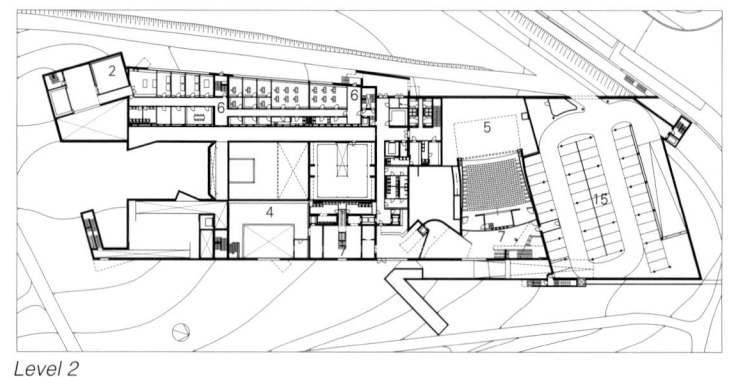

Level 2

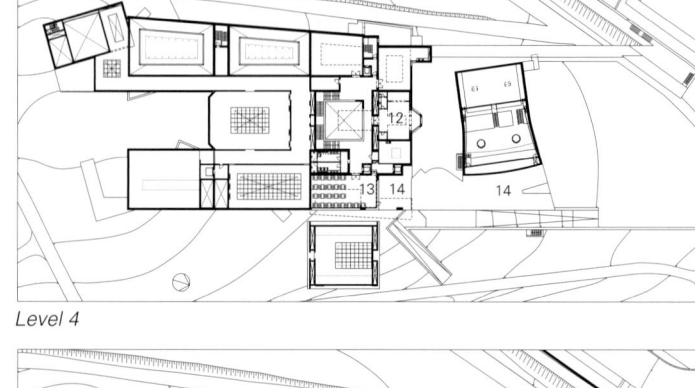

Level 4

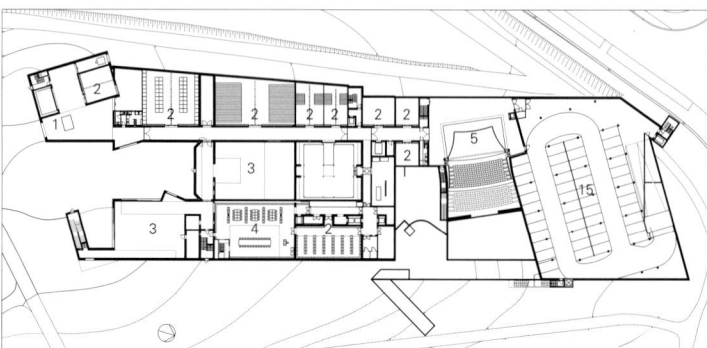

Level 1

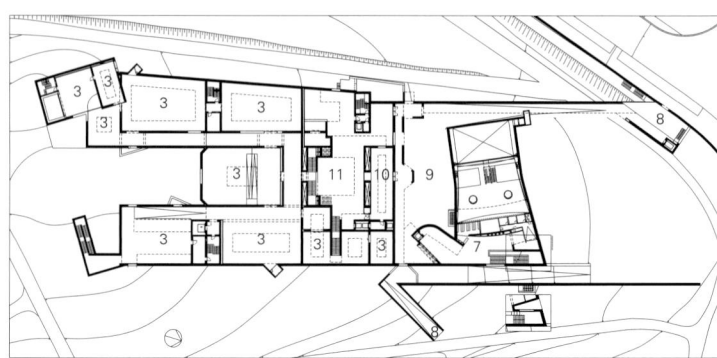

Level 3

クセス・エリアのなか、別のコートヤードをつくりだす。

建物は石あるいはスタッコの垂直面で包まれ、これらの壁の上端は同じ高さを保っているが、下端は、地盤の変化に従っている。

美術館

美術館への一般のアクセスは、敷地の一番高い部分に置かれ、屋敷を囲む既存の塀にある開口からである。この開口を抜けて、地下駐車場からの階段とエレベータ、幾つかの庭園からの小道が集中するパティオに出る。ギャラリーが美術館内部へ通じる広いコートヤード、そして独立したエントランスを抜けてオーディトリアムのホワイエまで続いている。

美術館エントランスの隣りには、レセプションとインフォメーション・デスクが置かれる。ここから、2層の高さを持ち、天井から光が差し込む正方形のアトリウムに至る通路が延びている。アトリウムは建物の輪郭を決めている長手軸線と横手軸線の中心にある。アトリウム内と隣接する部屋部屋の開口の位置は、軸性を視覚的に外へとあらゆる主要方向に向けて引き延ばす。

建物の幾何学構成の発生源であり、中心であるという機能の他に、このメイン・ホールには、美術館の各施設へ来館者を導く動線の出発点としての役割もある。入口階は展示室、ブックショップ、ギフトショップ。上の階はカフェテリアと遊歩道。下の階は図書室とオーディトリアム。

展示エリアは、大きさ、プロポーション、光、開口のタイプがそれぞれ異なるいくつかの部屋に分割されている。部屋同士は大きなU形のギャラリーで結ばれている。展示空間は入口階の大半を占め、一方の翼棟の低層階へ延びて行く。

各部屋をつなぐドアは、順路を変えたり、別の展覧会を同時に開催する際にも使われる。

Ramp to entrance on east 東側エントランスへの斜路

Cafeteria カフェテリア

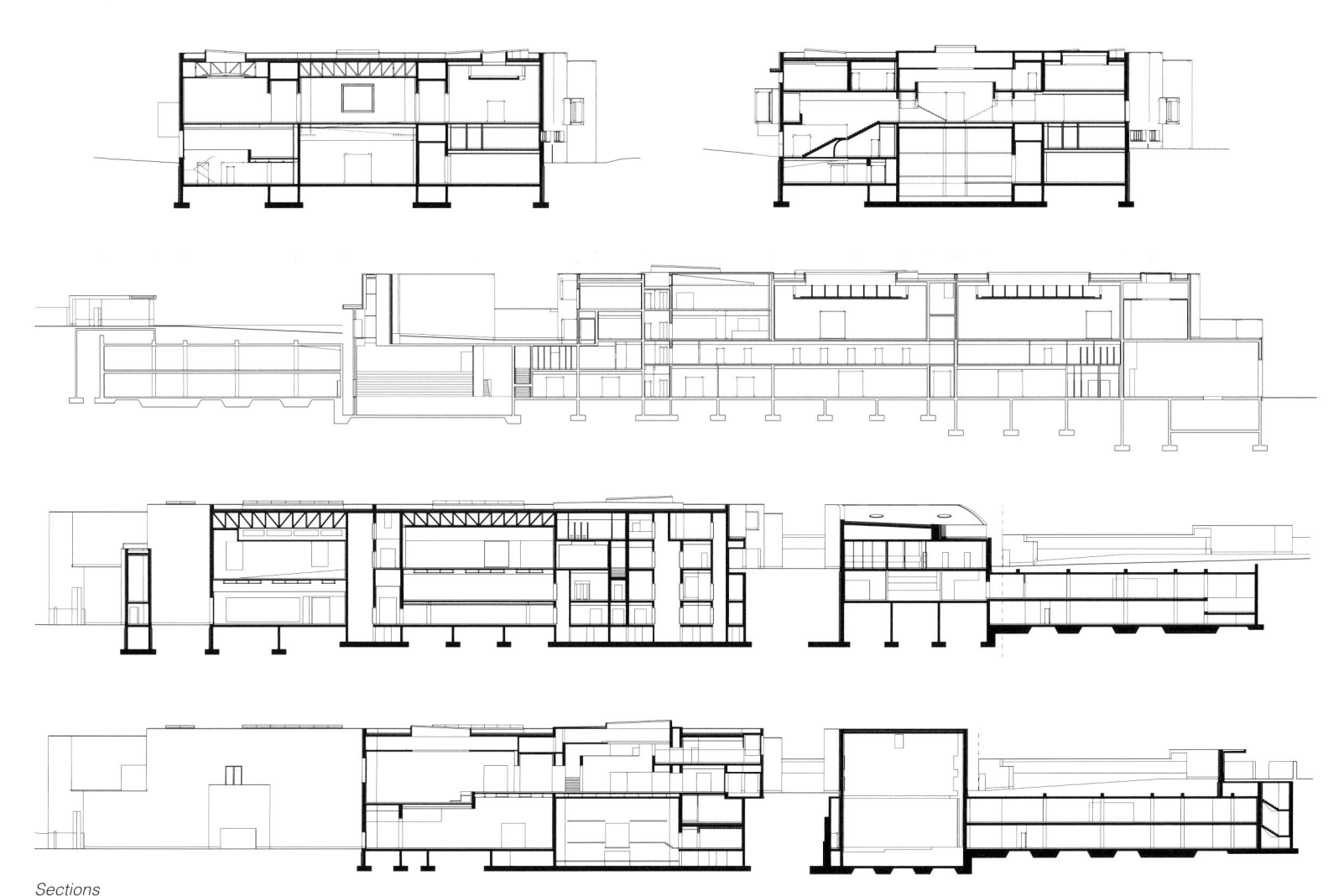

Sections

△▽ Gallery on entrance level　エントランス階展示室

Gallery on entrance level　エントランス階展示室 △▽

△▷ *Lower level: staircase to entrance hall* 　下階：エントランス・ホールへの階段

△▽ *Gallery on lower level* 　下階展示室

△▽ Library　図書館

1992–94
TADAO ANDO

NARIWA MUSEUM
Okayama, Japan

Nariwa is a municipality in the provinces of Okayama Prefecture along Nariwa River, a branch of Takahashi River. It is one of the most prominent fossils excavation spot in Japan. Situated north of this town is Kurashiki and its Ohara Museum with 70 years' tradition. Torajiro Kojima who played a major role in the acquisitions of its collection, was originally from Nariwa. Not only he had an extraordinary sense of beauty, he himself was an artist who has left a number of paintings.

Nariwa Museum is a facility of multiple functions such as the exhibition hall for Torajiro Kojima's personal collection of Oriental fine arts, the gallery, and the community center for the townspeople. On the site is a magnificent stone fence from the remains of the old mansion. To the south is a steep slope covered with rich greenery. The objective of the plan was to underline and further develop this environment endowed with history and nature in order to hand it over to the next generations.

We started out on creating a pond between the stone wall and the slope. On top of it were placed a static box of concrete and a dynamic line of motion, forming a vivid contrast to one another. The two-storied box was perforated with many large holes to provide water and greenery to the building where external and internal spaces would be linked three-dimensionally.

Anyone who tries to visit this museum is first blocked by the stone wall. With a mixed feeling of anxiety and expectation, one gets clear of the wall and finds the next scenery opening before the eye, only to be soon circumscribed by a concrete wall. As we make our way to the slope and go around a corner, the water surface and the thick green of the slope emerge into full view. The slope is an enormous partition screen, faintly presenting a hint of the existence of the world beyond and limiting the domain of the building. The entrance is located on the second level at the end of the slope.

Huge voids characterized by a water patio, an outdoor sculpture garden enclosed within walls, and a double-layered space of 9 meters high, are arranged between each exhibition room. The outer side of the building features spaces such as a plaza of steps leading down to the pool, a bridge, and a slope. The idea involved is a facility functioning as a 'plaza' in its true meaning, where people of the community gather to meet, and not just a place exhibiting paintings.

The green slope greets the visitors with flowers in the spring and colored leaves in autumn. The pond reflects and bonds such sceneries, the people, and the building. It is my hope that people would gather around the museum throughout the seasons to help it grow into a core of local community, transcending its role as a museum.

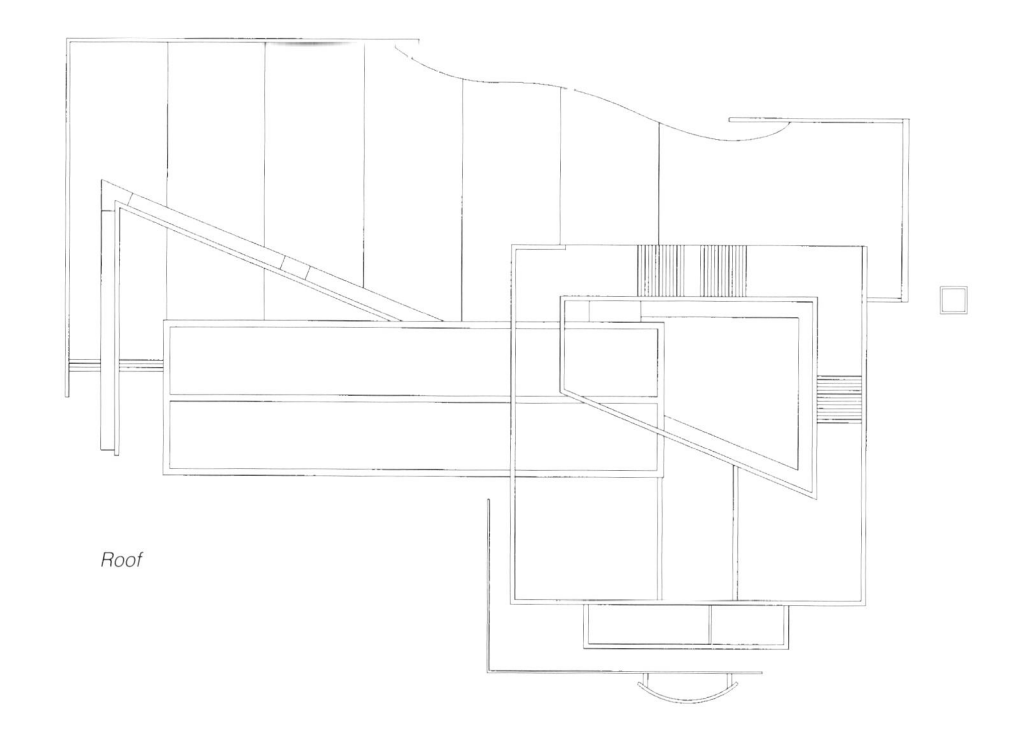

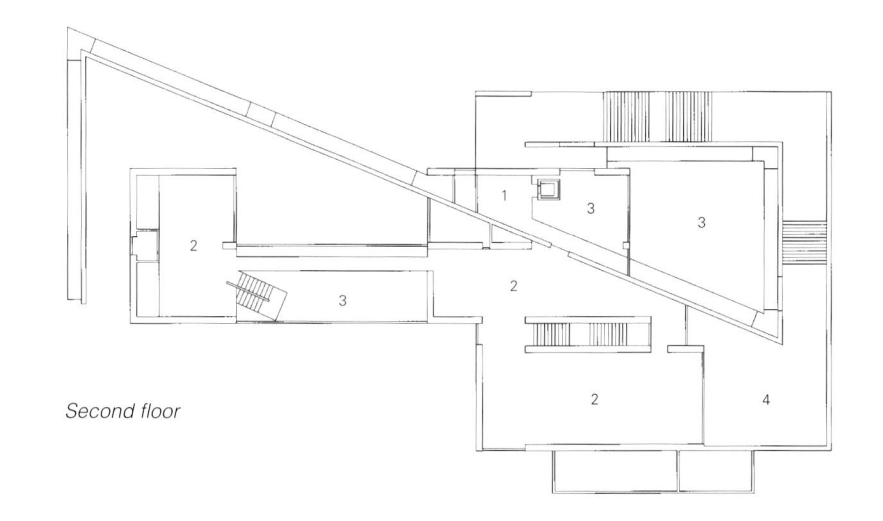

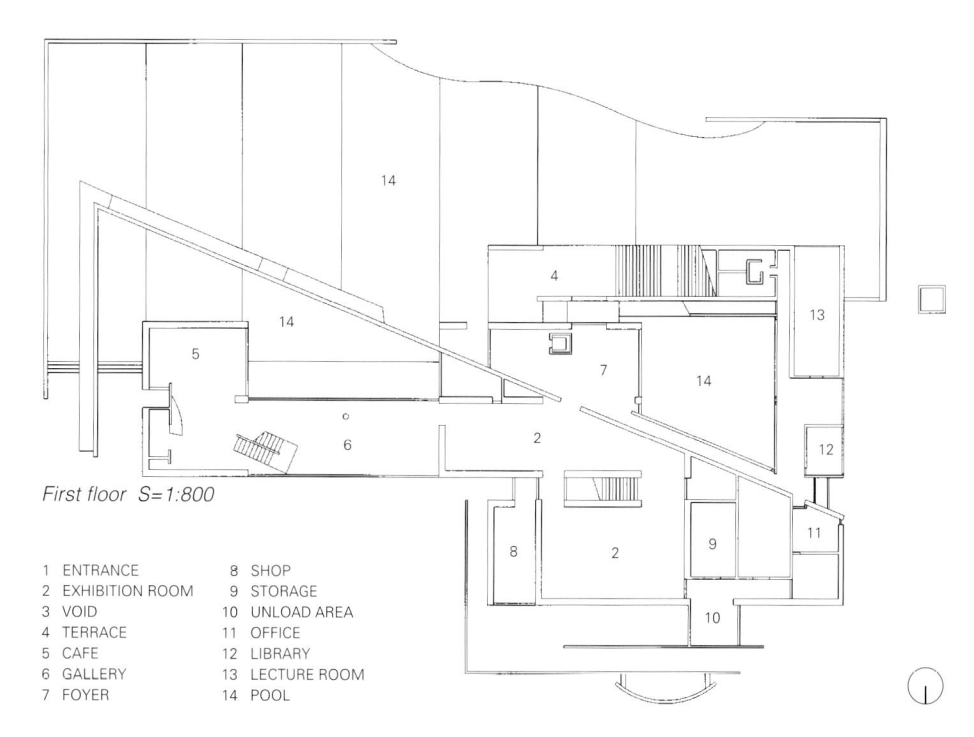

◁ *View from east*　東より見る

Roof

Second floor

First floor S=1:800

1 ENTRANCE
2 EXHIBITION ROOM
3 VOID
4 TERRACE
5 CAFE
6 GALLERY
7 FOYER
8 SHOP
9 STORAGE
10 UNLOAD AREA
11 OFFICE
12 LIBRARY
13 LECTURE ROOM
14 POOL

岡山県成羽町は、倉敷の北、高梁川の支流、成羽川の流れる地方都市であり、日本有数の化石の発掘地としても知られている。この町の南に位置する倉敷には昭和5年開館の伝統をもつ大原美術館がある。その収蔵品の買い付けに奔走した人物、児島虎次郎はこの成羽町の出身であった。優れた審美眼を持っていた彼は、同時に自ら筆を揮う画家でもあり、多くの作品を世に残している。

成羽町美術館は、児島虎次郎の残したオリエント美術のコレクションの展示、町民のギャラリーとしての機能、地域コミュニティセンターとしての機能などを併せもった施設として計画された。敷地には、旧屋敷跡の立派な石垣があり、その南側には豊かな緑の急斜面が迫っている。この歴史の香り高い自然に恵まれた環境を、建築によって顕在化、次代に引き継いでいけるような豊かなものとすることを目標として、計画を進めていった。

石垣と緑の急斜面の間に、まず人工の池を設けた。その上に静的なコンクリートの箱と、ダイナミックなアプローチの動線を、鮮烈な対比をもって配した。さらに2層からなる箱にいくつもの大きな穴を穿ち、それによって建物に水や緑を取り込み、内外空間を立体的につないでいくよう意図した。

この美術館を訪れた人は、はじめ石垣によって行く手を阻まれる。期待と不安を抱えながら石垣を越えると、次の世界が開けるが、すぐにコンクリートの壁が視界を限定する。スロープを徐々に進み、曲り角を折れると、水面と緑の斜面がその全貌を現す。緑の斜面は、巨大な衝立となって、その向こうの世界をほのめかしながら、建物の領域を限定する。エントランスは、スロープを進んだ先の2階レベルにある。

各展示室の間には水の中庭、壁に囲われた屋外彫刻庭園、高さ9mの吹抜け空間というそれぞれ特徴をもった巨大なヴォイドが配される。外部にも、水面へと降りていく階段広場、ブリッジ、スロープなどの空間を織り込んでいる。単に作品を陳列するだけの場所ではない、地域の人々が集う場所、真の意味での〈広場〉のような施設の在り方を目指した。

緑の斜面は、春には花を咲かせ、秋には紅葉する。池は、その様子と共に、人々や建物の姿を映し込み、それらを束ねていく。人々が四季を通してここに集うことで、美術館が美術館を越え、この地域社会の核として成長していくことを望んでいる。

Approach on east 東側のアプローチ

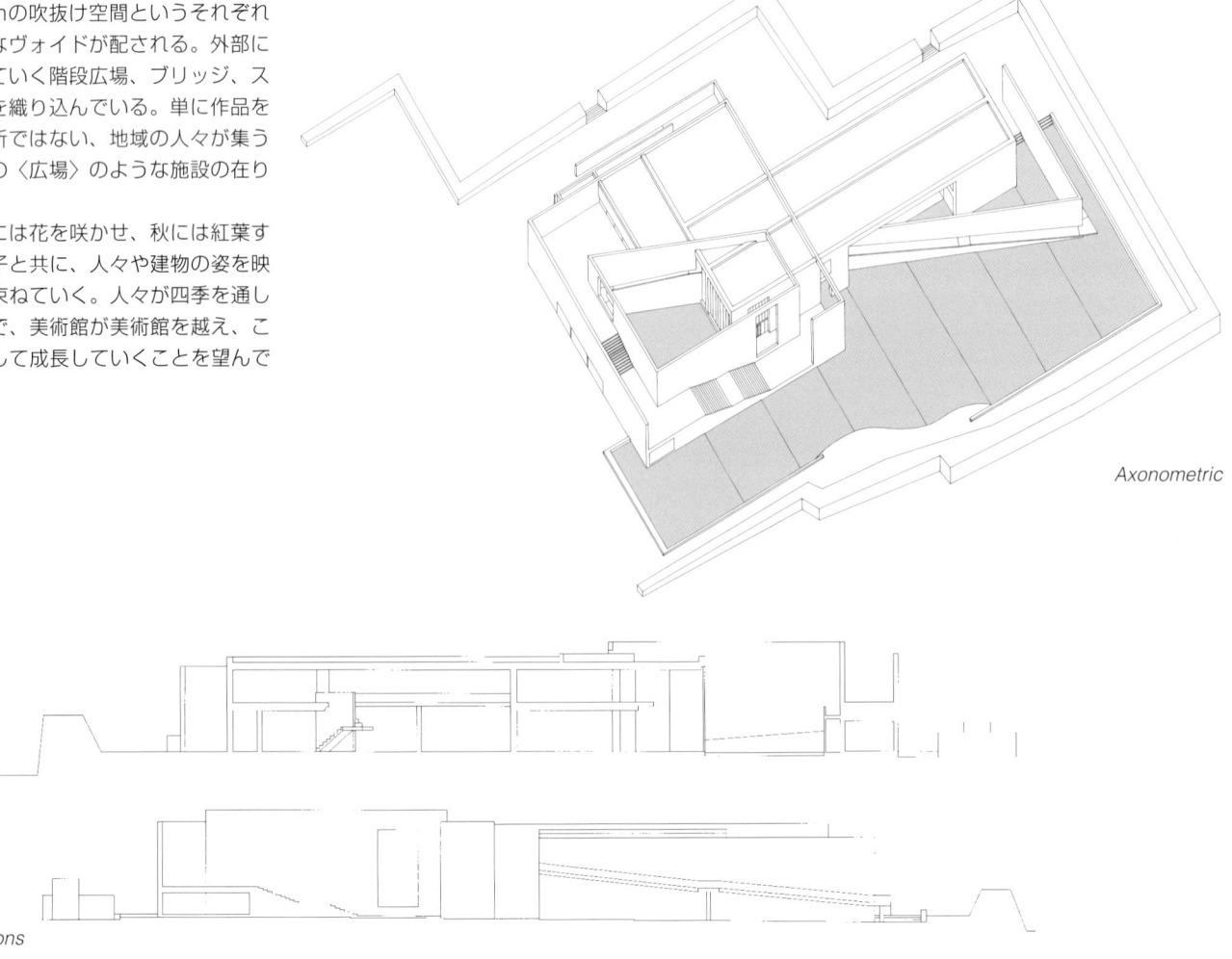

Axonometric

Sections

View from south 南より見る

View from north 北より見る

Foyer ホワイエ

View of foyer from ramp　斜路よりホワイエを見る

Gallery　ギャラリー

View from foyer　ホワイエより見る

Gallery: view toward west　ギャラリー：西を見る

Exhibition room　展示室

1992–96
I. M. PEI

MIHO MUSEUM
Shiga, Japan

Aerial view 航空写真

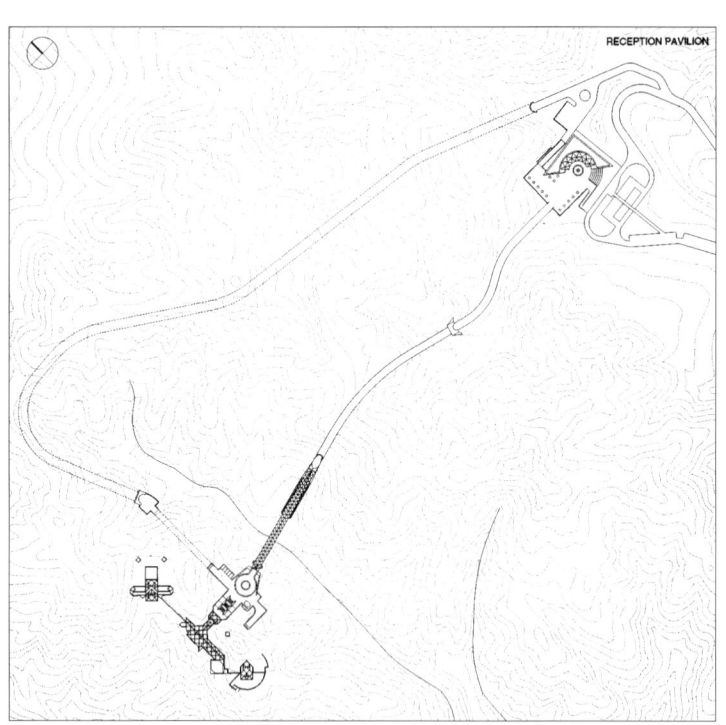

Site plan

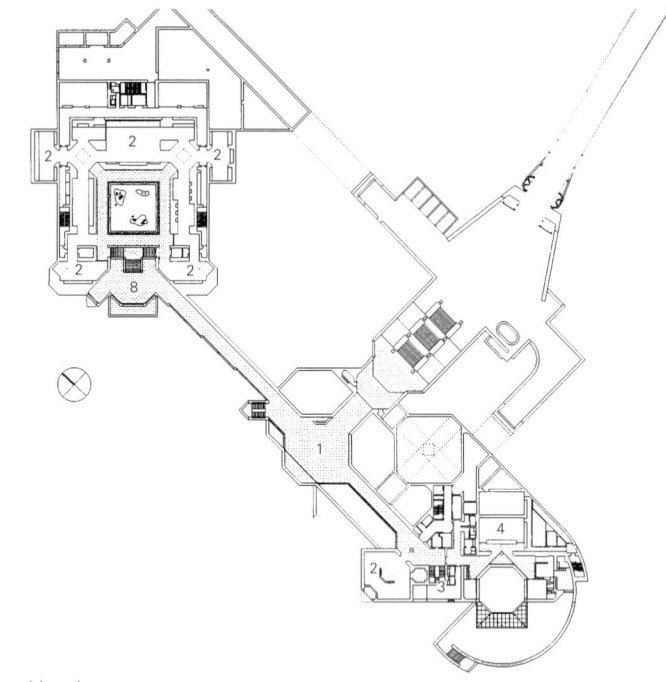

Ground level

1 ENTRANCE HALL
2 EXHIBITION ROOM
3 DIRECTOR'S ROOM
4 CONFERENCE ROOM
5 PLAZA
6 LECTURE ROOM
7 CAFE
8 LOBBY
9 OFFICE
10 TERRACE
11 COLLECTION STORAGE
12 LOADING DOCK

Basement 2

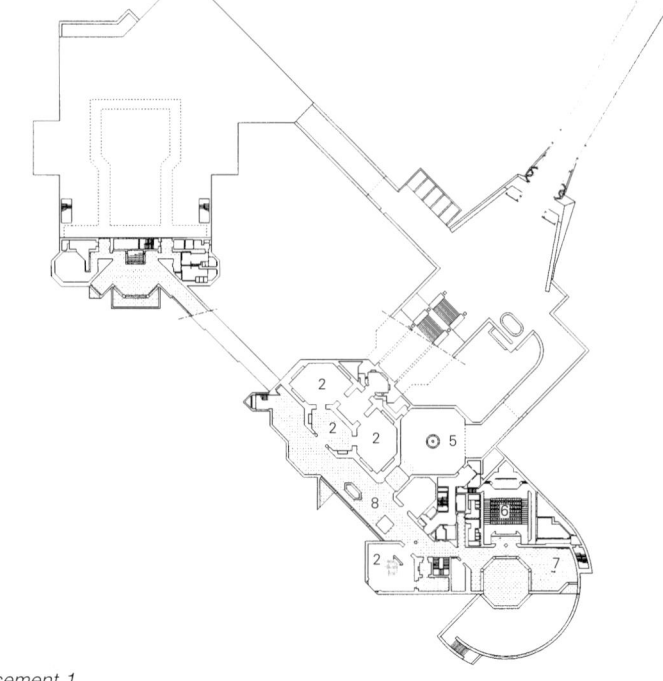

Basement 1

A museum nestled among the mountains of Shiga Prefecture. The building was inspired by a classic Chinese poem 'Peach Blossom Spring', depicting the discovery of a cave leading to a paradise lost.

Visitors take electric cars from the Reception Pavilion with its ticket booth through a 120-meter tunnel that opens onto a cable-stayed bridge spanning a valley, up to a plaza. Further up along the mountain side, they eventually reach the entrance hall of a building placed between the ridges. Only the glass roofs are visible over the mountainside, for 80 percent of the building is buried underground, conforming to legal restrictions.

As the visitors proceed into the public hall, the spatial scale shifts dramatically: up to this point, the building's full picture was concealed, whereas now it emerges under the huge skylight.

The silhouette of the skylights is an abstraction of traditional Japanese gabled roof. Organized of geometrical models, the three glass roofs are an assembly of reticulated triangles, and are each oriented in response to the topography. The skylight features a space frame incorporating a sunscreen composed of a series of angled metal tubes through which light is filtered inside.

Two wings constitute the museum, one housing works of Japanese art and another, of ancient Chinese and Middle and Near East. Space flows along the topography: the cubic volume of Egyptian art gallery, the square patio of Japanese art gallery, and glazed hallways stretching in between. The continuing yet winding sequence of views toward the external landscape emphasizes the framework of a scenario, making one's way into then outside the mountains.

滋賀県の山間に建つ美術館。建物は中国の古典『桃花源記』、洞窟の向こうに失われた桃源郷を発見する物語を元に発想された。

来館者は、切符売り場のあるレセプション・パビリオンから電気自動車によって、120メートルのトンネルを抜け、谷に架かるケーブル＝ステイ・ブリッジを渡り、広場に着く。ここから山に沿って上って尾根の間に配置された建物のエントランス・ホールへ至る。法的規制のため、建物の8割が地下にあるため、ガラス屋根だけが、山の斜面上に見える。

エントランスからパブリック・ホールへ進むと、空間スケールは劇的に変化する。見えなかった建築の全貌が、巨大なスカイライトとして姿を表す。

スカイライトのシルエットは日本の入母屋造の屋根を、抽象化したものである。このスカイライト・スペースは幾何学形態により構成される。網状に組まれる三角形の構成する三つのガラス屋根は、地形に対応して立ち上がっている。スカイライトは、メタル・チューブを連ねた日除けがスペース・フレームに組み込まれ、濾過された光を内部にもたらす。

美術館は二つのウイングからなる。一つは日本美術、一つは初期中国美術と中近東美術の展示空間である。空間は地形に沿って流れて行き、エジプト・ギャラリーの立方体のヴォリューム、日本ギャラリーの方形の中庭、その間に伸びるガラス張りの通路が所々に挟まっている。外の景色が見える場面が絶え間なく屈曲して続くことで、山の中を進み、また外へと進んでいく構成が強調される。

Bridge 橋

Night view of main entrance メイン・エントランスの夜景

View of entrance from east　東よりエントランスを見る

North wing　北ウィング

Entrance エントランス

Entrance hall エントランス・ホール

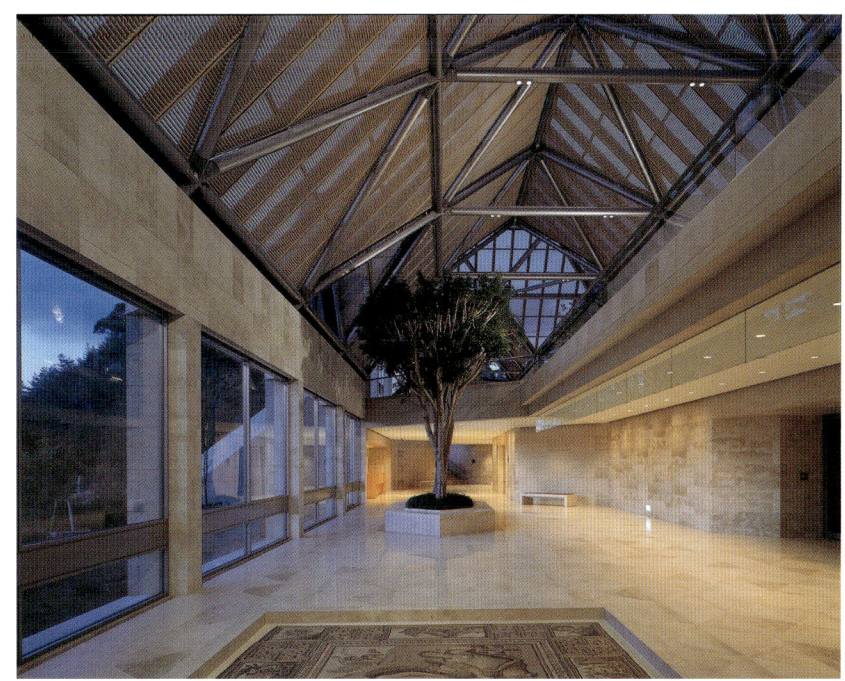

Lobby on basement 1 地下1階ロビー

Entrance hall エントランス・ホール

Cafe カフェ

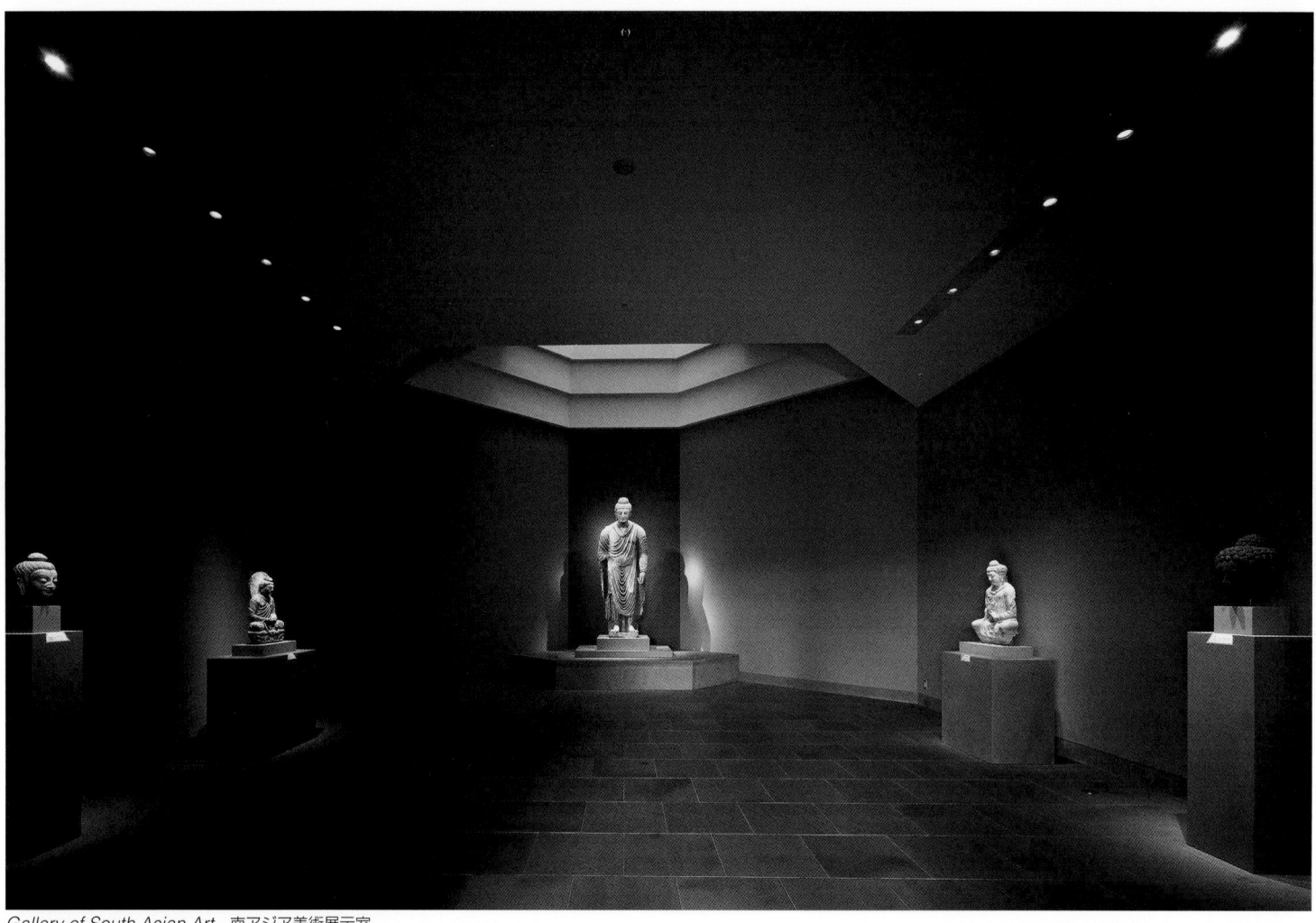

Gallery of South Asian Art　南アジア美術展示室

Gallery of Egyptian Art　エジプト美術展示室

Gallery of West Chinese Art　中国西域美術展示室

Gallery of Japanses Art　日本美術展示室

1992–97
STEVEN HOLL

KIASMA MUSEUM OF CONTEMPORARY ART, HELSINKI
Helsinki, Finland

View toward main entrance メイン・エントランス方向を見る

◁ *View from southeast* 南東より見る

East elevation 東面

The site is situated in central Helsinki in close proximity to Saarinen's Helsinki Railway Station and Aalto's Finlandia Hall.

The building's concept 'Kiasma (crossover)' is reflected in the architectural form as it weaves together the geometry of the city and of the landscape and the building itself.

Exhibition rooms are flexible by design, conforming to contemporary art's diversity of expressions. They are meant to be calm and quiet, yet never static. Irregularity creates individual differences.

Sunlight typical of Helsinki penetrates the building in a number of ways, due to the subtle variation given to the shape and size of the rooms produced by the gentle curves featured in the building's sectional plan. Such irregularity drives the motion that passes through a spatial sequence. The sequence unfolds itself along the curve, generating mystique and wonder. Visitors weave their experiences inside the museum—they witness an infinite sequence of changing perspectives linked to the overall concept of Kiasma, to unfold before their eyes.

The spatial system is open at the ends, implying an extent that lies beyond. The dynamic lines of motion inside consist of bowed slope and stairs, providing open views that interact with each other. These lines with open ends and contingency induce moments of rest, contemplation and discovery.

The problem common to museums having a number of overlaying gallery levels involves lighting: natural light reaches only the upper levels, leaving the lower levels to depend on artificial lighting. Here, it is resolved in two steps. First, the curved roof deflects horizontal light along the central axis. Also, its curve enables to arrange secondary skylights. As a result, both upper and lower levels are provided with natural light. Second, the 'refracting' skylight on the curved roof distributes natural light to galleries below the top level. In other words, natural light is introduced to every level as a consequence of the curved, intertwined figure of the building and the contortion of light and space entangled.

敷地は、サーリネンのヘルシンキ駅、アアルトのフィンランディア・ホールが近接するヘルシンキの中心部にある。

"キアズマ（交差）"というコンセプトによって、建物は都市と風景の持つジオメトリーと織り合わされ、それが建築形態に反映される。

展示室は、現代芸術の多様な表現に対応することを意図したものである。それらは静かであることを意図しているが、静止的ではない。その不規則性によって、個々に差異がつけられている。

ヘルシンキ特有の太陽光は、緩やかにカーブする建物断面から生まれる部屋の形と大きさの微妙なバリエーションにより、いくつもの異なった経路で差し込み、この不規則性が、空間のシークェンスを抜けて行く動きを進める。カーブしながら展開していくシークェンスは、神秘性と驚きの両方の要素を与えてくれる。訪問者は、内部体験を織り合わせ、つまりキアズマという全体のコンセプトに結びついた、変化するパースペクティヴの無限の連なりが次々に展開していくのを目にする。

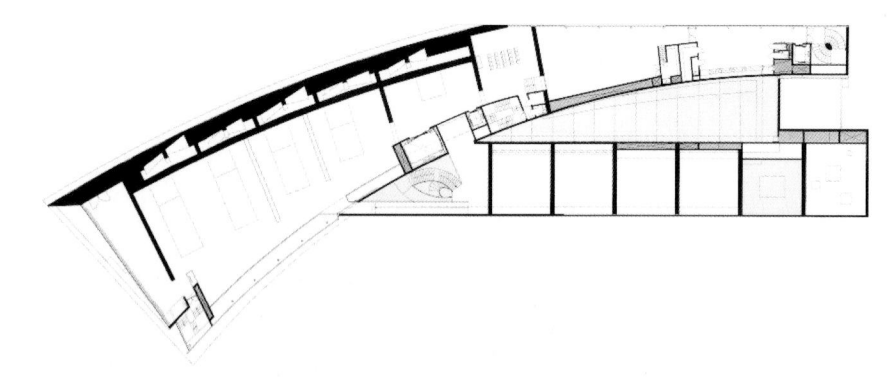

Fifth floor

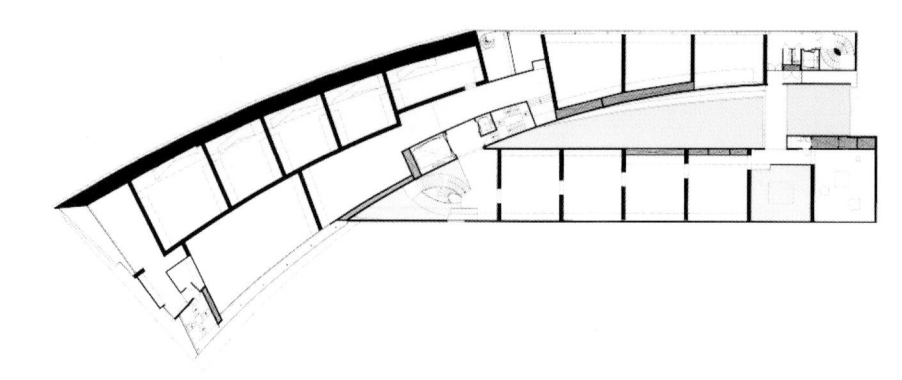

Fourth floor

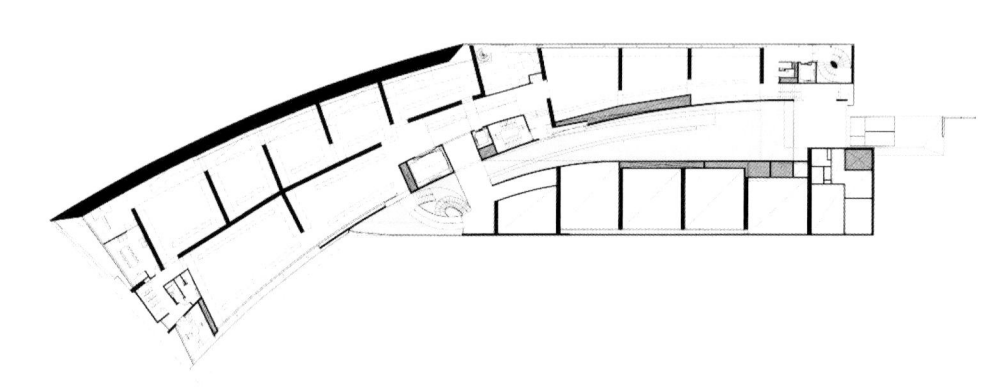

Third floor

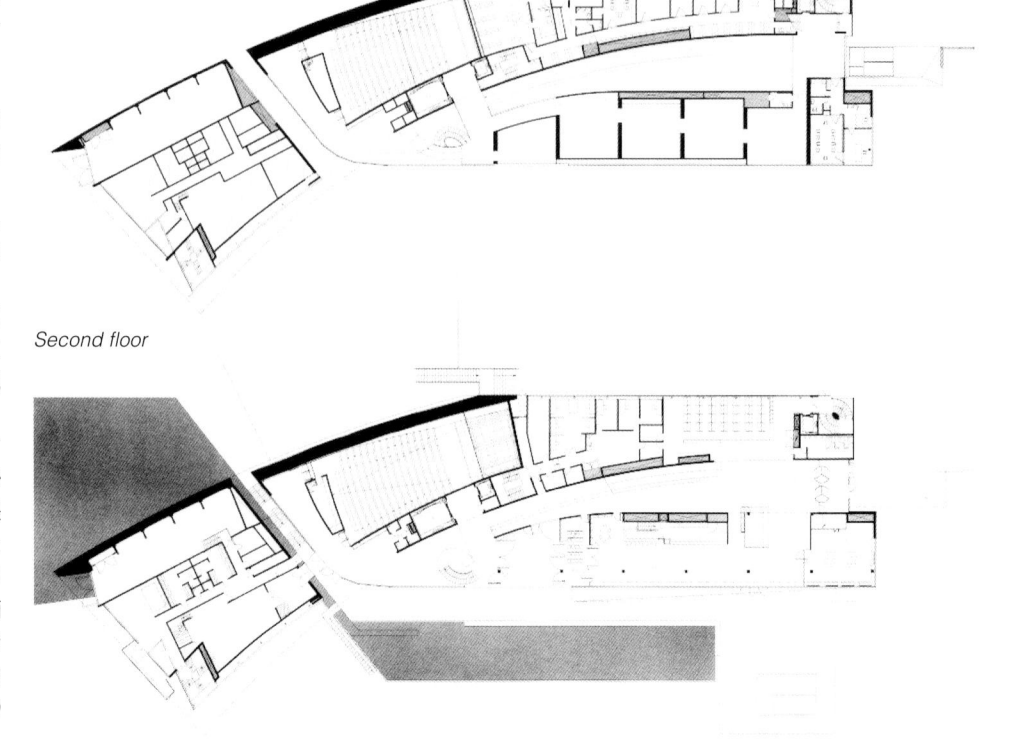

Second floor

Ground floor

オープン・エンドな空間システムは、その向こうに横たわる広がりを暗示する。湾曲する斜路と階段で構成されたダイナミックな内部の動線は相互に作用しあう開かれた眺めを提供する。このオープン・エンドで偶発性をもった動線は、休止、黙想、発見の瞬間を誘発する。

ギャラリーが何層にも重なっている美術館に共通する問題点は、積層するレベルの上層にしか自然光が入らず、下階は人工照明に頼らなければならないことであるが、ここでは2つの方法で解決している。第一に、カーブする屋根は、水平に入る光が中央に沿って屈折して注ぐ一方で、補助的なスカイライトを設置することができる。この結果、自然光は上階と下階の双方に差し込む。第2に、曲面屋根に付けられる、"屈折"した光を落とすスカイライトは、最上階より下の階のギャラリーに自然光を配分することになる。建物の湾曲し、絡み合った形態によって、また、空間と光の織りなす捻れによって、各階はそれぞれ自然採光されることになる。

View from north 北より見る

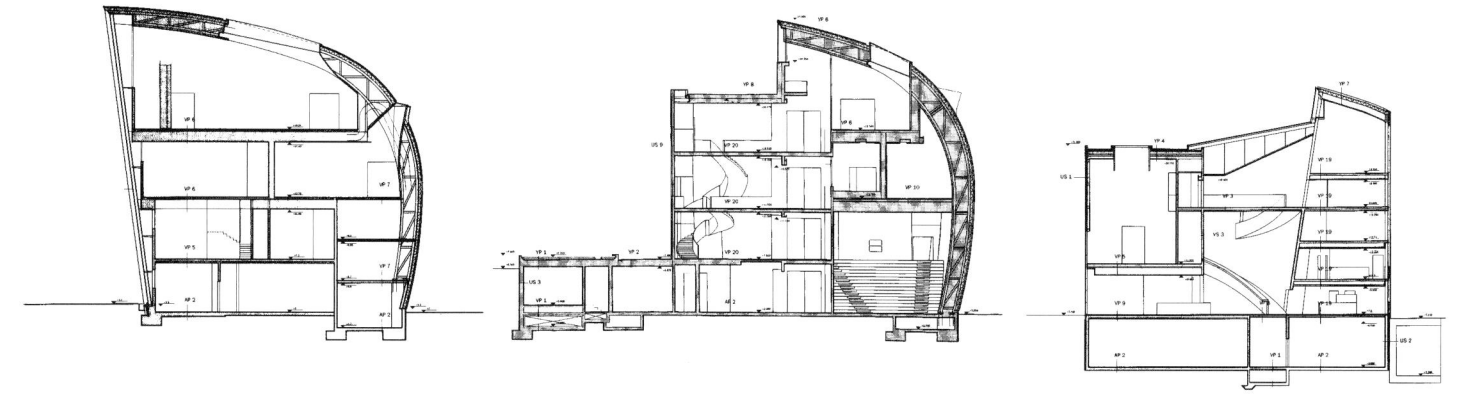

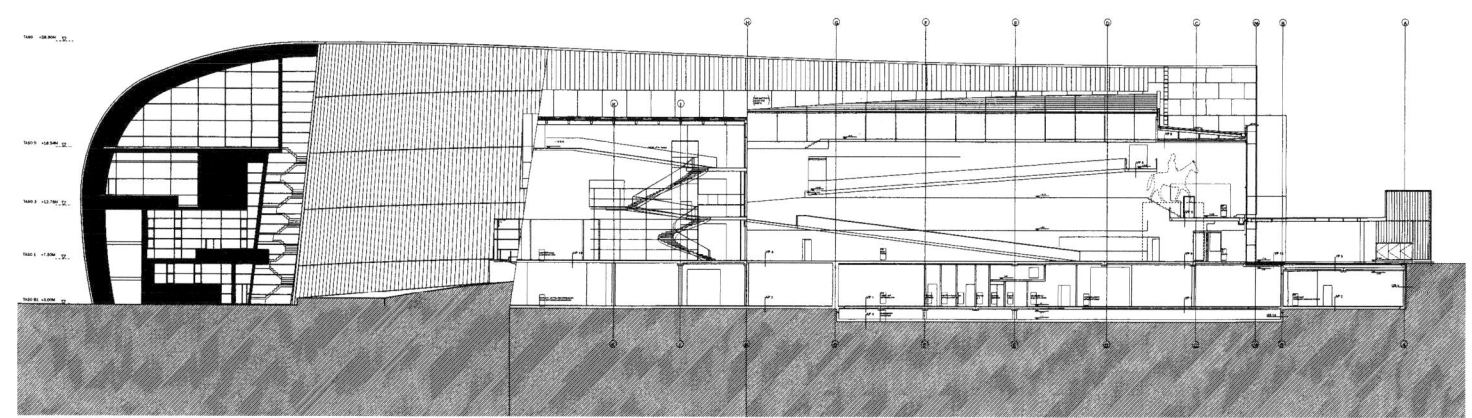

Sections

Atrium　アトリウム

Main entrance　メイン・エントランス

Spiral staircase　螺旋階段

Atrium: ramp　アトリウム：斜路

Exhibition space on second floor　2階展示室

Exhibition space on fifth floor 5階展示室

1993–94
COOP HIMMELBLAU

GRONINGER MUSEUM
EAST PAVILION
Groningen, The Netherlands

View from northwest 北西より見る

View from southeast 南東より見る

View from northeast 北東より見る

View from north 北より見る

303

The commission for the East Pavilion of the Groninger Museum was designed to house 16th Century to Contemporary art.

The galleries are part of a larger Museum complex, commissioned by the city of Groningen, with an overall design by Studio Mendini. Guest architects are; Coop Himmelblau, Philippe Stark, and Michele De Lucchi.

Our concept for the East Pavilion is based on the idea of the unfolding of positive and negative space and the continuation of the rooftop structure over the water to the canal bank, extending the Museum to the city.

The concept's intention is to establish different levels to experience art. The "inside skin" of the flexible exhibition system as well as the varying levels of the circulation allow for different points of view of the exhibited art.

The design process involved overlaying three dimensional studies of volumes of natural and artificial light with the original sketch drawing of the Pavilion concept. This process of layering resulted in a sketch model which used the power of the first emotional imprint, or psychogram of the concept, to dissolve the space. The design process further attempted to capture the random liveliness of this sketch model and translate its sculptural details to the scale of the actual building. As first developed in our project for the Folly No.6 in Osaka in 1989, a process of digitizing was employed which allowed us to maintain the original gesture of the sketch model and fix it precisely within a 3-dimensional grid. This digital model was then enlarged step-by-step in order to consider structural and spatial details, and ultimately was used directly in the production of the Pavilion's parts.

In order to achieve the goals of the tight budget and time frame for the project it was decided to use the local method of shipbuilding to construct the primary elements of the East Pavilion. Construction drawings of the geometrically complex steel plates were made directly from the computer model allowing the shipyard to construct the 300 tons of steel double-shelled panels enclosing the Pavilion extremely precisely. The steel plates arrived on site via barge completely prefabricated with structure, insulation, paint and edge details already intact. This streamlined process resulted in a very quick and economical construction term and a building whose all-welded details are more similar to those of a ship than a building.

フローニンヘン美術館の東館は16世紀から現代に至る美術作品を収容するものである。

このギャラリーはフローニンヘン市がステュディオ・メンディーニに全体設計を依頼した美術館コンプレックスの一部を構成する。メンディーニは、コープ・ヒンメルブラウ、フィリップ・スタルク、ミケーレ・デ・ルッキをゲスト・アーキテクトとしてコンプレックスの一部をデザインするように招待した。

東館に対するわれわれのコンセプトは、陽の空間と陰の空間を展開すること。屋根を延長して水の上から運河の岸まで掛け渡し、美術館を市内へと拡張してゆくというアイディアに基づいている。

アートを体験するためのさまざまに異なるレヴェルを設定した。変化するサーキュレーションの階高とフレキシブルな展示システムをも"内部の被膜"によって展示作品を異なった視点から観賞できる。

設計プロセスでは、コンセプトを表現する最初のスケッチと、自然光と人工照明の容量を検討する三次元的なスタディを重ね合わせていった。この重ね合わせのプロセスから最初の情緒的な刻印つまりコンセプトのサイコグラムの力を用いて空間を分解するスケッチ・モデルを導いた。さらに、スケッチ・モデルのもつランダムな活気を捕縛し、その彫刻的ディテールを現実の建物のスケールへと翻訳しようという試みへと進んだ。1989年の大阪の花博でのフォリーNo.6で最初に展開したように、スケッチ・モデルの最初の様相を保ちながら三次元グリッド上に精確に写し取るために計数化の手順を踏んだ。次に、この数値モデルを構造と空間のディテールを考えるために順次拡張してゆき、最終的に東館の部分を制作することに直接使用した。

厳しい予算と工期をクリアするために、東館の主要要素の建設にはこの地方で行われている造船技術を使うことに決めた。複雑な幾何学的形態をもつ鋼版の実施図面は、コンピュータ・モデルから直接制作されたもので、これによって、建物を非常な精確さで包む、300トンに達するスティールの二重シェル・パネルが造船所で制作された。この鋼版は、構造体、断熱材、塗装、端部のディテールを図面通り完全につくりあげた状態で、平底荷船で敷地に運ばれた。この能率的なプロセスは、非常に迅速で経済的な工期を可能にし、すべて溶接されたディテールは建物よりもむしろ船に似ている。

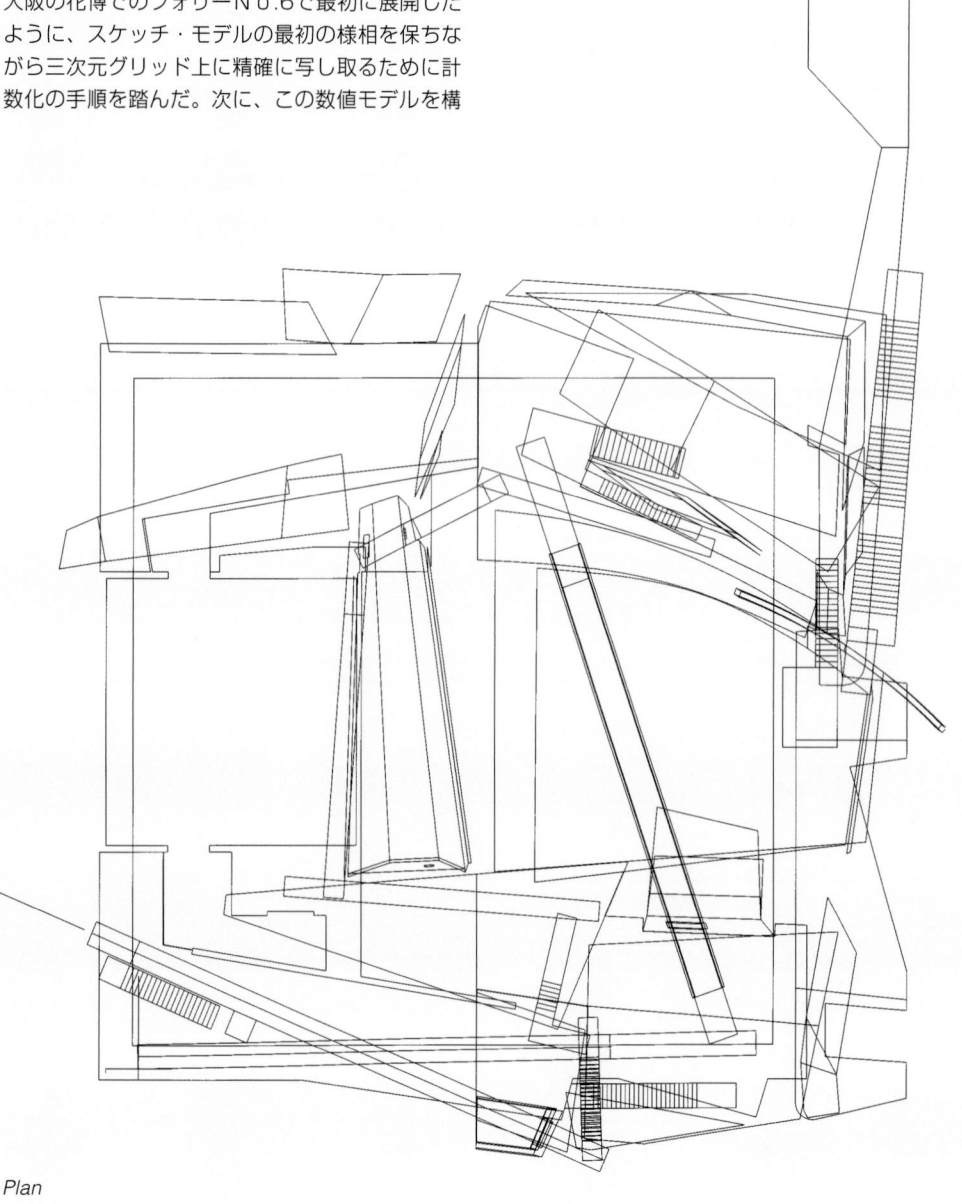

Plan

Building layers: circulation

Site plan

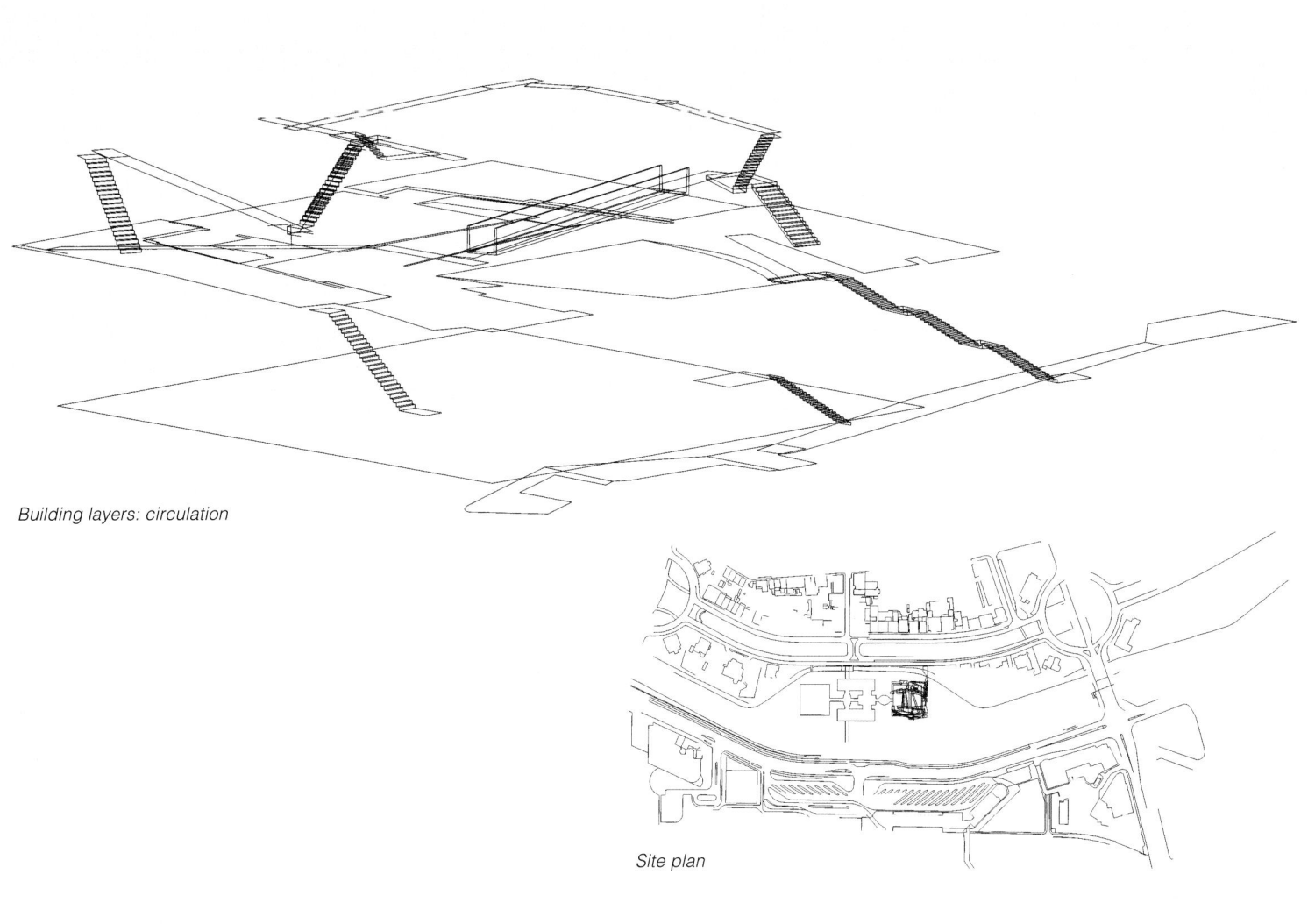

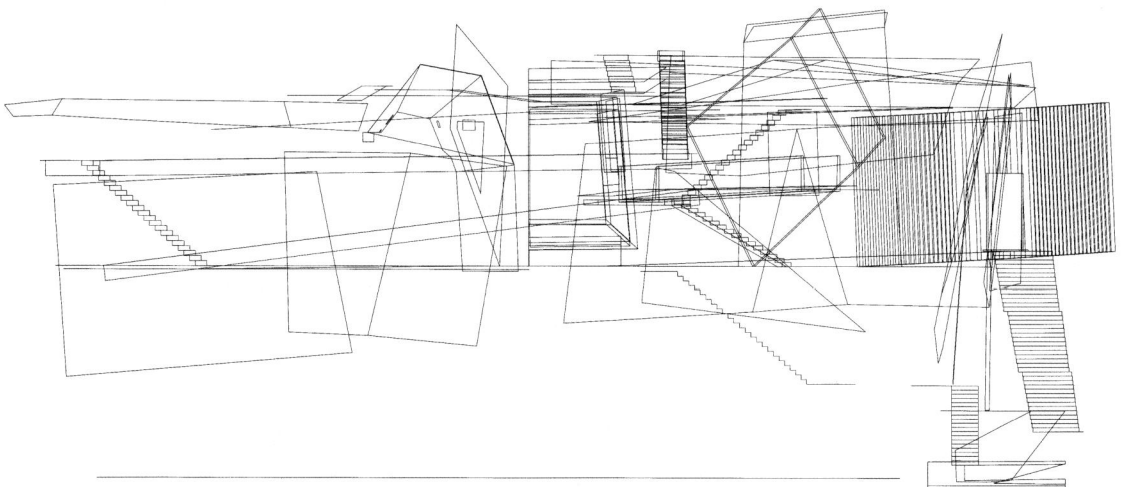

Elevation/section

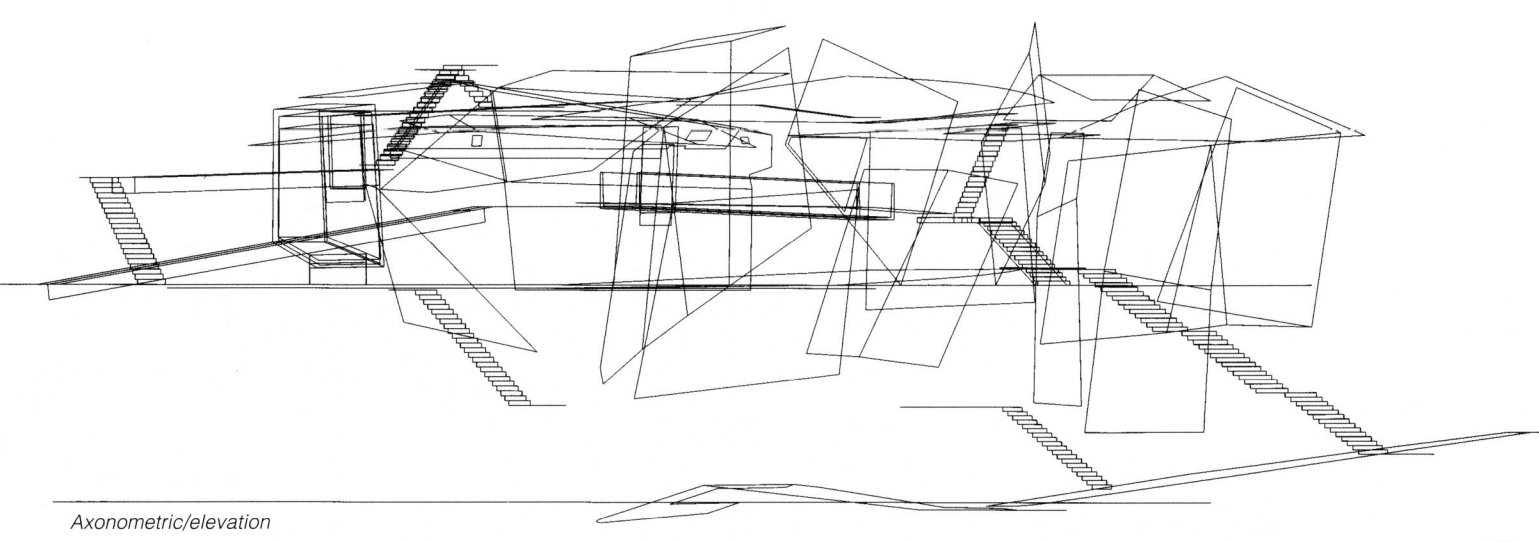

Axonometric/elevation

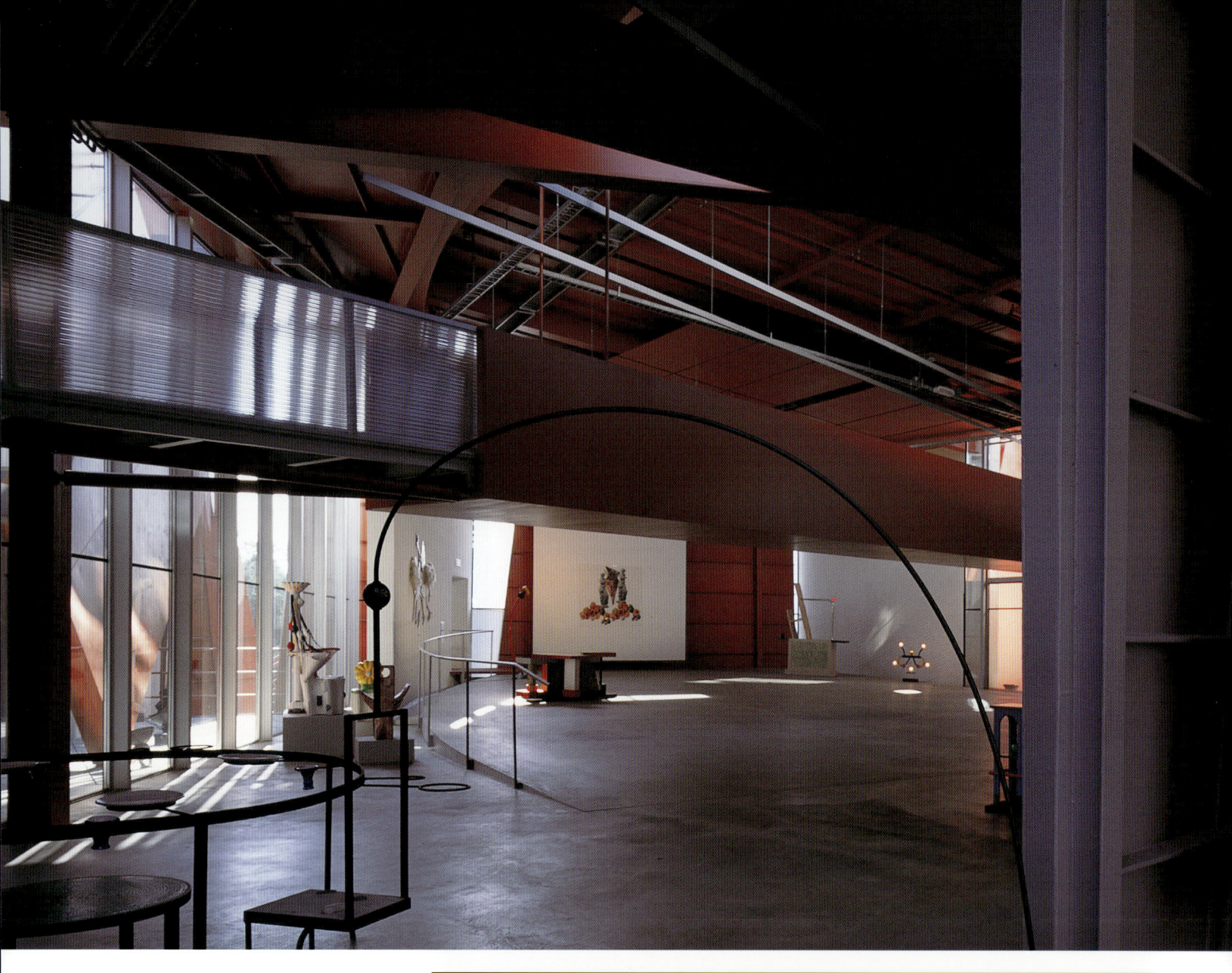

Exhibition space　展示室

307

Exhibition space　展示室 △▽▷

Axonometric

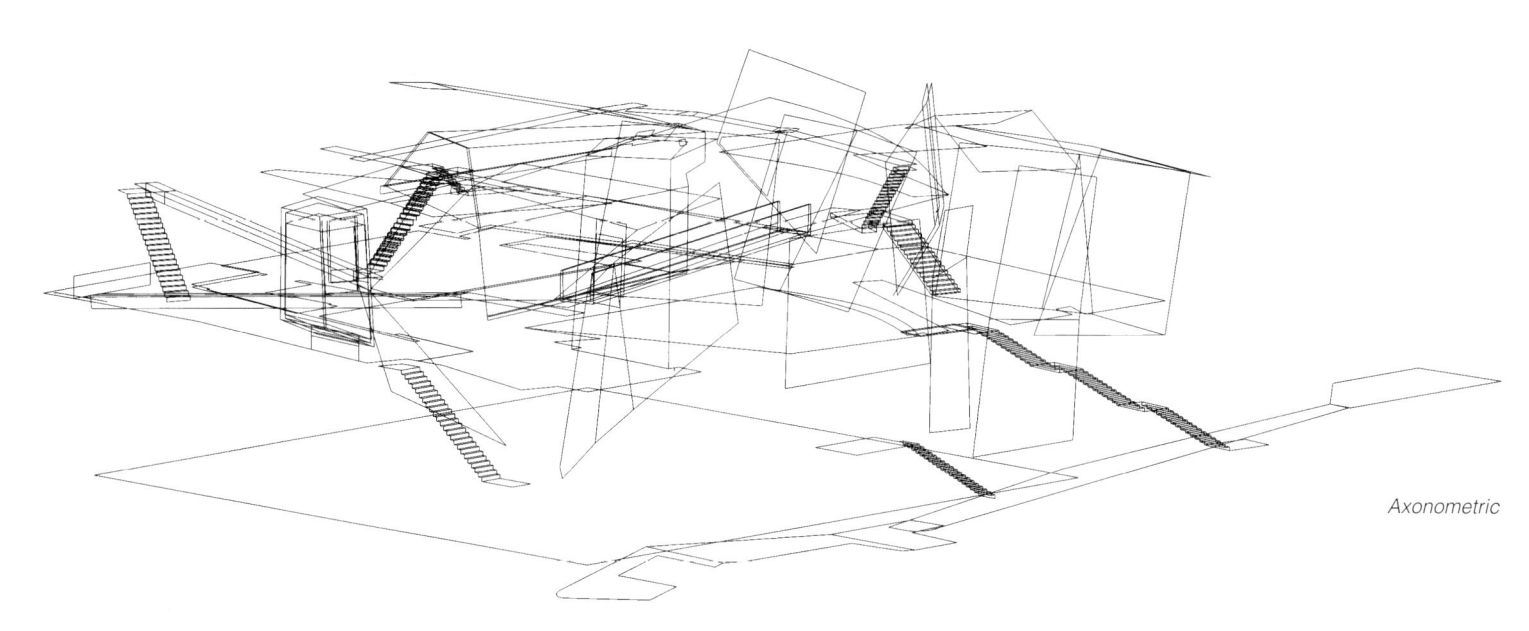

1995–99
KAZUYO SEJIMA + RYUE NISHIZAWA

O-MUSEUM
Nagano, Japan

Overall view from east　東より見る

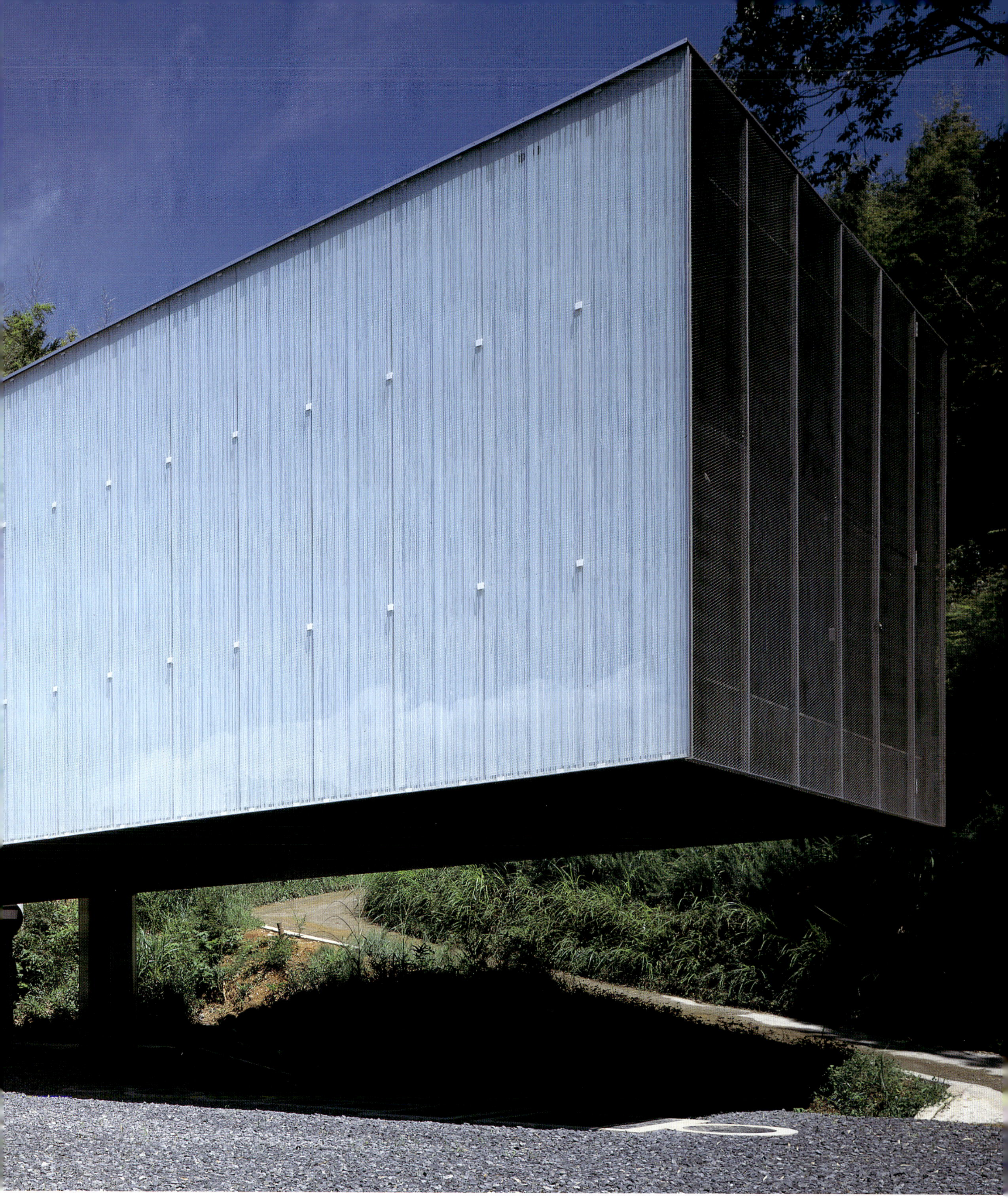

This building is a museum in a local city located in a mountainous area about four hours by car from Tokyo. It stands on the former site of the residence of the feudal lord and is halfway up the mountain on which the castle was built. The mountain rises behind the site, and in front, on a south-facing slope, stands a shoin-style building, the only surviving structure from the feudal period. Designated an Important Cultural Property (ICP) by the government, it is open to the public. At the bottom of the mountain are a village and fields. The museum is intended to exhibit arms and old documents handed down from generation to generation and everyday articles from the past, to show how the feudal lord lived and how the village once looked, and to enable visitors to access stored material.

We attempted to leave the things on the site in their existing state and to enable visitors to come into contact with them in as simple a way as possible. The building volume was determined largely by the required setback from the ICP-designated shoin and the presence of the mountain in the back. The long, slender volume is gently curved so as to blend in as much as possible with the natural and topographical features and the climate of the site. In addition, the volume is slightly raised to preserve and to make available to view the form of the site, which is itself historically important. A visitor passing under the building comes face to face with the mountain and is led to a ramp between the mountain and the building. As he gradually ascends the ramp, the shoin, which had been visible through a slit in the building and the ramp, disappears. As he approaches the entrance, a glass wall comes into view, and the shoin is again visible beyond it. From inside the entrance hall, the large beautiful roof of the shoin, which could only be looked at from below at ground level, is seen straight ahead. Walking through the building while looking at the exhibits, the visitor arrives at a small lounge. From there, the village, which provides a background for the exhibits and through which the visitor had passed on the way to the site, can be viewed once more. Thus this project is intended to be a museum for the entire environment, displaying not only the exhibits within the building but everything in that place.

Kazuyo Sejima + Ryue Nishizawa

Glazed wall detail ガラス壁のディテール

1 SPECIAL EXHIBITION ROOM
2 ENTRANCE HALL
3 EXHIBITION ROOM
4 LOUNGE
5 COLLECTION STORAGE 1
6 COLLECTION STORAGE 2
7 SECULITY OFFICE

Second floor

Ground floor S=1:400

Slope and pilotis　斜路とピロティ

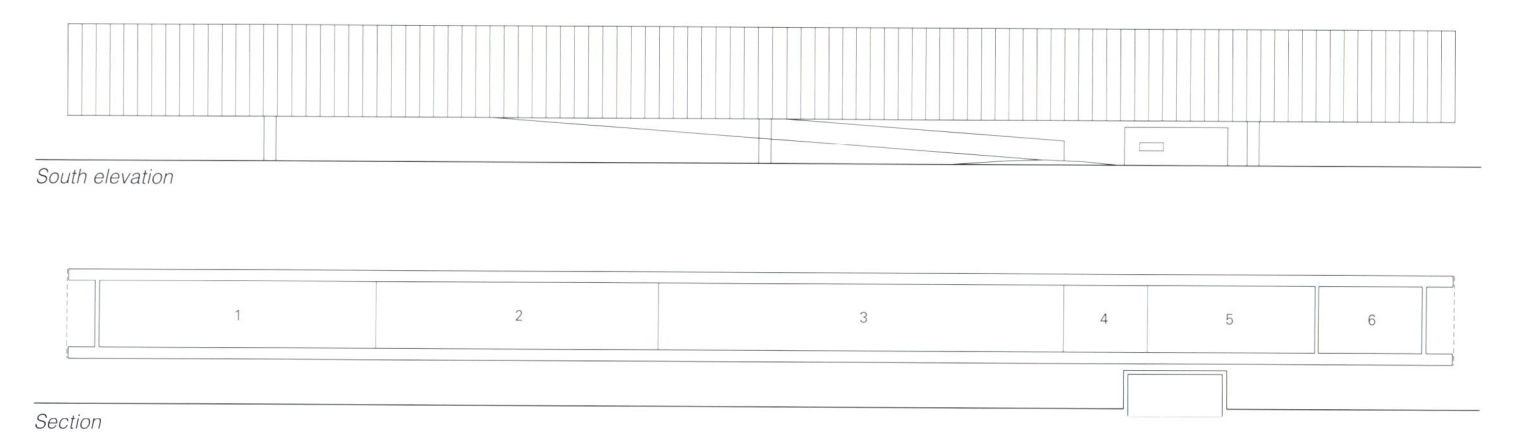

South elevation

| 1 | 2 | 3 | 4 | 5 | 6 |

Section

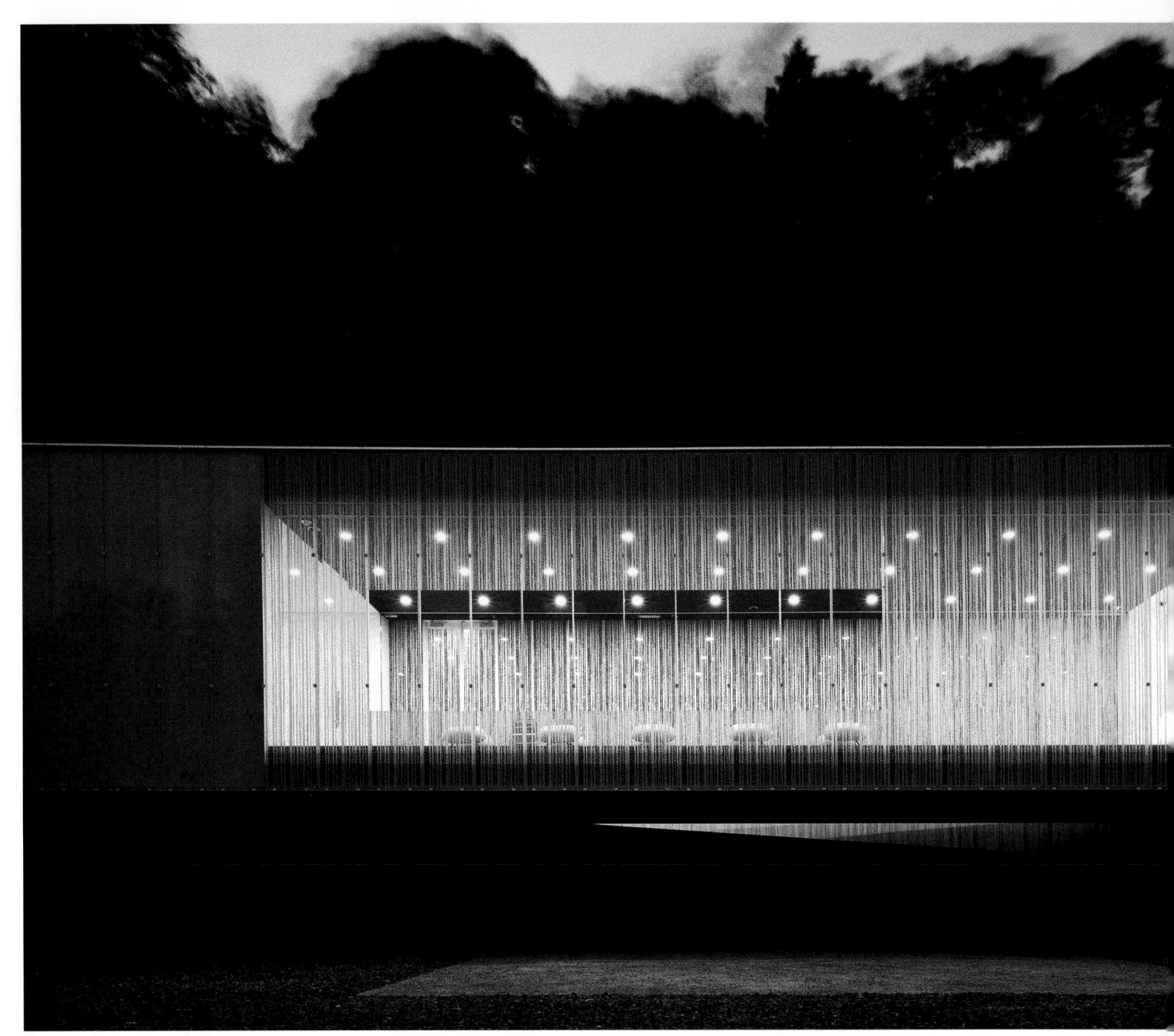

Evening view: entrance hall
夕景：エントランス・ホール

この建物は東京から車で約4時間程の山間部の地方都市に建つ資料館である。敷地はかつてこの地の領主居城のあった跡地で城山の中腹にある。敷地の裏側には城山が続き、前面の南側斜面には当時の建物としては唯一残る書院が国の重要文化財として保存・公開されており、そのふもとには里や田畑が広がる。この資料館は代々遺されてきた武具や古文書、古の生活を伝える品々などを展示し、領主の生活やこの里のかつてのすがたを伝え、また収蔵される資料を閲覧する施設として計画された。

私たちが試みたことは、その敷地にある既存の物を残し、そしてそれらにできるだけ単純な方法で触れることができる計画である。建物のヴォリュームは、重要文化財である書院からの後退距離と後ろの城山によりほぼ決定された。山際に沿うような細長いヴォリュームは、敷地にあふれる自然や地形や気候とできるだけ混じり合うように、ごく緩いカーブが与えられている。そして、重要な歴史的遺構の一つである敷地の形をそのまま残し視覚化するために、そのヴォリュームは少しだけ持ち上げられている。

敷地にやってきた人は、山を背景にして少しだけ浮かぶほとんどまっすぐのヴォリュームに出会う。庭を横切りながら少しづつ建物に近づくと、実は建物がカーブしていることを気づかされる。建物をくぐり抜けると、山にぶつかり、山と建物の隙間を走るスロープに導かれる。少しずつのぼっていくと、建物とスロープのスリットの中に見えていた書院が消えていく。エントランスが近くにつれガラスの壁面が現れはじめ、それ越しに再び書院が見えてくる。エントランスホールに入ると、地面からでは見上げることしかできなかった書院の大きな美しい屋根が正面に立ちはだかる。展示物を見ながら先に進むと小さな休憩室に出て、展示されていた物の背景となっている、そして敷地へのアプローチの途中通ってきた里の様子をあらためて眺めることができる。つまりこの計画では、建物内に展示される物だけではなくその場所にあるすべての物が展示物となるような、環境全体の資料館となるような建物のあり方を目指した。

（妹島和世＋西沢立衛）

Entrance hall エントランス・ホール △▽

View toward entrance hall from special exhibition room　特別展示室よりエントランス・ホールを見る

1994–2000
HERZOG & DE MEURON

TATE MODERN
London, U.K.

Overall view 全景

Turbine hall: north elevation タービン・ホール：北面

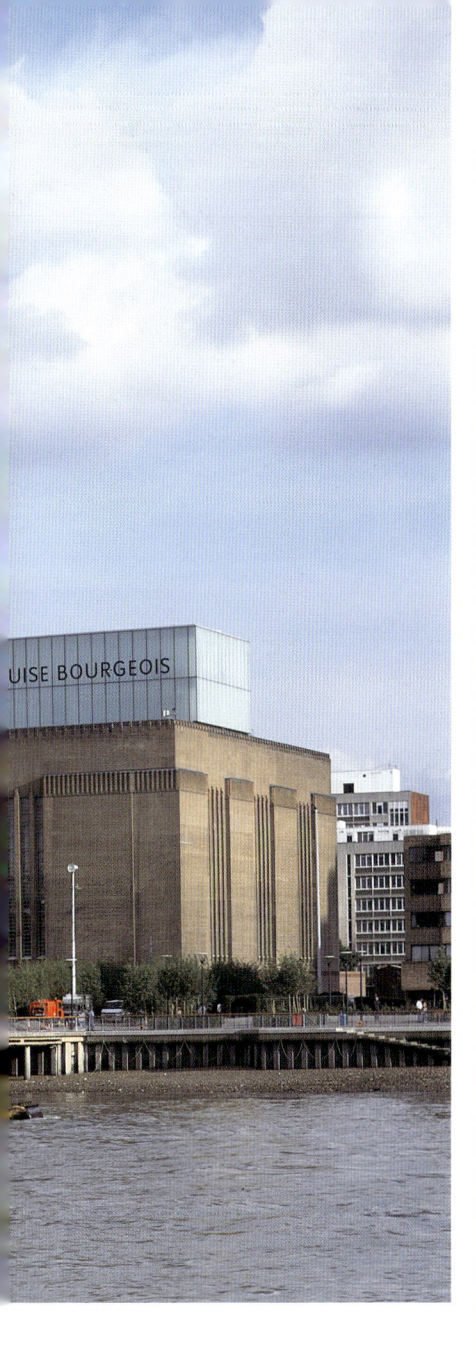

Turbine hall: view toward east　タービン・ホール：東を見る

317

A huge, Art Deco-style power station designed by Sir Giles Gilbert Scott was transformed into this museum of contemporary art, an architectural hybrid of traditional and present-time spaces. It is also an urban project with purposes of retaining the historical design of Bankside's brick architecture and giving it a role of a brand-new cultural landmark.

Turbin Hall in the center of this enormous complex is an area connecting the interior and the exterior, as it runs the whole length of the building in full height. Through a ramp, visitors are ushered into this Turbin Hall, the foundation level which is below River Thames' surface. From the Hall one can get the full view of the inner structure, from the entrance, shops, cafe, education area, auditorium, concourse, up to the exhibition spaces. The platform bridged in the middle of the Hall is the remains of the original floorplate that has once covered Turbine Hall's floor in its whole length.

Each one of the exhibition rooms on three levels is different in size and proportion from the others. Nevertheless, they are basically spaces of rectangular plans. Simplicity of the finishing not only brings about coherence with regard to this historical building, but also is appropriate for contemporary art exhibition spaces. The concourse facing each gallery levels accommodates vertical flow lines such as stairs and elevators giving access to all galleries.

The glass box floating on top of the museum roof is the lightbeam, accommodating a restaurant and a cafe on the top floor. It provides natural light into the fifth-floor galleries in daytime. By night, it reverses the direction of light to become a light belt illuminating London's sky as an urban 'device'.

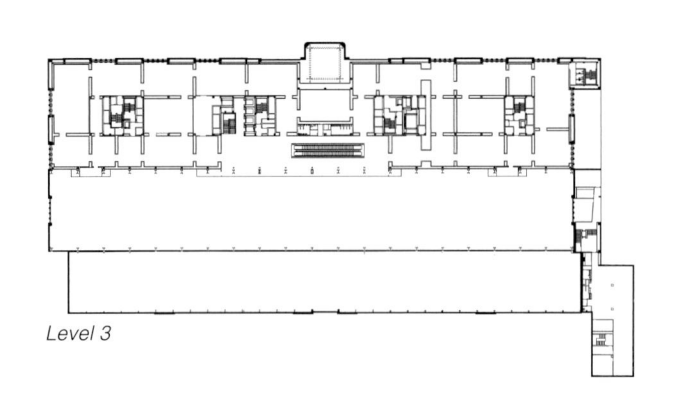

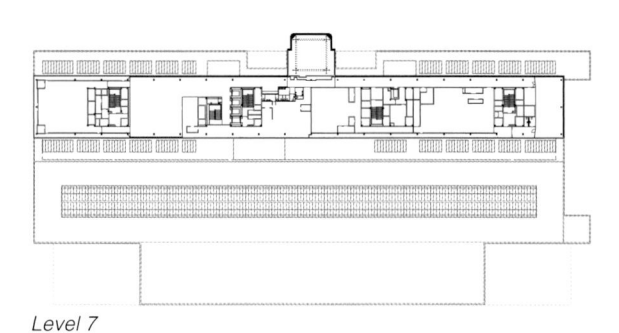

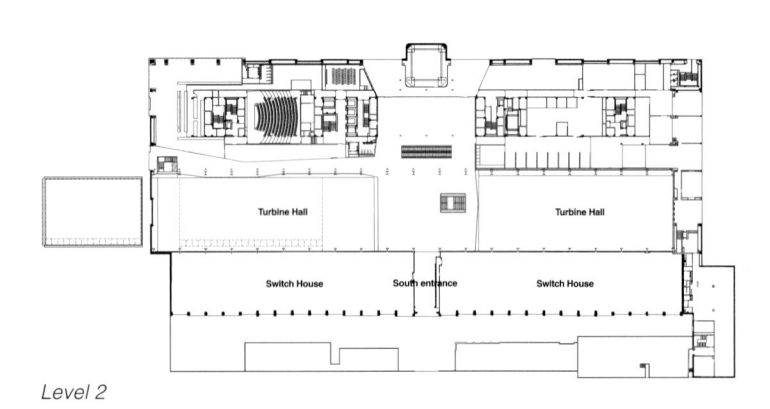

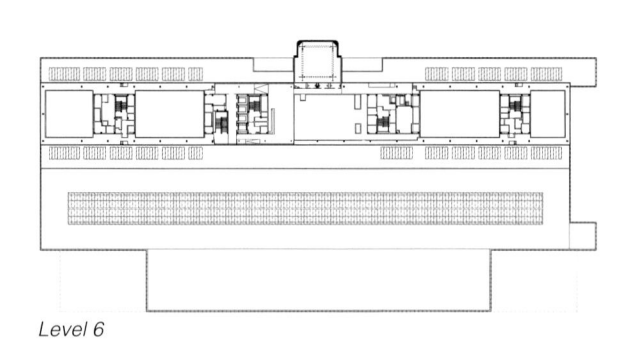

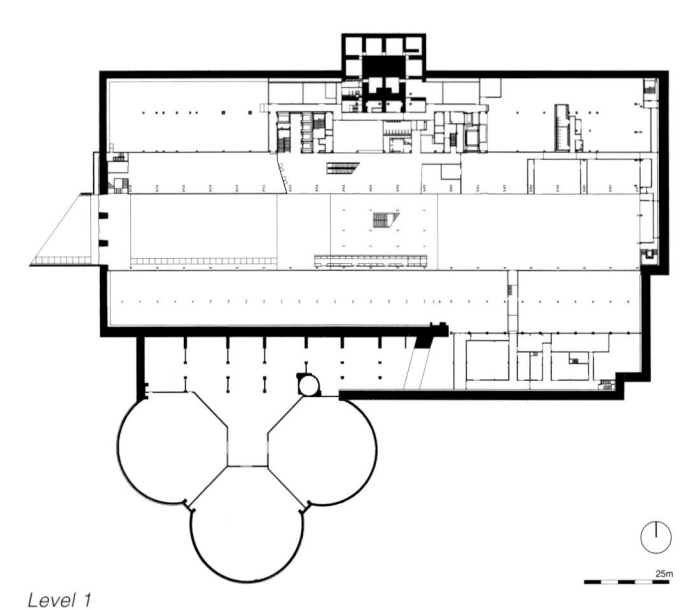

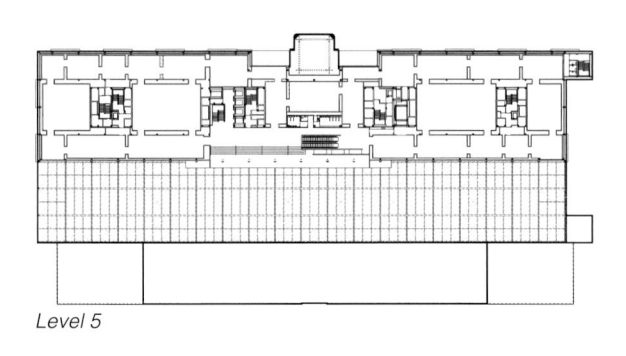

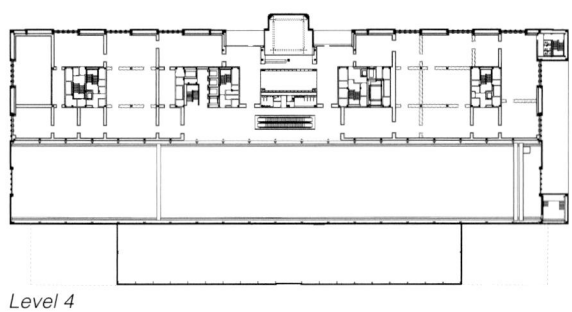

Level 3

Level 2

Level 1

Level 7

Level 6

Level 5

Level 4

ジャイルズ・ギルバート・スコット設計のアール・デコ様式の巨大発電所を改造した現代美術館。伝統と今日的な空間のハイブリッドとしての建築である。バンクサイドの歴史的な煉瓦造建築の意匠を十分に残し、新たに文化的なランドマークとして使命を与える都市的なプロジェクトでもある。

この巨大なコンプレックスの中心にあるタービン・ホールは内と外の間を連絡する領域で、道路のように、建物全長を建物の高さいっぱいの吹抜けとなって通っている。ランプによって、来館者はこのタービン・ホール、テムズ川の水面より低い位置にある基盤レベルへ導びかれる。ホールから、エントランス、ショップ、カフェテリア、教育施設、オーディトリアム、コンコース、展示場と並ぶ、その内部構成を一目で把握できる。ホールの中央にブリッジの様に架けられたプラットフォームは、かつてタービン・ホールの全長に渡って敷かれていた床板の残余である。

三層分のギャラリーは大きさやプロポーションは各々に違うものだが、それらは基本的に矩形のプランを持つ空間であり、シンプルな仕上げがされることで、この歴史建物と整合性をもたらし、また現代美術の展示空間として有用である。各展示階に面したコンコースは、垂直動線である階段やエレベータを収め、各ギャラリーへのアクセスを提供する。

美術館屋上の頂部に浮かぶガラスの箱——ライト・ビームは、最上階にレストランとカフェを収め、5階ギャラリーに昼光を注ぐ。夜は照明の方向を逆転させて、ロンドンの空に輝く光の帯になる都市的な「装置」となる。

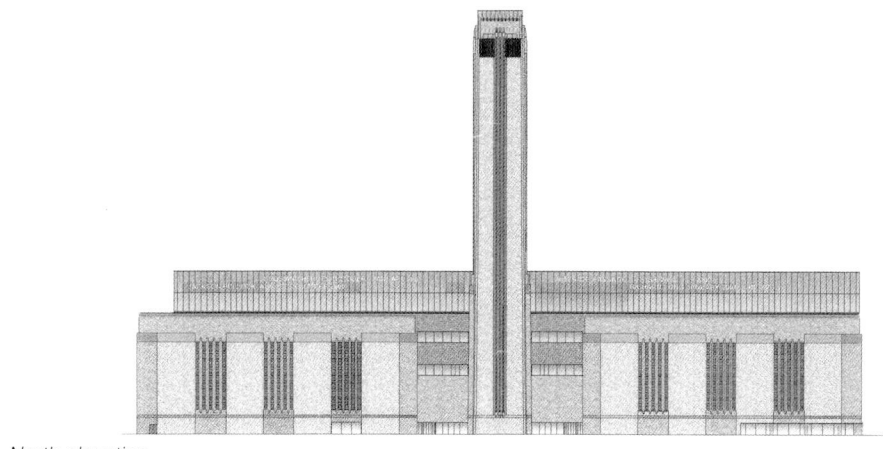

North elevation

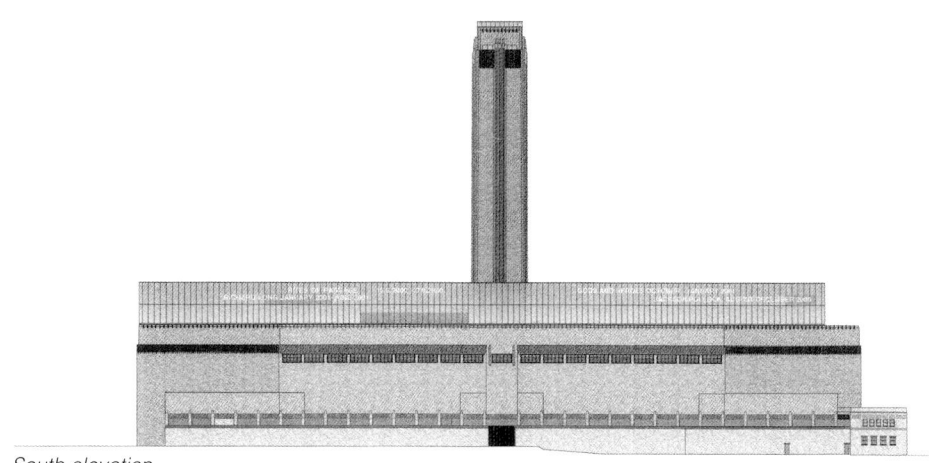

South elevation

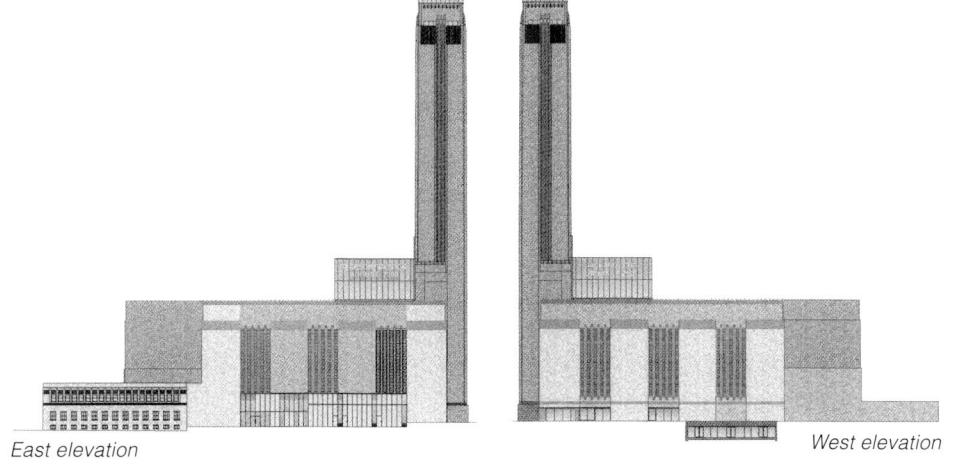

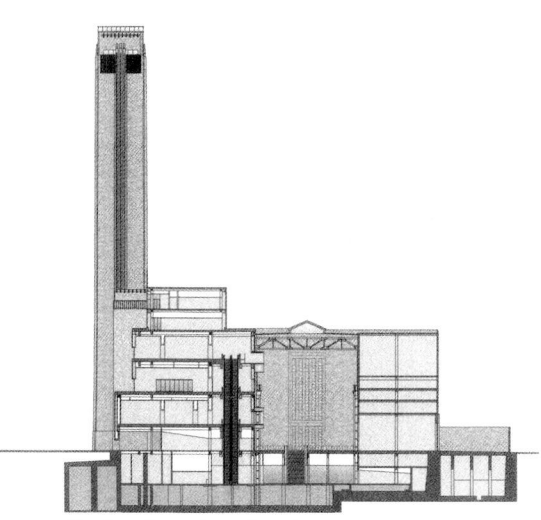

East elevation   *West elevation*

Section through north entrance

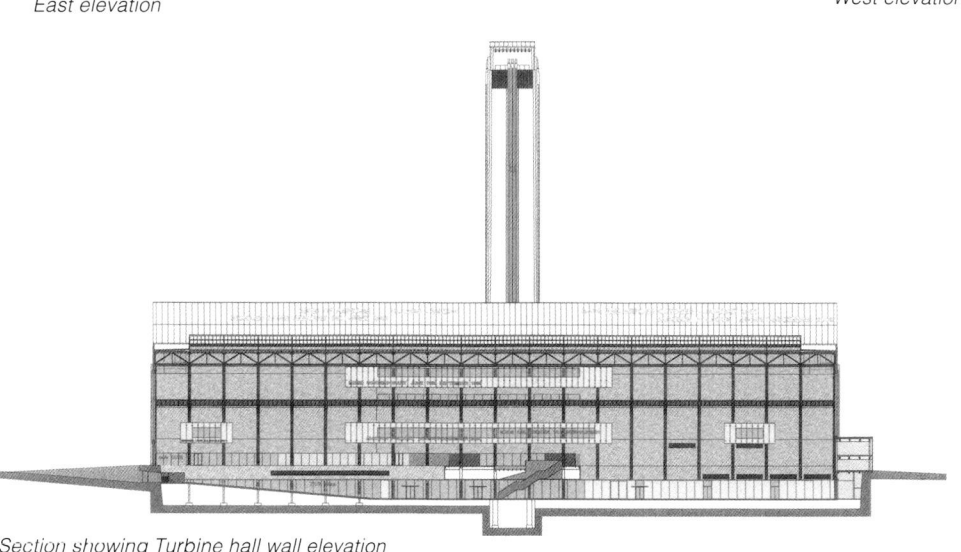

Section showing Turbine hall wall elevation

319

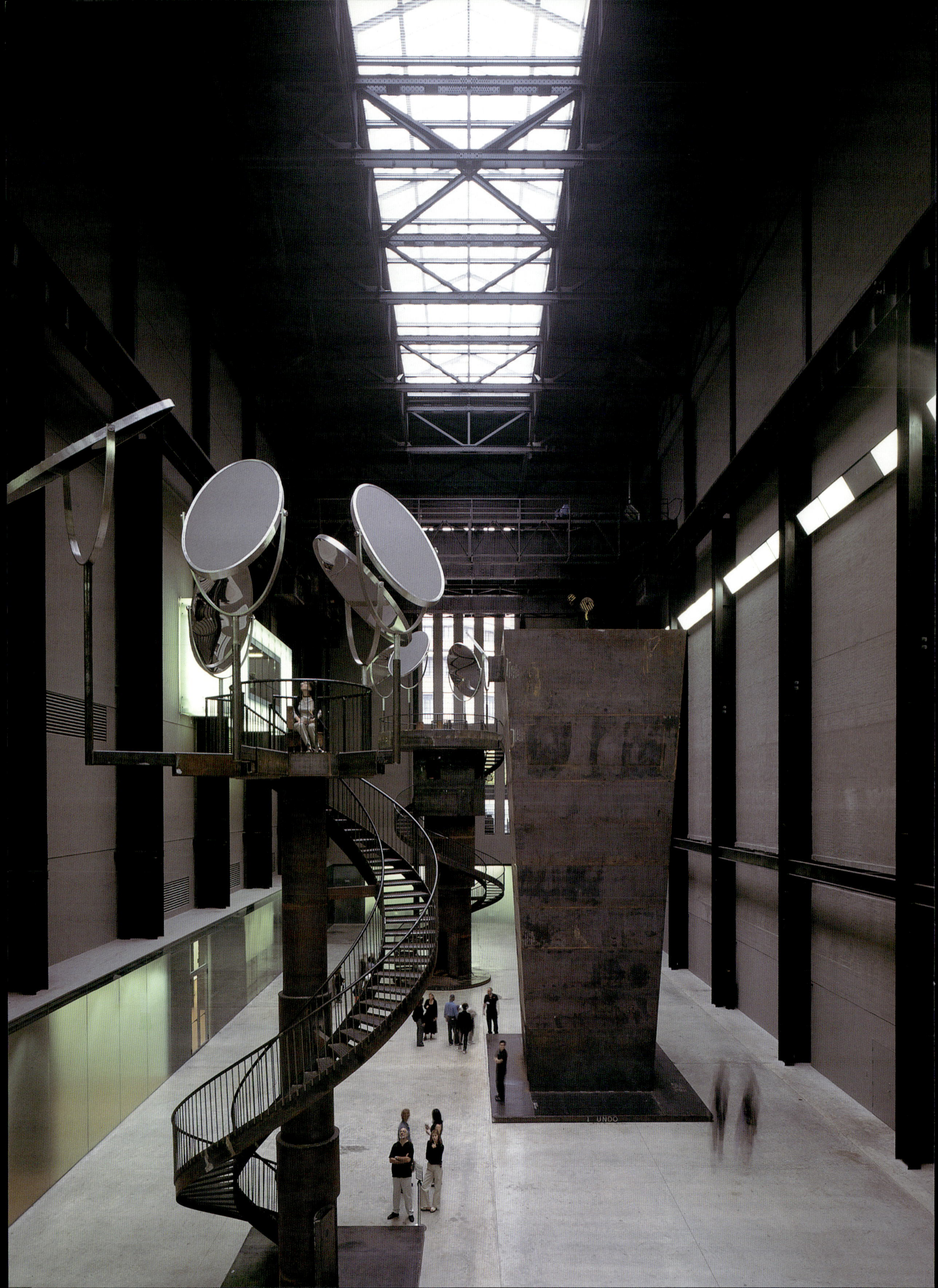

Level 1 レヴェル1

◁ *Turbine hall: view toward west* タービン・ホール：西を見る

Level 1: Turbine hall on right レヴェル1：右はタービン・ホール

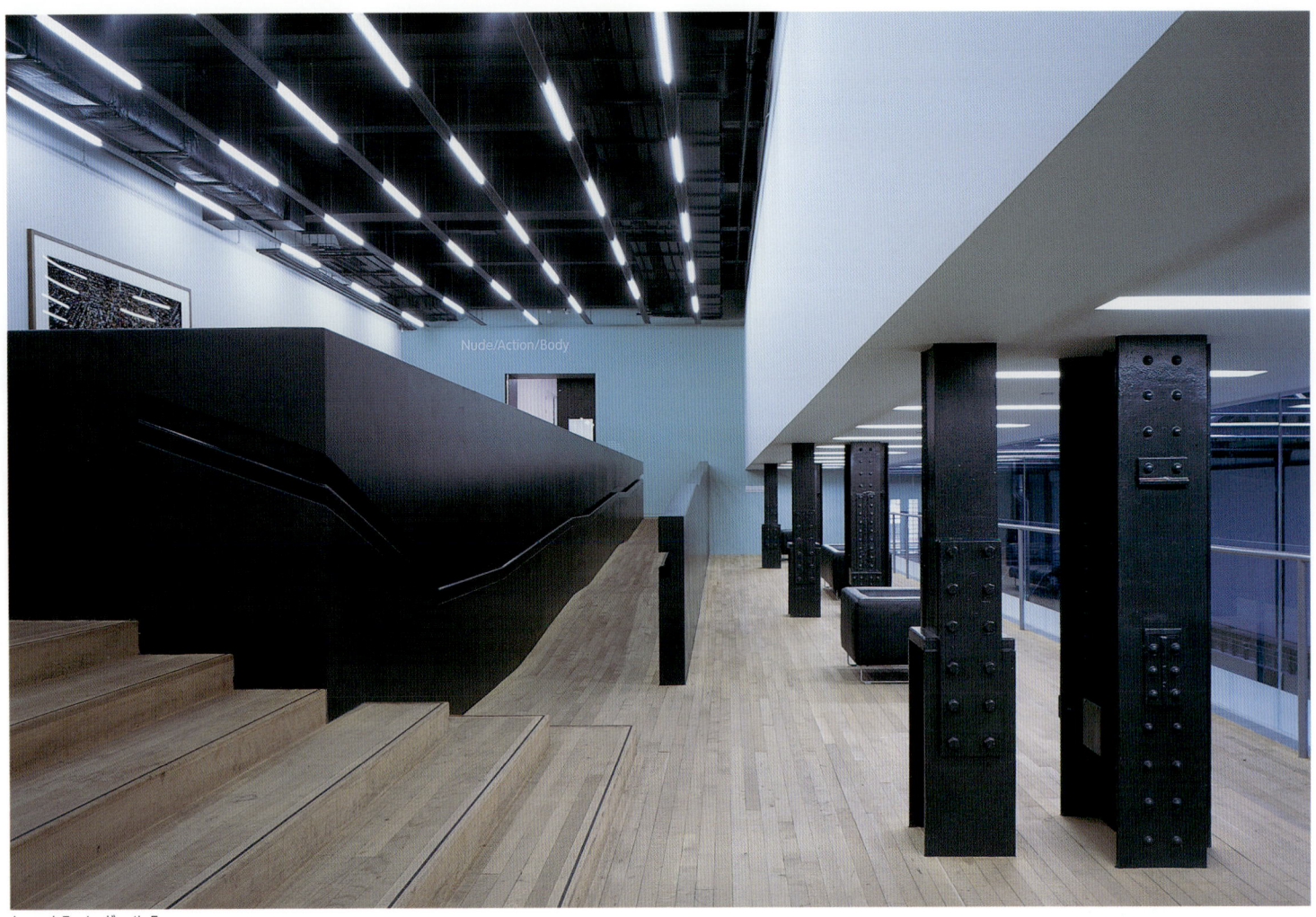

Level 5　レヴェル5

Level 3　レヴェル3

Level 7 レヴェル7   *Level 7* レヴェル7

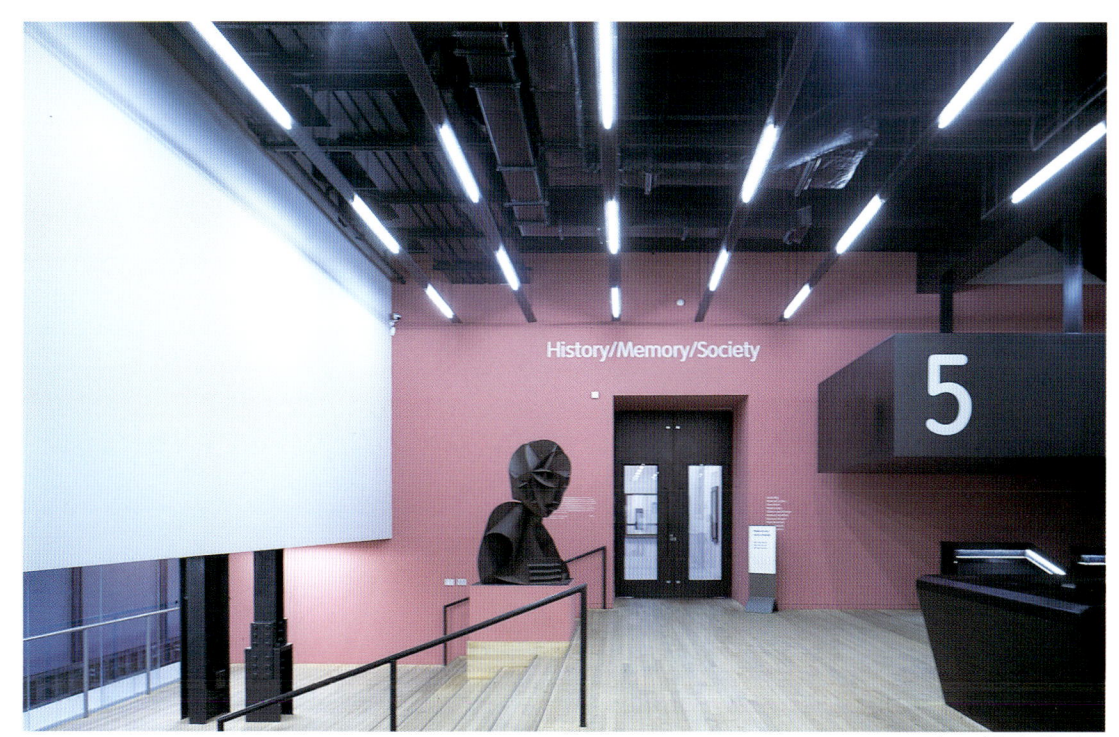

Level 5 レヴェル5

Exhibition room 展示室   *Staircase* 階段室

1998–2000
KENGO KUMA

BATO MACHI HIROSHIGE MUSEUM
Tochigi, Japan

Overall view 全景

In January 1995, newspapers had reported that a great number of original drawings by the painter Hiroshige Ando himself has been found from the Aoki's storehouse destroyed by the Great Hanshin Earthquake. These pieces of original drawings came to be contributed to Bato-cho Town in Tochigi Prefecture that had associations with the Aokis. This museum was planned with the purpose of housing this collection.

The mother of this project, Ms. Hisako Aoki, has come up with two requirements: one, to make use of the local, natural materials as much as possible; two, to make it the town's 'civic core', a place of human and cultural exchange.

Our plan proposed consisted of a gable-roofed volume of the simplest form piercing through the linear plaza commonly known as Hiroshige Kaido ('kaido' meaning 'highway').

The latter, a brand-new 'street' and a linear linkage between the Townhall Plaza and the hillside promenade at the back of the museum, would pierce through the building in an attempt to introduce a wide, urban-scale activity into the architecture. On the eastern side of Hiroshige Kaido are arranged the 'museum functions' in a classical sense. The western side is lined with restaurant serving the town's specialty cuisine and shops selling a wide variety of local products from pottery to vegetables. Representing tranquility and motion, the two domains would be bound together within the Kaido's multi-purpose covered space. Such mechanism would then literally open a hole into the closed exclusiveness of conventional museum architecture.

The gable-roofed volume is enveloped by a film of louvers made of local cedar plates (all having a section size of 30 x 60 mm, arranged basically at a pitch of 120 mm). Louvers of the same section size are used to cover the roof and the walls, but the film's property varies according to the requirements of the inner space. The exhibition room, where a most delicate environmental control is needed, features a roof of metal plates placed below the louvers, whereas other highly open spaces feature various combinations of materials according to the openness of the place, such as 'outer louvers + corrugated glass sheet + inner louvers' or 'outer louvers + stripe-shaped toplight + inner louvers', that would provide filter-like effects, allowing light particles of different characters to infiltrate and fill the rooms.

We sought to create, by means of filters, a sense of openness and an atmosphere inside

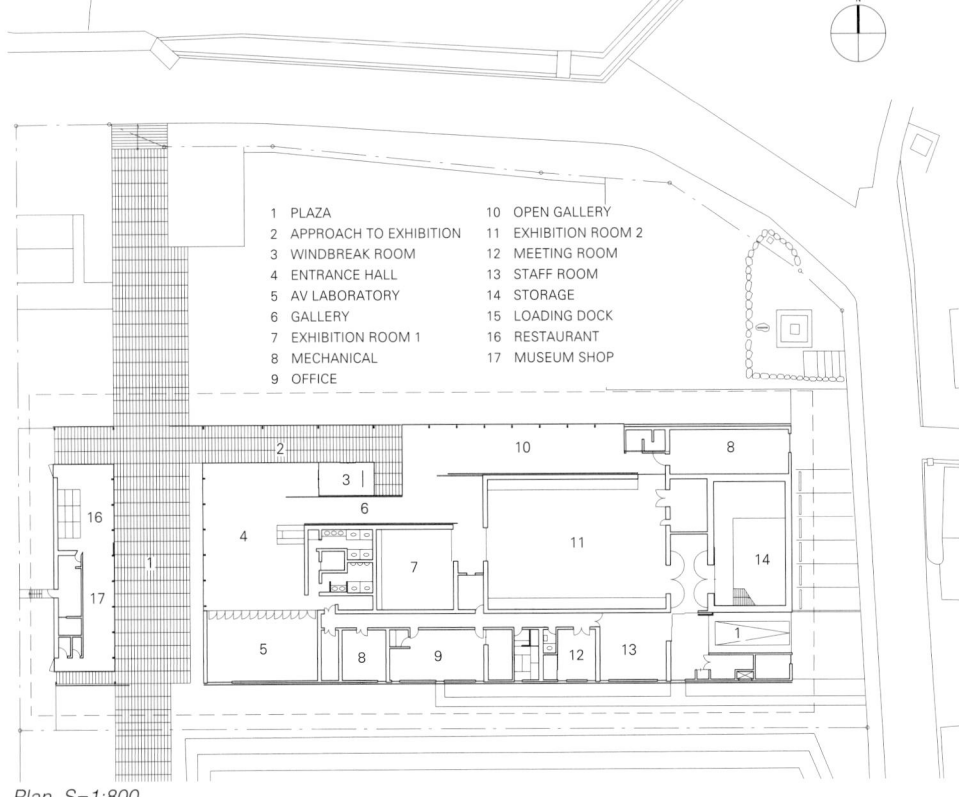

1 PLAZA
2 APPROACH TO EXHIBITION
3 WINDBREAK ROOM
4 ENTRANCE HALL
5 AV LABORATORY
6 GALLERY
7 EXHIBITION ROOM 1
8 MECHANICAL
9 OFFICE
10 OPEN GALLERY
11 EXHIBITION ROOM 2
12 MEETING ROOM
13 STAFF ROOM
14 STORAGE
15 LOADING DOCK
16 RESTAURANT
17 MUSEUM SHOP

Plan S=1:800

Approach: restaurant (left) and museum (right) 外部舗道：レストラン（左）と美術館（右）

which one has a feeling of being softly wrapped around. Our idea was that such atmosphere would be most suitable for the museum as a civic core—open and friendly. On the other hand, we felt that the subtle sandy texture produced by the louvers had something in common with Hiroshige Ando's Ukiyoe. Unlike Hokusai whose works are characterized by intense coloring and strong strokes, Hiroshige has made use of thin lines and minute dots to scan and put onto paper the Nature itself, and especially the flow of the fragile, ambiguous expressions of the light. Through this project, we have expected to reconstitute his work, using architecture as a tool.
Kengo Kuma

1995年1月、阪神大震災で倒壊した青木家の蔵から、安藤広重自身の筆による大量の肉筆画が発見され、新聞を賑わした。それらの肉筆画は、青木家とゆかりのある栃木県馬頭町に寄附されることとなり、それを収蔵する目的で本美術館は計画された。

プロジェクトの生みの親である青木久子氏は、最初に2つの条件を示した。一つは、地元の自然素材を可能な限り用いること。一つは馬頭町の核（シビック・コア）となるような、町内、町外交流の場となるということであった。

可能な限り、単純化された切妻型のヴォリュームを、通称、広重街道と呼ばれるリニアな広場が貫通するというのが、われわれの提案した配置計画であった。広重街道は、町役場前の広場と、美術館裏山の散策路と接続するリニアな広場であり、その新しい町の「通り」が建物の中を貫通することによって、建築に都市スケールのアクティビティを導入しようと試みたのである。広重街道の東側には古典的な意味での美術館機能が配置され、西側には、町の食材を供するレストラン、陶器から野菜までの地元の特産品を販売する売店が配置され、静と動の2つの領域が「街道」状の多目的な庇下空間によって束ねられる。その仕掛けによって、従来の美術館形式の閉鎖性に少しでも孔（文字通りの）が開けられればと考えた。

切妻型のヴォリュームは、地元産の八溝杉によってつくられたルーバー（すべて30×60ミリの断面形状を持ち、ピッチは原則として120ミリ）状の皮膜によって、包み込まれている。屋根から壁までが同一断面のルーバーによって覆われているが、皮膜の性能は内部のリクワイヤメントによって様々である。もっともデリケートな環境が要求される展示室においては、ルーバーの下部に金属板の屋根が葺かれ、開放性の高い空間では、その開放度に応じて、アウタールーバー＋波板ガラス＋インナールーバー、アウタールーバー＋ストライプ状のトップライト＋インナールーバーとの断面形状（すなわちフィルターの性状）がセレクトされ、フィルターによって濾過された粒子状の様々な光が室内を満たしている。

開かれながら、しかも物質にやわらかく包み込まれるような空気をフィルターによってつくりたかった。その空気の状態がシビック・コアとしての、開かれ、しかも親しまれる美術館にふさわしいと感じたからである。さらに、ルーバーがつくる繊細な粒子感は、安藤広重の浮世絵に通じると感じた。北斎のような強い色彩と形態とを用いることなく、細い線と小さな点を用いて、広重は自然、ことに光という自然の織りなす繊細にして曖昧な表情とその流動とを紙の上にスキャニングした。その作業を建築という道具を用いて、追いかけたいと思った。
（隈研吾）

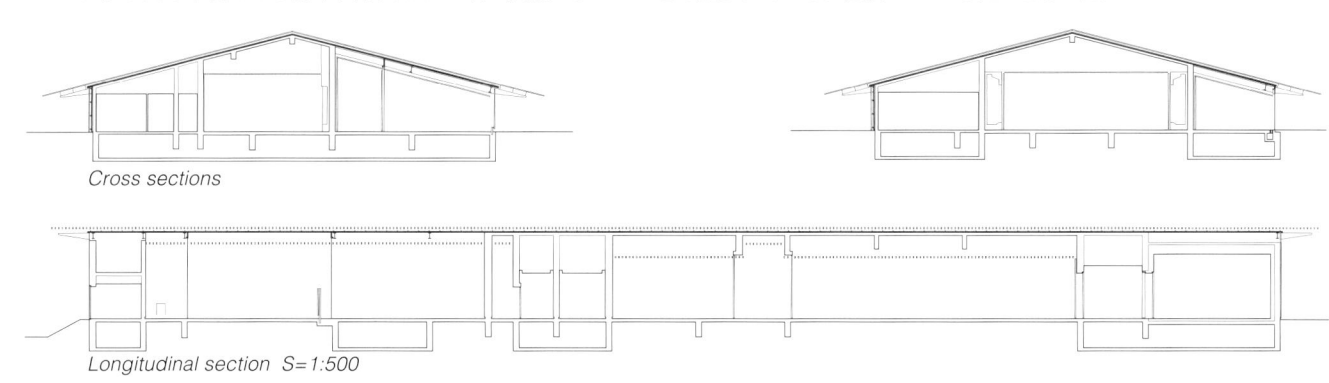

Cross sections

Longitudinal section S=1:500

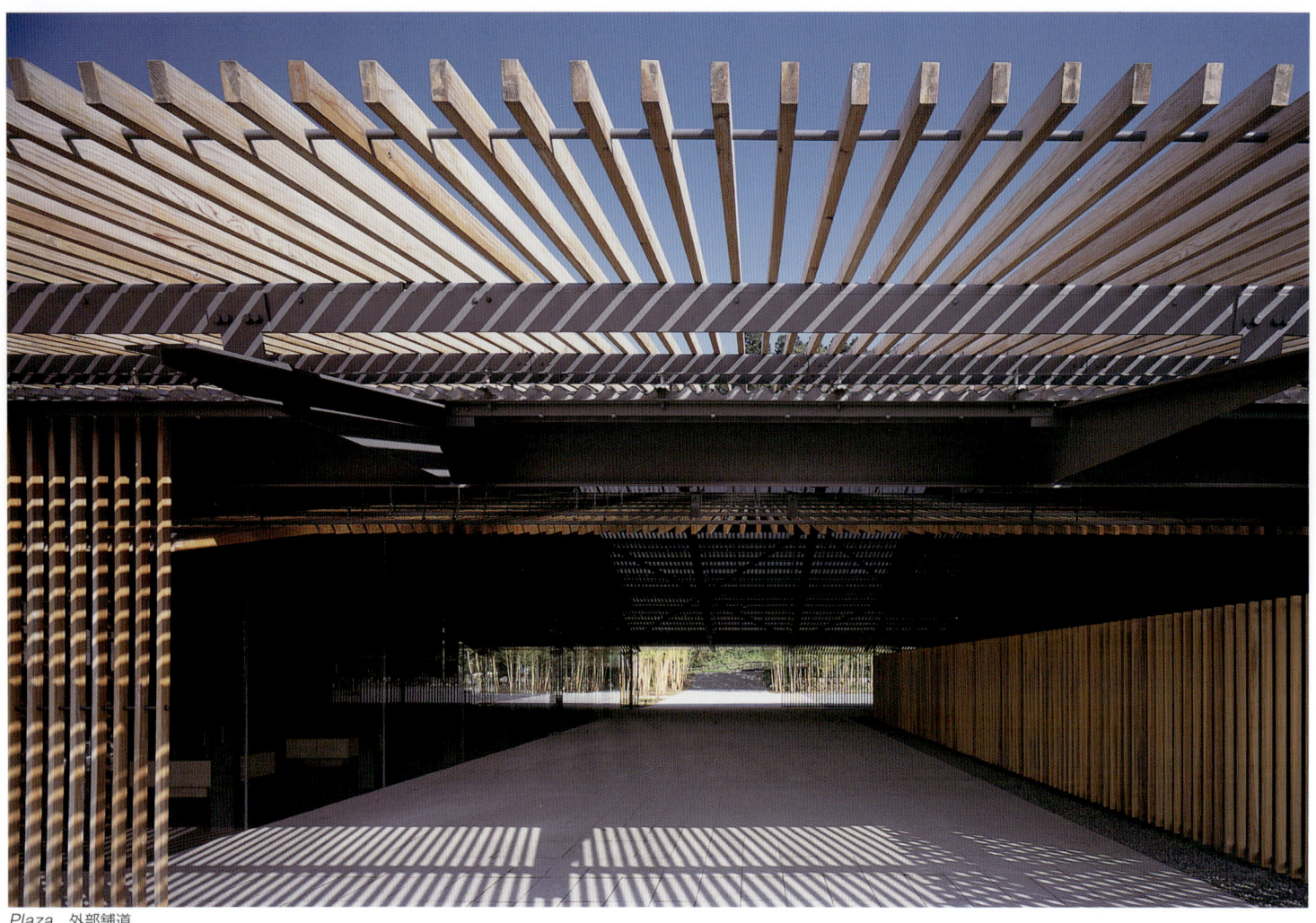

Plaza 外部舗道

Entrance hall エントランス・ホール

View from west 西より見る

View toward entrance hall エントランス・ホールを見る

View toward west from entrance hall　エントランス・ホールより西を見る

Gallery: view toward east　展示通路：東を見る

Entrance hall　エントランス・ホール

Exhibition room　展示室

1994–2000
NORMAN FOSTER

QUEEN ELIZABETH II GREAT COURT, BRITISH MUSEUM
London, U.K.

The courtyard at the centre of the British Museum was one of London's long-lost spaces. Originally an open garden, soon after its completion in the nineteenth century it was filled by the round Reading Room and its associated bookstacks. Without this space the Museum was like a city without a park. This project is about its reinvention. In terms of visitor numbers, over five million annually. In the absence of a centralised circulation system this degree of popularity caused a critical level of congestion throughout the building and created a frustrating experience for the visitor. The departure of the British Library to St Pancras in March 1998 provided the opportunity to recapture the courtyard and greatly enhance the Museum's facilities for coming generations. The clutter of bookstacks that filled the courtyard has been cleared away to give the building a new public heart, while the Reading Room has been restored and put to new use as an information centre and library of world cultures. For the first time in its history this magnificent space—its dome larger than that of St Paul's—is open to all.

The Great Court is entered from the Museum's principal level, and connects all the surrounding galleries. Within the space there are information points, a book shop and a cafe. Two broad staircases encircling the Reading Room lead to two mezzanine levels, which provide a gallery for temporary exhibitions with a restaurant above. Below the level of the Court are the Sainsbury African Galleries, an education centre and facilities for schoolchildren. The glazed canopy that makes all this possible is a fusion of state-of-the-art engineering and economy of form. Its unique triangulated geometry is designed to span the irregular gap between the drum of the Reading Room and the restored courtyard facades. The lattice steel shell forms both the primary structure and the framing for the glazing system, which is designed to maximise daylight and reduce solar gain. The Great Court is the largest enclosed public space in Europe. As a cultural square, it lies on a new pedestrian route from the British Library in the north to Covent Garden and the river in the south. To complement the Great Court, the Museum's forecourt has been freed from cars and restored to form a new public space. Both are open to the public from early in the morning to late at night, creating a major amenity for London.

Museum forecourt 博物館前庭

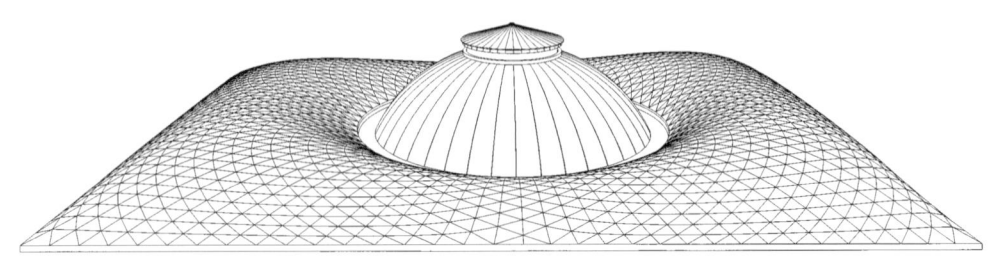

Wire frame drawing of roof

大英博物館の中心にあるコートヤードは、ロンドン市にとって長いあいだ失われていた空間であった。当初は広々とした庭であったが、19世紀に完成するとまもなく円形の閲覧室とその書庫によって埋め尽くされてしまったのである。この空間が存在しない博物館は公園のない都市のようなものであった。このプロジェクトは、その再建に関わるものである。来館者数に関して言えば、年間500万人を超えている。ここまで人が集まる場所となると、中心的なサーキュレーション・システムの不在は、建物全域に無視し得ないほどの混雑を招き、来館者は苛立ちを隠し得ない。1998年3月、大英図書館のパンクラスへの移転に伴い、コートヤードを復活させ、次世代に向かって博物館の施設を大きく強化するチャンスが生まれた。コートを乱雑に埋めていた書庫は取り壊され、博物館に新たな中心を与える一方、閲覧室は改装されて情報センターと世界文化図書館としての新しい役割を担う。セント・ポール寺院のそれより大きなドームに覆われた閲覧室の素晴らしい空間は、その歴史上はじめて、すべての人に公開されることになった。

グレート・コートへは博物館の主階から入り、周囲を囲むすべてのギャラリーがそこに結ばれている。その空間内にはインフォメーション、書店、カフェが配置された。閲覧室を取り囲む幅の広い2本の階段から2つのメザニン階に出ると、そこは特別展の会場で、上にはレストランがある。コートヤードの地下には、セインズベリー・アフリカン・ギャラリーと小中学生のための教育センター及び諸施設がある。こうした構成のすべてを可能としたガラス張りのキャノピーは、最先端技術

と無駄のない形態の融合にほかならない。三角形で構成された、その特異なジオメトリーは、閲覧室棟の円筒形と修復されたコートヤードを囲むファサードの間に生まれている不規則な空間を架け渡すためにデザインされたものである。鋼管ラチスによって組まれたシェルは主構造であると同時に、昼光は最大限に採り込み、熱取得は減少すべく設計されたガラス面を填め込む枠を提供する。グレート・コートは屋根や壁に囲まれた公共空間のなかでは、ヨーロッパ最大のものである。文化の広場として、それは北の大英図書館から南のコヴェント・ガーデンとテムズ川に至る新しい歩行ルート上に位置している。グレート・コートを補足して、博物館の前庭からは車が排除され、公共空間として整備された。2つの広場は、早朝から夜遅くまで一般に開放され、ロンドンの重要なアメニティとなっている。

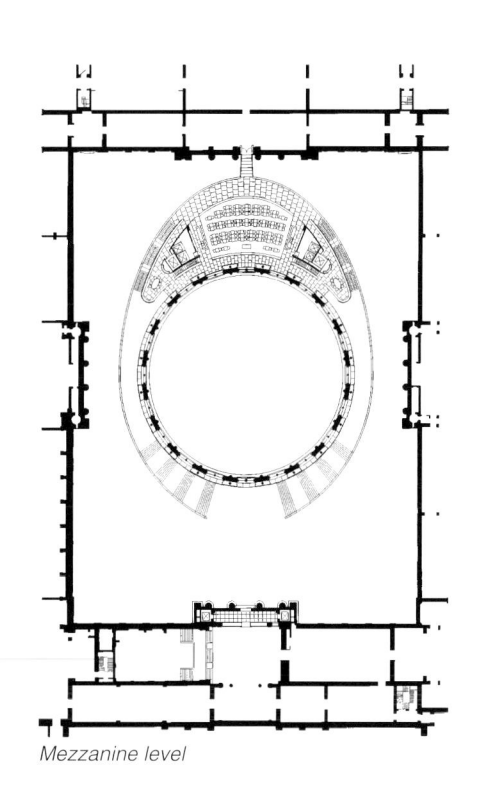

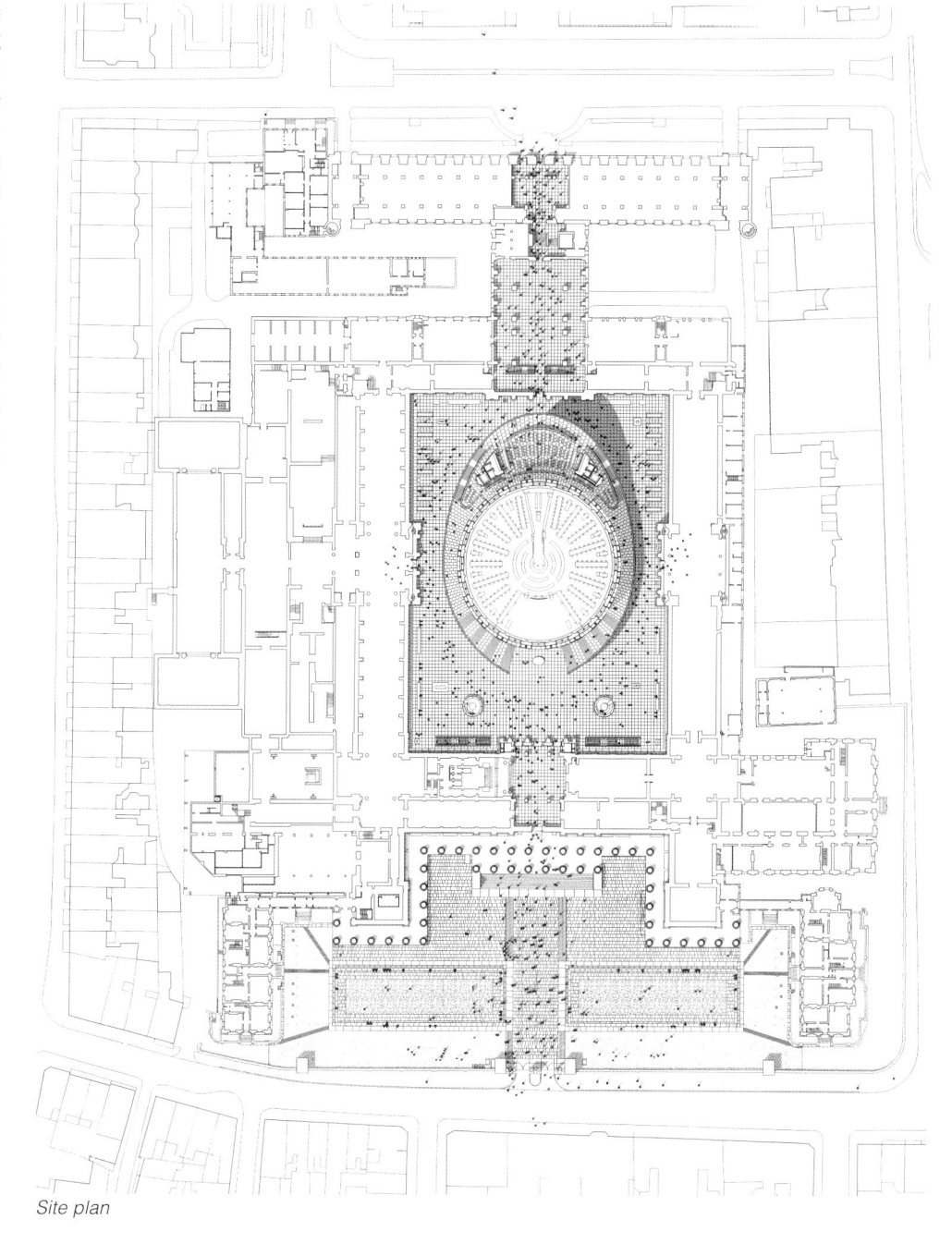

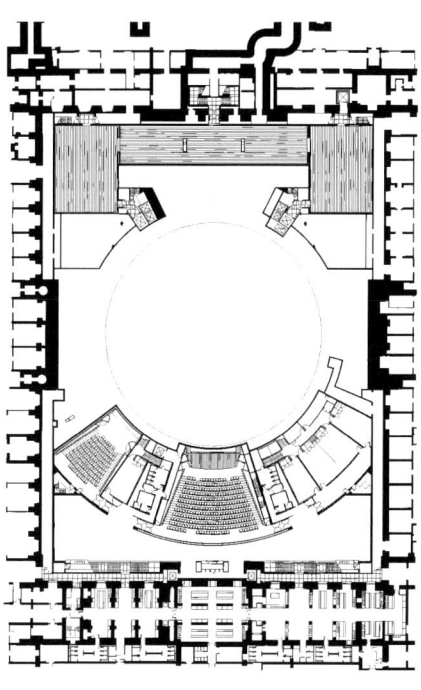

Mezzanine level

Site plan

Underground level

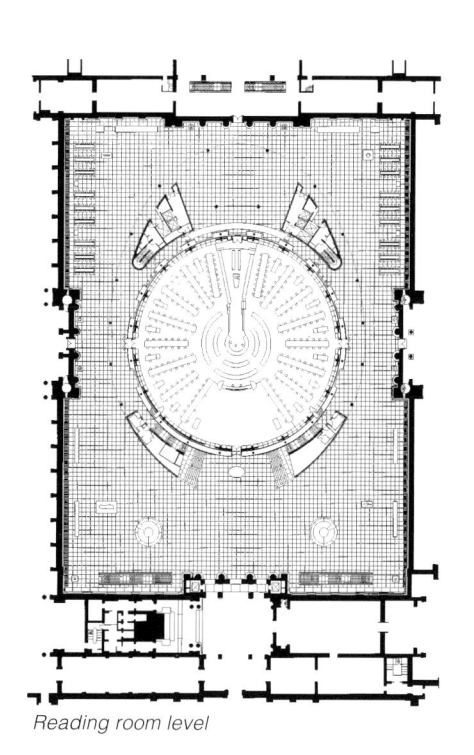

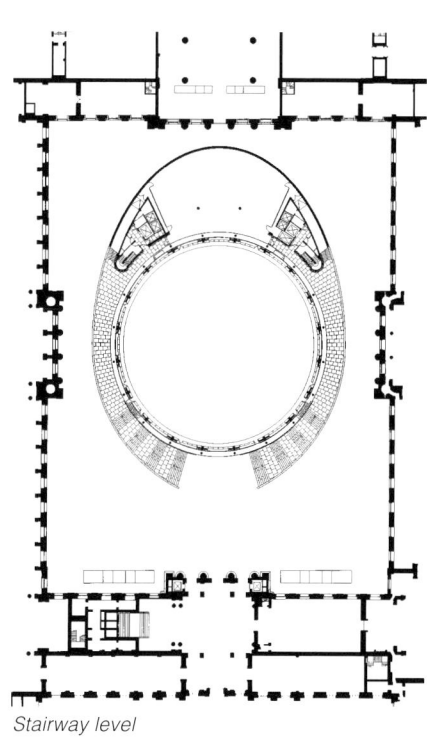

Reading room level

Stairway level

Glazed roof over Great Court　グレート・コートに架かるガラス屋根

Staircase 階段

Bridge connects with north wing 北ウイングと結ぶブリッジ

333

Restaurant on left 左はレストラン

North wing 北ウイング

Great Court グレート・コート

Staircase 階段

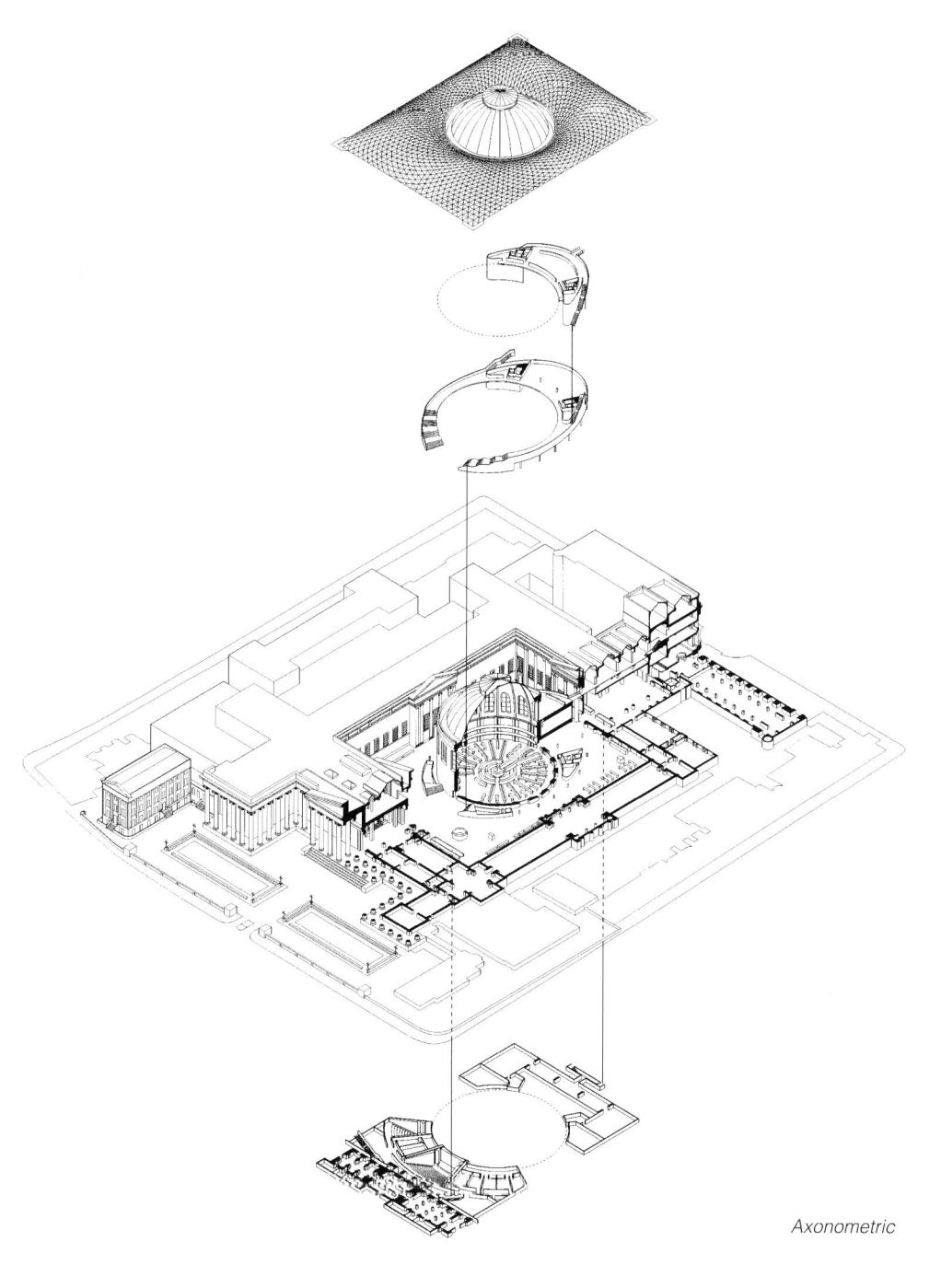

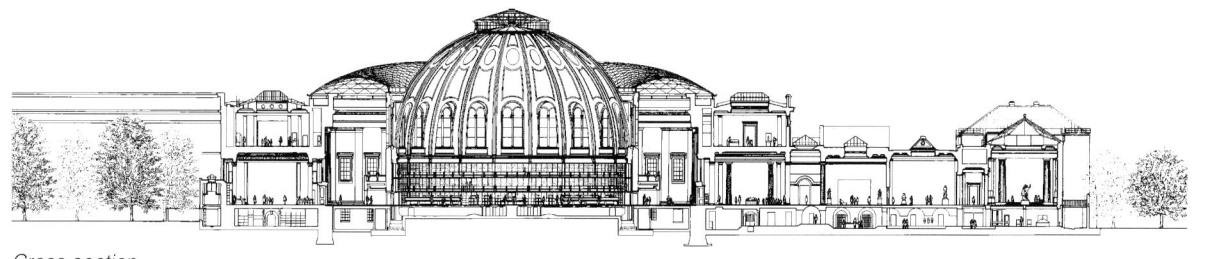

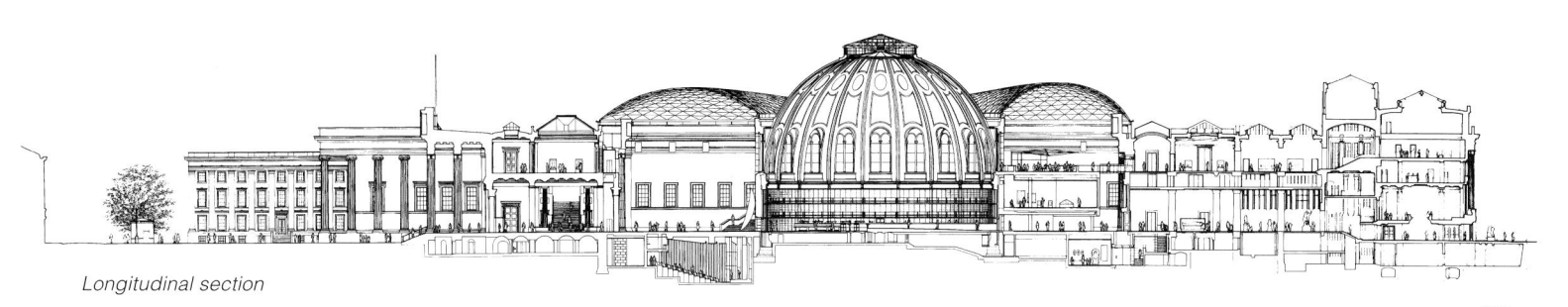

Axonometric

Cross section

Longitudinal section

335

GA Contemporary Architecture
Global Architecture

GA現代建築シリーズ 01
〈ミュージアム1〉

2001年12月20日発行
2015年 3月20日再版発行

企画・編集	二川幸夫
撮影	GA photographers
英訳	谷理佐 他
ロゴタイプ・デザイン	細谷巖
発行者	二川由夫
印刷・製本	図書印刷株式会社
発行	エーディーエー・エディタ・トーキョー 東京都渋谷区千駄ヶ谷3-12-14 TEL.(03) 3403-1581(代)

禁無断転載

ISBN978-4-87140-571-3 C1352